If we had wings we would fly to you

A SOVIET JEWISH FAMILY FACES DESTRUCTION, 1941–42

Jews of Russia and Eastern Europe and Their Legacy

Series Editor
Maxim D. Shrayer (Boston College)

Editorial Board
Karel Berkhoff (NIOD Institute for War, Holocaust and Genocide Studies)
Jeremy Hicks (Queen Mary University of London)
Brian Horowitz (Tulane University)
Luba Jurgenson (Universite Paris IV—Sorbonne)
Roman Katsman (Bar-Ilan University)
Dov-Ber Kerler (Indiana University)
Vladimir Khazan (Hebrew University of Jerusalem)
Alice Nakhimovsky (Colgate University)
Antony Polonsky (Brandeis University)
Jonathan D. Sarna (Brandeis University)
David Shneer (University of Colorado at Boulder)
Anna Shternshis (University of Toronto)
Leona Toker (Hebrew University of Jerusalem)
Mark Tolts (Hebrew University of Jerusalem)

If we had wings we would fly to you
A SOVIET JEWISH FAMILY FACES DESTRUCTION, 1941–42

KIRIL FEFERMAN

BOSTON
2020

Library of Congress Cataloging-in-Publication Data

Names: Feferman, K. (Kirill), author.
Title: "If we had wings we would fly to you": a Soviet Jewish Family faces destruction, 1941–42 / Kiril Feferman.
Other titles: Soviet Jewish Family faces destruction, 1941–42
Description: Boston: Academic Studies Press, 2020. | Series: Jews of Russia and Eastern Europe and their legacy | Includes bibliographical references.
Identifiers: LCCN 2019051618 | ISBN 9781644692905 (hardback) | ISBN 9781644692912 (paperback)
Subjects: LCSH: Ginsberg family--Correspondence. | Ginsburg, Efim, 1897–1973 | Holocaust, Jewish (1939–1945)--Caucasus, Northern. | World War, 1939-1945--Caucasus, Northern. | Jews--Persecutions--Soviet Union--History--20th century. | Rostov-na-Donu (Russia)--Biography
Classification: LCC DS134.85 .F44 2020 | DDC 940.53/1809224752--dc23
LC record available at https://lccn.loc.gov/2019051618

Copyright © 2020 Academic Studies Press
All rights reserved.

ISBN 978-1-64469-290-5(hardback)
ISBN 978-1-64469-291-2 (paperback)
ISBN 978-1-64469-292-9 (ebook, PDF)
ISBN 978-1-64469-352-0 (ePub)

Book design by PHi Business Solutions Limited.
Cover design by Ivan Grave.

Published by Academic Studies Press.
1577 Beacon Street
Brookline, MA 02446, USA

press@academicstudiespress.com
www.academicstudiespress.com

For my mother, Nellya Feferman (1947–2016)

Table of Contents

Preface	ix
Family Tree	xi
Timeline	xiii
Introduction	xv

PART ONE
Historical Background   1

Chapter 1.1. The Ginsburg Family in the North Caucasus	3
Chapter 1.2. Soviet Population Evacuation into the North Caucasus, 1941–1942	23
Chapter 1.3. The Holocaust in the North Caucasus	42

PART TWO
The Ginsburg Family Correspondence   55

Chapter 2. 1941	57
Chapter 3. 1942–1943	157

Conclusion   263

List of Letters in the Ginsburg Collection	266
List of Abbreviations	274
Bibliography	275
Index	287

Preface

This book was long in the making. It was about 2007 when I came across the Ginsburg correspondence in the Yad Vashem Archives. However, it took me some time to realize the unprecedented value of the letters and to figure out what could be done with them. My hope is that this book will serve as a literary monument to the unfortunate members of the Ginsburg family.

The first person who was able to appreciate the uniqueness of the Ginsburg collection was my mentor, the late Professor David Bankier. He did so during my 2009–10 postdoctoral project "To Stay or To Flee: Soviet Jews in the Northern Caucasus Facing the German Invasion in 1941–42" at Yad Vashem's International Institute for Holocaust Research. Professor Bankier's ideas were instrumental in helping me shape the narrative surrounding these letters. In this regard, I would also like to thank the staff of Yad Vashem's units, most specifically the people at the archives and library, who made my research so enjoyable and exciting.

I owe a special debt of gratitude to Anne Horenstein, my language editor, for meticulously and expertly working on the book. It is a pleasure to acknowledge financial support from Ariel University, which proved indispensable for editing and publishing.

My special thanks are extended to Professor Maxim D. Shrayer (Boston College), editor of the series Jews of Russia and Eastern Europe and Their Legacy from Academic Studies Press, for his encouragement and ability to truly appreciate the tremendous importance of the letters. I would also like to thank Ekaterina Yanduganova at Academic Studies Press for being a most kind, thoughtful, and patient editor.

Finally, I would like to acknowledge my father Mark and my wife Nastya for their support and inspiration while I struggled with my research and writing. I dedicate this book to my mother.

Family Tree

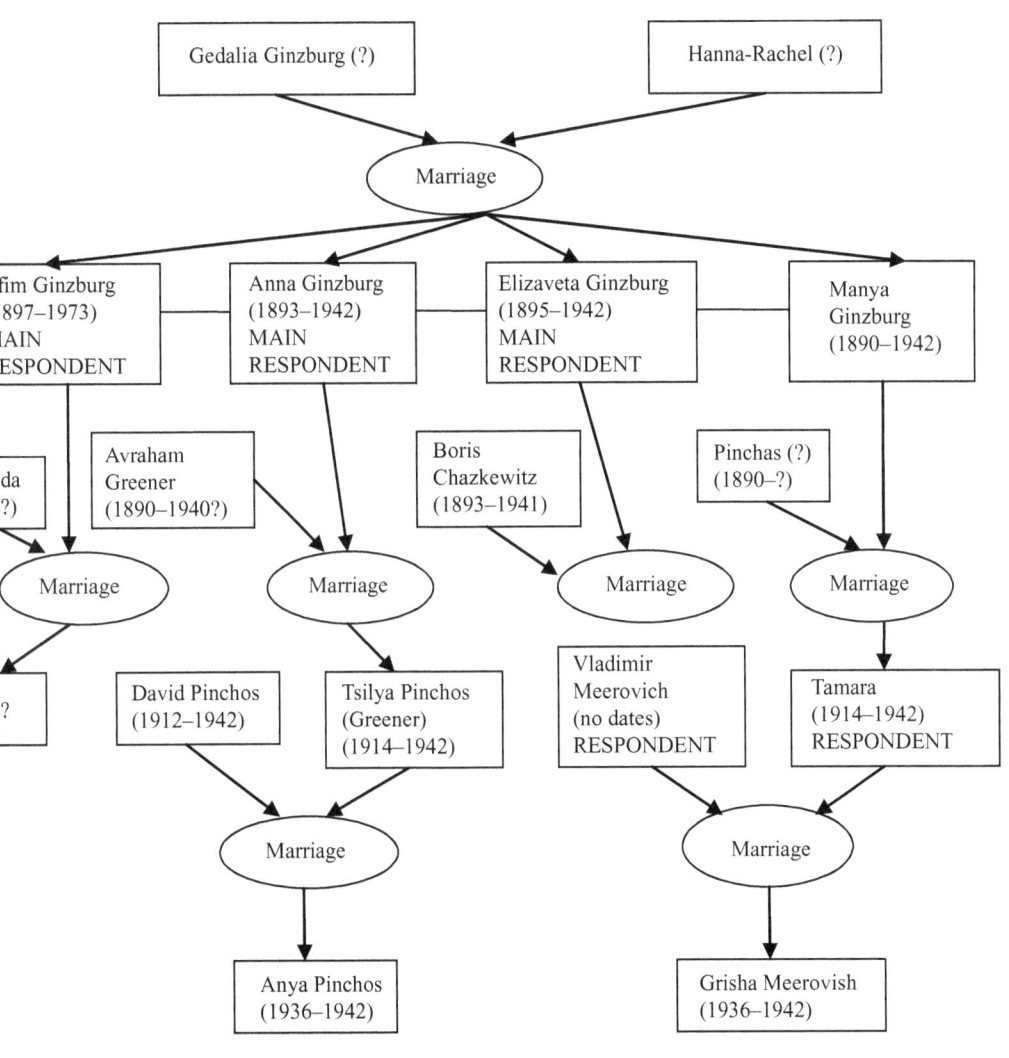

Timeline

Date	Event
August 23, 1939	Non-Aggression Pact between Nazi Germany and the Soviet Union (the Molotov–Ribbentrop Pact) signed
September 1, 1939	World War II begins
December 26, 1939	First letter in the Ginsburg correspondence
June 22, 1941	Start of Soviet-German War. Nazi Germany invades the Soviet Union
July–August 1941	David Pinchos conscripted in the army
Early August, 1941	German bombardment of Rostov-on-Don begins
Early September, 1941	German land advance towards the North Caucasus begins
September 18, 1941	Boris Chazkewitz passes away
September 19, 1941	Wehrmacht seizes Kiev
September 29–30, 1941	Murder of more than 33,000 Jews in Kiev
October 9, 1941	The Council for Evacuation approves evacuation of 30,000 women and children from the city of Rostov-on-Don
October 13, 1941	Families of Tamara Meerovich and Tsylya Pinchos are evacuated from Rostov-on-Don to Budennovsk
October 17, 1941	Wehrmacht seizes the city of Taganrog in the Rostov district
October 30, 1941	Murder of more than 1,800 Jews in Taganrog
October–November 1941	Volodya Meerovich fights in the ranks of the "Extermination Battalion"[1] defending Rostov-on-Don
Mid-November 1941	The Wehrmacht seizes the Crimean peninsula (except for Sevastopol)
November 21–22, 1941	The Wehrmacht seizes Rostov-on-Don for the first time
November 30, 1941	The Red Army liberates Rostov-on-Don from the Germans
December 5, 1941	German retreat in the Battle of Moscow begins
December 13, 1941	Ban on residents leaving Rostov-on-Don is imposed
Late December 1941	Families of Tamara Meerovich and Tsylya Pinchos move from Budennovsk to Vladikavkaz
December 30, 1941	Soviet forces land in the Crimea, begin their counter-offensive

---

1 On Extermination Battalions, see footnote 60 in chapter 1.1.

Date	Event
January 1942	The Wannsee Conference
Mid-February 1942	Ban on residents leaving Rostov-on-Don is moderated
February 26, 1942	David Pinchos is released from the Red Army
March 2, 1942	Volodya Meerovich returns to Rostov-on-Don
March 13, 1942	Tsylya Pinchos's family returns to Rostov-on-Don
April 21, 1942	Volodya Meerovich is conscripted into the Red Army
May 11, 1942	The Red Army is defeated at Kerch, Crimea
Late May 1942	The Red Army is defeated in the Battle of Kharkov
May 29, 1942	Secret order of the State Defense Committee on the preparation for the disablement of the strategically important oil enterprises in the North Caucasus, and the eviction from the region of "socially dangerous persons," "unreliable ethnicities," and foreign citizens
May 31, 1942	Tamara Meerovich's family returns to Rostov-on-Don
June 6, 1942	"Extermination Battalions" are secretly set up again in Rostov-on-Don
July 2, 1942	The Wehrmacht seizes Sevastopol
Early July 1942	*Operation Blau* directed at the North Caucasus begins
July 7, 1942	Tamara Meerovich's family is evacuated to the Rostov district
July 14, 1942	The rest of the Ginsburgs flee from the city to the Rostov district
July 18, 1942	The Soviet Authorities order evacuation of the local residents from the city of Rostov-on-Don
July 24–25, 1942	The Wehrmacht seizes Rostov-on-Don for the second time
August 11–14, 1942	Jews of Rostov-on-Don murdered
August 16, 1942	The Ginsburgs are murdered
August 1942	The Battle of Stalingrad begins
Early February 1943	The German Sixth Army surrenders at Stalingrad
February 14, 1943	The Red Army liberates Rostov-on-Don from the Germans
April 1943	Last letter from Volodya Meerovich
July 19, 1943	Last letter in the Ginsburg collection
Late August 1943	The Red Army liberates the entire Rostov district from the Germans

Introduction

This book is about one Jewish family, which was swept away by the Soviet-German War, the German invasion of Soviet Russia and the Holocaust—the Ginsburg family. The study draws largely on the letters that the members of the family sent to Efim Ginsburg, who was living in Soviet Central Asia. The letters cover a time span that was crucial for Soviet Jewry, stretching from the start of World War II to the murder of almost the whole Ginsburg family in August, 1942, during the Holocaust. The letters touch on many themes, including the wartime atmosphere, the correspondents' worsening living conditions, and, of course, the crucial question of evacuation.

The evacuation of Jews from the North Caucasus differed from the evacuation (of Soviet citizens, including Jews) from many areas that were quickly overrun and occupied by the Germans at the beginning of the Soviet-German War. Over many months, from 1941 to 1942, the frontline between the German and Soviet army positions remained static in this region. This allowed more time for the Jews living in the region to decide whether or not to relocate; significantly, this period provided an opportunity for the Jews to create written records, such as correspondence, which enable us to examine their decision-making processes. However, most such correspondence was lost in the maelstrom. The collection of Ginsburg letters preserved in the Yad Vashem Archives in Jerusalem is one of these rare records, as it sheds light on one Jewish family's long period of hesitation about evacuating from their home in Rostov-on-Don. I have employed this rich collection of Ginsburg family letters to illuminate the plight of the Jewish population of the North Caucasus, as Jewish family members deliberated and argued amongst themselves, over and over again, and finally made the fateful decision—whether to stay in their familiar local area, or to leave.

At the time of the German invasion of the USSR, the Ginsburgs, a Jewish family living in the city of Rostov-on-Don in southern Russia (the Russian gateway to the Caucasus), numbered eleven people, spread over three generations. Among the adults there were six women and three men, several of whom took part in the correspondence. The only member of the Ginsburg family living away from Rostov-on-Don was Efim Ginsburg (1897–1973). He was the recipient of almost every letter in this collection, and he managed to hold on to the collection and keep it safe, during and after World War II.

The Rostov-on-Don Ginsburgs (in fact, the family split up several times, but always remained close to the city) badly miscalculated the events of 1941 and 1942; they stayed in the Caucasus region and perished during the German occupation in the summer of 1942. Vladimir (Volodya) Meerovich, the sole family member from the Rostov-on-Don branch who wasn't murdered with the others, had been drafted into the Soviet army before the German attack on the Caucasus in June 1942; he survived until mid-1943. When he learned what had happened to his family, he began to take personal revenge on the Germans, by participating in some reckless reconnaissance raids. Life expectancy in these army units was extremely short.

The changing tides of the War had a direct impact on the correspondence. We can glean from the letters the unmistakably gloomy and deteriorating atmosphere, which was increasingly evident as the German armies approached the North Caucasus region the first time, from late summer to fall, 1941, and again in the summer of 1942. In contrast, the letters written in the early summer of 1941 and in the winter to spring of 1941–1942 are optimistic, citing both the real and imagined triumphs of the Red Army. Written in a country known for its keen interest in the inner thoughts of its citizens, these letters also could be read with an eye to the Ginsburgs' fear of the Soviet censorship, real or exaggerated.[1] Viewed from this perspective, the book sheds new light on the limits of what was permissible under Stalin[2] or, framed more broadly, on the principles of communication between people in the USSR.[3]

This communication revolves around one main issue that permeates all the letters—evacuation: that is, if, when, and how the family should leave their home city, in order to evade capture by the Germans. It should be remembered

---

1 See, for example, Tat'iana Voronina, "Kak chitat' pis'ma s fronta? Lichnaia korrespondentsiia i pamiat' o Vtoroi mirovoi voine," *Neprikosnovennyi zapas* 3 (2011): 162.
2 For example: Robert Kindler, "Famines and Political Communication in Stalinism. Possibilities and Limits of the Sayable," *Jahrbücher für Geschichte Osteuropas* 62, no. 2 (2014): 255–272.
3 For example, Malte Griesse, *Communiquer, juger et agir sous Staline. La personne prise entre ses liens avec les proches et son rapport au système politico-idéologique* (Frankfurt a.M. [et al.]: Lang, 2011).

that, in ordinary situations, people do not abandon their homes—it takes the direst of circumstances to convince them to leave. If someone has no way back, for one reason or another, he becomes a refugee.[4] On their way to a new life, refugees may cross borders, and, in case of hostilities, even front lines, ceasefire lines, etc.

Economic factors bring an additional dimension to this story, creating a constant and nuanced interplay with "life and death" factors. The greater the danger threatening potential refugees, the less place economic considerations played in their decision-making, responding to immediate threats. Other refugees made their decisions more as a strategic choice, that is, not in response to immediate threats, and as a result, they often avoided being trapped in a dilemma between "life and death" factors and economic calculations. Still, all those who considered evacuation had to reckon with the fact that they would incur many expenses due to their flight and subsequent resettlement, resulting in their impoverishment.

The flight of Jews from the Soviet Union's western regions into the interior, in the initial phase following the German invasion in June 1941, placed them in the category of refugees, as broadly defined above. Generally speaking, Jews who remained in territory under German rule faced the danger of physical extermination, but this is knowledge we only possess *a posteriori*. Soviet Jews considering flight could not acquire any definite and direct facts about what awaited them under German occupation. The physical destruction of Jews began only after June 22, 1941, and the Germans did their best to keep it a secret. Jewish flight from the deadly reach of the Germans should be viewed against the background of the Soviet evacuation program. This was a large-scale state-run project, aimed primarily at safeguarding the Soviet military industries and the manpower they employed from being taken over by the Germans. These state employees, often with their families, were evacuated, by government orders, to the country's hinterland; there were also Jews amongst this group. In addition, there were others who were ordered by their local employers to continue working, even until the last days of Soviet rule. With the exception of these two categories, all the others had to decide on their own whether or not they wished

---

4   In this book, the terms "refugee" and "evacuee" are used interchangeably to denote all those Jews and non-Jews who moved out of the threatened Soviet regions, whether under a government-initiated program or independently, unless stated otherwise. By the same token, the terms "evacuation," "flight" and "escape" are also used interchangeably to describe the ways in which people moved out of the threatened Soviet regions, whether under a government-initiated program or on their own, unless stated otherwise.

to join the evacuees, and to act accordingly. It was on them that the evacuation program had the biggest impact, by creating a certain psychological climate. This amounted to a paradox, as the totalitarian Soviet regime, preoccupied with its own survival, left masses of people to decide for themselves. Thousands of individual Jews had to make the fateful decision, alone, whether or not to leave their home and seek shelter elsewhere.

For residents of Rostov-on-Don, this decision was based on what they thought about the course of the Soviet-German War, and the likelihood and danger of German occupation of their city. Their perceptions were influenced in turn by the news they were hearing and reading, which was often a function of how the Soviet media presented such information. The Soviet media, an important, and often the only official news supplier, was not regarded as trustworthy by many Soviet people. However, its coverage created a certain climate, as did the specific measures that the local authorities implemented (even though we do not know for certain how the population, Jewish and non-Jewish, interpreted what they heard and read). These factors affected the decision of individual families about whether to stay or to go, along with other factors, such as age, gender, family situation, employment status, opportunities for evacuation, and the procedures to be followed, as well as fears about the dangers involved in the evacuation process itself. The Ginsburg letters, although written to pass censorship, do mention at least some of the factors that they were considering in determining what to do.

It could be anticipated that Soviet reporting would be confusing, as it reflected Soviet ideological maxims, including the claim that the Germans targeted all groups under their domination, not only the Jews.[5] Likewise, it could be expected that the Soviet media would be torn between the mutually exclusive goals of calming the public and raising people's spirits, by providing news during the War while not sowing panic.

But probably the most crucial question concerns the reliability of the Soviet media in the eyes of its consumers, and most specifically, in the eyes of potential evacuees. By the outbreak of the Soviet-German War in June 1941, the Soviet media was widely viewed as the most important instrument of propaganda, but not as a reliable supplier of news.[6] In order to gain the confidence

---

5 Karel C. Berkhoff, *Motherland in Danger: Soviet Propaganda during World War II* (Cambridge, MA: Harvard University Press, 2012), 134–166.
6 On Soviet newspapers in the 1920s, that is, during the stage framing this perception, see Matthew Lenoe, *Closer to the Masses: Stalinist Culture, Social Revolution, and Soviet Newspapers* (Cambridge, MA: Harvard University Press, 2004).

of its audience, or to put it simply, to make people believe its reports, the Soviet media definitely needed more than just to exercise a monopoly in supplying news; its news had to look credible to the Soviet people. Given the dubious reputation of the Soviet media in the eyes of many Soviet people, it is likely that the Jews had to rely on their ability to read "between the lines" in order to grasp the hidden messages, and especially to understand the course of the War. On the whole, as long as they perceived the situation as being relatively stable and did not view it as a clear mortal threat, then "conventional," that is, cost-benefit considerations played an important role in the decision-making of some Jews regarding evacuation.[7] But, once the situation became or seemed to become critical, economic factors were increasingly dismissed, and then Jews fled or attempted to flee, irrespective of all other arguments.[8]

With the benefit of hindsight, a contemporary reader might surmise that the correct answer to the dilemma confronting Soviet Jews in the threatened areas as to which would have helped them decide the best time to escape was to leave when the situation remained relatively calm, there was no disorder, personal property could be sold at a good price, and the Soviet evacuation program, not yet overstrained by an excessive influx of refugees, still functioned properly. The ideal destination for the evacuees would be one that offered a relative abundance of food and a milder climate, connections that could lead to employment, or, more broadly, help refugees survive there economically, and finally, was far enough away from the German armies.

If official sources did not suffice, Soviet Jews had to turn to indirect sources of information. Consequently, Jewish refugees moving into the Soviet-controlled area and talking about the German persecution of Jews appeared to be the most trustworthy sources of information. Indeed, Jewish refugees who fled from the German-controlled part of Poland (they came into the Soviet Union from September to December 1939), and those escaping from the western regions of Soviet Russia (after the German invasion of the USSR on June 22,

---

7   The emphasis here is on the words "relatively stable" and "some." This does not mean that political and moral considerations in their deliberations were entirely non-existent. But several hundred testimonies, analyzed in my book (Kiril Feferman, *The Holocaust in the Crimea and the North Caucasus* [Jerusalem: Yad Vashem, 2016]), roughly half of them pertaining to the Caucasus, point to the overwhelming importance of economic factors when the Jews were discussing their motives for evacuation from this region.
8   Anna Shternshis, "Between Life and Death: Why Some Soviet Jews Decided to Leave and Others to Stay in 1941," *Kritika: Explorations in Russian and Eurasian History* 15, no. 3 (Summer 2014): 478–479.

1941) could share with Soviet Jews what they knew about the various forms of anti-Semitic persecution, including sporadic killings.[9] But, as mentioned above, they could not tell the Soviet Jews about the all-encompassing genocide of the Jews in their homeland because it only began after June 22, 1941, when Nazi Germany invaded the Soviet Union.

But not every Jew contacted the refugees. Some were discouraged from doing so by Soviet admonitions against spreading alarmism. Furthermore, at times the influx of refugees would cease, if the frontline stabilized. When the flow of information coming from the refugees was cut back, and the role of other informal sources for one reason or another also decreased, the result was an information void. In such a situation, the proportional influence of the Soviet media would increase once more.

Viewed from a general perspective, this book considers the many factors affecting the Soviet-Jewish evacuation to potentially safer Soviet territories, far from the danger of German occupation, during World War II: the availability of information, individual discretion and consideration of outside factors, the effects of spontaneous relocation, and new local hostilities. Another key factor was what the local authorities did or did not do to encourage or facilitate evacuation. Finally, the big question is what evacuation opportunities and resources were available in Rostov-on-Don (and who could take advantage of them, and how), which could be another source for documenting patterns of flight.[10] While focusing on the evacuation of one Jewish family, the book considers their situation as a case study of the larger issues involved in evacuation. The Ginsburgs' personal deliberations and reflections and their recurring hesitation are set against the background of major wartime events in their region and in their home city of Rostov-on-Don, between 1941 and 1942. These events included the abrupt change from a peaceful life to destitution as a result of the German bombardment, the German capture of Rostov-on-Don in November 1941, its subsequent recapture by the Red Army, which held it for seven months, and the fall of Rostov-on-Don to the Germans, once again, in July 1942.

---

9 For example, Mordechai Altshuler, "The Distress of Jews in the Soviet Union in the Wake of the Molotov-Ribbentrop Pact," *Yad Vashem Studies* 36, no. 2 (2008): 85–88.

10 Unfortunately, the archives in Rostov and Moscow can only provide fragmentary material, inadequate for establishing the dimensions not only which share of the evacuees the Jews constituted (comparing the relative number of Jews and non-Jews in the local population), but also of the general evacuation program in the city. It seems likely that most records were destroyed or lost during the two occupations of Rostov-on-Don.

The major points of the book are to describe the Holocaust and the Soviet-German War through the Soviet Jewish lens.[11] The book seeks to find an answer to the painful question that haunted the pitiably few survivors from this family: why didn't the Ginsburg family escape to safety? Unlike Leningrad under siege,[12] Rostov-on-Don was not encircled and it was possible to leave the city, during most of the period under study. Who bears the responsibility for this family's fatal decision not to leave, in 1942, while they still had the chance? During that time, the German genocidal actions against Jews became known, and indeed some Jews were killed when Rostov-on-Don underwent the first brief German occupation, in November 1941. Although the Ginsburgs could have left the city before the first German attack, they did not do so. They conveyed their feelings and assessments of their situation, in letters to a relative who was living in a safe territory. The rich collection of correspondence between the members of the Ginsburg family helps us to understand their seemingly illogical decisions, and, more generally, to study some of the basic issues confronting Jews in a world threatened by a German invasion: the availability (or lack) of information, the attitudes of local authorities and local population groups, the changing tides of war and the knowledge of the mass murder of other Jews, the impact of these factors on individual Jews and their families, and, lastly, the fateful and difficult decisions that they themselves had to make.

Until recently, scholarship—whether Western, Jewish, or Soviet/Russian—has ignored the personal experiences of Jewish refugees in the wartime Soviet Union. The studies made of the evacuation have mainly been based on the official Soviet documentation.[13] In recent years, more studies have been published, analyzing the experiences of evacuees sent to remote Soviet regions, far away from the battlefields of the Soviet-German War.[14] Refugees

---

11 Scholarship on this topic is rapidly expanding. See, for example, Arkadi Zeltser, "How the Jewish Intelligentsia Created the Jewishness of the Jewish Hero," in *Soviet Jews in World War II: Fighting, Witnessing, Remembering*, ed. Harriet Murav and Gennady Estraikh (Boston, MA: Academic Studies Press, 2014), 104–129. Cf. David Shneer, *Through Soviet Jewish Eyes: Photography, War, and the Holocaust* (New Brunswick, NJ: Rutgers University Press, 2011).
12 Vladimir L. Piankevich, "The Family under Siege: Leningrad, 1941–1944," *The Russian Review* 75 (2016): 107–137.
13 For example, Albert Kaganovich, "Jewish Refugees and Soviet Authorities during World War II," *Yad Vashem Studies* 38, no. 2 (2010): 85–121. Cf. Vadim Dubson, "On the Problem of the Evacuation of Soviet Jews in 1941 (New Archival Sources)," *Jews in Eastern Europe* 3, no. 40 (1999): 37–56.
14 For example, Albert Kaganovich, "Evreiskie bezhentsy v Kazakhstane vo vremia Vtoroi Mirovoi voiny," in Alexander Baron (ed.), *Istoriia, pamiat', liudi. Materialy V mezhdunarodnoi konferentsii* (Almaty: Assotsiatsiia "Mitsva," 2011), 13–31. Cf. Zeev Levin, "Antisemitism

who were transferred to these areas were not directly threatened by the German onslaught. The experiences of refugees who were living in the areas that faced an immediate German threat (or who escaped from one threatened zone into another) are usually only mentioned in passing.[15]

One reason for this is that the question of evacuation or escape is one of the more elusive Holocaust subjects because the process is difficult to trace and analyze. The events resulting in Jewish flight were kaleidoscopic because Jews in immediately threatened regions often had to make critical decisions within just a few hours, based on a spontaneous reaction to dramatic events, such as the news of a German land offensive in the area, or the experience of German bombardments. As a result, few refugees left written records of their experiences in real time. Those fortunate enough to reach a safe haven, far from the threat of the German army, endured enormous hardships along the road, which often dominated the saga of their flight. Unfortunately, little information is available in the official records of Jewish escape into Soviet territories that were safe from the danger of German attack.

When the Jews considered the pros and cons of their flight from potentially threatened Soviet territories, they also had to take into account their ability to overcome numerous obstacles, including the attitude of their employers and the authorities in charge of issuing the necessary authorization. Another aspect of evacuation involved the need for the Jews to mobilize all their financial resources, an essential step in preparing properly for a long journey with an uncertain ending. Ideally, nothing valuable would be left at home, since there were no guarantees that they would be able to return to the same property, and because people anticipated that evacuation, although formally a free-of-charge state program, would nevertheless turn out to be an expensive undertaking. To cope with this problem, the preparations for evacuation involved converting their savings into easily movable valuables. In addition, although few people still owned their own homes in the Soviet Union,[16] the fate of the property (whether the evacuation would affect their eligibility to move back in again when they returned) weighed heavily on potential evacuees.

---

and the Jewish Refugees in Soviet Kirgizia, 1942," *Jews in Russia and Eastern Europe* 1 (2003), 191–203.

15 The notable exception is Shternshis, "Between Life and Death," 477–504.
16 On the Bolshevik policies in housing question before the war, see Steven E. Harris, *Communism on Tomorrow Street: Mass Housing and Everyday Life after Stalin* (Baltimore, MD: The Woodrow Wilson Center Press and the Johns Hopkins University Press, 2013), 45–47, 49–52, 55–70.

There was also the necessity to plan in advance for the care of people with special requirements, such as children and the elderly, to prepare for cold winters (procuring warm clothes) and economic uncertainties (it was worth taking items such as sewing machines, which would help their displaced owners find part-time work and survive in the future). Finally, evacuation proved to be largely a women's concern because an ever-growing number of men had been called up to the army. So the women had to figure out whether and how they would be able to organize their own and their dependents' evacuation.

It should also be realized that evacuation was not a guaranteed recipe for survival during the War. The advancing Wehrmacht troops sometimes forestalled the Jewish refugees, many of whom perished sooner or later in the German-occupied territories. Other causes of death were German bombs dropped on the trains carrying evacuees, starvation and illness when on the road and at the places of destination. Even the below-minimum supplies of basic food and commodities supposedly guaranteed and provided by the Soviet state were frequently unavailable. As a result, landlords, merchants, those involved in transporting the escapees, robbers, and many others exploited the Jewish evacuees' plight. However, in spite of all these problems, it should be clearly recognized that the evacuation did give the Jews a chance to survive, which they would not have had if they had stayed in the areas occupied by the German army.

In terms of the book's structure, I have set the scene with three background chapters. In chapter 1.1, I have briefly outlined the history of the Jewish presence in the North Caucasus, from their first settling in the region to the outbreak of the Soviet-German War in 1941, interwoven with the prewar history of the Ginsburg family. In chapter 1.2, I have analyzed the movement of civilians in the wartime Soviet Union, focusing on the movement of evacuees *into* the North Caucasus.[17] Chapter 1.3 gives an overview of the murder of Jews in the North Caucasus during the German occupation. However, the occurrences in the city and District of Rostov[18] have been interwoven in the chapters that directly refer to the Ginsburg family correspondence. By the same token, other relevant topics, such as the warfare taking place in various parts of the region and evacuation *from* the North Caucasus are integrated in the analysis of the Ginsburg family correspondence because the family explicitly discussed these subjects.

---

17 We can only speculate on why this movement of evacuees into the North Caucasus happened: for example, none of the Ginsburg respondents observed this movement (highly unlikely), or they did not deem it worth mentioning in their letters (more plausible).

18 On this issue, see Christina Winkler, "Rostov-on-Don 1942: A Little-Known Chapter of the Holocaust," *Holocaust and Genocide Studies* 30, no. 1 (2016): 105–130.

There are one hundred and sixteen letters in the Ginsburg correspondence, and also many unsorted pages. Some of the letters are long, covering many pages, containing discussion and information, and expressing the writers' emotions; others are condensed on postcards, where much had to be put on just one small page; there are also telegrams, with the briefest information. All the letters, except for the telegrams, were handwritten in Russian. From this collection, I selected and translated ninety-nine items that seem to best illustrate the themes of the book. Furthermore, some letters have not been translated in their entirety—often I only selected parts of the letters for translation. What guided me in the selection process? The most basic consideration is that the letters are extremely repetitive. One of the main explanations why they sent so many letters, sometimes more than one on the same day, is that the senders were not certain, and justifiably so, that their letters would ever reach the addressee. (The other explanation is probably the repetitive style favored by the authors themselves.) Although it is no doubt important for readers to know that some themes were particularly recurrent in the correspondence, reproducing all the letters would—in my opinion—make the book difficult, if not impossible, to read. In addition, in a small number of cases, it was impossible to identify the author and/or the date of the letters. Basic information about all the letters, including those not translated for the book, can be found in a list of the letters, at the end of the book, before the Bibliography. This information is also present in footnotes scattered throughout the book, in the most appropriate places, chronologically.

The analysis of the letters written by the members of the Ginsburg family constitutes the bulk of this book. I have divided the letters into three parts: those written in 1941, 1942, and 1943. I have tried as far as possible to reconstruct the atmosphere in which the Ginsburgs wrote their letters. To this end, my comments following each letter provide perspective not only on the changing relationships within the family but, most specifically, on the changing course of the War, as it affected the region in which they lived. I have described military developments in the entire North Caucasus, which would have been of significance to the Ginsburgs, if they had known about them in real time, but which they may or may not have learned about from the Soviet media.

To provide a further perspective on the outlook of the Ginsburgs, I have interwoven their correspondence with other contemporary testimonies relating to this period. Although, in many cases, it cannot be established whether the Ginsburgs shared some or all of these views, these documents provide an important additional context. To this effect, I have also cited relevant secondary sources that were published between June 1941 and July 1942 in Rostov-on-Don and other North Caucasian cities to which Jews were evacuated. These sources include the central Soviet newspapers (*Pravda* and *Izvestiya*) largely available in Rostov-on-Don, as well the local Soviet newspapers published in the North Caucasus, most specifically the newspaper *Molot* (*Hammer*), which was printed in Rostov-on-Don.[19]

In an attempt to understand how the Ginsburgs' perception of the events was shaped, I have also included other Soviet sources, indicating whether or not they would have been available to the Ginsburgs. Furthermore, in an attempt to present a relatively accurate appraisal of the strategic situation in the region, I have included contemporary articles from *The New York Times* and *The Washington Post*, expanding on the course of the War in the Caucasus. In many cases, these articles present a critical reading of Soviet and German military communiques, a unique and largely forgotten source of information on the course of the War. I recognized their value as a real-time source, even if they were not available to the Ginsburgs. To obtain a real-time update on the military situation in the region), first I had to strip off the layers of propaganda; I have commented on these communiques, as well as on all the other sources cited in the book.

In selecting which sources to include, I have given priority to the local media, assuming that, as a rule, the local population, including members of the Ginsburg family, were primarily interested in the news about their own locality. Furthermore, in many cases, the news from official Soviet newspapers did not reach them. Consequently, I have chosen local news (such as a report concerning fighting in the Rostov theatre) and major news from other sectors (such as a successful Soviet advance in some region other than the southern Soviet-German front). By the same logic, among publications from outside the Caucasus, I have selected only those that were of paramount importance in promoting Jewish awareness of the extensity of the German threat.

Where I have added information in the letters, for clarification purposes, I have used square brackets and italics. The word "Note" has been used where it refers to an official announcement by the Soviet authorities. The word "War," on its own, has been capitalized whenever it refers to the Soviet-German War. Other references to war, such as "wartime" and "time of war," are not capitalized.

---

19 For a brief overview of the Soviet newspapers during the War, see S. V. Shpakovskaia, "Sovetskie gazety v gody Velikoi Otechestvennoi voiny," *Voprosy istorii* 5 (2014): 64–74.

As regards names, where the married name of the sisters is known (in the case of Anya and Liza), I have given both their married name and maiden name (in parenthesis) throughout chapter 1.1 and the first time that one of them is mentioned in the other chapters, and only used their maiden name (Ginsburg) thereafter. For all three sisters, I have given their formal first names followed by their diminutive names (in parenthesis) throughout chapter 1.1 and the first time that they are mentioned in the other chapters, and only used their diminutive names thereafter. However, where their names are mentioned in the footnotes, I have used "Liza Chazkewitz and Anya Greener," as their letters to Efim are referenced in this way at Yad Vashem.

Part One
Historical Background

CHAPTER 1.1

The Ginsburg Family in the North Caucasus

The Ginsburg family came originally from Odessa, which was probably the most important trading center of the Russian Empire and a major harbor on the Black Sea. Home to more than 125,000 Jews in 1897, the city was a flourishing center of Jewish economic life from the second half of the nineteenth century.[1] However, it was also a difficult place for many Jews to live in; most of them could only eke out a miserable existence in the city as small-time traders, shopkeepers, and workshop employers.[2] They faced vigorous competition with one another—every third inhabitant of Odessa was Jewish—and with non-Jews.

The new generation of the Ginsburgs: the sisters Manya (Monya), Anna (Anya), Elizaveta (Liza), and their brother Efim, were born in Odessa between 1890 and 1897. It is likely that their parents (father Gedaliya and mother Hanna-Rachel) were frustrated by the tough competition and the need to provide for their growing family. It is also likely that they were scared into leaving Odessa, especially after the pogrom that broke out in the city in October 1905, which led to the murder of some 400 Jews—the bloodiest pogrom in the Russian Empire up to that point.[3] As a result, Gedaliya and Hanna-Rachel took their four children and left Odessa, somewhere before 1912, probably soon after the pogrom.

---

1 On the general history of the Jews in Odessa, see Steven J. Zipperstein, *The Jews of Odessa: A Cultural History* (Stanford, CA: Stanford University Press, 1985).
2 Jarrod Tanny, *City of Rogues and Schnorrers: Russia's Jews and the Myth of Old Odessa* (Bloomington: Indiana University Press, 2011), 30.
3 On this pogrom and more generally on the strained relationship between Jews and non-Jews in Odessa in the years preceding the pogrom, see Caroline Humphrey, "Odessa: Pogrom in a Cosmopolitan City," *Ab Imperio* 4 (2010): 27–79.

The Ginsburgs chose to move to the city of Rostov-on-Don, situated only 800 km to the east of Odessa, where they managed to survive the turbulent years of World War I and the Russian Civil War. When they arrived in Rostov-on-Don, it already had a substantial Jewish population. The city, founded in 1749, had its own distinct history, including the history of its Jewish residents. It was a part of what we refer to today as the "North Caucasus," all of which now belongs to the Russian Federation. The region first came under the sway of the Russian Empire in the eighteenth and nineteenth centuries. Russian penetration into these territories was met with occasional fierce armed resistance by the local inhabitants.[4] Still, the Empire prevailed, and from the early 1860s onwards, the region was subdued.[5]

The settlement of Ashkenazi Jews in most of the North Caucasus region was generally prohibited, as the area was situated outside the Pale of Settlement.[6] The only exceptions were the cities of Rostov-on-Don and Taganrog, which, until 1887, were part of the Ekaterinoslav *guberniya* (province), and thus part of the Pale. The first reference to a Jewish presence in the North Caucasus can be traced back to 1800, when ten Jewish *meshchane* (petty bourgeois) were registered as residents of the Rostov *uezd* (area).[7] As the Russian penetration into the region brought peace and prospects for economic development, Jews began to flock to the North Caucasus. Their prospects were doubtless better in these territories than in the overcrowded Pale of Settlement. As of 1838, some 6,000 Jews were registered in the Ekaterinoslav province, constituting 0.59% of the total population. According to another source, 26,069 Jews were living in the province in 1864.[8] In the same year, there were 289 Jews living in the city of

---

4 See, for example, Firouzeh Mostashari, *On the Religious Frontier: Tsarist Russia and Islam in the Caucasus* (London: Tauris, 2006); *Russian-Muslim Confrontation in the Caucasus: Alternative Visions of the Conflict between Imam Shamil and the Russians, 1830–1859*, ed. Thomas Sanders, Ernest Tucker, and Gary Hamburg (London: Routledge Curzon, 2004).

5 For example, Timothy K. Blauvelt, "Military-Civil Administration and Islam in the North Caucasus, 1858–1883," *Kritika: Explorations in Russian and Eurasian History* 11, no. 2 (Spring 2010): 221–255.

6 The Pale of Settlement was the area where Ashkenazi Jews were specifically permitted to live in the Russian Empire. Non-Ashkenazi Mountain Jews, who were regarded by the Imperial authorities as native peoples (*gortsy*), were permitted to live in the North Caucasus region, where they generally did not face the restrictions applied to Ashkenazi Jews. However, after 1887 Mountain Jews also experienced a deterioration in their standing. Ekaterina Norkina, "The Origins of Anti-Jewish Policy in the Cossack Regions of the Russian Empire, Late Nineteenth and Early Twentieth Century," *East European Jewish Affairs* 43, no. 1 (2013): 62–76.

7 Mikhail Gontmakher, *Evrei na donskoi zemle. Istoriia, fakty, biografiia* (Rostov-na-Donu: RostIzdat, 1999), 20.

8 Ibid., 20–21.

Rostov-on-Don (3.1% of the total population). There were also Jews among the soldiers and *kantonisty* stationed in the Dimitri Rostovski fortress.[9] Rostov-on-Don continued to attract Jews, and by 1866, their numbers had reached 2,500, almost 6% of the total population of the city.[10] One of the most important Russian Jewish industrialists and bankers, Samuil Polyakov, was active in the area from the late 1860s onwards.[11]

Towards the end of Alexander II's reign, the Tsarist government attempted to put an end to the semi-legal Jewish presence in the province. On May 22, 1880, the "Caucasian" parts of the *guberniya* were given to *Oblast' voiska Donskogo* (the Province of the Don Cossack Host), where Jews were explicitly banned from living and owning property. The new law was rigorously enforced, and all the Jews living in the region (which roughly includes the present-day Rostov district) with the exception of the two big cities, Rostov-on-Don and Taganrog, were expelled and sent back to the Pale of Settlement.[12]

The Tsarist government endeavoured to complete the expulsion of the Jews in 1887, when the area around Rostov-on-Don and Taganrog and the cities themselves were annexed by the Province of the Don Cossack Host. As a result, the residence and property ban was extended to include the Jews living in the two cities. Up to 10,000 Rostov Jews were due to be deported, but the decree was suspended after the Rostov City Council petitioned for its reversal on the grounds that it would be detrimental to the development of trade.[13]

The only population census conducted in the Russian Empire, in 1897, revealed the following statistical data regarding the presence of Jews (including Mountain Jews)[14] in the North Caucasus: there were 15,978 Jews in the Province of the Don Cossack Host, 2,196 in the area of the Kuban Cossackdom, and 6,582 in the area of the Terek Cossackdom.[15]

---

9 Ibid., 22.
10 Ibid., 23.
11 Ibid., 25–28.
12 Ibid., 29–31.
13 Ibid., 41–42.
14 The Mountain Jews were a small ethnic group, originally made up of Persian Jews, but much influenced by the surrounding peoples of the Caucasus region. See, for example, Sasha S. Goluboff, "'Are They Jews or Asians?' A Cautionary Tale about Mountain Jewish Ethnography," *Slavic Review* 63, no. 1 (2004), 113–140.
15 Sergei Markedonov, "Evrei v oblasti voiska Donskogo v kontse 19—nachale 20 veka," in *Trudy Vtoroi molodezhnoi konferentsii SNG po iudaike—"Tirosh"* (Moscow: Sefer, 1998), http://www.jewish-heritage.org/jr2a18r.htm, accessed November 30, 2011.

According to the Russian population census of 1897, among all other nationalities registered in Rostov-on-Don, the Jews had the highest level of literacy for men (71.7%) and one of the highest for women (54.7%). Unlike in other parts of the Empire, in the city of Rostov-on-Don relatively many who professed Judaism declared that Yiddish was not their mother tongue. This was due to the presence of many Mountain Jews.[16]

The North Caucasian Jews led an intensive religious and social life. In 1864, the local authorities recorded the presence of eleven synagogues and twenty-four prayer houses in the Ekaterinoslav province.[17] In the city of Rostov-on-Don, a soldiers' synagogue was opened in 1872, and the main synagogue was also inaugurated at that time.[18] In the 1880s, a Jewish hospital was opened in Rostov-on-Don.[19] By the end of the nineteenth century, the Rostov Jewish community could boast several *Talmudei Torah* (Jewish primary schools), a Jewish public college for girls, and a Jewish college acting under the auspices of the synagogue.[20]

As elsewhere in the Russian Empire, many of the younger generation of Rostov Jews became dissatisfied with the Tsarist regime, and joined the ranks of the revolutionaries.[21] In the second half of October 1905, a pogrom occurred in Rostov-on-Don, which also involved clashes between the Black Hundreds[22] and revolutionary-minded workers and young people. Some 150 Jews were slaughtered in the pogrom, which made it the second bloodiest pogrom in the Russian Empire (after Odessa) before the Russian Civil war.[23]

The next landmark in the history of Rostov Jewry was the arrival in the city of the fifth Lubavicher Rabbi, Rabbi Sholom Dov-Ber Schneerson, in 1915.[24] He spent five years there, until he passed away in 1920.

Contrary to what occurred in many other parts of the former Russian Empire, after the Bolshevik revolution in November 1917, the sympathies of at

---

16　Gontmakher, *Evrei na donskoi zemle*, 59–61.
17　Ibid., 20–21.
18　Ibid., 23.
19　Ibid., 38–39.
20　Ibid., 49.
21　Ibid., 55–56, 75–76.
22　The Black Hundreds (in Russian—*Chernaia sotnia*) was a vaguely defined Russian nationalist movement that started during the First Russian Revolution (1905–1907). It was vociferously anti-Semitic, and its members took an active part in pogroms against the Jews. On this movement, see Walter Laqueur, *Black Hundred: The Rise of The Extreme Right in Russia* (New York: Harper Collins Publishers, 1993).
23　Ibid., 109–111.
24　Andrew N. Koss, "War Within, War Without: Russian Refugee Rabbis during World War I," *AJS Review* 34, no. 2 (2010): 239–240.

least the more prosperous local Jews were with the White Russians. On December 13, 1917, A. Alperin, an important local merchant, delivered 800,000 rubles that had been collected by Rostov Jews to the *Ataman* of the Province of the Don Cossack Host for the fight against the Bolsheviks.[25]

In the course of the Russian Civil war in 1917–1920, the Jewish population in the North Caucasus found itself largely under the control of the White Russian movement. It is well known that a considerable number of White Russian troops espoused strong anti-Semitic feelings (see further on). In spite of this, in the North Caucasus the situation remained under control, obviously because of the relatively strong rule of the White administration, and there were no reports of significant anti-Jewish excesses there.[26] For some months, in the second half of 1918, part of the region, including the city of Rostov-on-Don, was occupied by the German army.[27] On the whole, under White Russian rule, independent internal Jewish life continued during these years, with a particular rise in Zionist activities.[28]

With the advent of the Bolsheviks, anti-Semitism in the region did not disappear but largely went underground.[29] Nevertheless, the infrequent reports published in a Rostov newspaper in 1929 depict vicious verbal attacks by local workers, who lashed out at their Jewish colleagues at the city's plants.[30] Still, the Jewish population in the region grew slightly in the period between the two World Wars, attracted by growing economic prospects and relatively plentiful food,[31] an important factor in the Soviet Union at that time. On the eve of the

---

25 *Kratkaia Evreiskaia Entsiklopediia* (Jerusalem: Hebrew University of Jerusalem, 1994), vol. 7, 402–404.
26 Markedonov, "Evrei v oblasti voiska Donskogo."
27 It seems that from the Jewish perspective, the German occupation of the region in 1918 brought about calm and relief from pogroms or from fear of pogroms. On the military aspects of the German drive to the region, see Reinhard Nachtigal, "Krasnyj Desant: Das Gefecht an der Mius-Bucht. Ein unbeachtetes Kapitel der deutschen Besetzung Südrußlands 1918," *Jahrbücher für Geschichte Osteuropas* 53, no. 2 (2005): 221–246.
28 Oleg Budnitskii, "Evrei Rostova-na-Donu na perelome epokh (1917–1920)," in *Rossiiskii sionizm: istoriia i kul'tura* (Moscow: Evreiskoe agentstvo v Rossii, SEFER, Dom evreiskoi knigi, 2002). Cf. Oleg Budnitskii, "The Jews in Rostov-on-Don in 1918–1919," *Jews and Jewish Topics in the Soviet Union and Eastern Europe* 3, no. 19 (1992): 16–29.
29 On one of the few examples of an open manifestation of anti-Jewish sentiments (directed against Mountain Jews), see Lyudmila Gatagova, "Caucasian Phobias and the Rise of Antisemitism in the North Caucasus in the 1920s," *The Soviet and Post-Soviet Review* 36 (2009): 42–57.
30 "Na bor'bu s antisemitizmom," *Molot* (Rostov-on-Don), December 14, 1928 and January 16, 1929. Quoted in: Gontmakher, *Evrei na donskoi zemle*, 167–168.
31 The emphasis here is on the word "relatively." Soviet famine in the 1930s also struck at the North Caucasus, albeit arguably on a lower scale than elsewhere in the country. Brian J. Boeck, "Complicating the National Interpretation of the Famine: Reexamining the

Soviet-German War, the small Jewish population was concentrated in several large North Caucasian cities, with Rostov-on-Don having by far the largest Jewish population in the region. According to the 1939 Soviet population census, 27,039 Jews (5.3% of the total population) lived in Rostov-on-Don,[32] while 33,024 Jews (1.1% of the total) lived in the whole Rostov District.[33] In addition, 4,600 Jews were registered in Kabardino-Balkaria, 2,100 in North Ossetia, 7,600 in the Krasnodar territory, and 7,100 in the Stavropol territory.[34]

The region was noteworthy for its unique Cossack population, well known for its anti-Semitic mindset. The Cossacks participated in the deportation of Jews by the Tsarist army during World War I,[35] and were actively involved in the pogroms in Ukraine, for example, in 1919.[36] The Bolshevik anti-Cossack crusade[37] (likely associated, one way or another, with the Jews, in the eyes of the local people in the region), included the Bolshevik onslaught on the Cossacks during the Collectivization period (presided over by Lazar Kaganovich, the only Jewish member of Stalin's inner circle).[38] The continuing anti-Semitic sentiment inculcated in the local people was latent, as it had almost no way

---

Case of Kuban," *Harvard Ukrainian Studies* 30, no. 1/4 (2008): 31–48. Cf. Andrea Graziosi and Dominique Négrel, "'Lettres de Kharkov': La famine en Ukraine et dans le Caucase du Nord à travers les rapports des diplomates italiens, 1932–1934," *Cahiers du monde russe et soviétique* 30, nos. 1–2 (Janvier–Juin 1989): 5–106.

32 *Vsesoiuznaia perepis' naseleniia 1939 goda. Osnovnye itogi* (Moscow: Nauka, 1992), 24, 26. According to German sources, in Rostov there lived from 200,000 to 300,000 civilians. Andrej Angrick, *Besatzungspolitik und Massenmord. Die Einsatzgruppen D in der südlichen Sowjetunion, 1941–1943* (Hamburg: Hamburger Edition, 2003), 561.

33 Evgenii Movshovich, "11 avgusta—60 let tragedii v Zmievskoi balke," *Shma* (Rostov-na-Donu) 7, no. 36 (May 15–July 24, 2002): 3. Cf. Vladimir Kabuzan, *Naselenie Severnogo Kavkaza v 19–20 vekakh: etnostatisticheskoe issledovanie* (St. Petersburg: Izd-vo "Russko-Baltiiskii informatsionnyi tsentr BLITS," 1996), 209.

34 Including Mountain Jews. *Distribution of the Jewish Population of the USSR 1939*, ed. Mordechai Altshuler (Jerusalem: Hebrew University, Center for the Research of East European Jewry, 1993), 13–15.

35 John Klier [as Dzhon Klir], "'Kazaki i pogromy': Chem otlichalis' voennye pogromy," in *Mirovoi krizis 1914–1920 gg. i sud'ba vostochnoevropeiskogo evreistva*, ed. Oleg Budnitskii (Moscow: ROSPEN, 2005), 55–56, 59–60.

36 Peter Kenez, *Civil War in South Russia, 1919–1920. The Defeat of the Whites* (Berkeley: University of California, 1977), 172. Cf. Iosif Shekhtman, *Pogromy Dobrovol'cheskoi Armii na Ukraine: K istorii antisemitizma na Ukraine v 1919–1920 gg.* (Berlin: Ostjüdisches Historisches Archiv, 1932), 31, 76.

37 Elena Khachemizova, *Obshestvo i vlast' v 30-e—40-e gody XX veka: Politika repressii (na materialakh Krasnodarskogo kraia)*, PhD diss., Maikop, Adygeiskii gosudarstvennyi universitet, 2004, 44–107.

38 E. A. Rees, *Iron Lazar: A Political Biography of Lazar Kaganovich* (London: Anthem Press: 2012), 110–111, 113, 121.

to express itself, before the Germans occupied parts of the region. But it was significant, judging by the noticeable number of active collaborators and quiet denouncers in the North Caucasus during the German occupation.[39] It was not all-encompassing, however, as evidenced by some manifestations of sympathy towards the Jews under Soviet rule before the German occupation in 1941–1942, and especially during the occupation.[40]

Finally, we should mention that the oppressive Soviet policies adversely affected the whole population of the North Caucasus, as they did the rest of the country. During the 1930s, some 42,000 Russian civilians were "repressed" (to adopt the Soviet term), that is, either shot down or incarcerated in the Azov-Chernomorsk territory (an administrative unit with the capital in Rostov-on-Don, which existed from 1934 to 1938).[41] The Cossacks, the Bolsheviks' bitter enemies during the Russian Civil war, suffered particularly as a result of these policies.[42] It is suggested that these policies affected local Jews, in a similar way to the rest of the population, but no worse.[43]

During the 1920s and the 1930s, most members of the Ginsburg family continued to live in Rostov-on-Don. It seems that following their relocation to a considerably more Russian and less Jewish city than Odessa, father Gedaliya changed his first name to Grigory, probably in order to improve his standing with his customers. But his wife kept her Jewish-sounding name, probably because she did not work outside their home. However, we cannot rule out that this behavior also reflected the different attitude of the husband and wife to assimilation. Presumably they died in the 1920s or the 1930s, but we do not know when or how they died, for the correspondence does not mention them even once.

The only family member who was not living in Rostov-on-Don at the end of the 1930s was the youngest brother, Efim Ginsburg (1897–1973). The brother of the three aunts, he received almost every letter in this collection and managed to keep them in his possession during and after World War II.

---

39 Feferman, *The Holocaust in the Crimea*, 427–435.
40 Ibid., 438–441.
41 Evgenii Zhuravlev, *Kollaboratsionizm na iuge Rossii v gody Velikoi Otechestvennoi voiny (1941–1945 gg.)* (Rostov-on-Don: Izd-vo Rostovskogo universiteta, 2006), 22–27, 42.
42 Natal'ia Bulgakova, *Sel'skoe naselenie Stavropol'ia vo vtoroi polovine 20-kh—nachale 30-kh godov 20 veka: Izmeneniia v demograficheskom, khoziaistvennom i kul'turnom oblike*, PhD diss., Stavropol, Stavropol'skii gosudarstvennyi universitet, 2003, 17–18.
43 Dissertations written in the North Caucasus by local researchers do not mention a noticeable Jewish presence among the regional power elites in the 1930s. Aleksandr Savochkin, *Massovye repressii 30–40-kh gg. 20 v. na Severnom Kavkaze kak sposob utverzhdeniia i podderzhaniia iskliuchitel'noi samostoiatel'nosti gosudarstva*, PhD diss., Vladimir, Vladimirskii iuridicheskii institut Federal'noi sluzhby ispolneniia nakazanii, 2008. Cf. Khachemizova, *Obshestvo i vlast'*.

Efim Ginsburg. 1930s. Courtesy of Yad Vashem Photo Archive.

His road from Rostov-on-Don to Moscow had been a very tortuous one. In 1921, Efim Ginsburg was imprisoned by the Soviet authorities on account of his "belonging to a socialist party,"[44] as recorded in the database compiled by the Russian "Memorial" society. If we try to interpret this meager information, it seems most plausible that Efim Ginsburg (who turned twenty in 1917) had been affiliated with one of the Russian socialist parties (but not with the Bolsheviks or with Jewish Socialist parties) even before 1917. I assume that most likely he was a member of the Menshevik faction,[45] or a Socialist Revolutionary party with their particularly high number of Jewish followers. This would

---

44 I would like to thank an anonymous reviewer of this book for providing me with the clue as to where to search for Efim Ginsburg's background during the prewar period. I contacted the Russian "Memorial" society, which gathers information on former members of Socialist parties in Russia. They had a couple of lines devoted to Efim Ginsburg and finally they were able to confirm that indeed we were talking about the same person.

45 On the Menshevik path in the Russian Revolution, see, for example, Abraham Ascher, "The Mensheviks in the Russian Revolution," *Zmanim: A Historical Quarterly* 27/28 (1988): 38–53 [Hebrew]. On the Socialist Revolutionaries, see, for example, Marc Jansen, *A Show Trial under Lenin: The Trial of the Socialist Revolutionaries, Moscow, 1922* (The Hague: M. Nijhoff, 1982).

account for his persecution by the authorities as early as 1921, that is, immediately after the Bolsheviks managed to consolidate their rule in Rostov-on-Don, at the end of the Civil War.

Unfortunately, there is almost no information about Efim Ginsburg's life between 1927, when he was released from prison, and late 1939, when he resurfaced in the Ginsburg correspondence.[46] So all we can do is to try to conjecture how he spent those years. The likelihood that the Soviet security agencies would have left him alone and that he was not hounded or discriminated against in that period would seem low. It is highly unlikely that Efim Ginsburg's socialist past would have been entirely erased from police records.[47] Formally, the rights of all those suffering from legal disenfranchisement were reinstated according to the 1936 "Stalin" Constitution.[48] But, in fact, people with such backgrounds were the first on the list of those targeted by the largest wave of the Big Terror in 1937–1938, and the odds were high that Efim Ginsburg would not have survived.

Yet he did survive, and this begs for an explanation. There were some, albeit minor, exceptions to the aforementioned trends in the Soviet policies. Some members of Socialist parties were able to change their banners and join the victorious Bolshevik regime. One of the most prominent examples is Andrei Vyshynsky, who, in 1917, as a minor official, signed the Provisional Government order to arrest Lenin. He formally switched allegiance from the Menshevik party to the Bolsheviks only in 1920, but was, nevertheless, able to rise to prominence in the Soviet Union, becoming a Chief Prosecutor in 1935–1939 and the Minister of Foreign Affairs in 1949–1953. Certainly even Vyshinsky knew that such a stain on his reputation could never be entirely removed. Presumably, this was the reason why he was particularly compliant in his dealings with the Soviet leaders, especially the security chiefs.[49]

In Efim Ginsburg's case, whatever his path during these turbulent years, by the end of 1939 (when he received the first letter from his family), he was living legally in Moscow, the capital of the Soviet Union, which indicates that

---

46 The only exception is few photos dating 1932 and 1936, which either featured Efim or were addressed to him.
47 David R. Shearer, *Policing Stalin's Socialism: Repression and Social Order in the Soviet Union, 1924–1953* (New Haven, CT: Yale University Press, 2009), especially pp. 158–180.
48 Golfo Alexopoulos, *Stalin's outcasts: Aliens, citizens, and the Soviet state, 1926–1936* (Ithaca, NY: Cornell University Press, 2003), 170–174. Disenfranchisement in the Soviet Union entailed a ban on participation in elections. It also meant receiving a reduced amount of food coupons, or not receiving them at all, a ban on certain types of employment, etc.
49 Valentin Berezhkov, *Kak ia stal perevodchikom Stalina* (Moscow: DEM, 1993), 226.

all previous charges against him had been formally dropped by that time. And yet, it seems obvious that he spent those years in constant fear, as did his family. This would account for the fact that, when the correspondence began, Efim Ginsburg was living separately from the rest of the family and probably had not communicated with them for many years. It may be the reason why the first letter in the correspondence (not analyzed in this book) was sent in late December 1939,[50] the year when the wave of terror after the Great Purges subsided.[51] Possibly, the Ginsburgs had decided that conducting a correspondence would no longer jeopardize the Rostov branch of the family, especially Volodya Meerovich, the highest-ranking member of the clan.

The fact that Efim (and, in a wider sense, the entire Ginsburg family) belonged to the circle of those oppressed by the Stalin regime certainly sheds a special light on the correspondence. By all accounts, the family members were predisposed to be particularly cautious in putting their "deviationist" (that is, different from the officially approved) thoughts down on paper, to a greater extent than ordinary Soviet people. It is a big question, whether and to what extent their experience was so unique, given the vast number of people who suffered from Stalinist repression.[52] But in any case, it adds an additional and extremely important layer to the considerations of the Ginsburg family members as to whether they should flee or not, and what to include or avoid mentioning in their letters.

We do not have any information about Efims's profession. The letters only allude to his important position and his being appreciated by his superiors (at least, in the eyes of his sisters). As the correspondence never mentions his wife or children, it seems most likely that he was not married and had no children at the time of the Soviet-German War. It indeed looks plausible, given his apparently turbulent prewar years. In July 1941, he was evacuated from Moscow to Omsk.[53] Then he was evacuated for a second time, from Omsk to Alma-Ata

---

50 Letter from Liza Chazkewitz in Rostov-on-Don, December 26, 1939, YVA: O.75/324, pp. 3–4.
51 See, for example, Michael Parrish, *The Lesser Terror: Soviet State Security, 1939–1953* (Westport, CT: Praeger, 1996), 1–51.
52 On the restrictions on communication under Stalin, see for example, Kindler, "Famines and Political Communication in Stalinism," 255–272.
53 On the evacuation to Siberia, see, for example, *Vo imia pobedy; evakuatsiia grazhdanskogo naseleniya v Zapadnuiu Sibir' v gody Velikoi Otechestvennoi voiny v dokumentakh i materialakh*, ed. L. Snegireva (Tomsk: Izdatel'stvo TGPU, 2005), vol. 1: *Iskhod*; Kristen E. Edwards, *Fleeing to Siberia: The Wartime Relocation of Evacuees to Novosibirsk, 1941–1943*, PhD diss., Stanford, CA, Stanford University, 1996.

(now Almaty in Kazakhstan).[54] The sad irony is that, since he did not die in the Holocaust, there was no one who could submit any information about him, apart from several small biographical details released by his widow, Ida, in the file submitted to Yad Vashem in 1989.

Towards the end of the Soviet-German War, Efim Ginsburg returned to Moscow. He married Ida Markovna Dektor sometime after 1943. Ida was a philologist, speech therapist, and translator. She taught at the Institute of Literature. The only thing we know about Efim's postwar pursuits is that in the 1960s "he wrote books on technical issues."[55] In 1973, only ten days after the end of the Yom Kippur War, the couple left the Soviet Union and immigrated to Israel. According to a handwritten note added by Ida Ginsburg-Dektor to one of the Ginsburg letters, he was granted special permission to take the entire correspondence with him abroad,[56] which was an unusually big concession for the Soviet authorities to make. The couple made their home in the city of Ramat Gan, where Efim died in 1973, only two months after arriving in Israel. His widow donated the vast correspondence that he had conducted with those members of the Ginsburg family who were murdered during the Holocaust to the Yad Vashem Archives in Jerusalem, in 1989. All my attempts to find Ida or any children they might have had, or any other member of his family have proved futile.

At the start of the Soviet-German War, the Rostov branch of the family numbered ten people, was made up of three generations. Among the adults, there were five women and three men, one of whom died a natural death in the fall of 1941. There were also two children in the family. The older generation was represented by three sisters. (The information about their husbands is also presented in this study.)[57] As can be seen from their correspondence, the three sisters thought of themselves as elderly, although by modern standards they were only middle-aged. This was because life expectancy in Soviet Russia was much lower than what is customary today in the developed world. In 1939, it was 49.7 years for women and 44.0 for men.[58]

---

54 On the evacuation to Kazakhstan, see, for example, Kaganovich, "Evreiskie bezhentsy."
55 Shulamit Shalit, "Mne rekomendovali vziat' psevdonim. (Mark Kopshytser, 1923–1982)," http://berkovich-zametki.com/2005/Starina/Nomer9/Shalit1.htm, accessed March 12, 2016. I am grateful to the anonymous reviewer of the manuscript who gave me the clue to search for Efim Ginsburg in this publication.
56 No date, YVA: O.75/324, p. 406.
57 See the section "August 1942" for details of when and how the members of the Ginsburg family were murdered.
58 Boris Urlanis, *Rozhdaemost'i prodolzhitel'nost' zhizni v SSSR* (Moscow: Gosstatizdat, 1963), 103–104.

1) Manya (Monya) (née Ginsburg) was born in Odessa in 1890 to Gedalia and Hanna-Rachel; she was married to Pinchas (Pinya). She was Tamara Meerovich's mother. She was murdered by the Germans in the Rostov District in August 1942.

Monya was the oldest family member. (We do not know her married name, so for the purposes of our book we will also refer to her as a Ginsburg, which was certainly her maiden name). She was not employed in 1941–1942, and mainly kept herself busy looking after her grandson, Grisha. She didn't take part in the correspondence with Efim.

2) Anna (Anya) Greener (née Ginsburg) was born in Odessa in 1893 to Gedalia and Hanna-Rachel; she married Avraham Greener (1890–1942),[59] also from Odessa. They had one daughter, Tsylya, who married David Pinchos, and one granddaughter, Anya.

Anya Greener. Courtesy of Yad Vashem Hall of Names.

---

59 Although in the information submitted to Yad Vashem, Efim Ginsburg's widow wrote that Avraham Greener had perished in 1942 during the Holocaust in the Rostov district, there is no reference to this in the correspondence.

Anya, the second sister, was *sluzhashchaia* ("functionaire" or "employee," in Soviet parlance). During 1941–1942, she did not work and was mainly in charge of the house and of buying food for the family. Anya almost never signed the letters sent to Efim, but her sister Liza, who appears as the principal correspondent from this part of the family, repeatedly emphasized that the letters were written by both sisters. She was murdered in the Rostov District in August 1942.

3) Elizaveta (Liza) Chazkewitz (née Ginsburg) was born in Odessa in 1895 to Gedalia and Hanna-Rachel; she married Boris Chazkewitz, and worked as a pharmacist.

Elizaveta (Liza) Chazkewitz. Courtesy of Yad Vashem Hall of Names.

Liza, the third sister, had no children. She had a profession, pharmacist, with which she could earn her living and even support her sister Anya, and sometimes even other members of the family. Liza was very actively involved in the correspondence. From the letters, it is clear that she always acted together with her older sister Anya, which gave them a high standing in the interfamilial relationship. She was murdered in the Rostov District in August 1942.

4) Boris Chazkewitz, born in 1893, was married to Liza Ginsburg; he died in Rostov-on-Don in September 1941.

Boris Chazkewitz. Courtesy of Yad Vashem Hall of Names.

Although he signed one letter, together with his wife, we know nothing about him, except for the fact that his health deteriorated dramatically in late summer 1941. He had to go on working, despite his illness. He died of natural causes on September 18, 1941, that is, two months before the first German occupation of Rostov-on-Don.

Anya and Liza were not evacuated from Rostov-on-Don in 1941; they survived the first German occupation of the city (November 21–28, 1941). They remained in Rostov-on-Don until July 1942, when the entire family moved to the village of Rogovskoe in the Rostov District, situated more than a hundred kilometers from the city. They were murdered there, after the Germans occupied the area in August 1942.

The younger generation was represented by the Meerovich and Pinchos families.

5) Tamara Meerovich was born 1913 in Rostov-on-Don to Pinya and Monya. She was married to Vladimir (Volodya) Meerovich and was the mother of Grisha. Tamara worked as a book-keeper.

Tamara Meerovich. Courtesy of Yad Vashem Hall of Names.

Tamara was actively involved in the correspondence, after she was evacuated from Rostov-on-Don in October 1941 together with her mother and son and the Pinchos family, first to the town of Budennovsk in the neighboring Krasnodar territory, and then, in late December 1941, to the slightly more remote city of Ordzhonikidze (now called Vladikavkaz), the capital of the Autonomous Republic of North Ossetia. Prior to her departure, it seems that she decided that the letters sent by Efim Ginsburg's sisters, Anya and Lisa, reflected her own point of view well enough or—this seems to be more likely—she did not wish to publicly voice her disagreement with her aunts, in order not to upset her uncle Efim.

Tamara was employed and was able to provide for her family. She stayed in Ordzhonikidze until early June 1942, when she returned to Rostov-on-Don. She was murdered, with the rest of her family, in August 1942, in the village of Rogovskoe in the Rostov District.

6) Vladimir (Volodya) Meerovich, date of birth unknown. Volodya was married to Tamara Meerovich and was the father of Grisha.

Vladimir Meerovich, Tamara, and their son Grisha. Courtesy of Yad Vashem Hall of Names.

Volodya was employed in a relatively important position in one of Rostov's plants, and was probably a member of the Bolshevik Party. In November 1941, he defended Rostov-on-Don fighting in the ranks of the so-called "Extermination

Battalion."⁶⁰ Then he was evacuated, together with his plant, to the nearby city of Ordzhonikidze. In early March 1942, Volodya and his plant were evacuated back to Rostov-on-Don. On April 21, he was conscripted into the Red Army. His last letters show that he was still alive in April 1943. He received information about the fate of his family before he was killed in action against the Germans in mid-1943, apparently intent on avenging their murder.

The Pinchos family consisted of:

7) David (Dod or Doda), born in Rostov-on-Don in 1912, was an "employee" (*sluzhashchii*). He was married to Tsylya Pinchos and was the father of Anya.

David Pinchos. Courtesy of Yad Vashem Hall of Names.

---

60 Extermination (*istrebitel'nyi*) battalions were established in accordance with the decree of the Council of People's Commissars from June 24, 1941 "On the protection of enterprises and institutions [against enemy spies and saboteurs] and the establishment of extermination battalions in the endangered areas." Their members (both men and women) were selected from people considered to be ideologically reliable. They underwent a short military training, and their service was regulated by the Military Code of the Red Army. At the same time, they continued with their usual employment. Several times a week (as the front line moved nearer, this frequency increased) they gathered for training and at night they guarded sensitive establishments, carrying their weapons. When the Germans approached the city, some of the extermination battalions participated in the fighting, while others formed the nucleus of future partisan units. On the extermination battalions in the North Caucasus, see Elena Nikulina, *Istrebitel'nye batal'ony Stavropol'ia i Kubani v gody Velikoi Otechestvennoi voiny: 1941–1945 gg.*, PhD diss., Pyatigorsk, Piatigorskii gosudarstvennyi lingvisticheskii universitet, 2005.

David served in the Red Army from fall 1941 to spring 1942. He was released from the Army in spring 1942 due to his very poor health. He returned to his family in Rostov-on-Don and was murdered with the others in the Rostov District in August 1942. He was not involved in the correspondence.

8) Tsylya, born in Rostov-on-Don in 1914 to Avraham and Anya Greener, was married to David Pinchos, and was the mother of Anya.

Tsylya Pinchos. Courtesy of Yad Vashem Hall of Names.

Tsylya seems to have had no formal profession, but took occasional side jobs as a tutor. She was evacuated with her daughter, together with the Meerovich family, first to Budennovsk, and then to Ordzhonikidze. She returned to Rostov-on-Don in early March, 1942. She was murdered in the village of Rogovskoe in the Rostov District in August 1942.

The youngest generation consisted of the two Meerovich and Pinchos children.

9) Grigory (his formal name, which the family never used. He was usually called Grisha) Meerovich was born in 1936 in Rostov-on-Don and murdered in the Rostov District in August 1942.

10) Anna (her formal name, which the family never used. She was usually called Anya, or Anechka) Pinchos was born in Rostov-on-Don in 1935, and was murdered in the Rostov District in August 1942.

Ania Pinchos. Courtesy of Yad Vashem Hall of Names.

On October 13, 1941, several days before the Germans seized Rostov-on-Don, Tamara Meerovich, her son Grisha, mother Monya, and her cousin Tsylya Pinchos with her daughter Anya were evacuated from the city by train to Budennovsk in the Ordzhonikidze District, situated some 580 km to the south-east of Rostov-on-Don.

In the first half of 1942, the two evacuee branches of the family returned to Rostov-on-Don. In March 1942, Tsylya Pinchos was the first to go back, with her daughter Anya. On June 2, 1942, Tamara Meerovich, with her son and her mother, returned to Rostov-on-Don from Ordzhonikidze. In the first half of July, they moved to the village of Rogovskoe in the Rostov District. They were murdered there during the German occupation in August 1942.

Grisha Meerovich and Anya Pinchos, 1936–1937. Courtesy of Yad Vashem Photo Archive.

CHAPTER 1.2

Soviet Population Evacuation into the North Caucasus, 1941–1942[1]

1. WARTIME EVACUATION OF THE POPULATION IN THE SOVIET UNION

When a central government initiates the partial or complete evacuation of a civilian population from territory threatened by an enemy, that initiative should be regarded as a part of its war strategy. In this sense, the evacuation envisioned and implemented by the Soviet government during the Soviet-German War had to take into account several considerations. On the one hand, the "scorched earth" policy with the complete removal of the population from the areas about to be seized had some advantages. It ensured that the Soviets would keep their human resources intact, whereas the Germans would have to count only upon their own scarce manpower in order to run the newly conquered regions. On the other hand, the complete depopulation of abandoned areas had serious disadvantages: it was hardly feasible on a practical level and it would leave no-one behind to wage a partisan war in the territory overrun by the enemy. In addition, it made sense to leave some of the population under the

---

1 In this chapter, I rely on some findings that have already been published in my previous articles. See Kiril Feferman, "A Soviet Humanitarian Action?: Centre, Periphery and the Evacuation of Refugees to the North Caucasus, 1941–1942," *Europe-Asia Studies* 61, no. 5 (July 2009): 813–831; idem, "Jewish Refugees under the Soviet Rule and the German Occupation in the North Caucasus," in *Revolution, Repression and Revival: The Jews of the Former Soviet Union*, ed. Zvi Gitelman and Yaacov Ro'i (Lanham, MD: Rowman and Littlefield, 2007), 211–244.

enemy's sway in order to capitalize on the inevitable friction between this population and the occupying power as time went on.

Particularly acute was the timing of any evacuation. The Soviets aimed at maintaining a probably impossible equilibrium: they tried to manage a gradual evacuation and, at the same time, keep the semblance of a normal life in order to avoid panic among the inhabitants and continue industrial production, including military industries, until the last moment. The evacuations were usually carried out until the position of the Soviet forces became indefensible.[2] Finally, there was the danger that massive evacuations would play into the Germans' hands, giving them an opportunity to bring German settlers who could fill the empty territories.

The decision of the Soviet government to start evacuating the general population during the War could be seen against the background of its prewar resettlement policies, which were applied to a number of Soviet nationalities and professional groups during the 1930s.[3] It may be said, cautiously, that, on a quantitative and geographic scale, the prewar population evacuation planning could not cope with the challenges as compared to the challenges presented by the actual German invasion. As with the industrial relocation plans,[4] the Soviet strategists failed to take into account that such a significant part of the country could possibly fall under the enemy's control.[5] It is noteworthy that, during the War, the Soviet authorities also tried to analyze and take into account the experience of Imperial Russia with respect to the eviction of the general population from the threatened areas during World War I.[6]

These considerations, compounded by a rapidly deteriorating strategic situation, guided the Soviet government when it made decisions to withdraw human resources from the Germans' reach, soon after the beginning of the War.

---

2 Rebecca Manley, *To the Tashkent Station: Evacuation and Survival in the Soviet Union at War, 1941–1946* (Ithaca, NY: Cornell University Press, 2009), 48–76.

3 Manley, *To the Tashkent Station*, 24–47. Cf. Alexander Statiev, "Motivations and Goals of Soviet Deportations in the Western Borderlands," *Journal of Strategic Studies* 28, no. 6 (2005): 977–983.

4 David R. Stone, "The First Five-Year Plan and the Geography of the Soviet Defense Industry," *Europe-Asia Studies* 57, no. 7 (2005): 1061.

5 Decree of the Executive Session of the Council of Labor and Defense "On the order of removal of valuable property, institutions, enterprises and human resources from the regions threatened by the enemy," April 20, 1928, Yad Vashem Archive (henceforth YVA): JM/24678. Source: Gosudarstvennyi arkhiv Rossiiskoi Federatsii (henceforth GARF): A-259/40/3028.

6 Aleksandr Kurtsev, "Bezhenstvo," in *Rossiia i pervaia mirovaia voina*, ed. N. N. Smirnov (St. Petersburg: Dmitrii Bulanin, 1999), 129–147.

The complete removal of the population was never under consideration. Rather, the government formulated its evacuation policy solely with regard to specific groups, which were singled out for their significance to the country's war effort and the survival of the Soviet regime. According to the directives, the evacuation of the general population was aimed first and foremost at safeguarding the lives of functionaries affiliated with the Communist Party, the Soviet government, and security agencies of all levels, together with their families. The next priority was to evacuate agricultural and industrial (mainly military-industrial) facilities together with their workers. Transferring all possible human resources away from the Germans' reach was the last item in the order of importance.[7] In addition, special emphasis was placed on the evacuation of children and elderly people,[8] although their relocation may be considered a humanitarian action, apparently not designed as part of the war efforts, however broadly they may have been interpreted.[9] Most organized evacuees fell into the third category.

There was also a considerable number of unorganized or independent refugees, who fled eastwards on their own initiative.[10] Many of them chose to escape because they feared that they would suffer under German rule. This group consisted of three major subgroups: Jews; members of the Communist Party, the Komsomol youth organization, and other Soviet functionaries; and families of officers of the Red Army.

The wartime evacuation of the population in the USSR was slated to be a highly centralized process. It was coordinated by the Council for Evacuation, created on June 24, 1941 in accordance with the joint decision of the Soviet government, called *Sovet Narodnykh Komissarov* (SNK or Council of the People's Commissars), and the Central Committee of the Bolshevik Party.[11] The head of the Soviet Trade Unions and Politburo Member Nikolai Shvernik was placed in

---

7 Decrees of SNK SSSR "On the evacuation of workers and employees of evacuated enterprises" and "On the order of evacuation of population during the war," Top secret, July 5, 1941, YVA: JM/24678. Source: GARF: A-259/40/3022. Cf. Dubson, "On the Problem of the Evacuation," 42–43.
8 The Council for Evacuation, "Transfer of children from the cities of Moscow and Leningrad to rural areas," Top secret, July 1, 1941, YVA: JM/24678. Source: GARF: A-259/40/3023.
9 I enlarge on this subject in my article, Feferman, "A Soviet Humanitarian Action?," 813–831.
10 K. Pamfilov, The Council for Evacuation's memorandum "On regulating the registration of the evacuated population and the improvement of information work; on location of the evacuated citizens," Top secret, December 25, 1941, YVA: JM/24678. Source: GARF: A-259/40/3014.
11 "Status and structure of Council for Evacuation. Attachment to the decision of SNK SSSR," Top secret, June 24, 1941, YVA: JM/24678. Source: GARF: A-259/40/3028.

charge of the Council.¹² This body was empowered to authorize the evacuation of all population groups, with the exception of residents in areas that were close to the front lines, in which case the evacuation fell under the jurisdiction of the military command.¹³ The decisions of the Council for Evacuation were binding for the local administrations and all-Union ministries.¹⁴ Overall, the Council presided over the evacuation eastwards of more than ten million Soviet citizens in 1941, as indicated in the report drawn up at the end of 1941 by Konstantin Pamfilov, the Deputy Chairman of the Council, in charge of the population evacuation.¹⁵

Following the military successes of the Red Army during the winter of 1941–1942, the Soviet leadership assumed that the stage of war-related evacuation was over. This prompted the liquidation of the Council for Evacuation and its replacement by a department of the RSFSR Council of the People's Commissars for the maintenance of the evacuated population on December 25, 1941.¹⁶ The central government even sanctioned a partial return of the evacuees (*reevakuatsiia*) into the central regions (Moscow, Tula, Kalinin) in the first half of 1942. However, when the German armies swept into the North Caucasus in summer 1942, the State Committee of Defense established on June 22 a new *Komissiya po evakuatsii* (Commission for Evacuation) staffed by the members of the disbanded Council for Evacuation and headed by Shvernik. This points to a continuity of Soviet evacuation thinking and policies, but the Commission appears to have enjoyed a lower status than the disbanded Council and certainly it was set up too late to effectively organize further civilian evacuation from the Caucasus. Nevertheless, according to the official Soviet data, more than eight million people were evacuated in summer and fall 1942, thus bringing the total number of evacuees during the War to about twenty-five million people.¹⁷

The organized evacuation of the population in the wartime USSR was carried out at the initiative of the central government. Local administrations

---

12 The first head of the Council was Lazar Kaganovich. On July 16, 1941, he was replaced by Shvernik.
13 Decree of SNK SSSR "On the arrangement of the population evacuation during the war," Top secret, July 5, 1941, YVA: JM/24678. Source: GARF: A-259/40/3022.
14 "Status and structure of the Council for Evacuation," YVA: JM/24678. Source: GARF: A-259/40/3028.
15 Report by K. Pamfilov, Top secret, December 25, 1941, YVA: JM/24678. Source: GARF: A-259/40/3014. A postwar Soviet study mentioned a lower estimate of 7.4 million people evacuated by the spring of 1942. I. I. Belonosov, "Evakuatsiia naseleniia iz prifrontovoi polosy v 1941–1942 gg.," in *Eshelony idut na Vostok. Iz istorii perebazirovaniia proizvoditel'nykh sil SSSR v 1941–1942 gg. Sbornik statei i vospominanii*, ed. Iu. A. Poliakov (Moscow: Nauka, 1966), 26.
16 Dubson, "On the Problem of the Evacuation," 38 (footnote 6).
17 Belonosov, "Evakuatsiia naseleniia iz prifrontovoi polosy," 28.

could submit their proposals on the character and timing of the evacuation, but specific decisions always had to be made by the center. This was a bureaucratic process that took time, even when the situation on the ground looked critical. The resulting delays could seal the fate of "last-minute" refugees.

Local administrations found it very difficult to accommodate masses of refugees and provide them with food, heating, and employment, all within a very short space of time. Like all projects not directly related to the war effort, the evacuation was underfunded, and local authorities had to find ways to fund it from local resources. These processes inevitably led to tension between the central government, on the one hand, and the local authorities and residents, on the other.[18] Often, the locals were forced to billet evacuees in their homes free of charge; there were fewer allocations from local budgets, which now had to be shared between the local residents and the incoming evacuees. So resentment against was the newcomers stirred up among the local administration and the local residents, as well as inter-regional and inter-ethnic animosity.[19]

2. THE NORTH CAUCASUS

2.1. The Local Population and the Jewish Evacuees

In the North Caucasus, Jewish evacuees came to constitute a considerable proportion of the newcomers who started moving into the region after the German invasion of Russia on June 22, 1941. On October 1, 1941, a local agency in charge of evacuation in the Krasnodar territory stated in its internal memorandum that Jews made up 73% of the 218,000 people who were received and given accommodation in the area.[20] Data of the Council for Evacuation pertaining to other areas indicates that, in summer and fall 1941, Jews constituted a majority of the newcomers throughout the North Caucasus:

---

18 E. Rees, "The Changing Nature of Centre–Local Relations in the USSR, 1928–1936," in *Centre–Local Relations in the Stalinist State 1928–1941*, ed. E. Rees (New York: Palgrave, 2002), 9–36.
19 For example, Fedor Kiselev, *Gosudarstvennaia politika po otnosheniiu k evakuirovannomu naseleniiu v gody Velikoi Otechestvennoi voiny. Na materialakh Kirovskoi oblasti i Udmurtskoi ASSR*, PhD diss., Kirov, Viatkskii gosudarstvennyi tekhnicheskii universitet, 2004, 77–85. Cf. Mariia Potemkina, "Evakuatsiia i natsyional'nye otnosheniia v sovetskom tylu v gody Velikoi Otechestvennoi Voiny," *Otechestvennaia istoriiia* 3 (2002): 148–156.
20 *Kuban' v gody Velikoi Otechestvennoi voiny, 1941–1945: Khronika sobytii*, ed. A. Beliaev and I. Bondar' (Krasnodar: Sovkuban', 2000), vol. 1, 76–77.

Distribution of the Registered Evacuated Population in the Regions of the North Caucasus, as of November 15, 1941, by Gender and Age, as a Percentage of the Total

	Men (16–59)	Women (16–54)	Children (0–7)	Children (8–15)
Krasnodar territory	19.2	39.1	16.7	15.0
Stavropol territory	18.7	26.2	14.2	15.9

Source: calculated by the author on the basis of data of Resettlement Departments processed by the Council for Evacuation, 1941. YVA: JM/24678. Source: GARF: A-259/40/3091.
Note: There is no information for the Rostov District.

This finding seems to contradict the widely held view that the Soviet government did not prioritize the evacuation of Jews[21] and must be explained. As mentioned above, in Soviet planning the region served as a reception area. However, the number of "unofficial" refugees who flooded into the Caucasus was considerably higher than the figures set for the organized evacuation. The reason for this influx of refugees was the geographical proximity of the North Caucasus to the Ukraine region with its sizeable Jewish population. Thus, the apparent contradiction may be reconciled in the following manner: although the Soviets did not prioritize the evacuation of Jews insofar as organized evacuation was concerned, they evidently allowed those Jews who had escaped independently and had reached the North Caucasus region to avail themselves of the facilities offered by the Soviet evacuation program such as provision of food, work, housing, warm clothes, fuel, medical aid, and school education for children.

It became apparent that the arrival of masses of predominantly Jewish evacuees led to an upsurge of anti-Jewish sentiments amongst the local population. This involved, among other factors, the refusal to allow Jewish evacuees to move into a place (the local inhabitants were recorded as saying: "We'll let Russians in, but not Jews"),[22] and the attempts to get rid of Jewish tenants with the tacit approval of local functionaries.[23]

---

21 Il'ia Al'tman, *Zhertvy nenavisti: Kholokost v SSSR, 1941–1945 gg.* (Moscow: Fond "Kovcheg": Kollektsiia "Sovershenno sekretno," 2002), 388–389. Cf. Yitzhak Arad, *The History of the Holocaust. The Soviet Union and the Annexed Territories* (Jerusalem: Yad Vashem, 2004), 177–202 [Hebrew]. Cf. Manley, *To the Tashkent Station*, 99–100, 166–167. Cf. Edwards, *Fleeing to Siberia*, 38–39.

22 The sources referenced here relate to the mixed Cossack-Russian localities (Krasnodar) and the indigenous North Caucasians (Kalmykia and unspecifiied North Caucasian indigenous localities). Senior Inspector Shklovskii, speech at session of the SNK of the Kabardino-Balkar ASSR, May 5, 1942, YVA: JM/24678. Source: GARF: A-259/40/3527.

23 Ibid.

Many Jewish testimonies also mention the atmosphere of anti-Semitism in the North Caucasus towards the Jewish evacuees.[24] This is how Vladimir Gel'fand who was evacuated to Essentuki, described the situation in his diary:

> In the streets and in the park, at a bread store, and in a line for kerosene, everywhere can one hear whispering—quiet, dreadful, cheerful, but hateful. They are talking about Jews. So far they speak awkwardly, while looking around. Jews are thieves. … Jews have money. … Jews don't like working. Jews don't want to serve in the Red Army. Jews live without being registered. Jews walk all over them [*seli im na golovu*]. In brief, Jews are the root of all misfortune.[25]

A Jewish refugee, who fled from Rostov-on-Don when it was captured by the Germans for the first time (late November 1941), stated in a postwar interview that, when:

> we entered local villages to seek food, the population was ill-disposed towards us and even behaved in a belligerent fashion. We were never invited to enter a house in order to clean ourselves up. There was even a feeling of terror.

Such attitudes did not diminish, but rather intensified, from May 1942 onwards, possibly in view of some change in the balance of forces in the region in favor of the Germans and the way that the local people perceived the situation. This was noted by a Jewish evacuee: "When [we] moved around North Caucasian localities, we sensed hostile attitudes on the part of the local population. 'Hitler will shoot you all the same,' they said. Often, we were denied water."[26]

Yet, in many cases it cannot be established whether the hostile attitude was due to the fact that the witnesses was Jewish, or the fact that they were refugees.

---

24 Saul Borovoi, *Vospominaniia: Pamiatniki evreiskoi istoricheskoi mysli* (Moscow: Evreiskii Universitet v Moskve, Jerusalem: Gesharim, 1993), 250, 252. Cf. Testimony of Anfisa Kalnitskaya, 1926, Hebrew University of Jerusalem, Institute of Contemporary Jewry, Department of Oral History (henceforth ICJ, DOH): TC 2759 (not transcribed). Cf. Testimony of Lyudmila Bradichevsky, May 13, 1996, ICJ: (217) 183, p. 3, and others.
25 Vladimir Gel'fand, *Dnevnik 1941–1946* (Moscow: ROSSPEN, 2015), 44.
26 Testimony of Yury Burakovsky, in *Evakuatsiia. Vospominaniia o detstve, opalennom ognem Katastrofy. SSSR, 1941–1945*, ed. Aleksandr Berman and Alla Nikitina (Jerusalem: Soiuz uchenykh-repatriantov, 2009), 91–92.

In contrast, a very limited number of sources noted that the Russian population displayed neutral or even positive attitudes towards Jewish refugees.²⁷ However, these few examples stand out as the exception to the trend, which was indicative of the increase in anti-Semitism among the local Slavic people on the eve of the German occupation of the North Caucasus.

More generally, the local authorities recorded an increase in anti-Semitic feelings as a reaction to the growing predominantly Jewish evacuation into the region. From the early stages of the War, many Jewish evacuees, especially those from recently annexed territories, were not conscripted into the Red Army. This could be explained by the Soviet concern about the political reliability of their new citizens, and also, by the general chaos surrounding the Soviet evacuation policy and its implementation. The local population in the North Caucasus was outraged to see many young Jews among the newcomers, whereas their own sons had already been drafted into the Soviet army.²⁸

As the German army approached the North Caucasus, animosity towards the Jews increased, as indicated by the following two quotes from Stavropol records. According to the memorandum of the District Committee of the VKP(b) prepared in September 1941, "the hostility towards Jews on the part of anti-Soviet elements was clearly on the rise in recent times in a number of areas."²⁹ On January 6, 1942, a lecturer in the VKP(b) Department of Agitation and Propaganda in the Stavropol territory communicated to the NKVD regional administration: "In the Libknekht area, the departure of draftees to the front took place in an anti-Soviet mood: 'Beat Yids and Communists!'"³⁰

Official Soviet records indicate that quite a number of ordinary people, and especially low-level functionaries, were convicted for "instigating nationally motivated animosity, namely anti-Semitism" in the context of the evacuation

---

27 Testimony of Sara Labinov, no date, ICJ: TC 2773, side A. Cf. Testimony of Ida Mandelblat, no date, YVA: VT/1911.
28 Information provided by the Head of the Military Department of Soldato-Akeksandrovsky *Raion* Committee of the VKP(b) B. Fadeev, Top secret, August 30, 1941, Gosudarstvennyi arkhiv noveishei istorii Stavropol'skogo kraia (henceforth GANISK): 1/2/64, pp. 8–10. In *Stavropol'e: Pravda voennykh let. Velikaia Otechestvenaia v dokumentakh i issledovaniiakh*, ed. V. Belokon', T. Kolpikova, Ia. Kol'tsova, V. Maznitsa (Stavropol: Stavropol'skii gosudarstvennyi universitet, 2005), 35.
29 Maksim Andrienko, *Naselenie Stavropol'skogo kraya v gody Velikoi Otechestvennoi voiny: otsenka povedencheskikh motivov*, PhD diss., Pyatigorsk, Piatigorskii gosudarstvennyi lingivisticheskii universitet, 2005, 57.
30 Ibid., 57.

into the North Caucasus.[31] We get little understanding, however, of what the NKVD in the North Caucasus regarded as manifestations of anti-Semitism subject to legal prosecution. Overall, the impression is that the central Soviet government tended to suppress anti-Jewish attitudes among the local elite and the inhabitants of the region (contrary to what we know about other evacuation reception areas[32]). Often viewed in conjunction with, or as explicit expressions of resentment against the Soviet regime and all too reminiscent of Nazi messages (to quote the Council for Evacuation envoy, "the enemy's hand is behind [these activities],")[33] they could not be ignored as in other regions: in late October 1941, the Wehrmacht had reached the gates of the North Caucasus.

2.2. The Macro View

2.2.1. 1941

Initially, the North Caucasus emerged as an important evacuation destination in early July 1941. Later, the Council for Evacuation designated three Russian districts of the North Caucasus (Rostov-on-Don, Krasnodar, and Stavropol) for the reception of 100,000 people in each city, to be evacuated from the Western Ukraine.[34]

In addition to the officially sanctioned plan, thousands of independent refugees thronged to the North Caucasus in summer and fall of 1941 because the region was situated on a natural escape route from Ukraine into the Soviet interior.[35] According to the data of a local agency in charge of the resettlement,

---

31 NKVD to Shvernik, November 25, 1942, YVA: JM/24678. Source: GARF: A-259/40/3529. Cf. Shklovskii, report "On the conditions of the evacuated population in Kabardino-Balkar ASSR," June 2, 1942, YVA: JM/24678. Source: GARF: A-259/40/3527.
32 Kiselev, *Gosudarstvennaia politika*, 79. Cf. Viktor Fedotov, *Evakuirovannoe naselenie v Srednem Povolzh'e v gody Velikoi Otechestvennoi voiny (1941–1945 gg.): Problemy razmeshcheniia, sotsial'noi adaptatsii i trudovoi deiatel'nosti*, PhD diss., Samara: Samarskii gosudarstvennyi pedagogicheskii universitet, 2004, 113. Cf. Mariia Potemkina, "Evakonaselenie v ural'skom tylu. Opyt vyzhivaniia," *Otechestvennaia istoriia* 2 (2005): 93–94.
33 Shklovskii, speech, YVA: JM/24678. Source: GARF: A-259/40/3527.
34 Decree of the Council for Evacuation "On the plan for the evacuation of members of families of workers and employees from Karelo-Finnish, Estonian, Latvian, Belorussian, Ukrainian (western areas), Moldavian SSR, districts of Murmansk, Leningrad and Smolensk," Top secret, July 7, 1941, YVA: JM/24678. GARF: A-259/40/258, p. 66.
35 Distribution of evacuees (registered by lists) by districts and republics of their origin on the grounds of the data of Resettlement departments as of November 15, 1941, YVA: JM/24678. GARF: A-259/40/3091.

37,165 evacuees arrived in the Krasnodar territory from July 19 to 25, 1941.[36] By early fall, this number had swelled considerably, and by September 10, it had reached 205,000.[37] The unofficial evacuees continued to arrive (see Table 1), despite the growing threat of a German thrust into the region. At that time, it was entirely unclear whether the German advance towards this region could be halted. The Soviet authorities considered the area to be under threat, as can be inferred from their intensive defensive preparations starting from mid-August 1941 in the Stavropol territory[38] and especially in the Rostov district.

The independent incomers to the North Caucasus viewed it as a destination area (intending to make a long-term stay) or simply as a transition point (intending to make only a short-term stay). They were usually not registered as evacuees prior to their arrival. Consequently, neither the central government nor the local authorities in the region anticipated their arrival. Nevertheless, they had to be provided for, much like the organized evacuees. Thus, since the regulations issued by the central government did not envisage giving a different treatment to unofficial newcomers and organized evacuees,[39] the considerable overstretching of the Caucasian resources from the start of the War led to the inappropriate treatment of refugees in the North Caucasus in 1941–1942. The local Caucasian inhabitants were receiving much reduced allocations of food, fuel, and other commodities following the arrival of so many evacuees, which would probably have increased their resentment towards the newcomers.

The authorities were extremely alarmed over the anticipated penetration of enemy agents disguised as evacuees, as the "Directive Letter of the Committee of the VKP(b) of the Krasnodar Territory on the Work with the Evacuees" from September 1941 demonstrates:

> Fascists are dispatching inhabitants of the occupied areas to the Red Army's rear, in order to carry out diversions, gather intelligence on the

---

36 Beliaev and Bondar', *Kuban' v gody Velikoi Otechestvennoi voiny*, vol. 1, 38–39.
37 Ibid., 56–57.
38 Information from the First Secretary of the Stavropol District Committee of the VKP(b) Mikhail Suslov on defensive preparations of the territory, Top secret, August 6, 1941, GAN-ISK: 1/2/63, pp. 113–114. In Belokon', *Stavropol'e*, 32.
39 With the exception of special one-time compensation paid to those evacuated in an organized manner. Decree no. 1791 of the SNK SSSR "On the payment of monetary allowances to those resettled from their locations on account of the relocation of their plants and institutions to other areas," July 1, 1941. In L. Snegireva (ed.), *Vo imia pobedy: Evakuatsiia grazhdanskogo naseleniia v Zapadnuiu Sibir' v gody Velikoi Otechestvennoi voiny v dokumentakh i materialakh* (Tomsk: Izdatel'stvo Tomskogo gosudarstvennogo pedagogicheskogo universiteta, 2005), vol. 1, 282–283.

deployment of Soviet units, send up rockets to signal to German planes the location of military units, [and] spread panic about the might of the German army [and] about its allegedly good behavior towards POWs and the [civilian] population.[40]

Echoing this appraisal, the Bolshevik Party Committee in one of the localities in the Krasnodar territory stated during this period that:

> Owing to the evacuation of the [civil] population of Western Ukraine and Western Belorussia [now Belarus] from the areas occupied by the enemy, we have refugees. It is a legal possibility to dispatch anyone [here], and it is probable that this is indeed being done on a large scale. People are arriving and telling such stories that cannot be described and [as a result], it creates an impression of panic . . . all kinds or rumors are being spread.[41]

Finally, on October 6, 1941, the NKVD Administration for the Krasnodar territory ordered a security check of all the newcomers.[42]

Evacuees were dispatched to locations all over the North Caucasus region, to towns[43] as well as villages,[44] including Russian localities and Cossack settlements (*stanitsy*).[45] According to a Soviet report, 226,000 people were evacuated to the Krasnodar territory in 1941, but only 51,353 remained there as of January 1942, out of whom 39,100 had been allocated to villages.[46] There is no record that the Jewish evacuees were ever sent to Muslim villages, which probably indicates the reluctance of the Jews to reside in an entirely unfamiliar setting.

---

40 Directive letter of the Committee of the VKP(b) of the Krasnodar territory on the work with the evacuees. In Khachemizova, *Obshestvo i vlast'*, 141.
41 TsDNIKK: 2507/1/3a, p. 47. In Khachemizova, *Obshestvo i vlast'*, 141–142.
42 Beliaev and Bondar', *Kuban' v gody Velikoi Otechestvennoi voiny*, 76–77.
43 Towns: Elista, Kislovodsk, Mozdok, and Nalchik. Testimony of Bradichevsky, ICJ: (217) 183, p. 1. Cf. Testimonies of Fiks, Rechister, Shaulov, Gisa, Bergman, Shaposhnikova, and Yury Piler, July 16, 1990, Yad Vashem Hall of Names (henceforth YVHN).
44 Villages: Naturbovo, Ivanovsky *raion*, Krasnodar territory; Russky farm, Stavropol territory. Questioning of Klavdia Parshikova, b. 1902, August 12, 1942, YVA: M.33/291, p. 98. Cf. Testimony of Brimer, YVA: 0.3/2501.
45 Labinskaya and Tbilisskaya *stanitsy*, Krasnodar territory. Questioning of Anna Suzdalenko, May 10, 1944, YVA: M.33/308, p. 29.
46 TsDNIKK: 1774-A/2/373, pp. 69–76. In Beliaev and Bondar', *Kuban' v gody Velikoi Otechestvennoi voiny*, 181–182.

2.2.2. In 1942

After the Red Army repelled the German advance in the North Caucasus in late November 1941, the situation on the Southern flank of the Soviet-German front stabilized. The Soviet victory at Rostov-on-Don, though limited, had several important repercussions. First, the Soviet civil and military administration became over-confident in its ability to check any further German advance. Therefore, in contrast to the previous months and despite the fact that the Germans remained camped only a few hundred kilometers away from Rostov-on-Don, the Soviet administration placed a ban on civilians leaving the city.[47] Second, some people, including a small percentage of the Jews, were enthusiastic about the Soviet recapture of Rostov-on-Don, and decided to return to the city of their own volition.[48] However, others, apparently the majority, remained skeptical.

Other North Caucasian areas situated further from the front line than the city of Rostov-on-Don became a destination of state-run evacuation from Leningrad, which was under siege. The decision was carried out in the winter months of 1941–1942, when evacuation from Leningrad was possible over the ice-covered Lake of Ladoga. Central Soviet planners designated the whole North Caucasus region and the Volga region for the evacuation of 11,000 people from Leningrad.[49] However, in April 1942, the local authorities recorded that 36,000 evacuees from Leningrad were accommodated in the Krasnodar territory alone.[50] In addition, many people from other threatened areas, such as the Crimea and Rostov-on-Don, were also evacuated by the authorities to the Caucasian interior in the first half of 1942.[51]

Thousands of Jews were evacuated to the region in 1942, among them the staff and, in particular, the students from Leningrad's institutions of higher education.[52] Sometimes they were accompanied by elderly family members.

---

47 Evgenii Movshovich, *Ocherki istorii evreev na Donu* (Rostov-on-Don: Donskoi izdatel'skii dom, 2006), 127.
48 See the testimony related to November 29, 1941 in this book.
49 Note on the work of Department of SNK RSFSR on the economic arrangements made for the evacuated population, October 14, 1942. In Snegireva, *Vo imia pobedy*, 308.
50 Beliaev and Bondar', *Kuban' v gody Velikoi Otechestvennoi voiny*, 249.
51 Memorandum of the Committee of the VKP(b) of the Karachaevo Autonomous Area, no later than June 24, 1943, GARF: 7021/17/8, pp. 2–3.
52 In Essentuki, Kislovodsk, and Pyatigorsk. Testimonies of Tsilya Gadleva, October 25, 1990, YVA: 0.3/4391, p. 9. Cf. Testimonies of Mira Idina, Anatoly Tukhshnaid, Khasya Epshtein, and Sima Royak, November 8, 1992, YVHN.

Occasionally, elderly people also arrived unaccompanied.[53] Again, there was a significant proportion of children: among 36,000 evacuees from Leningrad accommodated in the Krasnodar territory in April 1942, there were more than 10,000 children (almost 28%).[54] At the time of the German occupation in August 1942, the Jewish evacuees outnumbered the relatively insignificant number of native Jewish residents in the region.

The newcomers were settled in the region in an organized way. Once more, Jews were dispatched all over the North Caucasus, especially to the resort towns of the Stavropol territory.[55] They were also brought, albeit on a somewhat smaller scale, to villages,[56] again including Russian and Cossack settlements.[57] As in 1941, there were no records of Jewish refugees being sent to Muslim villages. In contrast to 1941, however, there is no evidence that Jewish refugees brought to the North Caucasus in 1942 were provided with employment. This may have been the result of the Soviets' logistic inability to provide masses of newcomers, including many white-collar workers, with suitable employment in the region. Alternatively, it is possible that the authorities did not consider that these evacuees would be staying in the Caucasus for a long period of time.

2.3. The Micro Level

2.3.1. Making Decisions

The Soviet Jews made their evacuation-related decisions on the basis of what they knew of the danger that the German occupation might cause them and the proximity of the German army. What did the Jewish evacuees and refugees

---

53 In Essentuki and Kislovodsk. Testimonies of Idina, Tukhshnaid, and Debora Shklovskaya, YVHN.
54 TsDNIKK: 1774-A/2/626, pp. 11–18. In Beliaev and Bondar', *Kuban' v gody Velikoi Otechestvennoi voiny*, 249.
55 Essentuki, Kislovodsk, and Pyatigorsk. Testimonies of Shklovskaya, March 5, 1991, Idina, April 1, 1991, Tukhshnaid, no date, Epshtein, November 8, 1992, and Royak, September 24, 1994, YVHN.
56 Novozavedennoe village, Soldato-Aleksandrovsky *raion*, Stavropol territory. Statement of Anna Shlaen, 1943, GARF: 7021/17/11, p. 114.
57 Kotlyarevskaya *stanitsa*, Maisky *raion*, Kabardino-Balkar ASSR. Report no. 75 of the local commission of the Extraordinary State Commission for Investigation and Establishment of the Crimes Committed by the German Fascists and their Henchmen in the Temporarily Occupied Soviet Territories of the Kabardino-Balkar ASSR, June 24, 1943, GARF: 7021/7/109, p. 171. Cf. Statement of the Commission of Aleksandriiskaya *Stanitsa*, Aleksandriisko-Obilnensky *Raion*, Stavropol Territory, January 25, 1943, GARF: 7021/17/9, p. 12.

in the Soviet Union know about the German treatment of Jews? By November 1941, the knowledge of the Soviet Jews about the Germans was acquired from official Soviet reporting, contact with refugees, and previous, often prewar information.

Regarding the media reporting, the situation was apparently more or less similar in the whole country[58]—the information was available, but it was not emphasized. However, local nuances were also at play. With respect to the Holocaust-related information available to the Jews living in the Caucasus up to mid-1942, little information could be acquired from listening to the radio.[59] The local press, such as the main newspapers of the Rostov district—*Molot* (*Hammer*), the Stavropol territory—*Ordzhonikidzevskaya pravda* (*Ordzhonikidze Truth*), and the Krasnodar territory—*Bolshevik*,[60] were a more important source of information. Precise analysis of relevant articles published in these newspapers is provided in the chapters dealing with the Ginsburg letters. Here I will confine myself to several general observations. Throughout the whole period from June 1941 to July 1942, not a single word was written about the evacuation *from* the North Caucasus. The dominant motive of the Soviet propaganda in this region, as seen from the local newspapers, remained "business as usual"—until the Germans reached the gates of the North Caucasus.[61] References to German mistreatment of Jews were rare,[62] and information on the advance of the German armies towards the Caucasus was clearly

---

58 Mordechai Altshuler, "The Holocaust in the Soviet Mass Media during the War and in the First Postwar Years Re-examined." *Yad Vashem Studies* 39, no. 2 (2011): 121–168. Cf. Karel C. Berkhoff, "'Total Annihilation of the Jewish Population': The Holocaust in the Soviet Media, 1941–1945," *Kritika: Explorations in Russian and Eurasian History* 10, no. 1 (Winter 2009): 61–105.

59 Inna Somova, *Kul'turnye i religioznye uchrezhdeniia Stavropol'skogo kraia v period Velikoi Otechestvennoi voiny*, PhD diss., Pyatigorsk, Piatigorskii gosudarstvennyi lingivisticheskii universitet, 2004, 47–48.

60 *Ordzhonikidzevskaya pravda* was published daily by the Ordzhonikidze Territorial Committee of the VKP(b), the District Council of the Deputies of Workers, and the Voroshilovsk Municipal Committee of the VKP(b). *Bolshevik* was published daily by the Krasnodar Territorial and Municipal Committee of the VKP(b) and the District Council of the Deputies of Working People. I looked through all the issues of these two newspapers from June 22, 1941 to late July 1942, when their publication ceased.

61 See editorial "O khode sbora urozhaia," and the Decree of the Bureau of the Ordzhonikidze Territorial Committee of the VKP(b) from July 9, 1942, *Ordzhonikidzevskaia pravda*, no. 159 (2534), July 10, 1942. Editorial "Rabotat' i ne shchadit' sily dlia fronta," *Bol'shevik*, no. 176 (1469), July 26, 1942.

62 A. Faigel'man, "V lapakh gitlerovskikh grabitelei," *Ordzhonikidzevskaia pravda*, no. 154 (2218), July 2, 1941.

outdated.⁶³ Finally, even though this information was sometimes available, its importance was partly offset by the skepticism that the average Soviet citizen felt towards the official propaganda.

Consequently, rumors coming mainly from refugees from such areas as Ukraine,⁶⁴ as well as from Red Army personnel (especially if there were Jews among them)⁶⁵ turned out to be a most important source of information. The effect of rumors is indicated in a postwar Jewish testimony pertaining apparently to the Krasnodar territory:

> The five members of my family stayed in the village of Ivanovka for [about] 4 to 6 weeks. In about November–December 1941, it was rumored that Jews gradually abandoned [their places of residence]. So, my family decided to move to Krasnodar.⁶⁶

With respect to Rostov-on-Don and the potential impact of incoming evacuees on the state of mind of local Jews, it should be noted that the city proved to be a very important transition point, through which thousands of refugees, including many Jews, fled eastwards. But when it came to the direct impact of rumors on decision-making by Rostov Jews, it seems to have been limited and diluted by Soviet propaganda more than was the case in the areas with weaker Soviet control, such as smaller towns and/or areas closer to the frontline.⁶⁷

The developments in the city were remarkable in another respect, namely, the unique fate of Rostov-on-Don and its Jewish population in 1941: the brief occupation of the city by the Germans from November 21–28, 1941 and its quick recapture by the Red Army limited the time available for attacking the Jewish population.⁶⁸ This experience would have made the rumors of the German threat less believable for the Rostov Jews.

---

63 Editorial "Otbit' napadenie vraga!," *Ordzhonikidzevskaia pravda*, no. 175 (2550), July 29, 1942. Editorial "Rabotat' i ne shchadit' sily dlya fronta," *Bol'shevik*, no. 176 (1469), July 26, 1942.
64 Testimony of Aleksandr Simakhov, January 8, 1998. In *Iskhod gorskih evreev: razrushenie garmonii mirov*, ed. Svetlana Danilova (Nalchik: Poligrafservis IT, 2000), 171. Cf. Testimony of Kalnitskaya, ICJ: TC 2759.
65 Testimony of Melinsky, YVA: 0.3/4342, p. 4.
66 Krasnodar was the largest city close to the village of Ivanovka, and it was much easier to join the evacuation from this city than from the village. Testimony of Gurevich, ICJ: TC 2761.
67 Shternshis, "Between Life and Death," 497–498.
68 These events are analyzed in depth in chapter 2.1.

The third source, that is, the Jews' previous, often outdated, knowledge about the German attackers seems to be the most difficult to describe properly. Yet it was frequently mentioned in testimonies. The degree to which the available information was understood and acted upon depended on the strength of the Jews' group identity, their level of intelligence, and their prewar whereabouts and contacts.

One factor the Soviet Jews used to decide on assess the German threat was the memories they retained about the attitudes of the German army towards Jews during World War I. At the outbreak of World War II, many North Caucasian Jews were newcomers to this region, so their conduct reflected their memories of the other regions in which they used to live, especially Ukraine.[69] In the North Caucasus, the only areas occupied by the German army during World War I were the Rostov district, and especially the city of Rostov-on-Don. Available testimony, from newcomers and Rostov Jews alike, point that Jews had good memories of the Germans' behavior in that earlier period, which influenced their unwillingness to move further away from the German advance.[70]

By and large, if we attempt to sum up the North Caucasian Jews' view of the Germans' attitude towards the Jews, available testimonies indicate that, in fall 1941, there were still a considerable number of Jews who were ignorant of the German persecution of the Jews in other places. In particular, many consciously chose to disregard the information that was available. The opinion of one Jewish intellectual: "I do not believe that the civilized nation of Goethe and Schiller can behave like barbarians"[71] is characteristic in this regard. However, by the summer of 1942, the number of Jews in these two groups had decreased to such a point that it can be claimed with certainty that an absolute majority of the Ashkenazi Jews living in the North Caucasus did not wish to stay under German rule.

---

69 On this issue, see, for example, Wolfram Dornik and Peter Lieb, "Misconceived Realpolitik in a Failing State: The Political and Economical Fiasco of the Central Powers in the Ukraine, 1918," *First World War Studies* 4, no. 1 (2013): 111–124; Pam Maclean, "Control and Cleanliness: German-Jewish Relations in Occupied Eastern Europe during the First World War," *War & Society* 6, no. 2 (1988): 47–69.

70 Testimony of Raisa Rakhlin, b. 1924, May 24, 1997, YVA: O.93/30459. Cf. Testimony of Tankha Otershtein, b. 1932, May 25, 1997, YVA: O.93/31823. Cf. Yaakov Krut, *Povest' o podarennoi zhyzni* (Petakh-Tikva: n.p., 2008), 9.

71 Professor Dobruskin from the Leningrad's Polytechnic Institute. See the institute's website, http://nashpolytech.ru/index.php?id=59, accessed September 16, 2019. See also Nicholas Poppe, *Reminiscences* (Bellingham: Western Washington, 1983), 161. See also Testimony of Klara Shcheglova, b. 1931, September 6, 1997, YVA: O.93/35826.

2.3.2. Implementing Decisions

Influenced by the Soviet media and/or rumors, many North Caucasian Jews came to view the situation as fraught with danger and reached the conclusion that they would be better off evacuating. Yet, there was a significant gap between their intentions and the feasibility of their plans. Jews often failed to leave because of illness and physical disabilities. The high proportion of mothers with children, unaccompanied children, and elderly persons among the Caucasian evacuees made this factor especially meaningful. People were also reluctant to leave their native area. The father of a witness from Nalchik suggested that they should leave, but the mother refused, asking: "Why should I abandon my house and go?"[72]

Additionally, the people were afraid of the economic hardships involved in the evacuation.[73] It should be noted that evacuation was a costly enterprise. The incoming evacuees had to pay most of their own expenses, as state subsidies did not suffice. It is no wonder therefore that potential evacuees, including Jews, endeavored to procure sufficient means, mainly movable assets like money, well in advance. This could be achieved by selling their possessions to those who were reluctant to evacuate. At this stage, the laws of the market came into play: if there was a massive flight, then very large numbers of refugees sold their valuables at the same time, and prices declined sharply. The following testimony, describing how a mixed Russian-Jewish family, on the eve of their evacuation from Grozny in Chechnya, sold their possessions, underscores the point. After returning from the city market in the summer of 1942, the Russian mother said:

> Do you know what's happening at the market [*tolkuchka*]? It is impossible to buy anything. Everyone is selling; they are almost ready to give their belongings away for nothing. Chechens are the only ones who are buying; they are really getting rich.[74]

As we see, this exchange did not have anything to do with anti-Jewish bias, but rather, it illustrates how expensive it was to become evacuees at this period.

---

72 Testimony of Elizaveta Nazarova, January 6, 1998. In Danilova, *Iskhod gorskih evreev*, 131.
73 Testimony of Liviia Digilova, b. 1936, August 19, 1999. In Danilova, *Iskhod gorskih evreev*, 45. Testimony of Nushum Shamilov, b. 1922, October 11, 1988, YVA: O.3/5157, p. 12.
74 Anatolii Skorokhodov, *Takoi dolgii, dolgii put'. Vospominaniia, razdum'ia, razmyshleniia* (Moscow: Izdatel'stvo Glavnogo arkhivnogo upravleniia goroda Moskvy, 2010), 217.

Once an individual Jew or a family decided to escape, they faced the Soviet bureaucracy in charge of this process. The incoming evacuees now formed the majority of the Jewish population in the North Caucasus. Most of them were officially unemployed, and therefore did not need official authorization in order to become eligible to apply for evacuation permits. However, a small minority of the newcomers and probably the majority of local North Caucasians were employed and had to go through the process of obtaining evacuation clearance.[75] This could take a longer or a shorter time, depending on the specific circumstances of each applicant, but if they wished to leave in an orderly manner, they could not avoid this process. It seems reasonable to assume that, before those Jews who were employed perceived that the situation was truly threatening, the vast majority of them were thinking of making an orderly evacuation.

Once Jews, individually or with their families, obtained all the necessary papers and received evacuation permits, they were entitled to leave. But still, this did not necessarily mean that all of them would succeed in realizing their plans. They could be prevented from doing so because of Soviet bureaucratic mistakes. For example, in Krasnodar, a Jewish woman received evacuation authorization, but was not allowed to leave until she had removed all the goods from her storage area.[76] A significant obstacle was the lack of the necessary transport services. The problem became particularly acute after the start of the German drive into the Caucasus, when the units of the retreating Red Army requisitioned all means of transport.[77]

We should also consider the impact of the food conditions in the region on the behavior of the Jewish refugees. In contrast to most other Soviet rear areas during the War, in the North Caucasus there was a relative abundance of food.[78] This was especially important for refugees coming from the besieged city of Leningrad, who had already suffered terrible starvation during the siege of the city since September 1941. Moving elsewhere from such a blessed region as the North Caucasus was fraught with uncertainty, and was therefore frowned upon by potential refugees.

Same as in other parts of Russia that were in the line of attack from the German army, the place of residence could also influence the intention and

---

75 Shternshis, "Between Life and Death," 500.
76 Testimony of Natalya Krechetovich, b. 1931, August 29, 1999, YVA: 0.33.C/5961.
77 Kislovodsk. Testimony of Gadleva, YVA: 0.3/4391, p. 9. Nalchik. Testimony of Nushum Shamilov, October 11, 1988, YVA: 0.3/5157, p. 12.
78 Kiril Feferman, "Food Factor as a Possible Catalyst for the Holocaust-Related Decisions: The Crimea and North Caucasus," *War in History* 15, no. 1 (2008): 85–87.

ability of the Jews in the Caucasus to escape from the approaching German forces. Other conditions being equal, a big city was the best place to get information about the German advance, and the best place to obtain Holocaust-related information. Especially favorable in this regard were large transportation centers through which Jewish refugees were trying to make their way eastwards. Conversely, it was more difficult to obtain information in smaller cities and towns, and in particular in villages, where geographical distance prevented Jews from learning about the proximity of the danger.[79]

However, in summer 1942 the situation changed. "Urban" Jews still seemed to be better informed with respect to the proximity of the German forces. But their ability to escape decreased dramatically because of the enormous transportation problems caused by the retreat of the Red Army and by the German bombardment of the main transportation centers. Conversely, Jews living in rural areas had some chance to escape on their own, provided that their point of departure was far enough away from the advancing German troops. Finally, it should be remembered that the evacuation from such a vast area as the North Caucasus was a multi-stage process: it was possible to escape the first wave of German attack in the region and still be swept away by the second wave.[80]

Moreover, the military developments in the southern part of the Soviet-German War zone in 1941–1942 were very confusing for those North Caucasian Jews who were trying to figure out whether and when they should run away. On the one hand, the victories of the Red Army during the winter campaign of 1941–1942[81] partly assuaged their fears. On the other hand, the fiasco of the Soviet forces near Kharkov in mid-May 1942 and the fall of Sevastopol on July 2 of that year prompted many Jews to consider immediate flight from the Caucasus.[82] This is analyzed in greater detail in the chapters dealing with the Ginsburg letters.

---

79 Villages of Dzhiginka in winter 1941–1942 and Ivanovka in November and December 1941. Testimony of Melinsky, YVA: 0.3/4342, p. 4. Testimony of Gurevich, ICJ: TC 2761.
80 Testimony of Aron Gurevich, no date, GARF: 7021/17/206, p. 329. See also Testimony of Lidiya Amchislavskaya, May 17, 1989, YVHN. Testimony of Izrail Tomachevsky, October 3, 1999, YVHN.
81 B. I. Nevzorov, "Sokrushenie blitskriga," in *Velikaia Otechestvennaia voina 1941–1945 gg.*, vol. 1, ed. N. M. Ramanichev (Moscow: Nauka, 1998), 248–284; idem, "Zimnee nastuplenie Krasnoi Armii," ibid., 285–318.
82 Testimony of Yakov Vinokurov, October 19, 1999, YVA: VT/2489 (not transcribed). Cf. Testimony of Barukh Yafit, September 4, 1999, YVHN.

CHAPTER 1.3

The Holocaust in the North Caucasus[1]

1. JEWISH COUNCILS, GHETTOS, AND CAMPS

In the North Caucasus, Jewish councils (Judenräte) were set up in the towns and cities with the largest Jewish communities: Essentuki, Kislovodsk, Krasnodar, and Stavropol.[2] In Cherkessk and Novorossiisk, their functions were assigned to a single person, the *starosta*.[3] Jewish councils were set up soon after the beginning of the occupation. Occasionally, the Germans explained this by citing the need "to protect the interests of the Jewish population" (Stavropol),[4] to ensure the proper arrangement of the Jewish community (Krasnodar),[5] or even "to improve the life [*byt*] of the Jews and to enable them to trade" (Novorossiisk).[6] Jewish Councils in the Caucasian towns were a convenient instrument in the German hands for the smooth enactment of the whole complex of

---

1 This chapter is a summary of my research on the Holocaust in the North Caucasus, as reflected in my book *The Holocaust in the Crimea*, 173–230.
2 Essentuki, Kislovodsk, Krasnodar. Statement of the Commission of the Town of Essentuki, July 10, 1943, GARF: 7021/17/4, p. 1. V. Karl, "The destruction of the Caucasian Jewry (descriptions of the Soviet writer Alexey Tolstoy following the eyewitnesses' testimonies of the anti-Jewish atrocities)," *Ha-tsofe*, no. 1842, January 26, 1944 [Hebrew]. Questioning of Nikolai Poznansky, January 10, 1944, GARF: 7021/16/462, p. 205.
3 Statement of the Commission of the Town of Cherkessk, July 13, 1943, GARF: 702/17/12, pp. 68–69. Memorandum of the Command of Krasnodar Group [*kust*] of Partisan Detachments, October 1942 (?). In Beliaev and Bondar', *Kuban' v gody Velikoi Otechestvennoi voiny*, 557.
4 Report of Abram Nankin, in *Chernaia kniga o zlodeiskom povsemestnom ubiistve evreev nemetsko-fashistskimi zakhvatchikami vo vremenno-okkupirovannykh raionakh Sovetskogo Soiuza i v lageriakh unichtozheniia Pol'shi vo vremia voiny 1941–1945 gg.*, ed. Vasilii Grossman and Il'ia Erenburg (Jerusalem: Tarbut, 1980), 272–273.
5 Questioning of Poznansky, GARF: 7021/16/462, p. 205.
6 Statement of the Commission of the Town of Novorossiisk, October 18, 1943, GARF: 7021/16/11, p. 1.

anti-Jewish measures: from registration of the Jewish population[7] to assigning Jews to forced labor.[8] Finally, the Germans compelled the Jewish Councils to collaborate with them in gradually depriving fellow Jews of their property[9] and in forcing the Jews to assembly places before being assigned to forced labor or killed.[10]

In the North Caucasus, the policy of confining Jews to ghettos was applied only to a few of the towns containing medium-sized (some hundreds) and small-sized (up to one hundred people) Jewish communities.[11] In the ghettos, the Jews were placed in separate locations hardly fit for human habitation and were forbidden to leave without the authorization of the Germans or the local administration, unless they were sent to perform forced labor.[12] The Jewish councils were not involved in running the ghettos: there were no councils in the town that had ghettos. The life of the ghettoized Jews was regulated solely by the Germans. The ghetto inmates did not work in industrial production, but only in humiliating jobs, such as cleaning lavatories and sweeping streets.[13] There were no payments in return for their labor. In order to survive, the Jews had to sell their possessions and rely on handouts from the local people when they went out to perform forced labor. As a result, the Jews suffered terribly from undernourishment.[14] In almost all ghettos in the North Caucasus, Jews were subjected to physical mistreatment and continual theft of their property.[15]

---

7   Essentuki, Krasnodar. Statement of the Commission of the Town of Essentuki, July 10, 1943, GARF: 7021/17/4, p. 1. Statement of Anna Sokolitskaya-Vasser, January 11, 1944, GARF: 7021/16/462, p. 204.
8   Statement of the Commission of the Town of Cherkessk, July 13, 1943, GARF: 702/17/12, pp. 68–69. Statement of the Commission of the Town of Pyatigorsk, GARF: 7021/17/3, p. 8.
9   Kislovodsk, Pyatigorsk. Statement of the Commission of the Town of Kislovodsk, June 21, 1943, GARF: 7021/17/5, p. 39. Statement of the Commission of the Town of Pyatigorsk, GARF: 7021/17/3, p. 8.
10 Krasnodar. NKVD Administration, Intelligence survey no. 21, October 6, 1942. In Beliaev and Bondar', *Kuban' v gody Velikoi Otechestvennoi voiny*, 461.
11 Elista, Zheleznovodsk. Report of the ESC, GARF: 7021/8/26, pp. 10–11. Statement of the Commission of the town of Zheleznovodsk, July 12, 1943, GARF: 7021/17/6, p. 1.
12 Cherkessk, Elista. Statement of the Commission of the Town of Cherkessk, July 13, 1943, GARF: 702/17/12, pp. 68–69. Report of the ESC, GARF: 7021/8/26, pp. 10–11.
13 Mikoyanshakhar—First ghetto, Zheleznovodsk. Statement of the Commission of the town of Mikoyanshakhar, June 20, 1943. GARF: 7021/17/10, p. 195. Statement of Kairov, GARF: 7021/17/6, p. 4.
14 Statement of the Commission of the Town of Mikoyanshakhar, June 20, 1943, GARF: 7021/17/10, p. 195.
15 Elista, Mikoyanshakhar, Zheleznovodsk. Report of the ESC, GARF: 7021/8/26, pp. 10–11. Statement of the Commission of the Town of Mikoyanshakhar, June 20, 1943, GARF:

Almost all the Jews in the ghettos were liquidated during the big wave of extermination in August–September 1942.[16]

2. TOWNS

The Germans' initial methods for dealing with the Jewish population differed from place to place. At times, the Germans personally approached the Jewish public or individual Jews in order to assuage their fears that Jews would be singled out in German orders.[17] The Germans also promised that absolute compliance with their orders would safeguard the Jews' future.[18] In many places, the Germans assured the Jews that the aim of "resettlement" was simply to send them to some other locality.[19] This policy should be regarded as part of their camouflage tactics.

Concurrently, the Germans' policy sometimes also involved threats against entire communities or individual Jews, such as Judenräte members. In such instances, the Germans warned the Jews that non-compliance with their orders would lead to heavy retribution, including capital punishment.[20]

It must be emphasized that in all of the aforementioned cases, the Germans were determined to prevent Jews from escaping from the occupied areas. In terms of the Germans' genocide policy—unlike an ordinary Soviet citizen, whose presence or absence usually mattered little to the Germans—a Jew was to be caught and killed in every town or village.

7021/17/10, pp. 195–196. Statement of the Commission of the Town of Zheleznovodsk, July 12, 1943, GARF: 7021/17/6, pp. 1–2.

16 Statement of the Commission of the Town of Cherkessk, July 13, 1943, GARF: 702/17/12, pp. 68–69. Report of the ESC, GARF: 7021/8/26, pp. 10–11. Statement of the Commission of the Town of Mikoyanshakhar, June 20, 1943, GARF: 7021/17/10, p. 196. Statement of Kairov, GARF: 7021/17/6, p. 4.

17 Krasnodar, Novorossiisk. In Krasnodar, the registration of the whole population took place in September 1942, that is, more than two weeks after the registration and destruction of the Jews. NKVD Administration, Intelligence survey no. 6. In Beliaev and Bondar', *Kuban' v gody Velikoi Otechestvennoi voiny*, 460–461.

18 Cherkessk, Stavropol. Landesgericht München I, Urteil gegen Johannes Schlupper, Heinrich Winterstein, Rudi Eschenbach, July 24, 1974, YVA: TR.10/956, pp. 34–35. Document of the Stavropol medical institute, July 2, 1943, GARF: 7021/17/294, p. 7.

19 Essentuki, Mineralnye vody. Jewish Anti-Fascist Committee [based on letters from the local inhabitants], "Caucasian Jews Crying Out," *Ha-tsofe* (Tel Aviv), no. 1702, August 4, 1943 [Hebrew]. Statement of Matvei Makogonenko, August 13, 1943, GARF: 7021/17/2, pp. 14–15.

20 Cherkessk, Stavropol. Statement of the Commission of the Town of Cherkessk, July 13, 1943, GARF: 702/17/12, pp. 68–69. Statement of the Commission of the City of Stavropol, July 11, 1943, GARF: 7021/17/1, pp. 95–96.

The German onslaught against the Jews in the North Caucasus involved several steps. First, in most Caucasian towns, immediately after occupation, the Germans forced the entire Jewish population to register.[21] This appeared to be a relatively mild step at first, because mass assembly of the Jews—for forced labor, ill-treatment, and eventual extermination—was not immediately ordered. Usually the registration process was organized by the Jewish Council, but sometimes the Germans themselves carried it out.[22] The local police only rarely participated in enforcing the registration orders.[23]

After registration, the next stage involved forcing adult Jews, including children over twelve years old, to wear six-pointed stars as identification badges.[24] The Germans applied this policy in most Caucasian towns.[25] In most cases, Jews were ordered to wear the stars immediately upon registration.[26] However, sometimes there was a short interval between the two procedures, as the Germans faced problems in applying the identification order.[27] This was due to anti-Jewish measures being poorly synchronized in some Caucasian towns located close to one another.

In the initial phases of the War, Caucasian Jews were occasionally physically ill-treated by their German oppressors.[28] This included German guards beating Jews and raping Jewish women in places where the non-Jewish population could not witness the abuse, such as in the apartments of Jews and in

---

21 Elista, Krasnodar. Report of the ESC on the atrocities of the German Fascist occupiers in the occupied *ulusy* and the town of Elista, no later than September 10, 1943, GARF: 7021/8/26, pp. 10–11. Statement of the Commission of the City of Krasnodar, June 30, 1943, GARF: 7021/16/5, p. 12.
22 Kislovodsk, Mineralnye vody. Testimony of Sklyar, YVA: 0.3/3934, p. 6. "How the Jews Are Murdered," *Ha-tsofe*, April 8, 1943 [Hebrew].
23 Testimony of Ya. Talyansky, no date, GARF: 7021/17/4, p. 31.
24 Kislovodsk. Testimony of Sklyar, YVA: 0.3/3934, p. 6.
25 Armavir, Zheleznovodsk. Statement of the Commission of the Town of Armavir, January 28, 1943, Tsentral'nyi arkhiv Ministerstva Oborony Rossiiskoi Federatsii (henceforth TsAMO RF): 51/958/52, pp. 91–92. Courtesy of the United States Holocaust Memorial Museum (henceforth USHMM). Statement of the Commission of the Town of Zheleznovodsk, July 12, 1943, GARF: 7021/17/6, p. 1.
26 Kislovodsk, Mineralnye vody. Testimony of Sklyar, YVA: 0.3/3934, p. 6. Statement of Pavlov, GARF: 7021/17/2, p. 13.
27 Essentuki and Krasnodar (?). Testimony of Belenkov, GARF: 7021/17/4, p. 24. Testimony of Krechetovich, YVA: 0.33.C/5961.
28 Cherkessk, Mikoyanshakhar. Statement on the atrocities and abuse committed by the German Fascist occupiers towards the peaceful population of Pregradnensky *raion*, June 28, 1943. In *Stavropol'e v Velikoi Otechestvennoi voine 1941–1945 gg. Sbornik dokumentov i materialov* (Stavropol: Knizhnoe izdatel'stvo, 1962), 135. Testimony of Nikeeva, GARF: 7021/17/10, p. 204.

detention centers.²⁹ But sometimes Jews were beaten in public or while performing forced labor.³⁰

If the Jews in the Caucasian towns were not killed immediately, they were compelled to perform forced labor.³¹ The forced labor orders applied to almost the whole Jewish population, including children over ten years old, pregnant women and those with small children, and old people up to ninety years of age.³² It was impossible to evade labor on medical grounds.³³

The Jews were only occasionally exploited for relatively easy work, for example, maintaining satisfactory sanitary conditions in the occupied towns, such as cleaning and sweeping the streets³⁴ or burying the corpses of dead people and animals.³⁵ Jewish labor was sometimes used for construction projects of military significance.³⁶ However, for the most part, the Jewish population was exploited for the most difficult and most humiliating work: cleaning lavatories and carrying huge stones.³⁷ In some occupied Soviet territories, the Germans

---

29 For apartments, see Essentuki. Testimony of Faina Gulyanskaya, July 2, 1943, GARF: 7021/17/4, p. 17. For detention centers, see Statement of the Commission of the Town of Cherkessk. July 13, 1943, GARF: 702/17/12, pp. 68–69. Statement on the resort Teberda, GARF: 7021/17/7, pp. 4–5.
30 For the public, see Mikoyanshakhar. Testimony of Nikeeva, GARF: 7021/17/10, p. 204. For forced labor, see Essentuki. Testimony of Belenkov, GARF: 7021/17/4, p. 23. Statement of the Commission of the Town of Essentuki, July 10, 1943, GARF: 7021/17/4, p. 1.
31 Essentuki, Kislovodsk, Zheleznovodsk. Letter by the painter L. N. Tarabukin and his wife D. R. Goldshtain to the writer Yu. Kalugin, [1943], YVA: M.35/25, p. 86. Testimony of Sklyar, YVA: 0.3/3934, p. 7. Statement of T. Z. Kairov, 1943 (?), GARF: 7021/17/6, p. 4.
32 Nalchik. "Nazis' Atrocities" [Hebrew], *Ha-tsofe*, no. 1717, August 19, 1943, p. 2 [source: Soviet diplomatic representatives in Washington; testimonies of fourteen Nalchik Jews on the fate of the Jews there]. Statement of the Commission of the Town of Essentuki, July 10, 1943, GARF: 7021/17/4, p. 1; Nalchik. Testimony of Avgosh Shamilova, January 8, 1998. In Danilova, *Iskhod gorskih evreev*, 26.
33 Essentuki, Zheleznovodsk. Testimony of Belenkov, GARF: 7021/17/4, p. 23. Statement of the doctor K. T. Gavrilova, 1943, GARF: 7021/17/6, p. 25.
34 Essentuki, Kislovodsk. Statement of the Commission of the Town of Essentuki, July 10, 1943, GARF: 7021/17/4, p. 1. Report of Evenson, YVA: P.21.2/1. Testimony of Sklyar, YVA: 0.3/3934, p. 6.
35 Zheleznovodsk. Statement of Kairov, GARF: 7021/17/6, p. 4.
36 Elista, Kislovodsk, Nalchik. Report of ESC, GARF: 7021/8/26, pp. 10–11. Statement of the Commission of the Town of Kislovodsk, July 5, 1943, GARF: 7021/17/5, pp. 35–36. In *Dokumenty obviniaiut. Sbornik materialov o chudovishchnykh zverstvakh Germanskikh vlastei na vremenno-okkupirovannykh Sovetskikh territoriyakh* (2nd ed., Moscow: Gospolitizdat, 1945), 140–142. Testimony of Shamilova, in Danilova, *Iskhod gorskih evreev*, 26.
37 Armavir, Essentuki. Statement of the Commission of the Town of Armavir. January 28, 1943, TsAMO RF: 51/958/52, pp. 91–92. Courtesy of USHMM. Statement of the Commission of the Town of Essentuki. July 10, 1943, GARF: 7021/17/4, p. 1.

paid the Jewish forced laborers, either with money or food, but in the Caucasian towns there was no payment.[38] Jews were exploited over the course of a lengthy working day, often without breaks,[39] and with no food supplied.[40] Jews fared better if the labor order was enforced by the Jewish Councils or heads of Jewish communities.[41] They fared far worse when either local collaborators or the Germans themselves were involved in enforcing the order.[42] Jews herded into small ghettos underwent the harshest treatment during their forced labor, as their entire lives (before, during, and after the day's labor) were regulated by a vicious German administration.[43]

In the North Caucasus, the Germans widely resorted to exerting economic pressure on the Jews. Imposition of monetary indemnity (*kontributsiia*) on the Jewish communities was one such measure.[44] The price of indemnity was high: for example, the community of Kislovodsk had to pay 100,000 rubles, the Jews of Cherkessk, 135,000 rubles, and the Jews of Mikoyanshakhar, 500,000 rubles.[45] The sum demanded bore no relationship to the actual number of Jewish inhabitants of the town in question: there were 2,000 Jews registered in Kislovodsk, while there were 820 in Cherkessk and only 129 in Mikoyanshakhar. The enormous size of the indemnity can be explained by the German assumption that the Jewish population, which consisted mainly of the evacuees from large Soviet cities, was well-off.

---

38 Kislovodsk, Pyatigorsk. Statement, July 5, 1943, GARF: 7021/17/5, pp. 35–36. Statement of the Commission of the Town of Pyatigorsk, GARF: 7021/17/3, p. 8.
39 Statement of the Commission of the Town of Essentuki, July 10, 1943, GARF: 7021/17/4, p. 1.
40 Essentuki, Nalchik. Ibid. See also Testimony of Shamilova. In Danilova, *Iskhod gorskih evreev*, 26.
41 Statement of the Commission of the Town of Pyatigorsk, GARF: 7021/17/3, p. 8. Statement of the Commission of the City of Cherkessk, July 13, 1943, GARF: 702/17/12, pp. 68–69.
42 Nalchik, Tikhoretsk. Testimony of Shamilova. In Danilova, *Iskhod gorskih evreev*, 26. See also Beliaev and Bondar', *Kuban' v gody Velikoi Otechestvennoi voiny*, 464–465.
43 Elista, Mikoyanshakhar, Zheleznovodsk. Report of the ESC, GARF: 7021/8/26, pp. 10–11. Statement of the Commission of the Town of Mikoyanshakhar, June 20, 1943, GARF: 7021/17/10, p. 195. Statement of Kairov, GARF: 7021/17/6, p. 4.
44 Cherkessk (?), Essentuki. Landesgericht München I, Urteil gegen Schlupper, YVA: TR.10/956, p. 63. Statement of the Commission of the Town of Essentuki, July 10, 1943, GARF: 7021/17/4, p. 1.
45 Commission of the Town of Kislovodsk, June 21, 1943, GARF: 7021/17/5, p. 39. Testimony of Nikeeva, GARF: 7021/17/10, p. 204. To the best of my knowledge, there is no authoritative source on what the ruble was worth compared with major international currencies during the War.

The indemnity order was combined with other German steps aimed at dispossessing the Jews. The example of Kislovodsk underscores this point. Alongside the indemnity worth "100,000 rubles in cash," the German authorities demanded that the Jewish committee delivered "530 articles made of gold or silver, rings, watches, cigarette cases, 105 dozen silver spoons, 230 pairs of shoes, men's suits, coats, and carpets."[46] Usually "organized" plunder took on the form of orderly arranged "requisitions," effected largely by means of the Judenräte[47] or under the pretext of legal searches of Jewish apartments for weapons or for unregistered Jews.[48] It is noteworthy that there exists no record of "non-organized" plunder of Jewish property in the Caucasus. The reason is the strictly enforced discipline in the Wehrmacht, which was also extended to the local population of the Caucasian towns under German control. In many localities, the Germans confiscated all Jewish property.[49] In other places, similarly to many other occupied Soviet regions, less valuable articles were left for the local policemen,[50] and then sometimes distributed, sold, or left for the local population.[51]

In a few Caucasian towns, regardless of the size of the Jewish population, Jews were subjected to various forms of economic or political boycott. However, this boycott was far from being a comprehensive and consistent policy in the Caucasian towns. Rather, it seems that, given the brevity of the period prior to the annihilation of the Jews in the North Caucasus, the majority of the Jewish population did not suffer from boycotting. Nevertheless, even single events of this kind could influence the public opinion about the Jewish population.

As mentioned above, the Germans sometimes employed segregation, another component of their restrictive policy towards the Jews in the Caucasus, against the background of general residence and movement restrictions. The

---

46   Statement, July 5, 1943, GARF: 7021/17/5, pp. 35–36.
47   Essentuki, Kislovodsk. Statement of Professor Vladimir Dik, June 27, 1943, GARF: 7021/17/4, p. 9. Report of Evenson, YVA: P.21.2/1.
48   Essentuki, Nalchik. Testimony of Belenkov, GARF: 7021/17/4, p. 24.
49   Cherkessk, Mikoyanshakhar. Statement of the Commission of Pregradnensky *Raion*, June 28, 1943. In *Stavropol'e*, 135. Testimony of Nikeeva, GARF: 7021/17/10, p. 204.
50   Pyatigorsk, Stavropol. Statement of the Commission of the Town of Pyatigorsk, GARF: 7021/17/3, p. 8. Report of Nankin, in Grossman and Erenburg, *Chernaia kniga*, 272–273.
51   Elista, Essentuki. Statement of D. Babkina, July 20, 1943, GARF: 7021/8/27, p. 91. Testimony of Belenkov, GARF: 7021/17/4, p. 26.

German restrictive policies were relatively lenient in the region, but there were several deviations from this pattern.[52]

After the Germans occupied a town, it took them from one or two weeks to four months between registering the Jews and ordering their assembly and mass extermination.[53] Jews were often threatened with severe physical punishment for failure to comply with register and assembly orders.[54] Jews were required to leave most of their belongings in their apartments, but were permitted to take with them a certain amount of money, valuables, and personal possessions.[55]

The German administration normally proclaimed the order to assemble, although very occasionally the local authorities or the Jewish Council issued the order.[56] For the most part, the Germans openly intervened only at the assembly points, which they did by ordering armed guards to prevent the Jews from leaving these locations.[57] In cities and bigger towns, the Germans assembled the Jews in the urban squares, and then immediately marched them out towards execution sites.[58] In smaller towns, they herded the Jews into one location and kept them there for up to two days, usually without food or water, before driving them to extermination sites or placing them in gas vans.[59]

---

52 Essentuki, Novorossiisk. Statement of the Commission of the City of Essentuki, July 10, 1943, GARF: 7021/17/4, p. 1. Questioning of Alekseeva, GARF: 7021/16/11, p. 77. Cf. Alexei Tolstoi, "Korichnevyi durman," *Pravda*, August 5, 1943.
53 Krasnodar, Stavropol. NKVD Administration, Intelligence survey no. 21, October 6, 1942. In Beliaev and Bondar', *Kuban' v gody Velikoi Otechestvennoi voiny*, 461. Report of Nankin. In Grossman and Erenburg, *Chernaia kniga*, 272–273. Essentuki, Kislovodsk. Statement of the Commission of the Town Essentuki, July 10, 1943, GARF: 7021/17/4, p. 1. In *Dokumenty obviniaiut*, 140–142; Statement of the Commission of the Town of Cherkessk, July 13, 1943, GARF: 702/17/12, pp. 68–69; Statement on the Resort Teberda, GARF: 7021/17/7, pp. 4–5.
54 Essentuki, Stavropol. Statement of the Commission of the Town of Essentuki, July 10, 1943, GARF: 7021/17/4, p. 1. Statement of the Commission of the City of Stavropol, July 11, 1943, GARF: 7021/17/1, pp. 95–96.
55 Kislovodsk, Pyatigorsk, Teberda. Testimony of Sklyar, YVA: 0.3/3934, p. 7. Statement of the Commission of the Town of Pyatigorsk, GARF: 7021/17/3, p. 8. Statement on the Resort Teberda, GARF: 7021/17/7, pp. 4–5.
56 Statement of the Commission of the Town of Essentuki, July 10, 1943, GARF: 7021/17/4, p. 1. Statement of the Commission of the Town of Pyatigorsk, GARF: 7021/17/3, p. 8; Cherkessk. Der Untersuchungsrichter 115 Ks 6a-c/71, Strafsache gegen Schlupper, Vernehmungsniderschrift Schluppers, December 14, 1971, YVA: TR.10/1081, p. 56; Krasnodar. NKVD Administration, Intelligence survey No. 21. In Beliaev and Bondar', *Kuban' v gody Velikoi Otechestvennoi voiny*, 461.
57 Cherkessk, Novorossiisk. Statement of the Commission of the Town of Cherkessk, July 13, 1943, GARF: 702/17/12, pp. 68–69. Questioning of Silina, GARF: 7021/16/11, p. 28.
58 Stavropol. Statement, July 14, 1943, GARF: 7021/17/1, pp. 3, 5.
59 Cherkessk, Essentuki. Statement of the Commission of the Town of Cherkessk, July 13, 1943, GARF: 702/17/12, pp. 68–69. Testimony of Belenkov, GARF: 7021/17/4, pp. 25–26.

The Germans conducted killing operations in the Caucasian cities and towns throughout almost the whole of the occupation period. Annihilation of the Jewish population was only limited by the logistics necessary for the Germans to prepare the ground, so that the extermination actions could be carried out smoothly (most specifically, by the deployment of the Einsatzgruppe forces). In August, killing operations began against the Jews of Stavropol and Krasnodar, the most populous and presumably the most important regional centers of the German-controlled Caucasus. In Stavropol, 4,000 Jews were murdered.[60] The number of victims in Krasnodar was either 1,800 to more than 3,000 Jews, according to various estimations.[61]

In one month, September 1942, the Germans wiped out the bulk of Caucasian Jewry, primarily in the four neighboring resorts of Stavropol region: Essentuki, Kislovodsk, Mineralnye vody, and Pyatigorsk. There were almost 10,000 victims in total.[62] After that date, the pace of annihilation of the Jews in Caucasian towns slowed down. The last large-scale wave of actions swept the towns in the form of "mopping-up" operations, in light of a possible German withdrawal from the North Caucasus.[63]

After the extermination actions in the Caucasian towns and cities, the Germans found some Jews still in hiding, following all-encompassing security steps directed against the general population. However, due to the relatively mild character of the occupation in the Caucasus, the Germans rarely conducted such searches. Round-ups of Jews in the Caucasian towns,[64] in which whole areas were cordoned off for house-to-house searches in the wake of the extermination action,[65] were rare. Most of the Jews in

---

60 GARF: 7021/116/11a, p. 24.
61 NKVD Administration, Intelligence survey No. 21, October 6, 1942. In Beliaev and Bondar', *Kuban' v gody Velikoi Otechestvennoi voiny*, 461. Statement of the Commission of the City of Krasnodar, June 30, 1943, GARF: 7021/16/5, pp. 11–12, 14. Military court of the North Caucasian Front, Krasnodar trial, July 14–17, 1943. In *Dokumenty obviniaiut*, 104.
62 Statement of the local Commission on the investigation of the Nazi German atrocities, January 21, 1943, TsAMO RF: 51/958/52, p. 85. Courtesy of USHMM.
63 Statement of the Commission of the Town of Mikoyanshakhar, June 20, 1943, GARF: 7021/17/10, p. 195. Statement on the Resort Teberda, July 5, 1943, GARF: 7021/17/7, pp. 4–5. *Dokumenty obviniaiut*, 163–164.
64 Stavropol. Strafsache gegen Bierkamp, Auswertung der Vernehmungsprotokolle russischer Zeugen von Bl. 1/92-65/40 d. Acte. B. 7–8, Iwan D. ab Okt. 41 bei der Tataren-Komp. Woroschilowsk—K, YVA: TR.10/1147, p. 576.
65 Stavropol. "Those are the First News ... What the Nazis Do towards the Jews before their Retreat from Russia," *Davar* (Tel Aviv), no. 5366, February 24, 1943 [source: Moscow, special telegram to *Davar* dated February 22, 1943]. [Hebrew].

hiding were caught as a result of denunciations by Russian and Ukrainian civilians.[66]

On the whole, the milder nature of the German occupational regime in the Caucasus in comparison to other areas[67] and the short time that it lasted did enable some Jews to survive. The swift withdrawal of the German forces from the region in late 1942 contributed to the rescue of a certain number of people who were already in detention; in all probability, there were also some Jews amongst them.[68]

3. RURAL AREAS

In the rural Caucasian areas, Jews were required to register only in some villages. At times, German orders included explicit threats directed not only against any Jews who failed to register, but also against any local people who gave shelter to Jews.[69] The registration of Jews was ordered primarily by the military administration.[70] Sometimes it demanded that Jews wear identifying stars immediately upon having being registered.[71] But infrequently, Jews were not required to register at all, only to wear identifying bands.[72]

The Germans widely employed Jewish forced labor in rural areas, primarily for gathering the harvest[73] and, to a much lesser extent, for military construction work[74] or for humiliating cleaning jobs.[75] Their conditions while performing

---

66 Kislovodsk, Krasnodar. Testimony of Leina Faina, no date, GARF: 7021/17/206, p. 85. Krasnodar trial. Interrogation of Ivan Paramonov, June 26, 1943, Akademiia Federal'noi Sluzhby Bezopasnosti Rossiskoi Federatsii: H-16708, p. 657. Courtesy of USHMM.
67 On the German *Judenpolitik* in another Russian area (Pskov district in the North-Western part of Russia), see Johannes Enstad Due, *Soviet Russians under Nazi Occupation. Fragile Loyalties in World War II* (Cambridge: Cambridge University Press, 2018), 60–87.
68 Mozdok. Testimony of Alexander Guseev, after 1976, YVA: 0.3/6970, pp. 4–5.
69 Statement of the Commission of *Stanitsa* Novo-Aleksandrovskaya, GARF: 7021/17/11, p. 28.
70 Statement of the Commission of *Stanitsa* S[taro?]-Shcherbinskaya, GARF: 7021/16/12, p. 195.
71 Villages Blagodatnoe and Zolskoe. Statement of the Commission of Shpakovsky *Raion*, GARF: 7021/17/12, p. 55. Statement no. 90, GARF: 7021/7/109, p. 186.
72 *Stanitsy* Labinskaya and Gulkevich. Conversation of the ESC member V. Grizodubov with Mariya Doragan, June 4, 1943, YVA: M.33/298, p. 17. Questioning of Anastasy Gur (Kondrat'ev), May 15, 1944, GARF: 7021/16/435, p. 130.
73 *Stanitsy* Bekeshevskaya and Sovetskaya. Statement of the Commission of Suvorovsky *Raion*, GARF: 7021/17/12, p. 3. Statement of the Commission of *Stanitsa* Sovetskaya, August 15, 1943, GARF: 7021/16/435, p. 184.
74 Statement of the Commission of *Stanitsa* of Novo-Aleksandrovskaya, GARF: 7021/17/11, p. 28.
75 Vorontsovo-Aleksandrovskoe village. Statement of Lidiya Brailovskaya, 1943, GARF: 7021/17/10, p. 33.

forced labor depended on the extent to which the German occupying forces were present. When the Germans supervised the laborers, their existence was made unbearable and involved physical cruelty, allocation of the most difficult assignments, and dangerously unsanitary conditions, which resulted in a high mortality rate.[76] Jews faced very long working days and unachievable production norms.[77] The Germans gave them no food and stopped the local population from giving them any.[78] The Jews were better off, relatively, when the local collaborators supervised their labor.[79]

In contrast to the towns, in the villages the Germans and their local collaborators looted Jewish property, without restraint, in addition to carrying out orderly "requisitions."[80] The German military and security command seemed to tacitly approve of this free-hand policy. It applied not only to those whose direct responsibility it was to "handle" the Jewish question (the officers and soldiers of the Einsatzgruppen[81] and Kommandaturen),[82] but also to other sectors of the German army, which only had casual contacts with the Jewish population,[83] and to local collaborators.[84] The German commanders were less

---

76 Statement of the Commission of *Stanitsa* of Novo-Aleksandrovskaya, GARF: 7021/17/11, p. 28. Statement of the Commission of the Village Menzhinskoe, June 27, 1943, GARF: 7021/17/10, pp. 155–156.
77 Menzhinskoe village, *stanitsa* Bekeshevskaya. Statement of the Commission of the Village Menzhinskoe, June 27, 1943, GARF: 7021/17/10, pp. 155–156. See also Statement of the Commission of Suvorovsky *Raion*, GARF: 7021/17/12, p. 3.
78 *Stanitsa* Bekeshevskaya. Statement of the Commission of the Village Menzhinskoe, June 27, 1943, GARF: 7021/17/10, pp. 155–156.
79 *Stanitsa* Sovetskaya and Troitskoe village. Statement of the Commission of *Stanitsa* Sovetskaya, GARF: 7021/16/435, p. 184. Testimony of Lilia German, August 16, 1943, GARF: 7021/8/27, p. 55.
80 Villages Olginskoe and Stepnoe. Statement of A. Kureshov, June 25, 1943, GARF: 7021/17/10, p. 162. Statement of the Commission of Stepnoe Village, July 22, 1943, GARF: 7021/17/11, p. 147.
81 On the Einsatzgruppen, see C. Earl Hilary, *The Nuremberg SS-Einsatzgruppen Trial, 1945–1958* (Cambridge: Cambridge University Press, 2009), 4–8; See also Peter Klein (ed.), *Die Einsatzgruppen in der bezetzten Sowjetunion 1941/42: Die Tätigkeits- und Lagerberichte des Chefs der Sicherpolizei und des SD* (Berlin: Edition Hentrich, 1997), in particular Andrej Angrick's "Die Einsatzgruppe D," ibid., 88–110.
82 *Stanitsa* Aleksandriiskaya, Sukhoe village. Statement of the Commission of *Stanitsa* Aleksandriiskaya, GARF: 7021/17/9, p. 12. Statements of the inhabitants of Sukhoe village: N. Zhdanova, A. Parashuk, O. Sankova, 1943, GARF: 7021/17/10, p. 137.
83 Izobilnensky *raion*, Stavropol territory. Statement of the Commission of Izobilnensky *Raion*, June 29, 1943, GARF: 7021/17/10, pp. 121–122.
84 Villages Beluevsky in Libknekhtovsky *raion* (?) and Blagodatnoe. Statement of Nina Zaitseva, 1943, GARF: 7021/17/10, p. 166. Statement of the Commission of Shpakovsky *Raion*. GARF: 7021/17/12, p. 55.

concerned with local public opinion in the countryside. Thus, they turned a blind eye to the lawless behavior of the Wehrmacht personnel, assisted by the local collaborators, who looted Jewish property. In addition, the German authorities hoped to gain the sympathies of the local inhabitants by distributing the looted property to those who the Germans defined as having been discriminated against under the Soviet regime.[85] Furthermore, in many cases the local population in the rural areas was more ill-disposed towards Soviet power and everything associated with it, including Jews, and therefore was more inclined to adopt a favorable stance towards the German onslaught against the Jews.[86]

Occasionally, Jews living in the rural areas were subjected to movement and residence restrictions. The Germans tried to register the entire rural population in the Caucasus, in order to prevent the infiltration of Soviet agents.[87] The German regulations contained a special emphasis on idnetifying those who had arrived in a given locality after the outbreak of the War, meaning evacuees or refugees: "Heads of municipalities have to draw up [lists]. ... The second list encompasses strangers in a given locality who settled down there after June 23, 1941. Jews and foreigners have to be specially marked."[88] The local authorities in the villages were also required to state the nationality of the newcomers, with a particular emphasis on Jews.[89] This was followed by the murder of the registered Jews.[90]

---

85 Clarification of Krivokhatsky, the *Oberbürgermeister* of Stavropol, sent to the *starosta* of Spitsevka village to inquire about the property of the murdered citizens, October 1942. In *Stavropol'e v period nemetsko-fashistskoi okkupatsii (avgust 1942–ianvar' 1943): Dokumenty i materialy Komiteta po delam arkhivov Stavropol'skogo kraia, Gosudarstvennogo arkhiva Stavropol'skogo kraia, Tsentra dokumentatsii noveishei istorii Stavropol'skogo kraia*, ed. Valeriia Vodolazskaia, Mariia Krivneva, and Nelli Mel'nik (Stavropol: Knizhnoe izdatel'stvo, 2000), 48.
86 Anlage zu II./Pol.Rgt., Einsatz- und Tätigkeitsbericht des Bataillons für die Zeit vom 1.–31.8.1942 (Auszug aus dem KTB), September 12, 1942, Rossiiskii gosudarstvennyi voennyi arkhiv (henceforth RGVA): 1358/1/9, p. 106. Cf. Merkblatt für das Verhalten gegenüber kaukasischen Völkern, no date, RGVA: 1323/2/263, p. 219.
87 Service instruction of the Councilor of the military administration Dr. Mantel on the establishment of the new order, directed to heads of areas and towns, Article 4, September 19, 1942. In Vodolazskaia, Krivneva, and Mel'nik, *Stavropol'e v period nemetsko-fashistskoi okkupatsii*, 44–46. Cf. Letter-instruction of *starosta* of the Aragir regional administration [*raiuprava*] sent to the *starosta* of Mussa-Ardzhin village, Stavropol *krai*, October 27, 1942, GARF: 7021/17/14, p. 34.
88 Service instruction of Dr. Mantel.
89 Ibid. Cf. Statement of the Commission of Troitskoe Village, GARF: 7021/8/27, p. 54.
90 Villages Troitskoe and Levokumskoe. Statement of the Commission of Troitskoe Village, GARF: 7021/8/27, p. 54. Memoirs of Petr Belokurov, November 13, 2002, YVA: 0.33/6783, pp. 3–5.

The local authorities ordered those Jews who were staying in the Caucasian villages to present themselves at assembly points, which were mainly in public buildings, such as schools[91] or *Kommandaturen* posts.[92] The Germans only rarely used enforcement measures, mostly to ensure that the Jews did not try to evade the order to assemble.[93] After the assembly, Jews were isolated for some time and then marched out to be murdered—usually in the immediate vicinity of the village.[94] Jewish women were sometimes raped during the killing operations.[95] On the whole, during the Holocaust in rural Caucasian areas, the small German forces carried out this final stage of the annihilation of the Jews quite smoothly, as compared to the previous stages.

Jews were murdered in the Caucasian villages throughout the whole period of the German occupation of the region. In September and October 1942, hundreds of Jews were murdered, and the bulk of the rural Jewish population was destroyed. The pace of annihilation decreased in November, but in December 1942 the North Caucasian villages were swept by a new wave of killings. As in the towns, it consisted of last-minute mopping-up actions in the whole region (on the eve of the possible German withdrawal from the Caucasus), and the "cleansing" of all undesirable elements, including Jews. Remnants of the legally registered Jewish population, such as inmates of camps[96] and those detected as a result of intensified searches, were killed during the German retreat from the region in January 1943.[97]

---

91 Menzhinskoe and Bogdanovka villages. Minutes of the Plenary meeting of the Ordzhonikidze District Committee of the VKP(b) on the terror regime of the occupiers in the occupied territory and their plans to use the lands of *kolkhozes* and *sovkhozes*, March 9, 1943. In Vodolazskaia, Krivneva, and Mel'nik, *Stavropol'e v period nemetsko-fashistskoi okkupatsii*, 81.
92 Stepnoe and Starominskaia villages. Statement of the Commission of Stepnoe Village, GARF: 7021/17/11, p. 147. Statement of the Commission of Starominsky *Raion*, December 12, 1943, YVA: M.33/302, p. 32.
93 Statement of the Commission of Bogdanovka Village, GARF: 7021/17/10, p. 158.
94 Borguevsky rural council. Statement of the Commission of Suvorovsky *Raion*, GARF: 7021/17/12, p. 2.
95 Ladozhsky *raion*. Statement of the Commission of *Stanitsa* Ladozhskaya, February 1, 1943, YVA: M.33/292, p. 30.
96 *Stanitsa* Goryachevskaya. Interrogation of Miroshnichenko, GARF: 7021/17/10, p. 74.
97 Kirov *kolkhoz*. Statement of the Commission of Kirov *Kolkhoz*, January 15, 1943, GARF: 7021/17/11, p. 151.

Part Two
THE GINSBURG FAMILY CORRESPONDENCE

CHAPTER 2

1941

The Ginsburg correspondence began on March 26, 1939. The first letter in our collection was written on this date, but it does not appear the very first letter to have been sent after a long interval. Rather, it is most likely that there were some previous letters, which Efim did not keep. The general impression given in the eight letters in the collection that were written before the War[1] shows that the Ginsburgs were a harmonious family, whose members did their best to take care of one another, despite the distance separating them. This is demonstrated by the warm congratulations sent by the Rostov Ginsburgs to Efim Ginsburg on his birthday (they sent not only ordinary letters[2] but also telegrams, which were much more expensive)[3] and the greetings that they sent him on the New Year.[4] The latter telegram may indicate the family was sufficiently acculturated to view January 1 as a Soviet holiday, devoid of its Christian underpinnings, which Jews could celebrate just like any other Soviet people.

---

1 Unless stated otherwise, all letters quoted in this book were written by the family members from Rostov-on-Don to Efim Ginsburg in Moscow. All those letters were written by the Ginsburg sisters, Anya and Liza, except one letter from Tamara. In addition to the letters analyzed in this section, the prewar part of the correspondence also includes the following letters: from Liza Chazkewitz, YVA: O.75/324, pp. 21–22; from Liza Chazkewitz, May 31, 1941, ibid., pp. 25–26, and from Liza Chazkewitz, June 22, 1941, ibid., pp. 7–30. The last letter contains no reference whatsoever to the War and was likely written and sent before the official announcement made at 12:00 pm on June 22, 1941.
2 From Anya Greener, April 1939, 1940, or 1941, ibid., p. 179; from Liza Chazkewitz, March 18, 1941, ibid., pp. 15–16; from Liza Chazkewitz, April 10, 1941, ibid., pp. 17–18.
3 From Anya Greener, Liza Chazkewitz, and Boris Chazkewitz (telegram), March 28, 1940, ibid., pp. 7–8; from Liza Chazkewitz (telegram), December 30, 1939 or 1940, ibid., p. 375.
4 From Liza Chazkewitz (telegram), December 30, 1939 or 1940, ibid., p. 375.

For his part, Efim reciprocated by congratulating the Rostov family members on their birthdays[5] and by sending a package containing items that were available in Moscow but not in Rostov-on-Don. It should be noted that the package was not sent by regular mail but delivered by an acquaintance who had travelled from Moscow. The family was deeply grateful to this person for his assistance, and for the token of Efim's consideration for them. There was only one indication about the actual contents of the packages: the Ginsburg sisters particularly appreciated the gift of sugar.[6] There is no doubt that the family lived frugally. Before the War, Efim had occasionally visited Rostov-on-Don, apparently, on business trips. These reunions were very important events for the family.[7] As for other ideas and reflections, apart from family issues, the Rostov Ginsburgs were cautious not to put down on paper anything other than their feelings, wishes, and congratulations.

April 1941

The first unconventional letter, containing ideas beyond those centered on the family and, most specifically, including thoughts related to the war, was sent on April 18, 1941 by Tamara Meerovich from Rostov-on-Don to her uncle Efim Ginsburg in Moscow:

> Grisha is turning five. Soon he'll go to school, and we'll grow old just like that. But there is nothing we can do about it. I am only frustrated by the fact that we are spending our youth during such a difficult period. Apart from work and troubles (*zaboty*), there is nothing good happening. Let's hope that this is a temporary situation and that something better awaits us. The only good thing is that we haven't suffered the horrors of a war; the rest is really a trifle.[8]

All was still quiet in the Soviet Union, as the cataclysmic war was being waged elsewhere in Europe. And this, according to twenty-eight-year old Tamara

---

5 From Tamara Meerovich, April 18, 1941, ibid., p. 19. See section entitled April, 1941 below.
6 From Liza Chazkewitz and Anya Greener, September 8, 1940, ibid., pp. 11–12.
7 From Anya Greener, no date, apparently written before the War, ibid., p. 347.
8 From Tamara Meerovich, April 18, 1941, ibid., pp. 19–20.

Meerovich, was the only "good thing" in her life. It is possible that her dissatisfaction stemmed from her age or the sense that she could not lead a more fulfilling life, one way or another. Whatever the case, in her only letter written before the War engulfed her country Tamara appears to be a pessimist by nature. This was a significant admission in a society in which people were expected to be happy with their lot.[9] And yet, she was able to recognize and appreciate the quiet of peacetime. But Tamara's "only good thing" was not going to last for very long.

Efim Ginsburg. Before the war. Courtesy of Yad Vashem Photo Archive.

THE WAR

June 1941

On June 22, the Soviet Union was invaded by Nazi Germany and some of its allies (Croatia, Finland,[10] Hungary, Italy, Romania, and Slovakia).

---

9 On this subject, see, for example, Jeffrey Brooks, *Thank you, Comrade Stalin! Soviet Public Culture from Revolution to Cold War* (Princeton, NJ: Princeton University Press, 2000), esp. 83–105; Lewis Siegelbaum and Andrei Sokolov, *Stalinism as a Way of Life. A Narrative in Documents* (New Haven, CT: Yale University Press, 2000), 207–281.

10 Finland joined the War on June 25.

> German military planners set their eyes on the North Caucasus region, not only as the result of a "natural" expansion eastwards, in pursuit of living space, but as part of a deliberate drive eastwards with the aim of capturing the Soviet oilfields, which were of major strategic importance.[11]
>
> The significance of the Caucasus region as an oil reservoir during the Second World War stemmed primarily from three major facts:
> - Nazi Germany badly needed oil to keep its war machine going.
> - Major oil reserves had been located and explored in the Caucasus region, especially on the Caspian Sea shelf near Baku. The North Caucasus itself possessed important oil refinery facilities at Maikop and Grozny.
> - Britain was supplied with oil from the Iraqi oilfields near Mosul; at a later stage of the global war, Germany planned to advance towards Iraq in order to gain access to this oil and prevent it reaching Britain. Here, too, capturing the Caucasus was critical for the Germans, as their road to Iraqi oil had to be pushed eastwards through the Caucasus.

According to a local witness, the Rostov inhabitants dispersed "without comment" after the Soviet government announcement about the German invasion on June 22.[12] This may be indicative of the shock that the announcement caused to the local residents. The outbreak of war also caused some anti-Soviet feelings to be expressed, when a local inhabitant rejoiced at the news of the German invasion, "This is the beginning of the end of Soviet power."[13] Still, it seems that at the onset of the War such sentiments were only shared by a minority, while many of the older residents were afraid to express their feelings about these earth-shattering events, and preferred to sit on the fence.

On the same day, a general conscription was proclaimed in the North Caucasian military district,[14] and three days later, the Rostov-on-Don newspaper *Molot* described how that draft decree was in fact carried out in the city. According to the

---

11 Joel Hayward, "Too Little, Too Late: An Analysis of Hitler's Failure in August 1942 to Damage Soviet Oil Production," *Journal of Military History* 64, no. 3 (2000): 769–794. Cf. idem, "Hitler's Quest for Oil: The Impact of Economic Considerations on Military Strategy, 1941–1942," *Journal of Strategic Studies* 18, no. 4 (1995): 94–135. Cf. Wilhelm Tieke, *Der Kaukasus und das Öl: Der deutsch-sowjetische Krieg in Kaukasien 1942/43* (Osnabrück: Munin, c.1970).
12 K. S. Karol, *Solik: Life in the Soviet Union, 1939–1946*, translated from the French by Eamonn McArdle (Wolfeboro, NH: Pluto Press, 1986), 75.
13 Manley, *To the Tashkent Station*, 90–91.
14 Krasnodar, Stavropol. Beliaev and Bondar', *Kuban' v gody Velikoi Otechestvennoi voiny*, vol. 1, 25–26. Decree of the Presidium of the Supreme Council of the USSR on enlistment of conscription-age persons from a number of areas. 22 June 1941. In *Stavropol'e*, 27.

newspaper, every single draftee duly presented himself to the municipal conscription offices.[15] This statement might seem to be somewhat of an exaggeration, more like propaganda than fact. However, it is in keeping with many testimonies that pointed to an immediate upsurge of patriotism throughout the country, among many young people, who had been brought up entirely under the Soviet system.[16]

The frontline was far away, Rostov-on-Don was not yet within the range of German bombers, but four days after the War broke out, on June 26, 1941, the Soviet military command in the city imposed its initial, though still minor, limitations on the free movement of the urban population. These steps were made public when *Molot* published "Order No. 3 of the Commander of Rostov-on-Don's anti-aircraft defenses on limiting the movement of vehicles without special permits at night."[17] Such a measure could hardly be expected to make an impression on the Ginsburgs, since it only affected the small number of people who owned automobiles. But the next day, the Rostov newspaper published a small note on the last page: "For violations of blackout regulations, a person will be sentenced to five years of imprisonment by decree of the Military tribunal of the North Caucasian Military District."[18] The warning served to indicate that the Soviet military command in Rostov-on-Don was seriously considering the possibility that the city might come under German air attack. In another report, published on June 29, 1941, *Molot* informed its readers that punishment would be imposed on violators of the curfew.[19] Noteworthy is the fact that no formal announcements about the blackout and curfew decrees appeared in Rostov's official media. Most probably, announcing such decrees in print would have made an explanation necessary, and the authorities preferred to present the populace with a *fait accompli*.

The local population's awareness of the War may have increased following a decision of the Bureau of the Rostov District Committee of the VKP(b), the most powerful authority in the city and the region. On June 25, it issued a decree "On the activities towards the establishment of Extermination Battalions to fight against the enemy's airborne forces."[20] The order was not made public.

---

15 L. Vaisman, "Vtoroi den' prizyva. V Rostove," *Molot* (Rostov-on-Don), no. 147, June 25, 1941.
16 For example, Kiril Feferman, "'The Jews' War': Attitudes of Soviet Jewish Soldiers and Officers towards the USSR in 1940–1941," *The Journal of Slavic Military Studies* 27, no. 4 (2014): 585–586.
17 *Molot*, no. 148 (6027), June 26, 1941.
18 *Molot*, no. 149 (6028), June 27, 1941.
19 "V oblastnom upravlenii militsii," *Molot*, no. 151 (6030), June 29, 1941.
20 Party's archives of the Rostov district: 9/1/304, pp. 224–225. In *Na zashchite Rodiny. Partiinye organizatsii Dona v Velikoi Otechestvennoi voine*, ed. V. M. Rezvanov (Rostov-on-Don: Rostovskoe knizhnoe izdatel'stvo, 1980), 45–46. This order was based on the decision of

However, since this decree affected hundreds of Rostov-on-Don's citizens from whose midst this battalion had be raised, it increased the possibility that eventually the Ginsburgs would take note of these measures and realize that the War might be closer than they had previously believed.

On June 25, the Soviet government issued a ban on keeping radio sets at home. This was done in order to prevent Soviet citizens from listening to German propaganda broadcasts.[21] Although not announced publicly, the decree was immediately applied in the Rostov District, and all residents were required to hand in their individual radio sets—every radio set in the USSR was registered—to the militia within twenty-four hours.[22]

The early days of the War saw a turnabout in the Soviet propaganda approach to presenting the Nazis' anti-Jewish policies. The Bolshevik stance in regard to this issue had already been noticeable in a prewar Soviet movie, entitled *Professor Mamlock*, which featured Nazi persecution of Jews in Germany. The film, depicting a Jewish doctor and his communist son, describes the abuse they suffered at the hands of the Nazis.[23] *Professor Mamlock* was released in the Soviet Union on November 7, 1938, and was shown in the first half of 1939, but it was suppressed following the Soviet-German Pact of Non-Aggression in August 1939.

Almost immediately after the outbreak of the German-Soviet War, *Professor Mamlock* was advertised quite conspicuously in the Rostov newspaper as an "anti-Fascist movie" (on June 25, 26, 28, and 29, 1941), and was shown in the Ruzh Theater.[24] Furthermore, it took the city's most important Gorky Theater only three days after the outbreak of war to stage a live performance of *Professor Mamlock* by F. Volf; the première took place in the theater as early as June 25.[25]

---

the Politburo of the Central Committee of the VKP(b) of June 24, 1941 "On the actions to combat saboteurs and parachutists."

21 Christopher J. Butsavage, *German Radio Propaganda in The Soviet Union: A War of Words*, MA thesis, College Park, MD, University of Maryland, 2012.

22 Aleksandr Malyshev, *Sredstva massovoi informatsii Iuga Rossii v gody Velikoi Otechestvennoi voiny: Na materialakh Dona, Kubani, Stavropol'ia*, PhD diss., Rostov-on-Don, Rossiiskii gosudarstvennyi universitet stroitel'stva, 2001, 45–46. Cf. Karol, *Solik*, 75.

23 Olga Gershenson, *The Phantom Holocaust: Soviet Cinema and Jewish Catastrophe* (New Brunswick, NJ: Rutgers University Press, 2013), 14–19. *Professor Mamlock* is available in Russian on YouTube at https://www.youtube.com/watch?v=-Qh20Dvdt_0, accessed November 14, 2011. Some sections with English subtitles are available at https://www.youtube.com/watch?v=-Qh20Dvdt_0, accessed November 14, 2011.

24 *Molot*, no. 147 (6026), June 25, 1941. *Molot*, no. 148 (6028), June 26, 1941. *Molot*, no. 150 (6029), June 28, 1941.. *Molot*, no. 151 (6030), June 29, 1941.

25 Tat'iana Zelenskaia, *Kul'turno-prosvetitel'nye uchrezhdeniia Dona i Kubani v period Velikoi Otechestvennoi voiny 1941–1945 gg.*, PhD diss., Rostov-on-Don, Rostovskii gosudarstvennyi universitet, 2005, 67.

Another prewar Soviet film featuring the persecution of Jews in Germany was revived in response to Germany's new status as the enemy. In Rostov-on-Don, the screening of *The Oppenheim Family*, based upon Lion Feuchtwanger's novel *The Oppermanns*, was advertised in the city's cinema theaters (June 26, July 9–13, August 5, 1941).[26] It is a tale of four German-Jewish siblings during the period from November 1932 to April 1933, as they face the danger that Hitler's government will take over the business built up by their grandfather. All of them become targets of Nazi physical abuse and legal persecution.[27] The film showed the ideological darkness and anti-Semitism in the heart of Germany. The following excerpt from the review of *The Oppenheim Family* published in *The New York Times* on May 24, 1939, sheds some light on the movie screened in Rostov-on-Don movie theaters soon after the outbreak of the War:

> The members of "The Oppenheim Family" are almost purely symbols, and incongruously enough, whether by accident or satirical design, the young Jewish hero is the most Nordic-looking of them all. The literary professor who spouts party idiotology [*apparently a misprint—it should be "ideology"*] to his classes, and ultimately drives the young man to suicide, has what racial theorists might regard as a conspicuously "non-Aryan" appearance. The persecution and heroism of the German Communists, though a parallel theme, is handled with positively heroic restraint.[28]

In the same vein, on June 26, a lengthy article on the establishment of the ghetto in Warsaw appeared in *Pravda*:

> Early last year, brick walls began to go up at certain street crossings. ... In November 1940, an order was handed down that all Jews (up to the third generation) should move to this neighborhood. ... As the eviction proceeded, the Jews were totally dispossessed. ... From the surrounding towns, they rounded up all Jews who had survived the abuse and concentrated them in this neighborhood in Warsaw. ... Now, some 600,000 people

---

26 *Molot*, no. 148 (6028), June 26,. *Molot*, nos. 159–163, 182 (6038–6042, 6061), July 9–13, 1941; August 5, 1941. The movie is available on YouTube, but only in Russian, at https://www.youtube.com/watch?v=LIz0DQnLz9s. See also Jonathan Skolnik, "Class War, Anti-Fascism, and Anti-Semitism: Grigori Roshal's 1939 Film *Sem'ia Oppengeim* in Context," in *Feuchtwanger and Film*, ed. Ian Wallace (New York: Peter Lang, 2009), 237–243.
27 Skolnik, "Class War, Anti-Fascism, and Anti-Semitism." See also Gershenson, *The Phantom Holocaust*, 23–27.
28 "The Screen; 'The Oppenheim Family,' Soviet Film Version of a Feuchtwanger Novel, Arrives at the Cameo," *The New York Times*, May 24, 1939.

have been packed into the ruins and semi-destroyed streets. ... A minimal quantity of bread is distributed once every two weeks. They dwell in half-demolished buildings. ... The Jewish masses are a ghastly sight: tattered, driven to the brink of insanity, starving, wretched to no end. ... People are simply dying of starvation, not only of diseases, dying in the streets.[29]

On the same day, the Rostov newspaper published a report about German persecution of Jews in the entire German-held part of Poland:

In the General-Gouvernement[30] Jews and Poles receive lower rations than Germans. In the areas annexed to the Reich, up to 1.5 million Jews and Poles were evicted from their homes and all their property confiscated. The Jewish population is actually placed beyond the law and driven into ghettos; in cities they are fenced off by barbed wire. Jews above the age of ten are obligated to wear a large yellow or green star. Jews are forbidden to use public trams. Every Jew has to work for two years without pay in a labor camp. In Dombrow, a synagogue full of praying Jews was set ablaze.[31]

Such publications should be seen first and foremost against the background of a mounting Soviet anti-Nazi propaganda attack. There is no doubt that information about Nazi abuse of Jews in Europe was known to the Soviet authorities before the German attack on the Soviet Union, but this persecution was kept secret in order to preserve the Soviet alliance with Nazi Germany. This article was the first important signal for the Soviet Jewish population in Rostov-on-Don, a warning about what could await the Jews under German rule, including initial references to physical annihilation.[32]

Molot continued its exposure of Nazi anti-Jewish policies. On June 27, 1941, the newspaper published a short report on the German abuse of Jews in Serbia: "All Jews are ordered to wear a yellow armband with the inscription 'Jew' on it. Jewish property is being confiscated everywhere by the German

---

29 T. Krushevskii, "'Nenavist' k germanskim okkupantam bezgranichna,' Pis'mo iz Varshavy," *Pravda*, June 27, 1941. In Altshuler, "The Holocaust in the Soviet Mass Media," 126–127.
30 This was the official title used by the Germans for the political unit they created in the occupied part of Poland. The Soviets simply rendered it as it sounded in German.
31 S. Borisov, "Pod piatoi Germanskogo fashizma," *Molot*, no. 148 (6027), June 26, 1941.
32 On presentation of the Holocaust in the Soviet media during the War, see, for example, Berkhoff, "'Total annihilation'"; Kiril Feferman, *Soviet Jewish Stepchild: The Holocaust in the Soviet Mindset, 1941–1964* (Saarbrücken: VDM Verlag, 2009), 9–43.

authorities."[33] In a similar vein, on June 28, 1941, the Rostov newspaper mentioned a *numerus clausus* (fixed maximum number) policy enacted for Jews in France, setting a 3% quota of Jews who could enter university.[34] The Soviets pointed to anti-Jewish policies being implemented elsewhere in German-dominated Europe, even in the countries where for a long period there had been no discrimination against Jews, let alone physical violence. Still, Soviet propaganda fell short of explicitly stating that this was part of a master plan to "solve the Jewish question." To give the Soviets the benefit of the doubt, it is possible that there was not enough verified information to form such a conclusion. Thus, Jewish consumers of Soviet propaganda, including the Ginsburg family, had no choice but to try to bring together various pieces of information about the German-orchestrated anti-Jewish frenzy, and to draw their own conclusions about their implications.

July 1941

At the start of the Soviet-German War, the battles and the German air strikes took place a long way away from Rostov-on-Don.

> In the first months of the Soviet-German War, the main theaters of operation were far away from the North Caucasus. The major thrust of the German armies was directed at Moscow, and, in descending order, at Leningrad and various localities in Ukraine. The Axis forces fighting in the southern sector of the front, advancing towards the Caucasus, included the German forces grouped in the Army Group South (*Heeresgruppe Süd*) and the Romanian troops that were subordinate to the German Command in terms of the conduct of operations. Of all the German Army groups formed for the purposes of the War, Army Group South was the weakest, and it was opposed by the mightiest of the Red Army groups deployed along the Soviet-Romanian border. It is no wonder, therefore, that the pace of advance of the German-Romanian forces in the southern sector of the Soviet-German front was the slowest in the first two months of the War, compared with the northern and central sectors.

However, on July 2, 1941, only ten days after the outbreak of hostilities, the Rostov District Committee of the VKP(b) and the Rostov Executive Committee

---

33 "Rezhim terrora v Serbii," *Molot*, no. 149 (6028), June 27, 1941.
34 *Molot*, no. 150 (6029), June 28, 1941.

ordered mandatory preparations for anti-aircraft defense, to be made by the entire population. In retrospect, this seems to have been a prudent step, which saved lives when the German bombardment of the city began a month later. It is quite likely that such measures, encompassing masses of people, could have introduced Rostov-on-Don's inhabitants to the realities of war, and prompted some of them to escape from the city at this very early stage of the War.

On July 3, 1941, only eleven days after the outbreak of hostilities, new and much stricter military regulations were introduced in the city:

1. Entry of persons who are registered [as living] outside the cities of the Rostov district into these cities is forbidden.
2. No movement of vehicles or pedestrians is permitted in the cities of the district from 24.00 to 4.00.
3. No photography is permitted in the district.[35]

This order accounts for the scarcity of photographs showing Rostov-on-Don under Soviet rule in 1941–1942. It was also the first attempt by the local authorities to block refugees from entering the Rostov district, including the city of Rostov-on-Don. Although this step might appear harsh, it should be interpreted in the context of the bitter experience gained by the Soviets in fighting German agents in the country's westernmost regions, compounded by Stalin's fear of espionage everywhere. However, it is noteworthy that the eastward road was left open, putting no obstacles in the way of those inhabitants of Rostov-on-Don who were eager to leave.

But judging by Liza Chazkewitz's letter to her brother Efim Ginsburg from July 3, 1941, the Ginsburg clan in the city was in no mood to leave:

> Dear Efim!
>
> Yesterday we received your letter from June 28 [and] were very content [to hear that] you were in good health and that everything fared well. We are all in good health too, and everything fares well with us, too. That's all for the time being, our dear one. Please be healthy and happy. Hearty greetings from Monya, Anya, Tamara, Tsylya, the men, and in particular, [our] dear children. We all kiss you fervently, several times.

---

35 "On arranging public order and state security in the city of Rostov-on-Don and the Rostov district". Order No. 4 of the commander of the garrison of the city of Rostov-on-Don and the Rostov district from July 2, 1941," *Molot*, no. 154 (6033), July 3, 1941.

Our only hope and desire is that the accursed enemy that has shattered the peace of the entire people of our Soviet Union (especially of the Jews) will be smashed as soon as possible. We believe firmly that the enemy will be destroyed, and the victory will be ours.[36]

Extensively employing Soviet propaganda clichés, such as "shattered peace" and "the enemy will be destroyed, and the victory will be ours," Liza's letter looked like a typical Soviet newspaper clipping. This should come to us as no surprise, especially on this day, when Stalin delivered his famous "Brothers and sisters" speech.[37] According to a local witness, the speech made a tremendous impression on Rostov inhabitants.[38] Set against this background, Liza's special emphasis on Jews being singled out in this War, a fact often played down in Soviet propaganda, is particularly noticeable. Liza provided no explanation for her remark, which appeared evident to her and her addressee, even at this very early stage of the War. Although there was still no news available about the total physical destruction of the Jews, as this phase of the "Final Solution" began only later with the German invasion of the Soviet Union, Liza and Efim already felt that the Jews would be especially victimized in this War.

In early July 1941,[39] the Central Committee of the Bolshevik party issued a secret decree, "On Local Newspapers and Journals," ordering:

… a substantial reduction in the number of copies of newspapers and a temporary cessation of many area-level (*raionnye*) publications, owing to a severe shortage of paper, conscription of journalists into the Red Army, as well as the expansion of military media.[40]

The decree was immediately implemented in Rostov-on-Don, when on July 3, 1941, the Bureau of Rostov District Committee of the VKP(b) (the highest executive body in the city and the district) decided "… to temporarily cease the publication of the district Komsomol newspaper *Bolshevistskaya*

---

36 From Liza and Borya Chazkewitz, July 3, 1941, YVA: O.75/324, p. 35.
37 For the full text of the speech in English, see http://www.ibiblio.org/pha/policy/1941/410703a.html.
38 Karol, *Solik*, 76.
39 We do not have an exact date.
40 Tsentr dokumentatsii noveishei istorii Rostovskoi oblasti (henceforth TsDNIRO): 9/1/306, p. 102. In Zhuravlev, *Kollaboratsionizm na iuge Rossii*, 166.

smena, as well as of *Leninskie vnuchata*, *Koster* magazine, and twenty-four other newspapers."[41]

The impact of this measure on the local population in the long run should not be underestimated. From now on, for each city there remained only one local newspaper, whose circulation was soon artificially limited due to the shortage of paper. The circulation of such newspapers was even further curtailed in compliance with the decree of the Soviet government from August 20, 1941 (discussed below). Furthermore, it became considerably more difficult for Rostov-on-Don's citizens to obtain major Soviet newspapers because the authorities placed limits on the number of issues of central newspapers that reached the Rostov district.[42] Thus, fewer media sources remained from which Rostov's Jews, including the Ginsburgs, could have received up-to-date information about the peril that they faced.

In addition to limitations placed on their freedom of movement, Soviet citizens had to pay a high financial price for the War. On July 4, 1941, *Molot* published a Decree of the Presidium of the USSR Supreme Council.[43] The decree did not state the exact size of the tax increase but stipulated that these measures would remain in effect for the entire duration of the War.[44] While it is probable that the restrictions on available media and the additional taxes were onerous, the Ginsburgs would not have mentioned such complaints in their correspondence at this stage of the War. We may surmise that they avoided doing so, either because of their fear of Soviet censorship or because they did not wish to upset Efim.

This Ginsburg family correspondence was not a private diary intended for home use. In some respects, it had a semi-public nature, as the letters sent by mail could have been read by the Soviet censors.[45] These censors had been intercepting the private letters of Soviet citizens regularly even before the War broke out,[46] and there is little doubt that the Soviet people were well aware of this censorship. However, the situation changed after the outbreak of hostilities,

---

41 Gosudarstvennyi arkhiv Rostovskoi oblasti (henceforth GARO): r-4248/1/1b, p. 4. In Zhuravlev, *Kollaboratsionizm na iuge Rossii*, 167.
42 TsDNIRO: 9/1/318 (a), p. 117. In Zelenskaia, *Kul'turno-prosvetitel'nye uchrezhdeniia*, 62.
43 Declared one day before.
44 *Molot*, no. 155 (6034), July 4, 1941.
45 On the division of Soviet wartime letters into private and public, see Voronina, "Kak chitat' pis'ma s fronta?," 161–162.
46 On the prewar Soviet interception of private letters, see for example, Peter Holquist, "'Information Is the Alpha and Omega of Our Work': Bolshevik Surveillance in Its Pan-European Context," *Journal of Modern History* 69, no. 3 (1997): 415–450. Cf. Vladlen S. Izmozik, "Voices from the Twenties: Private Correspondence Intercepted by the OGPU," *Russian*

as the Soviet government decided to publicly admit the existence of a certain form of censorship, but only the one concerning rumor-mongering. On July 6, 1941, the Presidium of the USSR Supreme Soviet promulgated a decree "On the responsibility for spreading rumors stirring up concerns in the midst of the population during the War." Military tribunals were empowered to punish rumor-mongering with prison sentences ranging from two to five years, unless—ominously—"this infringement deserved a more severe punishment."[47]

However, sometimes the alarmist rumors that the authorities were so eager to stifle circulated widely. This could happen even in the early days of the War, when the supply of up-to-date information was suddenly cut off. On the evening of July 8, due to a malfunction, central Moscow radio fell silent in the Rostov District. This event had disastrous consequences on public morale, with the report of the Rostov District Party Committee describing it as a "mass panic."[48]

On July 9, 1941, limitations were imposed on the contents of letters sent within the country. This was publicly admitted by the Rostov-on-Don newspaper:

> In view of the state of war in the country and in order to prevent the dissemination of state and military secrets, the State Commissariat of Communications has decreed:
> 1) To forbid from putting in letters and telegraphs any information of military, economic, or political nature, whose disclosure might result in damage to the state
> 2) To forbid all mail offices from receiving or delivering postcards with views, photographs, etc.[49]

From now on, Soviet citizens were warned that they could be charged with alarmism and spreading defeatism as a result of information that they included in their letters. The decree was immediately enforced, but, unfortunately, official Soviet statistics do not allow us to gauge how many people were punished

---

Review 55, no. 2 (1996): 287–308. For a more general view of the Soviet censorship under Stalin, see, for example, Tat'iana Goriaeva, *Politicheskaia tsenzura v SSSR, 1917–1991 gg.* (Moscow: ROSSPEN, 2009), 246–283.

47 "Ob otvetstvennosti za rasprostranenie v voennoe vremia slukhov, vozbuzhdaiushchikh trevogu sredi naseleniia," *Vedomosti Verkhovnogo Soveta SSSR* 32 (1941).
48 Letter by B. Dvinsky to Shcherbakov, July 11, 1941, RGASPI: 17/125/73, pp. 29–30. In Berkhoff, *Motherland in Danger*, 30.
49 Information on the order of receipt and delivery of postal and telegraph correspondence during the War, *Molot*, no. 159 (6038), July 9, 1941.

throughout the country for not being cautious enough when putting their thoughts on paper. However, we do have details on the enforcement of this decree in individual cities such as the city of Krasnodar. In the second half of 1941, in Krasnodar alone, eighteen people were found guilty of this violation; in comparison, only one person was condemned for draft evasion.[50] According to official Soviet statistics, 47,987 people were convicted in 1941 of defeatism and spreading rumors.[51] Given Efim Ginsburg's background as a "marked" individual, it is likely that the Ginsburgs self-censored their letters, probably to a further degree than Soviet citizens who had never been in trouble with the authorities.

Soviet propaganda also made a point of proving to Soviet citizens that their government was serious in its struggle against spreading alarmism. On July 19, 1941, *Molot* provided an example of how the new regulations were enforced:

> The Military Tribunal of the Voroshilov Railroad sentenced I. L. Shulga, a former railroad employee, to five years' imprisonment and three years of subsequent disenfranchisement for the dissemination of provocative rumors and slander among the population.[52]

We would expect that the Ginsburgs' probable awareness of such punishments would result in more self-censorship. Given Efim Ginsburg's background, the letters should be read in this context. As already mentioned, such concerns can be traced back to the prewar period.[53]

The first weeks after the outbreak of the War, when the situation around Rostov-on-Don continued to be relatively stable, saw the continuation of this trend. In mid-July 1941, *Molot* mentioned an interesting example of the Bolshevik ideological struggle against the Nazi racial theory. On July 16, a lecture, "On the Racial Gibberish of Fascism," was delivered by docent (an academic rank below professor) V. P. Drozdov in the Rostov Municipal Lecture Hall. The newspaper even provided a short description of the lecture. The inclusion of this plan testifies to the importance of the subject for Soviet propaganda:

---

50 Natal'ia Garazha, *Deiatel'nost' organov vlasti po mobilizatsii rabochego klassa na pobedu v gody Velikoi Otechestvennoi voiny 1941–1945 gg.: Na materialakh Krasnodarskogo kraia*, PhD diss., Maikop, Adygeiskii gosudarstvennyi universitet, 2005, 128.

51 Oleg Mozokhin, *Statistika repressivnoi deiatel'nosti organov bezopasnosti SSSR na period s 1941 po 1943 gg.*, http://www.fsb.ru/history/authors/mozohin.html, accessed January 3, 2012.

52 "Provokator nakazan," *Molot*, no. 168 (6047), July 19, 1941.

53 However, Jochen Hellbeck does not view self-censorship as the underlying reason for Soviet people editing their diaries. See his *Revolution on My Mind: Writing a Diary under Stalin* (Cambridge, MA: Harvard University Press, 2006), 103, 359, 384.

1. What is fascism like?
2. Fascist gibberish about upper- and lower-level races.
3. Racism as a pseudo-scientific justification of the German fascists' plans.
4. Marxism-Leninism on races.[54]

There were no further statements in the Rostov media showing that these activities were continued. Although we know that Soviet propagandists pursued this theme in a series of books published during the War,[55] it is doubtful whether, given the wartime chaos, any of these publications reached Rostov-on-Don in 1941 and 1942.

In the meantime, more Soviet films featuring German persecution of Jews were shown in Rostov-on-Don in July 1941. In addition, a famous prewar film, *Bolotnye Soldaty* (*Frog Soldiers*)[56] was shown in the city's cinema theaters on July 20, 23, 24, and 26, 1941.[57] *Frog Soldiers* was a rousing war film about a German anti-Nazi underground activist caught and imprisoned in a camp, who escaped with the aid of his comrades.

On July 23, Liza wrote another letter to her brother Efim, who in July 1941 had been evacuated from Moscow to the city of Omsk in Siberia:

> Dear Efim!
> … We are all alive and in good health. It is still all quiet with us.
> Our dear one! Don't regret that you went there. We assume that it will be better there; we feel confident about you there and wouldn't mind being near to you. But it is difficult and even impossible. It is highly desirable that the confounded fascism will fail truly, very soon, so that we will again be close to each other…
> Best wishes from all of us.
> Kisses, Liza.[58]

---

54 *Molot*, no. 165 (6044), July 16, 1941.
55 For example, Nikolai Derzhavin, *Fashizm—zleishii vrag slavianstva* (Moscow: Akademiia nauk SSSR, 1942); Ernst Fischer, *Die faschistische Rassentheorie* (Moskau: Vlg. für fremdsprachige Literatur, 1941); Vasilii Struve, *Fashistskii antisemitizm—perezhitok kannibalizma* (Moscow: Akademiia nauk SSSR, 1941).
56 The Russian version is available at https://www.youtube.com/watch?v=z7woSoUu7xE. See Gershenson, *The Phantom Holocaust*, 19–23.
57 *Molot*, no. 169 (6048), July 20,1941, *Molot*, nos. 171–172 (6050–6051), July 23–24, 1941, *Molot*, no. 174 (6053), July 26, 1941.
58 From this point, all letters from Liza were sent to Efim Ginsburg in Omsk, until stated otherwise. From Liza Chazkewitz, July 23, 1941, YVA: O.75/324, p. 38.

A change in Liza's mood is discernible here. At this point, she did not mind leaving Rostov-on-Don in principle, but could not do so because of seemingly "difficult" and "impossible" logistical difficulties. (This phrase could be probably understood in the context of Volodya Meerovich's service in the secretive Extermination Battalion, of which we will learn from later correspondence.) Her confidence in an imminent Soviet victory and the ensuing defeat of the Germans was not as strong as in her previous letter; victory was now said to be "highly desirable" while the entire situation in Rostov-on-Don was only described as "still quiet."

In the meantime, Efim began his long journey as an evacuee well acquainted with privation and suffering. We can only guess at his feelings, relying on what his relatives wrote to him, because his own letters, with one exception, were not preserved in this collection. Almost certainly he was evacuated from Moscow as part of an orderly, arranged process. It was no doubt a shock for him to move away from Moscow, the most prosperous Soviet city and a symbol of success for every Soviet citizen, and in his letters he described this frankly, as well as the enormous difficulties he faced as an evacuee. We will see how this contributed to creating a negative image of the life of evacuees in the eyes of other family members. Later on, they would cite Efim's own letters when they needed to justify their decision not to leave Rostov-on-Don.

These motives were implied in the next letter, written by Liza on July 27, 1941:

> It is all quiet with us still. ... We hope that the enemy will be entirely smashed soon. Then you, our dear one, will come back and live as you did previously.
>
> We all embrace you. Liza.[59]

This is the first of fifty letters in the correspondence, which bears the stamp "Reviewed by military censorship." In the letters sent in 1942, this stamp also mentions "Rostov-on-Don," which apparently means that the letters underwent vetting by military censors stationed in the city. None of the other letters bore this stamp, which most likely indicates that the other letters were not read by the military censors. We can also speculate that occasionally military censors read and stamped letters that arrived in Rostov-on-Don, including some letters sent by Efim Ginsburg and read by the Rostov branch of the family. At any rate,

---

59 From Liza Chazkewitz, July 27, 1941, ibid., p. 40.

it is certain that Efim Ginsburg was aware that the letters coming from Rostov-on-Don were sometimes read by the censors. It is most likely that such open form of censorship contributed to the Ginsburgs' perception of being watched, and hence, to special caution in expressing their inner thoughts in letters (which was in keeping with the Soviet government's policies aimed at curbing the flow of sensitive information during the War).

When was the military censorship openly imposed in Rostov-on-Don? In other words, when did military censors stamp letters sent from the city? As mentioned earlier, the first letter in the Ginsburg collection that bears this stamp is dated July 27, 1941. This policy continued unabated till early October, reflecting the worsening military situation around the city. None of the letters sent from Rostov-on-Don from October till December 10 bears this stamp. This can be attributed to the failure of military censorship, owing to a general loosening of Soviet control in the city as the German armies drew closer. The censorship was re-imposed after December 10 (date of the first letter sent by the Ginsburg sisters after the liberation of the city). With some inexplicable pauses, the censorship continued until February 7, 1942. Evidently, by that time, the authorities saw the situation around Rostov-on-Don as being more stable.[60] Military censorship was re-imposed for just a few days in early March 1942, and re-imposed again, on an ongoing basis, from April 21. The last letters sent by the Ginsburgs from the city in July 1942 bear the censors' stamps, and presumably, censorship was still active after that date.

The re-impositions of the censorship could provide clues as to how the authorities viewed the situation. In all probability, the Ginsburgs were aware of these signs. Perhaps, this caused them to censor their own letters more carefully than previously. Yet in retrospect, it seems unlikely that the family, at least the Rostov branch, fully perceived the return of open military censorship in April 1942 as a sign of the growing Soviet concern and anxiety about the military situation around Rostov-on-Don.

On July 31, 1941, *Izvestiya* printed an article containing a confession by a German prisoner-of-war, who described how he, together with some SS men, rounded up hundreds of Jewish women and children on a bridge over the Vistula River and smashed the children's heads in, as their parents watched.[61] We will see the impact of such horrifying news on the Ginsburgs in their correspondence.

---

60 The ban on civilians leaving the city was also lifted around this time.
61 I. Shuster, "Razgovor s plennymi soldatami," *Izvestiia*, July 31, 1941. In Altshuler, "The Holocaust in the Soviet Mass Media," 129–130.

August 1941

Despite the German advance on all fronts, the Soviet media went out of its way to create the impression that the situation remained under control. One example of this approach is an announcement placed in the Rostov newspaper. On August 1, 1941, *Molot* informed its readers that a new academic year had begun at Rostov's institutions of higher education.[62]

On August 7, Liza sent a new letter to her brother Efim in Omsk:

> Dear Efim!
> I hasten to report to you that we are all in good health; it is still all right here. ... Monya is also all right; the children are fine; everyone is working. ...
> Boris's health is deteriorating. ...
> Be healthy and happy, Liza.[63]

For the time being, everything seemed to be fine, except for the health of Liza's husband, which was deteriorating due to natural causes. But apparently because of Liza's fear of censorship, she said nothing about the first German bombardments of Rostov-on-Don, which had begun in early August. The word "still" is the only sign that could indicate the growing anxiety among the Rostov Ginsburgs.

Soviet anti-fascist propaganda continued ceaselessly. In early August 1941, the Rostov-on-Don Theater of Dolls presented its new anti-fascist program based on the works of local writers: *Budet Gitleru Konets* (*There Will Be an End to Hitler*), created by the theater's chief producer, D. Meltser.[64] The goal of the performance, staged in the Gorky Municipal Park of Culture, was to boost the confidence of Rostov's residents. The people were alarmed by evident factors such as the intensifying German bombardment of the city, as well as by successful German land advances, which they could only guess about.

> In late July and early August 1941, a major change in the German war strategy took place. Faced with the dilemma, in which direction to make the major thrust, the German political and military leadership vacillated between two options. The first one, supported by the Wehrmacht High Command (OKW), was to commit its main forces to the thrust against Moscow.

---

62   *Molot*, no. 179 (6058), August 1, 1941.
63   From Liza Chazkewitz, August 7, 1941, YVA: O.75/324, p. 43.
64   Zelenskaia, *Kul'turno-prosvetitel'nye uchrezhdeniia*, 68.

Arguably, this would precipitate the fall of Moscow, the Soviet capital, and the most important political and economic center. Some German leaders hoped that this would also bring about the downfall of the entire Soviet state. However, it is known today, from recently disclosed documents, that the Soviets were resolved to continue fighting even after the surrender of Moscow and made preparations to this effect. Furthermore, this move would have exposed German troops to attack by the sizable Soviet forces entrenched in Ukraine. The second possibility contemplated by Hitler was to divert some forces from the Moscow direction southwards, and to ensure the destruction of the Soviet armies in Ukraine.

Hitler attempted to reconcile both options. In Directive no. 34, signed on August 12, 1941, he ordered the Army Group Center to turn south to strike Ukraine and Crimea first, smashing the remaining Soviet forces there and capturing major economic and strategic objectives, before resuming the drive towards Moscow.[65] In this southward drive, the German forces seized Ukraine, the Donets Basin and the Crimea, destroying or capturing immense Soviet forces. Quite probably Moscow was spared thanks to this move, but the fate of the hundreds of thousands of Ukrainian Jews was sealed. The future of the Caucasian Jewry was also put into jeopardy.

On August 10, *Izvestiya* published an article based on the testimony of a witness who had fled from Minsk several weeks earlier. On July 21, the witness related, the Germans forced the Jews to dig pits, bound them by hands and feet, threw them into the pits, and ordered the Belorussians to bury them alive. The Belorussians refused, and in response the Germans shot forty-five Jews and thirty Belorussians.[66] Despite the stress on the "fraternity of peoples," characteristic of the Soviet media, the theme of indiscriminate murder of Jews in the "core" Soviet areas[67] was now mentioned, probably for the first time, by the Soviet propaganda tools that would have been available to the Ginsburg family. A similar story about the murder of Jews in Minsk appeared in *Pravda* on August 11, 1941.[68]

---

65 Befehl Hitlers, OKW/WFSt/Abt. L, Nr. 441412/41 g.Kdos.Chefs., 21.8.1941, in KTB/OKW, Bd. 1, S. 1062f. In Johannes Hürter, *Hitlers Heerführer. Die deutschen Oberbefehlshaber im Krieg gegen die Sowjetunion 1941/42*, 2nd edition (Munich: R. Oldenbourg Verlag, 2007), 292–293.
66 "Nemetsko-fashistskie zverstva v Breste i Minske," *Izvestiia*, August 10, 1941. In Altshuler, "The Holocaust in the Soviet Mass Media," 133.
67 That is, excluding the areas annexed after the outbreak of the Second World War.
68 "Izdevatel'stvo liudoedov," *Pravda*, August 11, 1941. In Altshuler, "The Holocaust in the Soviet Mass Media," 133.

Molot continued to publish more information on Soviet measures against alarmism. This included the above-mentioned ban on keeping radio sets at home. On August 13, 1941, the newspaper reported that an inhabitant of Rostov-on-Don was sentenced to five years' imprisonment for concealing a radio set.[69]

Of special interest is the way the Rostov newspaper covered the German bombardment of Rostov-on-Don. On August 12, 1941, *Molot* reported that German planes carried out air raids on Moscow, causing civilian casualties and much destruction. But nothing was said about the bombardment of Rostov-on-Don itself.[70] The only hint was to be found in an article on a large-scale drill carried out in Rostov-on-Don for extinguishing incendiary bombs,[71] an article that appeared in the same issue of the newspaper. Publishing any information about the outcome of the German bombardments was strictly forbidden by the Soviet censors, as evidenced by the almost total silence in the local newspapers in the North Caucasus. However, there were several cases when the newspapers violated this ban. For example, a newspaper called *Vpered (Forward)* in the small center of Bataisk, situated very close to Rostov-on-Don, reported that, as a result of the German bombardment, the electrical network and water supply were damaged.[72] This information was brought to the attention of *Glavlit* (the Soviet agency in charge of censorship), and the newspaper was punished (we do not know in what way).[73]

More information on German policies towards Jews appeared in *Molot* on August 15:

> In locality G[74] Hitler's bandits placed forty Jews, men and women, in a square, and shot all of them down. The hangmen locked ninety elderly persons and children in a barn and set out to shoot them with automatic rifles.[75]

This was the first time that the physical destruction of Jews in the occupied Soviet territories was reported by the Rostov-on-Don newspaper. Although, as we now know, the Soviet media generally captured the new, genocidal phase of the "Final

---

69 *Molot*, no. 189 (6068), August 13, 1941.
70 *Molot*, no. 188 (6067), August 12, 1941.
71 Ibid.
72 TsDNIRO: 9/5/39, p. 85. In Malyshev, *Sredstva massovoi informatsii Iuga Rossii*, 51.
73 Ibid.
74 In their public reports the Soviets frequently refrained from identifying localities for fear of disclosing their sources.
75 A. Tarasov, "Prezrennye palachi i ubiitsy," *Molot*, no. 191 (6070), August 15, 1941. Cf. Berkhoff, "'Total annihilation,'" 71.

Solution" in the occupied Soviet regions, failure to identify the location where this atrocity allegedly took place may have led skeptical Soviet readers to regard this report as just another example of "spin" by the Soviet propaganda machine.

In the same issue, it was announced that *Professor Mamlock* was to be staged in Rostov-on-Don. The première took place in the Gorky Theater on August 16–18.[76]

On August 15, *Izvestiya* reported that Rostov-on-Don's Komsomol launched an initiative for the city's youth to go to work voluntarily on one of the coming Sundays (*voskresnik*).[77] This short item demonstrates how the Rostov media promoted a "business as usual" mood. Many similar reports were published in almost every issue of the newspaper.

On the same day, Liza sent a short note to her brother:

Dear Efim! …
We are all fine and in good health. … Best wishes from everybody.
Kisses, Liza.[78]

This letter can be best summed up as a "no news is good news" update, describing an interim situation in the city.

Given what was published in the Soviet media and what the inhabitants of Rostov-on-Don may have sensed in this period, it is illuminating to juxtapose this limited information with *The New York Times*' view of the strategic situation in the region. The article "Oil in the Caucasus, Abundant and Accessible," published on August 18, 1941, read as follows:

> The relentless Nazi drive towards the Caucasus has at long last disclosed to the world that Hitler's foremost quest is for petroleum, the very lifeblood of every modern war machine. … With the Nazi dream of a short war shattered, Hitler must either acquire new supplies of the black liquid, or face the certain prospect of seeing his superb war machine gradually coming to a standstill. The Caucasus alone contains the solution to the most desperate problem Hitler has yet had to face. … The Caucasus is by reason of its economic and strategic significance truly one of the decisive fronts of this war.[79]

---

76 *Molot*, no. 191 (6070), August 15, 1941.
77 "Vsia molodezh' Rostova vyidet na voskresnik," *Izvestiia*, no. 192 (7568), August 15, 1941.
78 From Liza Chazkewitz, August 15, 1941, YVA: O.75/324, p. 44.
79 Isaac Stone, "Oil in the Caucasus, Abundant and Accessible," *The Washington Post*, August 18, 1941.

The author explicitly depicted the Caucasus as the direction of the next German thrust. This was evident to American journalists not because they possessed unattainable insider intelligence but rather because they had a macro view of the Soviet-German War and could predict events correctly. The author of this article realized that, apart from serving ideological goals, the War was also a competition for resources. In this respect, the Caucasus proved to be the most natural direction for the next German advance. However, at this stage of the War, the members of the Ginsburg family residing in Rostov-on-Don failed to develop their own strategic view of events. Nor was such a view provided by the Soviet media, which preferred to focus on depicting local and tactical warfare.

On August 20, 1941, the Soviet government issued decree no. 1905/898c: "On regulating the periodicity of publication of all daily republican, district, and area newspapers." From now on, all newspapers were to be issued "three times a week x four pages. Komsomol newspapers merged with the general media; area newspapers to be published three times a week."[80] We cannot establish whether, how often, or if at all, Rostov's inhabitants read Soviet newspapers. But the practical outcome of this step was, as already indicated, a sudden and substantial reduction in the number of sources from which they could receive critical updates (albeit filtered by Soviet censors and propagandists) on the German danger, information that might have led them to flee Rostov-on-Don.

Another Soviet measure aimed at preventing leaks of information involved *Glavlit*'s August 1941 ban on sending area (*raionnye*) newspapers outside their respective areas, city newspapers outside their cities, and district (*oblastnye*) newspapers outside their respective districts.[81] Coupled with the ban on civilians keeping radio sets in their homes and a sharp cutback in public radio broadcasting, due to scarcity of funding,[82] this order was ultimately bound to negatively affect the ability of Soviet civilians, including the members of the Ginsburg family, to learn about the proximity of the German forces.

At the same time, to partly make up for the loss of information, in August 1941, Rostov authorities set up 260 newspaper stands at the city's most crowded locations, carrying the country's two most important newspapers, *Pravda* and

---

80   GARO: r-4248/1/1b. In Zhuravlev, *Kollaboratsionizm na iuge Rossii*, 166. Cf. Berkhoff, *Motherland in Danger*, 16.
81   Zhuravlev, *Kollaboratsionizm na iuge* Rossii, 172.
82   Malyshev, *Sredstva massovoi informatsii Iuga Rossii*, 45.

Izvestiya, as well as Rostov-on-Don's *Molot*.[83] Thus, with respect to the printed media, we can assume that Rostov's population was kept informed, albeit less so than in normal times, about what the central Soviet government desired to convey to Soviet citizens nationwide. This news included information, however diluted, about German ill-treatment of Jews in Europe and the occupied Soviet territories. However, specific details about the proximity of the German armies, which could be received from other regions, were not available to Rostov-on-Don's inhabitants, and what little was published in the city's media on this subject was entirely inadequate.

It is noteworthy that an important meeting of the representatives of the Jewish people, held in Moscow on August 24, 1941, was reported in newspapers across the country.[84] On August 26, 1941, *Molot* published the representatives' appeal to "Jewish brothers in the entire world," as they tried to arouse the sympathy of world Jewry.[85] The meeting was also shown in Soviet newsreel no. 84 and screened in cinema theaters all over the Soviet Union, including in Rostov-on-Don, on August 30.[86] If the Ginsburgs actually received this information—the letters do not give a clear-cut answer to this question—this could have been an important trigger in raising their awareness of the growing danger to them as Jews.

A small satirical article (*felyeton*) published in *Molot* on August 26, 1941 was the only reference in Rostov-on-Don media to the German air raids that had been striking the city for more than three weeks. The article urged the population not to exaggerate the magnitude of the bombardments, as it claimed that "People are making a mountain out of a molehill."[87] But this was no molehill: the effectiveness of the German air raids on Rostov-on-Don, which were carried out from late August 1941 onwards, can be gleaned from the postwar testimonies of the city's non-Jewish inhabitants, published in 2006. They mention the numerous civilian casualties of the German air strikes.[88]

---

83 Ibid., 43. Cf. Zhuravlev, *Kollaboratsionizm na iuge Rossii*, 168.
84 For example, in the neighboring North Caucasian city of Krasnodar. *Bol'shevik* (Krasnodar), no. 201 (1183), August 26, 1941.
85 *Molot*, no. 200 (6079), August 26, 1941.
86 *Soiuzkinozhurnal*, no. 84, August 30, 1941, Rossiiskii gosudarstvennyi arkhiv kino- i fotodokumentov (henceforth RGAKFD): record 4644, http://pobeda-vov.ru/Lib/pages/item.aspx?itemid=10496, accessed March 18, 2010. Cf. Jeremy Hicks, *First Films of the Holocaust: Soviet Cinema and the Genocide of the Jews, 1938–1946* (Pittsburgh, PA: University of Pittsburgh Press, 2012), 45–54.
87 "Prodavtsy slonovoi kosti," *Molot*, no. 200 (6079), August 26, 1941.
88 Testimonies of M. Vdovin, A. Kotliarova, B. Safonov, S. Lyubimova, V. Lemeshev. In Vladislav Smirnov, *Rostov pod sen'iu svastiki* (Rostov-on-Don: ZAO "Kniga," 2006), 45–49, 51.

In the meantime, on August 26, the Rostov authorities introduced food rationing—of bread, sugar, and confectionary items—in the city as of September 1. Notably, the circulation of these basic commodities was only limited to the point of rationing after two full months of the War, which means that the region, known for its abundance, was then still far from the fronts and relatively well provided for. Nevertheless, the realities of war gradually made themselves felt in the Rostov District too. Many thousands of evacuees and Soviet military personnel passing through the city had to be fed despite a growing shortage of working hands in agriculture during the harvest, as capable men were drafted in the Army. It can be assumed that the partial introduction of food rationing had a stabilizing effect on conditions in Rostov-on-Don by guaranteeing staple food for the local population during the growing crisis. As the Ginsburg correspondence shows, none of the family members complained about the food conditions in Rostov-on-Don, in contrast to the towns to which they were evacuated.

At the very end of August, all the fear that the Ginsburg family had tried to conceal in their previous messages was revealed. It began with the letter sent by Anya and Liza on August 30:

> Dear Efim!
> … We are still alive and healthy, but do not know how long we will be healthy. We live in a state of great alarm and anxiety. We worry a great deal, because we do not know what the future is preparing for us. We would like to be near to you but apparently this is entirely impossible.
> For the time being, we are wishing you all the best: be healthy and happy. Greetings from all and each one of us. Kissing you. It is only too bad for the children. The children send you kisses.[89]

A new motive in the letter is the fate of the children, or to be more precise, of the sisters' grandchildren. Apparently the family felt strong enough to face the difficulties, but the fate of Anya (Anechka) and Grisha (Grishenka), who, like the other family members, had to suffer from the growing wartime privations, was becoming a particular concern. Probably in time, worry about the children would have induced the family to move away from their home city. The next letter, sent on August 31, provides more factual insights into the sisters' gloomy mindset:

---

89 From Liza Chazkewitz, August 30, 1941, YVA: O.75/324, p. 10.

Dear Efim! ...

We are very anxious and concerned. Yesterday evening we sat in a shelter for 3 hours; it was already the third time, how ... dreadful it is when an air raid alarm starts up. We don't know what is going to happen to us. Borya can hardly move, yet he must go to work and wake up the children. If we had wings, we would fly to you, because we think that it is quiet in your place. ...

That's all for the time being. It doesn't look good, but let's hope that it will be good, one can't lose hope. ...

Yesterday, David was sent somewhere.[90]

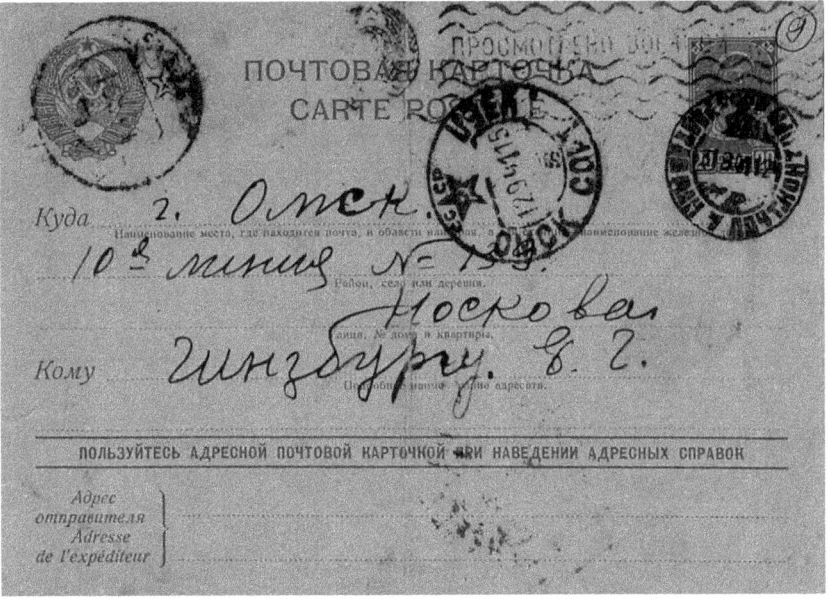

Envelope. YVA: 0.75/324, p. 9. Courtesy of Yad Vashem Archives.

The letter is full of pessimism. Everything was linked together: Boris's worsening state of health and David being dispatched on some war-related mission. This is also the first reference in the Ginsburgs' correspondence to the German bombardments that made the family spend many hours in shelters. As this letter shows, the air raids had the greatest impact on the Ginsburgs' state of mind. The city, as we have already seen, was severely damaged.

---

90 From Liza Chazkewitz, August 31, 1941, ibid., p. 46.

But we should ask ourselves the most important question for our story. How did the family interpret these bombings? Did they realize that the Germans were now getting closer? More generally, to what extent could air strikes serve as a sign of the ensuing ground advance? From the history of World War II, we have contradictory answers. The civilian population in England suffered from massive German air strikes, which weren't followed by a ground offensive, even though a land-based assault had been envisaged by the Germans in case the air attacks were successful. Moreover, the German civilian population was also suffering from growing Allied bombing, starting from 1942, but the ground offensive materialized only in mid-1944 and was not initially directed against the Reich proper. However, the Allied air strikes did affect public morale in Germany.[91] In contrast, in many other places, such as Poland in September 1939, ground advances were preceded by air strikes. Therefore, there were no particular reasons for the Ginsburgs to interpret the Rostov air raids one way or another. Their initial reaction to the bombardments, as expressed in the above letter, seems to signal the lack of any decision.

In addition to air raids, a new factor emerged in Rostov-on-Don in the course of August 1941: many old people and youngsters were sent to dig anti-tank trenches.[92] From this fact, the inhabitants of the city could infer that the German land advance towards Rostov-on-Don was a threatening possibility.

September 1941

> From early September 1941, the German armies began their advance towards the North Caucasus.[93]

On September 7, 1941, a local newspaper in the neighboring North Caucasian city of Stavropol published an article on the heroic Soviet defense of the Ukrainian capital, Kiev. The article made it clear that the German armies were

---

91 Neil Gregor, "A Schicksalsgemeinschaft? Allied Bombing, Civilian Morale, and Social Dissolution in Nuremberg, 1942–1945," *The Historical Journal* 43, no. 4 (December 2000): 1051–1070.
92 Testimony of L. Shabalina. In Smirnov, *Rostov pod sen'iu svastiki*, 43.
93 For the analysis of the Battle of the Caucasus in 1941, see Ernst Klink, "The Conduct of Operations," in *Germany and the Second World War*, vol. 4: *The Attack on the Soviet Union*, ed. Horst Boog, Jürgen Förster, Joachim Hoffman, Ernst Klink, Rolf-Dieter Müller, and Gerd R. Überschär (Oxford: Oxford University Press, 1998), 613–627.

slowly but steadily approaching the North Caucasus.[94] However, the Ginsburgs could not read this important article, since, as mentioned above, there was a ban on distributing newspapers from other districts, and no such article appeared in the Rostov-on-Don media.

At the same time, *Molot* continued to mention the Nazi persecution of Jews. On September 7, 1941, the newspaper featured a major article written by a Jewish author. The article focused on the *Professor Mamlock* performance staged in the Rostov Gorky theater, although the word "Jew" was mentioned only once in the article.[95] On the one hand, such a publication had the potential to raise the Ginsburgs' awareness of the danger. On the other hand, with the German armies approaching the North Caucasus, the family's options had narrowed.

It is against this background that the following letter written by Liza Chazkewitz in Rostov-on-Don on September 7, 1941, should be read:

> Dear Efim!
>
> … Don't worry about our financial means. It is not so important now. What really matters is that the barbarous enemy be smashed soon. It will be the best thing for everyone!!! From September 1, it is quiet here, but we are not quiet in our hearts; we are alarmed and live in a state of anxiety. None the less, we haven't lost hope and wait for good news [*expecting*] to see each other again. …
>
> Tamara has received your telegram and is waiting for your letter. Certainly, it is extremely difficult to go to you, because it is not so easy now to travel. On the other hand, if we did go, we would have someone with whom to stay. Otherwise, it is very bad, all the more so since we have absolutely no [*financial*] means. But generally, I don't want to go anywhere, since it is a very sad story. …
>
> Well, my dear, that's all for the time being. Let's wait and hope, and we'll be spared. We are working as before. Best wishes from all of us. We all send you kisses and wish you all the best, hoping for a joyful meeting after the victory.[96]

It is difficult to establish whether in writing about the imminent defeat of the Germans, Liza was still mouthing Soviet propaganda messages, due to her

---

94 A. Krasnov, "Geroicheskaia oborona Kieva," *Ordzhonikidzevskaia pravda* (Stavropol), no. 212 (2276), September 7, 1941.
95 I. Brailovskii, "Professor Mamlock," *Molot*, no. 211 (6090), September 7, 1941.
96 From Liza Chazkewitz, September 7, 1941, YVA: O.75/324, pp. 47–48.

fear of censorship, or trying to reassure herself and her brother. It seems, however, that more cracks between the official Soviet propaganda line and the way it was perceived by the Ginsburg family are discernible in this letter, compared to the previous period.[97] In this respect, the use of strong statements at the very beginning of the letter—apparently out of context—suggests that these optimistic phrases were purposefully written in a noticeable place in the text, for the benefit of the censors and at the same time, in an attempt to strike a hopeful note.

Liza's letter reflects growing anxiety and uncertainty. At this point, the Ginsburgs had not ruled out the possibility of escape, even if only as a theoretical option for the time being. Still, at this stage, the fear of a long journey to uncertainty and worries about their limited financial resources outweighed their fear of the Germans, and they were clearly reluctant to take practical steps in this direction.

It is important to keep in mind that the Soviet media misrepresented the precarious situation by conveying "everything is under control" messages to the local population. There is no sufficient space in this book to cite the hundreds of articles exemplifying this approach, which were published in every newspaper. But the following is an example of this recurrent motif in Soviet propaganda. On September 10, 1941, a *Molot* editorial urged local inhabitants to make sure that "complete and warm wintering (*zimovka*) for cattle" would be prepared.[98] Editorials in Soviet newspapers tended to emphasize the most important messages that the regime was interested in conveying at any given point of time. If preparation for wintering cattle was given priority, this constituted a public declaration that the Soviet administration would continue to function in the coming winter and that there was no need to fear that the city might be seized by the Germans. Hence, this editorial implied that there was no need for civilians to leave Rostov-on-Don.

On September 14, 1941, *Molot* again advertised the performance of *Professor Mamlock* on the stage of the Rostov Gorky Theater.[99] In the absence of other material on Nazi persecution of the Jews, this publication, as well as the very fact that the performance was still being staged in a city threatened by German armies, could also have served as a reassuring signal for Rostov's Jews.

---

97 Kiril Feferman, "To Flee or Not to Flee: The Conflicting Messages of Soviet Wartime Propaganda and the Holocaust, 1941," *Cahiers du monde russe* 56, nos. 2–3 (April–September 2015): 526–27.
98 *Molot*, no. 213 (6092), September 10, 1941.
99 *Molot*, no. 217 (6096), September 14, 1941; *Molot*, no. 218 (6097), September 16, 1941.

On September 14, 1941, Stavropol's newspaper published an editorial article reprinted from *Pravda* from September 13, 1941. The article mentioned the murder of Jews in the Western part of the Soviet Union, albeit only in passing and together with other national groups.[100] However, even this information remained unavailable to the Jews of Rostov-on-Don.

On September 17, 1941, Liza wrote a new letter to her brother:

> Dear Efim!
> ... It is still all right here; let's hope this will continue. ...
> We received your money [*transfer*], dear one, and feel sorry about it. Why did you send it to us? We don't need it. I want to send it back, and await your instructions.
> Our mood is somehow not really good [*ne akhti*]. We are not quiet at heart. But let's wait and hope to receive only good news. There is no news from David; we don't know where he is.[101]

The Rostov branch of the Ginsburg family felt more and more anxious as the situation in the Soviet south appeared to be worsening. Still, they did not know how close the Germans were and therefore could not assess the gravity of the situation. Official Soviet sources emphasized fighting that was taking place far away from Rostov-on-Don: newsreel no. 91, released on September 18 and shown all over the Soviet Union, including Rostov-on-Don, described the Soviet preparations to defend Odessa.[102]

Yet, as revealed from their internal correspondence, Soviet security agencies were well aware of the gravity of the situation. On September 18, 1941, the Krasnodar Territorial Administration of the NKVD gave the order to evacuate its own archives, as well as the archives of the Krasnodar territory, to Soviet Central Asia.[103] (Krasnodar is only 250 km to the south of Rostov-on-Don.) However, this information was not shared with the Soviet population.

Fresh information on the Nazi abuse of Jews in the Soviet Union appeared in Stavropol's newspaper: on September 18, 1941, *Ordzhonikidzevskaya pravda*

---

100 Editorial "Mest' i smert' fashistskim sobakam," *Ordzhonikidzevskaia pravda* (Stavropol), no. 218 (2282), September 14, 1941.
101 From Liza Chazkewitz, September 17, 1941, YVA: O.75/324, p. 50.
102 *Soiuzkinozhurnal*, no. 91, September 18, 1941, RGAKFD: record 5361, http://pobeda-vov.ru/Lib/pages/item.aspx?itemid=10503, accessed August 5, 2010.
103 To the city of Aktyubinsk. A. Fedoseev, "K voprosu o provedenii evakuatsionnykh meropriiatii na territorii Krasnodarskogo kraia v 1942 g.," in *Vtoraia mirovaia i Velikaia otechestvennaia voina: aktual'nye problemy sotsial'noi istorii* (Maikop: Adygeiskii gosudarstvennyi universitet), 173.

mentioned the murder of Jews in Lvov.[104] But this important report was not published in Rostov-on-Don.

On September 21, 1941, Liza wrote a long letter:

> Dear Efim!
>
> … We are very glad that you are in good health; to us it is all that matters!! … But there is nothing to be done; what really counts is your being in good health; then, everything [*else*] will be all right. Accursed fascism, I wish it were smashed and destroyed entirely. Then, you would return to Moscow again, and we would live as we used to do.
>
> It is still the same with us; we are very anxious. No one is thinking yet about evacuating, because where could we go? Besides, in order to do so [*become an evacuee*], one needs first, health, second, a lot of money (precisely as you wrote). And we have neither. Most importantly, fall is getting closer, then winter; it is terrible for us to even think about moving… We wish to be spared this. Everyone would be really happy, if this War were over and this barbarous fascism were destroyed forever. Our dear one, we are moved by your anxiety about us. …
>
> David has long since been drafted; he was sent to work; there was only one letter from him, dated September 8, and on September 12 the area was heavily bombed. God knows whether he is alive.
>
> There is one more misfortune. Boris passed away quietly at 6:30 in the morning on September 18… Now he doesn't need to be anxious. He can only take care of us so that all of us should be alive and in good health and there would be no need to run away anywhere and that barbarous Hitler would be tomorrow where Boris is. It is sad for me to write all this to you. But from now on, I am not going to write anything bad. I only wish to write about good news from today onwards, so that the first good news will be the triumph over fascism! …
>
> My dear one, forgive me for everything. There is nothing good about it; we all are very worried and anxious … Best wishes from everyone to everyone, especially from our dear children Anechka and Grishenka. We all send you hugs and kisses, our dear one. So far we are sleeping well. I hope it will continue. Liza.[105]

---

104 Vanda Vasilevskaia, "Zapadnaia Ukraina istekaet krov'iu," *Ordzhonikidzevskaia pravda* (Stavropol), no. 219 (2283), September 18, 1941.
105 From Liza Chazkewitz, September 21, 1941, YVA: O.75/324, pp. 51–55.

What is special about this letter? It is noteworthy that the Rostov branch of the Ginsburg family appeared so anxious about the well-being of Efim Ginsburg in Siberia. Indeed, the living conditions of Soviet evacuees were very difficult. But still, in view of the family's own problems—namely, the fact that the Germans were advancing closer and closer to Rostov-on-Don and their very lives were at stake—their preoccupation with the economic hardships of their brother, who was living in a much safer place, seemed to be an attempt by the Ginsburg family in Rostov-on-Don to divert Efim's and their own attention from the real danger. The Rostov Ginsburgs also appeared to be extremely frightened by Efim Ginsburg's description of all he had suffered during his evacuation to Omsk.

Nevertheless, they were not opposed to leaving in principle. But they preferred to think about evacuation in practical terms, involving a strain on both their budget and their health—and of course, the notorious Russian winter, which came early in 1941 and was particularly severe.

> The movement of refugees and North Caucasian Jews *from* the North Caucasus eastwards had been conspicuous since summer 1941, when the possibility of a German offensive towards the region was still slight. For many Jewish refugees, the North Caucasus only served as a transition point on their way eastwards, to areas safe from German attack.[106] Others, however, were asked or forced to settle in the Caucasus and were often dispatched to remote Caucasian areas.[107]
>
> In 1941, quite often "local" evacuation took place, when refugees were dispersed *within the North Caucasus*[108] instead of being dispatched further eastwards. This left them still inside the endangered region and contradicted the main imperative of central evacuation policies, which were aimed at moving refugees safely away from the Germans. This may have been due to the general disorder prevalent in the evacuation process at the local level and the excessive confidence felt by the authorities regarding the ability of the

---

106 Elista, *stanitsa* Starominskaya. Testimony of Bradichevsky, ICJ: (217) 183, p. 1. Cf. Borovoi, *Vospominaniia*, 256.
107 *Stanitsa* Labinskaya, villages Slavyanskaya and Vyselki. Questioning of Raisa Niminskaya, August 24, 1943, YVA: M.33/292, p. 105. Cf. Diary of Ioffe, entry from November 10, 1941, State Archive of the Autonomous Republic of the Crimea (Derzhavnyi arkhiv avtonomnoi respubliki Krym, henceforth DAARK): R-156/1/31, p. 31. Cf. Testimony of Kalnitskaya, HUJ, ICJ, DOH, cassette no. TC 2759 (not transcribed).
108 Statement of Sara Igla, August 18, 1944, GARF: 7021/9/6, p. 79. Cf. Testimony of Kalnitskaya, ICJ: TC 2759.

Soviet forces to hold on to the North Caucasus. But it is also possible that these Jews consciously did not wish to go too far away, estimating that any German advance into the region would be duly thwarted.

Some of the local North Caucasian Jews also took the opportunity to evacuate, as Soviet authorities continued to evacuate residents from the region in the fall of 1941. As in other localities, it was not explained to the Caucasian Jews that they would be specially targeted by the Germans for ill-treatment and annihilation. Furthermore, it seems that, unlike refugees and evacuees who moved into the region from western areas, it was psychologically more challenging for the North Caucasian Jews to leave, because it was their first evacuation. However, the advance of the German armies in the southern sector, coupled with news of German ill-treatment of Jews, often conveyed by Jewish refugees from the west, did lead some North Caucasian Jews to leave their homes.

Those living in the Rostov district were certainly no exception to the trend, with only a part of the Jewish population choosing to leave.[109] The evacuation of civilians from the Rostov region was launched during September–October 1941. Approximately 100,000–150,000 civilians were evacuated and about 50–100,000 fled the region at their own initiative. Among the organized evacuees, there were 7–10,000 Jews,[110] and it is estimated that a similar number of Jews fled independently.[111] The majority of those evacuated from Rostov-on-Don in an organized fashion were women, elderly people and children, including those from the orphanages. Many evacuees were professionals, including doctors and university personnel.[112] According to the German occupational administration, up to 50,000 Jews remained in the Rostov region in November 1941.[113]

It is noteworthy that, in the fall of 1941, Jews fleeing from the North Caucasus were still able to avail themselves of the partially crippled, but still

---

109 Testimony of Valeriia Margolis, 1941, in Berman and Nikitina, *Evakuatsiia*, 142.
110 Movshovich, "11 avgusta—60 let tragedii v Zmievskoi balke."
111 Evgenii Movshovich, "Rostov-na-Donu," in *Entsiklopedia Kholokosta na territorii SSSR*, ed. Il'ia Al'tman, 2nd edition (Moscow: ROSSPEN, 2011), 866.
112 Al'tman, *Zhertvy nenavisti*, 273.
113 Operational report no. 16 from occupied Eastern territories, in *The Einsatzgruppen Reports: Selection from the Dispatches of the Nazis' Death Squads Campaign against the Jews (July 1941–January 1943)*, ed. Yitzhak Arad, Shmuel Krakowski, and Shmuel Spektor (New York: Holocaust Library, 1989), 358.

active transportation system.[114] At the same time, they already experienced serious problems: it was extremely difficult to get tickets and often the tickets were not honored; there were far more would-be escapees than the actual number of seats and trains available;[115] it was not easy to move away from remote localities, because of the unavailability of transport.[116] The sporadic German bombardment of railways and railway stations caused casualties among the Jewish refugees,[117] and resulted in delays in railway traffic.

It is surprising—but only at first glance—that the death of one of the family members is only mentioned as the last "news item" in the letter. Apparently, the deterioration in Boris's health was so obvious for those living with him that they had become accustomed to the idea of his imminent death. Nevertheless, it is remarkable that his passing is entirely overshadowed in the letter by the concerns of the living. This order of subjects in the letter indicates that the Rostov Ginsburgs, or at least Liza, realized that their own lives were now in danger.

The conscription of one of the family members, David, to the Red Army raises the question of a "fighting" response by the Ginsburg family. However, his enlistment is not necessarily indicative of a "fighting" mood among the Ginsburgs because David did not join the army voluntarily.

Soviet troops on Rostov-on-Don's streets. 1941–42. Central Archive of Moscow's Electronic and Audio-Visual Materials, 0-94365. Courtesy of Russian Holocaust Center.

---

114 Diary of Ioffe, entry from November 9, 1941, DAARK: P-156/1/31, p. 31. From Liza Chazkewitz and Anya Greener to Efim Ginsburg in Alma-Ata (henceforth all letters are addressed to Efim Ginsburg in Alma-Ata, until stated otherwise), November 18, 1941, YVA: O.75/324, p. 74.
115 Diary of Ioffe, entries from November 28 and 29, 1941, DAARK: P-156/1/31, p. 34.
116 Testimony of Mandelblat, YVA: VT/1911.
117 Testimony of Lidiya Yundina, October 4, 1988, YVHN. From Liza Chazkewitz and Anya Greener, November 18, 1941, YVA: O.75/324, p. 77.

What would have been the patriotic response? This is a difficult question. With the exception of self-evident propaganda maxims (absolute obedience and self-sacrifice expected of everyone),[118] the Soviet government itself refrained from providing specific guidance in some less clear-cut cases. For example, it did not prescribe how people living in the areas threatened by the Wehrmacht were expected to behave: to leave before the Germans arrived, or to stay. In this regard, the great dilemma confronting patriotically minded Soviet civilians, including Jews, was how to best combine their contribution to the country's war effort, broadly defined, with the desire to survive the War.

Also of interest is the first reference to God in the Ginsburg letters. Having looked through all their letters, I was under the impression that the family was entirely secular; prior to this letter, God, with or without a capital letter, was never mentioned. But, as sometimes happens, when danger becomes real, God may return to a person's conscience. Also noteworthy was the family's assumption that Boris would somehow watch over them, an assumption that suggests a hidden vein of religious feeling in this otherwise secular family.

Another indication of religious feeling in this family is the phrase used in the last paragraph: "Forgive me for everything," which seems to be somewhat misplaced. What should Efim forgive his sisters for? But September 21, 1941 was the date of the Jewish New Year, Rosh Hashana. This holiday marks the beginning of the ten Days of Awe, which end with Yom Kippur, the Day of Atonement. It is customary for Jews to ask each other for forgiveness on this day. This may have been an innocuous way for the Ginsburg family to demonstrate their religious feelings without arousing the suspicions of the Soviet censors.

Judging from what we know from many other stories, Liza states correctly that evacuation was a very expensive undertaking. People with means were the first to get away; those who had no money were far less likely to leave. She is also right in pointing to the Ginsburg sisters' poor health as a major impediment to their taking part in the evacuation. Relocation to an area with inadequate sanitary and health conditions would have been very likely, as the Rostov Ginsburgs learned from Efim's letters. This probability, as well as the likelihood of encountering others, unknown, problems along the road, could deter even young and strong people from leaving. And yet, all these considerations applied only as long as there was no mortal danger.

Further anxiety is manifest in a short letter sent on the very same day, September 21, 1941.

---

118 Berkhoff, *Motherland in Danger*, 35–67.

Dear Efim!

... We are very glad that you are all right and in good health. Our dear one! Don't worry about us so much! That won't help us, and it only hurts you. There is no good news; we are all very worried and anxious. ...
Liza.[119]

The Red Army was incurring great losses in Ukraine. This was given prominence in *The New York Times* report on the encirclement of the Soviet forces near Kiev, dated September 21, 1941:

> Berlin, Sept. 20—Surrender of the Kiev garrison, mopping up operations in the Ukrainian capital and progress in liquidation of 200,000 Russians trapped in the triangle between Kiev, Priluki and Kremenchug to the east were featured in today's German Supreme Command communiqué.[120]

It goes without saying, however, that the Soviet media left the Ginsburgs in the dark, along with all the other ordinary Soviet citizens, regarding this drastic defeat of the Soviet forces, a defeat with fearful implications for the German drive towards their own region, the North Caucasus.

However, the Soviet populace learned to compensate for the lack of candor in their press by getting frontline updates from refugees who had arrived in their city. These refugees included Jews who had managed to flee Kiev and reach Rostov-on-Don. For example, here are the words of a Jewish man who escaped from Kiev to Rostov-on-Don in mid-September 1941: "When Hitler occupied Kiev, the Red Army told us: 'Run for your dear life' ... They gave us the option to go. We didn't have money to buy train tickets."[121] The man was later settled in a kolkhoz and put to work. Important for our story is that he and other refugees were a significant source of information for local Jews. But if the Ginsburgs received such communications, it was never mentioned in their letters. However, they may have been afraid that, if such a letter were intercepted, the Soviet censors could accuse the Ginsburgs of disseminating panic.

Information coming from outside was often instrumental in spurring Rostov Jews to escape. This is underscored by the following account. In 2006, a Russian author interviewed inhabitants of Rostov-on-Don who were

---

119 From Liza Chazkewitz, September 21, 1941, YVA: O.75/324, p. 49.
120 C. Brooks Peters, "Kiev mopped up, Nazis announce. Russians Held Thwarted in Effort to Escape Trap after Flight of Their Leaders," *The New York Times*, September 21, 1941.
121 Testimony of Fritzi Schiffer, b. 1922, March 29, 1995, YVA: O.3/7873.

youngsters at the time of the Soviet-German War, but had been old enough to remember details. This is what one of his interviewees recollected:

> Many people were evacuated. Our entire courtyard was full of possessions left behind, which they [*the evacuees*] could not take [*with them*]. In particular, there were many books about Marxism-Leninism and political literature. ... Among the books, we boys happened to find a letter from Moscow sent to a Rostov addressee. It said that there was panic in Moscow, and that evacuation was underway. The addressee was strongly advised to leave Rostov as soon as possible. The letter was sent to Kaganovich, who lived in our courtyard. ...[122]

The Kaganovich family did indeed leave Rostov-on-Don; they survived the War and later returned to the city.

As the Red Army failed to halt the continued thrust of the Wehrmacht towards the Caucasus, even official Soviet propaganda had to address the alarming situation at the front, albeit in a veiled manner. On September 26, 1941, the Rostov newspaper published on its front page a major article, "The German Fascists Will Not Tread on Don Steppe!" about a meeting of former partisans and participants in the Civil War at *stanitsa* Razdorskaya.[123] This was the first clear signal in the local Rostov media indicating the growing threat of the German advance towards the city. The serious situation on the southern front was also reflected in a short note published in *Molot* on September 27, 1941, which mentioned the defense of Odessa.[124]

On September 27, *Izvestiya* published an article "The People's Hatred," signed by a certain N. Petrov.[125] The article stated that, according to fascist ideology, the "Jews, who, Fascism claims, bring disasters to Germany, must be destroyed."[126] This was an important statement, and, taken separately, was at odds with the official Soviet outlook at the time, as the government did not acknowledge the Germans' genocidal goals until the joint Moscow Declaration in December 1942. Nevertheless, such a vague claim would hardly have sufficed

---

122 Testimony of A. Agafonov. In Smirnov, *Rostov pod sen'iu svastiki*, 46.
123 *Molot*, no. 227 (6106), September 26, 1941.
124 Mayor-General I. E. Petrov, "Oborona Odessy," *Molot*, no. 228 (6107), September 27, 1941.
125 The prominent contemporary Dutch scholar, Karel Berkhoff, has inferred that this could be none other than the nominal Soviet head of state, Mikhail Kalinin. Karel Berkhoff, "'Total Annihilation,'" 72.
126 N. Petrov, "Nenavist' naroda," *Izvestiia*, September 27, 1941.

to convince Soviet Jews, among them members of the Ginsburg family, that the German occupation would bring disaster for them.

This was counterbalanced by a flow of reports emphasizing a "business as usual" mood. For instance, one day later, on September 28, 1941, a newspaper in Stavropol reported on the regular performance of regional agricultural work in the fall.[127] Similar trends were still discernible in *Molot* at that time.

In late September, the Rostov Theater of Musical Comedy was the first cultural institution of the city to be evacuated.[128] This event was not advertised, but local inhabitants, including the Ginsburgs, may have learned about it and drawn their own conclusions.

October 1941

On October 1, 1941, Liza wrote to Efim Ginsburg:

> Dear Efim!
>
> … We haven't received any letters from you in a long time.
>
> We are beginning to worry. … Boris is better off than we are: he rests there in peace!!! But we are quite uneasy, and do not know what awaits us. Nor do we know what to do. The most awful thing is the fact that winter is getting closer. …
>
> David is in good health; he has written to us. Everyone sends you their best wishes and kisses. Liza.[129]

The letter speaks for itself. Apart from the panic clearly sweeping the family, we should also keep in mind that it was sent on Yom Kippur, and it is possible that the ominous mood of this day affected the Ginsburg family in Rostov-on-Don.

On October 2, 1941, a newspaper in Stavropol, a city in the North Caucasus situated some 350 km to the southeast of Rostov-on-Don, published an article titled "The enemy stretches his hands out to Donbass."[130] This publication was a clear acknowledgement of the growing vulnerability of the Soviet

---

127 Editorial "'O vypolnenii osennikh sel'khozrabot v krae,' Postanovlenie shestogo plenuma Obkoma VKP(b) ot 24 sentiabria 1941 g.," *Ordzhonikidzevskaia pravda*, no. 230 (2294), September 28, 1941.
128 To Sochi. GARO: p-4144/1/10, p. 4. In Zelenskaia, *Kul'turno-prosvetitel'nye uchrezhdeniia*, 74.
129 From Liza Chazkewitz, October 1, 1941, YVA: O.75/324, pp. 63–64.
130 M. A. Suslov (Secretary of the Ordzhonikidze District Committee of the VKP[b]), "Velikaia Otechestvennaia voina i zadachi partiinykh organizatsii," *Ordzhonikidzevskaia pravda*, no. 233 (2297), October 2, 1941.

North Caucasus, but because of Soviet policies, it remained unavailable to the inhabitants of Rostov-on-Don, including the Ginsburgs.

Growing anxiety was manifest in Liza's letter written the next day, October 3:

> Dear Efim!
>
> We received your letter dated September 19. As always we were very glad; on the other hand, it greatly upset us that you were so worried and suffering about us! Don't do this, our dear one, because you are so lonely. Right now, we are not considering relocating anywhere, because, for the time being, the question is not yet so acute for us. Let's hope that we won't need to go anywhere. In any case, we don't even think about going to you, since it is so far away. If need be, we'd better not go too far. Don't think about sending us money or selling anything. It won't help anything. We don't need it; if necessary, we'll write to you about it.
>
> Take care of yourself. Best wishes and kisses from all of us, Liza.[131]

Noticeable is some change in the Ginsburgs' vacillation between "stay or go." The situation appears to have been gradually deteriorating, although there was little indication of this fact in the Rostov media. So, the Rostov Ginsburgs were ready, for the first time, to weigh the possibility of flight as a practical solution—but only "not too far away." Emotional phrases, such as "it won't help anything," showed a growing panic among the family. Also noteworthy is the Ginsburgs' persistence in rejecting monetary support from their relative, as they stated that "we don't need it." Obviously, this was an illusion: the Rostov Ginsburgs did require funds in order to be able to evacuate, as they themselves acknowledged in earlier letters, but they clearly did not want to take money from their brother, who was also in need.

On October 5, *Izvestiya* published an article "On the Don River Bank," depicting the normal life that continued in Rostov-on-Don at that time. Alongside pictures of workers excelling themselves in producing armaments for the Red Army and the city's inhabitants engaged in some type of military training, there were also photographs of sportsmen preparing for a sailing championship on the River Don and of the city's preparations for winter. *Izvestiya* was a Soviet-wide newspaper, available to Efim Ginsburg, but this article was probably a source of misinformation for him and might have persuaded him to some degree that for the time being there was no need for his relatives to leave the city.

---

131 From Anya Greener, October 3, 1941, YVA: O.75/324, pp. 66–67.

In contrast to the frivolous pictures that served as an accompaniment, the article's particular value was in its portrayal of the German occupation of Rostov-on-Don and the adjacent area in 1918. According to this article, the Germans had plundered the city and also physically abused the local population. The last message was of particular importance to the older generation of Ginsburgs, who, in all probability, had personally witnessed the German occupation during the First World War in Rostov-on-Don and could compare their own experiences with what was described in *Izvestiya*. The Ginsburgs must have remembered the "good" Germans from that war,[132] which rendered this type of Soviet propaganda ineffective for the family and perhaps increased their confusion. In all possibility, such articles were counterproductive with respect to those among the Jews who had themselves witnessed the German occupation during the First World War or had close relatives whom they could ask for their first-hand account of this period.

The next letter was sent from Rostov-on-Don on October 6, 1941:

> Dear Efim!
>
> … There is no reason for you to think that we are angry [*with you*], because you cannot receive us at your place. It is just ridiculous [*to imagine*] where you are and where we are. Besides, winter is getting closer. … We are not considering any trip now, because it is entirely impossible. We shall wait. For the time being, there is no mass evacuation, and hopefully there probably won't be one. Hitler won't get us. It is hard to travel because of the children; our health is not good; there are no men; the only one is Volodya, and he cannot do anything. So we have to stay here and hope that everything will be all right. That's all for now; it is difficult to say what lies ahead.
>
> With love and kisses, Liza.[133]

The letter reveals the Ginsburgs' continuous reluctance to move, which comes as no surprise. They had plenty of good reasons why they should not go anywhere. More surprising is their apparent passivity and probably even resignation: "We shall wait. …" The transition from "stay" to "go" had begun, but it was too slow and would not keep pace with the advancing German forces.

In the meantime, as mentioned in the chapter dealing with the evacuation, in fall 1941, Rostov-on-Don turned into an important center of Jewish

---

132   On this issue, see, for example, Maclean, "Control and cleanliness."
133   From Liza Chazkewitz, October 6, 1941, YVA: O.75/324, pp. 60–61.

evacuation. It appears that quite a number of newcomers were observant Jews, and they contributed to the revival of Jewish life in the city. October 6, 1941 was the first day of the Jewish holiday of Sukkot. This is how the holiday was described by a Jewish officer stationed in the city:

> On the first day of Sukkot, I received a day off and tried to find a synagogue. I almost failed and became so desperate that I wanted to return to the base, but suddenly I came across a bearded man dressed in a festive way and a little boy next to him holding a bag with a *tallis* [*prayer shawl*]. I followed them till they entered a certain house, evidently a dwelling. I realized that I had been walking in a circle around the synagogue for almost thirty minutes. My entrance to the building in a uniform spurred tension in the midst of those praying. It turned out that a number of refugee families were living in the *ezras noshim* [*women's prayer section*]. … I explained to the *gabai* [*the manager of the synagogue*] in Yiddish that I am a "Westerner" [*he was born in Grodno*] and requested a *machzor* [*prayer book*]. The tension subsided.[134]

Did the Ginsburgs make contact with such refugees? There are no references to this in the correspondence. Several factors weigh against such a possibility. We see from the officer's testimony that the newcomers were understandably cautious about talking to strangers. It also stands to reason that the local people, including Jews, were careful about approaching the newcomers. Soviet spy mania was bound to affect everyone. Besides, there were other barriers, such as language (many Jewish refugees did not know Russian, while there is no indication that the Ginsburgs knew Yiddish) and time (refugees came and went; it was difficult to forge long-term relationships with them).

On the same day, October 6, Liza sent another letter to Efim Ginsburg:

> We ask you, our dear one, in strong terms, not to worry about us so much, because in any case you cannot help us. We understand very well that you are eager to help us; but it is impossible! How can we think about making a long trip to you at this difficult moment, especially in winter? It is frightening to think about it, especially if we take into account our poor health and the fact that we need to travel with children. Besides, Volodya is the only one who could accompany us, but, for the time being, he is unable to do so. Right now, we are staying here and going to wait for what may come. Let's take the chance [*avos'*] that it will turn out all right, and

---

134   Avshalom Daigi Dashot, *A Walk in the Ways of My Life* (n.p., 2008) [Hebrew], 43–44.

we won't need to leave Rostov. We pray and think about it day and night, hoping that we won't have to move away. Don't send us any money; don't sell anything.

With love and kisses. Best wishes from all of us and from the children, Liza.[135]

What is remarkable about this letter? First, it is noteworthy that the sisters sent two letters conveying more or less the same message. It seems that the Ginsburgs did not feel they had made a convincing case in the first letter, in which they claimed they could not leave at that time. They were still instinctively reluctant to move away, but they needed to explain this decision logically to their brother. They concluded by deciding to "wait and take a chance," using a typical Russian expression (*avos'*). The sisters' consistent lack of resolution, despite the steadily aggravating circumstances, may be better understood if we consider the fact that they had been schooled in the prewar Soviet system, which did not encourage Soviet citizens to act on their own agency or to show individual initiative; the state was expected to take care of everything.[136] Also notable is a religious reference ("we pray"), a significant turnabout from their prewar, apparently secular mindset.

On October 9, the Evacuation Council sanctioned the evacuation of 30,000 women and children from the city of Rostov-on-Don and 30,000 more from Taganrog, the second largest city of the Rostov district—and only 67 km to the west of Rostov-on-Don—which would be occupied by the Germans just eight days later. The decision came as a response to the request lodged by the Rostov District Committee of the VKP(b) in early September, which asked for permission to evacuate the children and their mothers from these two cities.[137] This example is indicative of two major evacuation-related issues: it shows that the center needed a significant time to authorize evacuation, and it also indicates that evacuation was focused on of specially designated groups. All others, including the Ginsburg sisters, had to wait for other opportunities to be evacuated.

The German air strikes against Rostov-on-Don did not stop and only intensified as the Wehrmacht marched closer to the Caucasus. *Molot* referred to

---

135 From Anya Greener, October 6, 1941, YVA: O.75/324, p. 65.
136 On Soviet paternalism, see, for example, Lewis H. Siegelbaum, "'Dear Comrade, you ask what we need,' Socialist paternalism and Soviet rural 'notables' in the mid-1930s," in *Stalinism: New directions*, ed. Sheila Fitzpatrick (London: Routledge, 2000), 231–256.
137 GARF: A-259/40/3070, pp. 1, 4. In Manley, *To the Tashkent Station*, 70.

them, but in a characteristically veiled fashion: on October 9, 1941, an article by a Soviet general described how airborne forces operated and how one could fight against them.[138] Of course, the local inhabitants were well aware of the bombardment of their own city, so the reluctance of the local Soviet media to report these facts served only to diminish the trust of the Rostov people.

On October 11, 1941, *Molot* mentioned battles around Mariupol, a Ukrainian city some 180 km to the west of Rostov-on-Don, signaling an increasingly strained situation in the area.[139] This appeared to be a departure from the Soviet trend of under-reporting. However, here it was a case of reporting in a markedly delayed and thus misleading fashion: the city of Mariupol had actually been seized by the Germans on October 8, three days before the date of the article. Moreover, the credibility of this source had long since been undermined.

A Russian witness remembers how panic burst out in Rostov-on-Don at this time:

> Approximately one month before the Germans' entry to Rostov, panic began in the city. Probably this was a result of panic in Moscow. The rumor was that the Germans were breaking through towards Rostov. All the bosses abandoned the city. All this took place within two-three days. In this atmosphere of anarchy, people began to loot shops. ... They took away everything they could. ... Policemen began to threaten to use weapons and shoot in the air. One policeman injured a woman. Several Red Army soldiers, who were passing by, approached and killed the policeman on the spot. There was terrible havoc and mess.[140]

The German armies were approaching, getting closer to Rostov-on-Don itself, and by then the Soviet press could keep silent no longer. On October 12, 1941, *Molot* published on the front page a passionate appeal to "to all working people of Rostov-on-Don", "To Turn Rostov into a Defense Fortress! To Rise as One Man to Defend our City!" The newspaper finally clamed that "a grave danger threatens our beloved city of Rostov-on-Don." The article mentioned "hordes of German fascists" and listed the measures that would be taken to cope with the danger. The appeal was signed by the Commander of the North

---

138 Mayor-General M. Filippovski, "O vozdushnykh desantakh i kak s nimi borot'sia," *Molot*, no. 238 (6117), October 9, 1941.
139 "Na Mariupol'skom sektore," *Molot*, no. 240 (6119), October 11, 1941.
140 Testimony of A. Karpetian. In Smirnov, *Rostov pod sen'iu svastiki*, 54.

Caucasian Military District, Fedor Remezov, and the Secretary of the Rostov municipal committee of the VKP(b), Boris Dvinsky.[141]

With hindsight, we can understand that this article was a self-evident Soviet defensive measure, resulting from the course of the War. However, the local inhabitants were without doubt unprepared for this appeal. No previous Soviet propaganda had even hinted at the possibility that there could be a battle for the city of Rostov-on-Don. Instead, the War was depicted as a relatively remote event. One could read "between the lines" that the Germans were slowly approaching, but for the average inhabitant of Rostov-on-Don, who was only "fed" information by the official news, and who was unaware of other sources and neglected other signs (for example, the bombardments), this announcement came totally out of the blue. Concurrently, it is also likely that the sudden "enlightenment" of the Soviet newspaper, especially at this critical hour, could have boosted its credibility in the eyes of the local readership.

This same issue of *Molot* also mentioned more fighting near Mariupol.[142]

An influx of organized evacuees and refugees, who were fleeing from the advancing German armies, found themselves in the North Caucasus, causing panic among the local authorities.[143] On October 14, 1941, *Molot* wrote that "fascists dispatch to us their agents, whose task is to spread panic in the midst of the population by circulating various provocative rumors." An example was a certain Valentina Alferenko, mentioned as arrested by "state organs."[144]

How can we interpret this report, and how is it connected to our narrative? There were many evacuees and refugees, including large numbers of Jews. The odds were high that the information they possessed would have been shared with local Jews, thus prompting the latter to leave. At the same time, the ever-suspicious Soviet authorities tried their best to prevent the flow of this information, and in all likelihood, were largely successful.

On October 14, the Evacuation Council issued a secret directive on the evacuation of equipment from several garment, knitted goods, and shoe factories from Rostov-on-Don to the country's interior.[145] This is one of a very few Soviet

---

141 *Molot*, no. 241 (6120), October 12, 1941.
142 Ibid.
143 Feferman, "A Soviet Humanitarian Action?," 821–822.
144 *Molot*, no. 243 (6122), October 14, 1941.
145 GARO: R-3737/5/34, pp. 29–30. Rebecca Manley mentions the order by the "North Caucasus Military Soviet" (apparently she means the Military Council of the North Caucasian Front or the Military Council of the North Caucasian District) "to evacuate the city of Rostov in mid-October" (Manley, *To the Tashkent Station*, 72). However, for lack of archival

documents that shed light on the evacuation from the city. Careful planning is evident. It was made clear where equipment from each plant would be removed to, and how many carriages would be necessary. The last column showed the number of carriages allocated for the evacuation of "workers, engineers, and technical personnel, as well as members of their families." These figures differ significantly from one plant to another, but overall they are impressive: it was envisaged that altogether 204 carriages would be allocated for the evacuation of civilians, as compared to 428 carriages for the removal of equipment.

It is important to understand how such measures influenced public opinion in Rostov-on-Don. The evacuation decree impacted directly only those who were employed in these factories, as they were ordered to leave. Their family members could choose whether to accompany them or not, but in most cases they did so, and the number of allotted carriages was calculated to provide space for them. However, this evacuation had its greatest impact on people outside these two circles, namely, more distant relatives and friends of the evacuees, as well as the general public, including Jews, who drew their own conclusions from observing such a relatively large-scale evacuation. That said, other plants and their personnel, particularly food and military plants employing many people, were not evacuated at this time, and, in the eyes of the general public, this acted as a counterweight to the evacuation of the garment, knitted goods, and shoe factories.

Faced with the dangerous proximity of the German armies, the Soviet military authorities in Rostov-on-Don responded by further tightening security measures in the beleaguered city. On October 14, 1941, the military authorities in Rostov-on-Don enacted a night curfew, forbidding movement from 8 pm to 5 am. Severe penalties, up to and including capital punishment, were imposed for hooliganism.[146] This would have been considered a relatively minor transgression in normal times, and the fact that the authorities resorted to such draconian measures testified to their nervousness. Moreover, the local media made it immediately clear that these measures would be rigidly enforced. On October 15, the Rostov newspaper reported that "train conductor S. Degtyar told unfounded stories, causing concern among the population." He was sentenced to five years' imprisonment and three years of subsequent disenfranchisement.[147]

---

reference, it is impossible to define the precise character of the military order and its likely impact on the population, beyond the fact that the two decrees were synchronized in time.

146 Order no. 4 in the Rostov garrison. *Molot*, no. 241 (6120), October 12, 1941.
147 "Razoblachennyi sheptun," *Molot*, no. 244 (6123), October 15, 1941.

For the Soviet military, the civilian population was not only a burden, but a threat and a liability. It could be infiltrated and had to be protected from the enemy. However, it was also an asset that could be employed in defending the city. Thus, on October 15, 1941, the Rostov-on-Don newspaper called upon civilians to construct barricades in the city.[148]

Of special note is the article, "To Hold On!" published by a prominent Soviet writer of Jewish origin, Ilya Erenburg.[149] Initially, the article appeared in the central Soviet press, and on October 15, 1941, the piece was reprinted in Rostov-on-Don:

> They say that they fight against Communists. It is a lie. They are against all citizens of our country. ... They say that they are against Jews. It is a lie. They also have their own Jews whom they favor. These Jews have an inscription in their passports: "WJ," "valuable Jew."[150]

Much is condensed here in a few lines. This was the clearest admission, until then, in the Soviet media that the Germans, at least in their declarations, singled out Jews for abuse. But the article could have also misled Jews into believing that—if deemed valuable—they could survive under German rule. This second inference was important, especially as it was voiced by a Jew. The overall message of the article for the Jews was highly ambiguous and could have been interpreted either way.

Bolshevik party leaders joined the military in their appeal to Rostov's civilians. On October 16, 1941, *Molot* published a front page article "Slogan: Everyone is a Fighter; Everyone is a Warrior." The article cited the Secretary of the Lenin Regional Committee[151] of the VKP(b), Sorokin, who called upon the citizenry "to turn Rostov into an unassailable defense fortress."[152]

These appeals were immediately translated into action on the ground. On October 16, 1941, the Rostov military commander ordered:

---

148 "Barrikady," ibid.
149 On Ilya Erenburg's background and his anti-Nazi writings, see, for example, Yosef Govrin. "Ilya Ehrenburg and the Ribbentrop-Molotov Agreement," *The Israel Journal of Foreign Affairs* 7, no. 2 (2013): 103–108. Cf. Katerina Clark, "Ehrenburg and Grossman: Two Cosmopolitan Jewish Writers Reflect on Nazi Germany at War," *Kritika: Explorations in Russian and Eurasian History* 10, no. 3 (Summer 2009): 607–628.
150 *Molot*, no. 244 (6123), October 15, 1941. Cf. Berkhoff, "'Total annihilation,'"69.
151 In this case "Lenin" was the region's name.
152 *Molot*, no. 245 (6124), October 16, 1941.

... to conscript for the performance of labor involving the construction of defensive installations the entire male population of the city and District of Rostov (men between the ages of 15 to 55 and women [*aged*] 16 to 45). Failure to comply with the order will be punished in accordance with martial law [*po zakonam voennogo vremeni*].[153]

Some 130,000 people worked on constructing Rostov's line of defense every day.[154] These measures were conspicuous and clearly indicative of the worsening of the situation. These sights doubtlessly affected the mood of the Ginsburg family, although from their correspondence we cannot infer that any of them was actually involved in this construction. Indeed, it is likely that, because of their ages and occupations, the order did not apply to them.

Construction of barricades on Rostov's streets. Central Archive of Moscow's Electronic and Audio-Visual Materials. Courtesy of Russian Holocaust Center.

Rostov's inhabitants, including the Ginsburgs, were unable to learn exactly to what extent circumstances had deteriorated, or to put it more bluntly, where the German armies actually were at this point in time. By mid-October, the Germans had succeeded in making inroads not only in the North Caucasus but in the Rostov district itself, where they captured the city of Taganrog. However, this success was not reported in international newspapers, judging by the article published in *The New York Times* on October 22, 1941. The article mentioned the capture of a very important Soviet industrial center on the road to the

---

153 Ibid.
154 Zelenskaia, *Kul'turno-prosvetitel'nye uchrezhdeniia*, 74.

Caucasus, Stalino (now named Donetsk), some 160 km to the north-west of Rostov-on-Don, but not the capture of Taganrog, further east and much closer to Rostov:

> While closely guarded official silence continued to hide the progress of the battle for Moscow, the German High Command in a special communiqué today claimed new successes at the northern and southern ends of the eastern front—the occupation of the Island of Dagoe and thus the "liquidation of the enemy in the entire Baltic area," and the occupation of the town of Stalino in the Donets Basin.[155]

On October 24, the Gorky Theater, was evacuated to Makhachkala.[156] It was not advertised in the city, but, given the importance of the theater, this departure would have been widely known to the local inhabitants. There remained only one source of entertainment in Rostov-on-Don: *Kontsertno-estradnoe byuro* (Bureau of entertainment and performances), which continued to give performances in the city until mid-November 1941.

Several days later, the German army reported the seizure of Kharkov, another important industrial Soviet center on the road to the Caucasus, situated more than 450 km to the north-west of Rostov-on-Don. On October 26, 1941, *The New York Times* wrote:

> The city was the chief center of economic life in the vast agricultural Ukraine. Kharkov, whose capture, the Germans claimed yesterday, was the chief hub of economic life in Ukraine, occupying an extremely strategic position on the main routes between Moscow to the north and Crimea and the rich Caucasus oil lands to the south.[157]

Again, there was no reference to this strategic conquest in the Rostov newspaper, nor was any information about the fall of Kharkov published in the central media that was available in Rostov-on-Don.

Even though Rostov's inhabitants were not provided with factual information about what was occurring on the frontline, the rapidly deteriorating situation made itself felt in the next letter written by Anya and Liza, sent from

---

155 "Stalino claimed by Nazis in South. Capture of Donets Steel City Extends Threat to War-Vital Region, Berlin Asserts," *The New York Times*, October 22, 1941.
156 GARO: p-4140/1/123, p. 2. In Zelenskaia, *Kul'turno-prosvetitel'nye uchrezhdeniia*, 74.
157 "Loss of Kharkov is a serious blow," *The New York Times*, October 26, 1941.

Rostov-on-Don on October 26, 1941. The letter described dramatic family events:

> ... I [*hereby*] inform you that Anya and I stayed in Rostov. Our beloved Monya, Tamara, Tsylya, and the small children were evacuated on October 13 to Budennovsk (Ordzhonikidze territory). Volodya was unable to get evacuation permits [*evakolisty*] for us. That's why we remained. We were very anxious before we got a message from them saying they were all alive and in good health and arrived there all right. But Tamara describes their terrible living conditions; it is better to die at home. We don't know any longer what to do, either to get to them and to suffer with them or to anticipate the end of our lives here.
>
> Borya is no longer with us; he passed away on September 18. But he is better off than we are!!! We envy him that he didn't live to see these dreadful things, and most important is the fact that the most horrible things are yet to come; we don't know what awaits us.
>
> We wish strongly that we could be together with you in Alma-Ata, because we could feel calm and safe there. But apparently it is absolutely impossible! Now we are all dispersed, and it is hardly possible that we will see each other again!!! If at all!! How difficult it is to endure and to suffer all this. But of course, we shouldn't lose our temper; let's hope that we all will be alive and see one another again, God willing.
>
> Please write to our relatives about everything and also write what we should do, although if we take into account when you will receive this letter and when we get your reply, a great number of things may have occurred and changed by then. Still, write about everything. Maybe we will survive and be alive and well. ...
>
> Volodya is here in Rostov; David has left and there is no word from him, but he came here for several days. ...
>
> Be healthy and happy! Write us about the road, how you settled down, what is the arrangement with the apartment, work and the rest.
>
> We send you our love, our dear one, many times. Saying to you "See you again" [*do svidaniia*].
> Liza and Anya.[158]

The family had split up. The older generation decided not to decide, that is, its response was to stay at home. In contrast, the younger generation opted

---

158 From Anya Greener, October 26, 1941, YVA: O.75/324, pp. 65–71.

for flight. Of course, the older generation appeared to have a solid reason not to move away: they had not received evacuation permits. But as we know from many other sources, at this time it was possible for people to escape on their own, without a permit. At least, they could try. Instead, the sisters preferred to stay and to wait; they seem to have chosen to succumb to the inevitable. They did not know exactly what would happen, but the letter was full of macabre forebodings: "the most horrible things are yet to come;" "it is hardly possible that we will see each other again," and so forth. At the same time, the older Ginsburgs tried not to fall into despair, indicating that their evacuated relatives might have made a mistake when they moved away: "it is better to die at home." But they were now in panic: dreaming about joining their brother in Alma-Ata, asking him for advice, the sisters did not know what to do.

Let us now examine what was published in the newspaper in the town to which the younger generation of the Ginsburgs had been evacuated, Budennovsk. (They stayed in the town until late December, 1941.) This town was situated some 580 km to the southeast of Rostov-on-Don.

Budennovsk (east of Stavropol) was not taken during the first German occupation of the North Caucasus in the fall of 1941, but it was captured in the summer of 1942, and its entire Jewish population was wiped out during August and September 1942. Yet, in the meantime, life in the town was taking its own course between war and peace. On October 29, 1941, Budennovsk's newspaper *Bolshevistskaia pravda* published a major article, "To Fight Relentlessly against Whisperers and Panic Mongers."[159] As in Rostov-on-Don, the search for the "threat behind the frontline" was also evident in Budennovsk. There is no doubt that such attitudes on the part of the local authorities could have affected the behavior of the evacuated Meerovich and Pinchos families, causing them to reduce their contact with those refugees who might possess information about the Germans, their policies towards the Jews, and the proximity of the German army. They may also have refrained from recording this critical information in letters.

Contemplating the situation from afar, the central Soviet authorities also recognized that the situation was worsening. On October 28, 1941, the Council for Evacuation issued a decree ordering the authorities in the Rostov District (as well as in several districts located in areas other than the North Caucasus) "to direct the evacuated population through Stalingrad to Kazakh and Uzbek SSR."[160] The decree was a clear indication that by that time, the central Soviet

---

159 *Bol'shevistskaia pravda* (Budennovsk), no. 142 (1723), October 29, 1941.
160 Council for Evacuation, Decree no. 14603se, Top secret, October 28, 1941, YVA: JM/24678. Source: GARF: A-259/40/3068.

government no longer considered escape routes that went through the North Caucasus safe enough for the evacuees. And certainly from the Council of Evacuation's standpoint no refugee should have to stay anywhere in the region; they were to be directed to faraway Central Asia. We can hypothesize that if the families of Tamara Meerovich and Tsylya Pinchos had waited a little longer and had been evacuated after the decree of the Council for Evacuation went into effect, they might have found themselves close to Efim Ginsburg in Alma-Ata, and safe.

However, the decree never went into effect in the Rostov District because it was sent back from Rostov-on-Don "due to lack of communication." This is a very important fact indicating that more than three weeks before the actual German occupation of the city, communications between Moscow and Rostov-on-Don were brief at best, and sometimes they failed completely. Leaving aside the acute problem of the chaos reigning in the Soviet Union at that time, this episode points the local administration made increasingly autonomous decisions regarding evacuation in the city and the district during the critical weeks before the German conquest.

In Budennovsk, the situation was also far from safe. This can be seen from another announcement published in the local newspaper, only too reminiscent of what had previously appeared in Rostov-on-Don's *Molot*. On October 29, 1941, the headquarters of the Budennovsk anti-aircraft defense announced rules of behavior during an air raid. German bombardments were now regarded as a real and imminent danger.[161]

On October 29, the *Sonderkommando* 10a (part of the Einsatzgruppe D) destroyed the entire Jewish population, some 1,800 people, of the city of Taganrog in the Rostov District.

The sisters, Anya and Liza, who had remained in Rostov-on-Don, continued to keep their brother updated of the situation, as far as they knew it. On October 30, 1941, they wrote:

> Dear Efim!
> … Most important is that you should be happy and healthy; then you'll be all right. This is already the second letter to you. Now I am repeating that Anya and I stayed in Rostov, while Monya, Tamara and Tsylya as well as our children were evacuated. …
> Just guess what we felt when they went and we stayed [*behind*]. It is difficult to describe it; before we received their first letter, we thought that

---

161 Ibid.

we would go mad. It was said that they would be taken far away, although without any precise details. But they were only brought to Budennovsk (formerly Prikumsk) at the railway siding; if need be, it would be very difficult to get out of there.

Upon their arrival, they wrote that it would be better to die at home. Thanks to the three girls who traveled with them, they were provided with a room that has an earthen floor and may easily go to pieces; eight persons live there together; they are in need of many bare essentials that cannot be procured. In order to heat that hut [*khata*], they need to pay 15–20 rubles a day for wood; it is impossible to procure kerosene; all in all, it is very difficult in every respect. Three of them sleep on one bed without a mattress. They took very little bedding; they didn't even take a feather bed for Anechka, not even a single mattress. Nor did they take any saucepans or buckets, so they have nowhere to cook or to collect water, or many other necessities.

Now, after their letter, our dear one, we (Anya and I) don't know what to do, whether we should stay here or move to them. There is no rescue there, either, and then, where else can we move to? In particular, given our financial resources. So we don't know ourselves what to do and whether we should make up our minds to perish. Maybe, you, our dear one, will give us advice on what to do and how to behave, if we have enough time to get your letter? …

That's all for the time being. We are all dispersed, and God knows when we shall see each other, if at all. It is bitter and hard—what did we come to? And what shall we come to? It is dreadful even to think about it. Take care and be happy. I hope you will get this letter at least.

With love, Anya and Liza.[162]

The sisters were not certain whether Efim received their previous letter, so they thought it necessary to repeat the main points from the previous message, including the evacuation of the younger generation from Rostov-on-Don and their own continued residence in the city. The sisters were not sure whether their decision to stay was the right one. Still, the contents of this letter suggest that those family members who were evacuated to Budennovsk suffered

---

162 From Liza Chazkewitz and Anya Greener to Efim Ginsburg in Alma-Ata (henceforth, all letters are addressed to Efim Ginsburg in Alma-Ata, until stated otherwise). October 30, 1941, YVA: O.75/324, pp. 72–76.

hardships; financially, the situation of the evacuees was far more difficult than the conditions in Rostov-on-Don. Obviously, they had no family connections there. Moreover, they had not been evacuated sufficiently far away. In other words, Anya and Liza Ginsburg assumed that if the Germans could invade Rostov-on-Don, they could also reach Budennovsk—an assumption that proved to be wrong in 1941, but correct in 1942.

At that stage, nowhere in the correspondence is it explicitly mentioned why there was a need to escape from the Germans. The unspoken danger seems to have been clear to all the correspondents, even if they were unaware of what happened in their immediate vicinity, for example, what had occurred in Taganrog the day before, because no word had reached them on the massacre of Jews there. Overall, it appears that staying as well as fleeing looked terrible to both branches of the Ginsburg family.

November 1941

Fierce fighting that had taken place on the Crimean peninsula, close to the North Caucasus, was mentioned by Krasnodar's newspaper, on November 2, 1941.[163] But even this report did not explain how critical the situation of the Soviet troops in the Crimea was, and what the repercussions were for the people in the Caucasus. Moreover, even such meager news was not available to residents of Rostov-on-Don,

The answer to this question was to be found in an article published in *The Washington Post* on November 3, 1941:

> The situation in the Crimea, site of Russia's chief southern naval base and a "short cut" to the Caucasus, admittedly was growing critical. ... Berlin reported ... the capture of Simferopol, the Crimean capital, last night, in a drive apparently for a flank attack on already-menaced Rostov. To the north ..., Berlin claimed the capture of more of the Donets Basin industrial area by troops, which apparently aimed at cutting off southern Russia.[164]

The unstable situation in Rostov-on-Don was made clear in the letter sent by the Ginsburg sisters to Efim on the same day, November 3, 1941:

---

163 TASS special communiqué, *Bol'shevik*, no. 260 (1242), November 2, 1941.
164 "Crimea's situation critical, Reds say," *The Washington Post*, November 3, 1941.

We have already sent you two letters to your new address, but I wonder when you will get them and when we will get your reply. Because every hour of life matters.

I have already written to you that our relatives left for Budennovsk, but we stayed here, because at that moment Volodya could not obtain an evacuation permit [*for us*]. Now it is possible to get the evacuation permit, but it is terrifying to be on the road, so we foresee the end of our lives here. It is very difficult for our people to be there. My only wish is that they will be in good health.[165]

The letter sheds more light on the mood of Anya and Liza Ginsburg during the weeks before the first German occupation of Rostov-on-Don. The sisters admitted that the road eastwards to the Soviet hinterland was open, but they refused to move away. What happened? Why did they decide to stay and surrender to their fate, if they obviously had no illusions about what would await them under the German rule? After all, the sisters have written, "… we foresee the end of our lives here."

Apart from the reasons frequently cited in the Ginsburg's previous letters, such as their poor health, material hardships, and so forth, there was an additional psychological consideration. By early November 1941, the Wehrmacht had not yet lost a single battle in World War II. To many people living in 1941 in Europe, including the Ginsburg sisters, the German army looked invincible. It is hard for us to guess what they felt at that time, but it appears that Anya and Liza Ginsburg expected the Wehrmacht to wear down the Soviet divisions, one after another, and thrust its way eastwards in every sector of the Soviet-German front. Paralyzed by fear, they felt that the German conquest was unstoppable and that trying to escape would only postpone the inevitable.[166] This must be the most important reason why the sisters did not flee Rostov-on-Don in November 1941.

On November 5, 1941, G. Ivanchenko, the Secretary of the Bolshevik Regional Party Committee in Budenovsk, attempted to boost the morale of the town's residents, now including the Meerovich and Pinchos families, with an article published in a local newspaper, "Let Us Give Everything for the

---

165 From Liza Chazkewitz and Anya Greener, November 3, 1941, YVA: O.75/324, p. 81.
166 For example, Oleg Budnitski and Jason Morton, "The Great Patriotic War and Soviet Society: Defeatism, 1941–1942," *Kritika: Explorations in Russian and Eurasian History* 15, no. 4 (Fall 2014): 767–797.

Victory over the Enemy!" The article did not refer, however, to any specific developments on the southern front.[167]

Despite the bravado of their public proclamations, the Soviet authorities in the North Caucasus made some preparations in case the Wehrmacht were to break through to the region. On November 12, 1941, Petr Seleznev, the Secretary of the Krasnodar Territorial Committee of the VKP(b), and Konstantin Timoshenkov, the Head of the NKVD Territorial Administration, issued a joint directive to the Party secretaries of the municipal and regional committees and the local leaders of the NKVD in the Krasnodar territory, ordering them "to prepare clandestinely for destruction the copies of local newspapers and archival material kept at the local organizations in case the territory should be occupied by the enemy."[168] Needless to say, these measures were not made public. Still, these steps certainly indicated that the Soviet authorities had seriously considered the possibility of an impending German occupation of the North Caucasus, including and far beyond the city of Rostov-on-Don, in the fall of 1941.

On November 16, the central Soviet government ordered the Rostov authorities to immediately evacuate 10,000 children from the city to various locations in Siberia. We do not have any information whether or not this decree, which would have affected many of the remaining inhabitants of Rostov-on-Don, was implemented. It seems safe to say that the local authorities were unable to fulfill the decree due to the dangerous proximity of the Wehrmacht. Yet, it shows us how the Soviet evacuation program functioned. When it came to a strategic evacuation, that is, moving large and well-defined population groups, the central government decided when the evacuation would start and where the people would go. The local administration had only some tactical leeway to implement the order.

On November 18, 1941, the Krasnodar newspaper reported on the German advance in the Crimea.[169] This report failed to mention the fact that the Soviets had already lost almost the entire Crimean Peninsula (with the exception of Sevastopol). But even this incomplete information was not made available to the residents of Rostov-on-Don.

On November 18, 1941, Liza and Anya sent what would be their last letter before the German occupation of Rostov-on-Don:

---

167 *Bol'shevistskaia pravda*, no. 145 (1726), November 5, 1941.
168 Fedoseev, "K voprosu o provedenii evakuatsionnykh meropriiatii," 167–168.
169 "Ozhestochennye boi za Krym," *Bol'shevik*, no. 273 (1255), November 18, 1941.

> I am writing to you to tell that we are all alive and in good health. Monya, Tamara, Tsylya, and the children are in Budennovsk. …
>
> We stayed here; now we do not know what to do, whether to go to them and to suffer with them, or to wait for death to come here? We are very anxious about you, our dear one, and you are worried about us even more. We do not know anything about [*what is happening to one*] another, and have received no messages whatsoever; it is really painful. We want everything to pass well and in peace, so that they will be able to return to Rostov, to their home, to us. And not the other way around, that we would have to go to them. They are suffering tremendously there and are deprived of everything. …[170]

The letter was written at a critical moment, only three days before Rostov-on-Don was overrun by the German armies. We do not know what was published in the city's newspaper, since, to the best of our knowledge, none of its November 1941 issues was saved in the archives. However, the letter shows how little information on the actual state of affairs around Rostov-on-Don was available to the Ginsburg sisters. Three days prior to the German occupation, they were still contemplating the possibility of escaping eastwards, a route that was doubtless no longer feasible.

Still, there was something particularly gloomy in the air, which left its imprint on the contents of the letter. The Ginsburg sisters wrote openly about their impending death; they felt it was coming closer, but did not know what to do. The sweeping fear of the Germans that paralyzed Anya and Liza was getting stronger. As they saw it, there was no chance to escape from the advancing Wehrmacht—sooner or later they would conquer everywhere and would catch everyone.

Another letter was sent to Efim Ginsburg on the same day, November 18, 1941. This time, it was from Tamara Meerovich in Budennovsk:

> Upon our arrival here, I sent a postcard to you in Omsk that you did not get, probably due to your transfer to Alma-Ata. …
>
> We left Rostov by train on October 13. We did an unforgivably foolish thing. On October 9, after Mariupol was seized, a terrible panic spread in Rostov; everyone started to run. This mass escape affected the state of mind of the rest and carried them away; most important, the future does not bode well but [*only promises*] horrors. We made several decisions in

---

170 From Liza Chazkewitz and Anya Greener, November 18, 1941, YVA: O.75/324, p. 77.

the course of one day: a few times we [*decided to*] evacuate; at other times we decided that it is better to die on the spot than along the road, in a foreign land. But frequent bombardments and the approach of the frontline unsettled us completely [*vybilo iz kolei*].

With great difficulty, through the District Executive Council [*oblispolkom*] … Volodya managed to procure the evacuation permits for us, but only for five persons. Therefore, only Tsylya, [*my*] mother and I, and the children left. Certainly, it was very difficult for us to part from Aunt Anya and [*Aunt*] Liza, but there was no other solution. In addition, they were inclined to stay there and not to go anywhere. At the same time, Volodya promised to make every effort in case of an extreme emergency to help them move away and get to us. How envious we are of them, that they remained at home and did not experience the hardships of evacuation. Of course, their life is not easy either, but still they are at home, in the warmth, and, most importantly, wherever we are, apparently the same thing awaits all of us. It was promised that we would be taken to Baku, then to Central Asia. But to our great sorrow, it did not happen. During the journey, the destination was changed to Budennovsk, previously Prikumsk. We were very upset over this. First, we haven't moved far away from the frontline. Second, the station of Budennovsk is [*only*] a siding; the railway does not continue any further. Upon our arrival, it was proposed that we go to kolkhozes situated some 50–70–100 km away from Budennovsk, but we decided to stay in the town.

We live with our fellow travelers, two wives of military men, in the room allocated by the Military Commissariat [*voenkomat*]. The living conditions are terrible. There is an earthen floor; it is cold, and there is nothing with which to heat the place. Initially, we endured a lot of hardships; the children fell ill; just imagine how awful it is to live in such conditions. Besides, it is not quiet here; there were air-raid warnings when Min[eralnye] Vody was bombed. So it is not difficult to figure out how we feel. You may call it a "rescue." Many of the evacuees began to move away from here to Makhachkala [*on the Caspian Sea*], and from there by ship further on. But rumors were circulating: that it was impossible to reach Makhachkala; that on the way people were taken off [*the train*] and dispatched to kolkhozes; that an epidemic of typhus broke out in Makhachkala; that people must wait for a month or so in order to board a steamer. It would be insane for us to go on such a journey with children and without a man.

At this time, I was offered work as a bookkeeper in a kindergarten. We decided not to move anywhere, because the conditions may be worse there, and [*because we did not want*] to be housed too far away from our family. I work as a bookkeeper in the kindergarten of the railway station. My salary is 300 rubles, but most importantly, we were provided with a room and firewood. … People experience enormous hardships [*muchaiutsia, literally "undergo tortures"*] regarding fuel; coal cannot be bought at any price. In order to get wood, we need to spend twenty rubles a day. The children attend kindergarten; I work; my mother is in charge of the household, and Tsylya is in charge of "procurements." So, compared to other people, we are really well off; many are envious of us.

But we are very concerned about the current situation, and we are afraid that we'll have to escape from here. If Rostov does not hold fast, then there will be a [*front*] line beyond the Caucasus. Where are they going to evacuate us to, then? Maybe into Central Asia and then, hopefully, it would be possible to meet you. Volodya's letters from October 25 reassured us; he wrote that the enemy was pushed back beyond Taganrog and that there is no need for us to fall into despair, that as soon as the situation improves he will arrive and take us [*away*]. But his last letter, dated November 12, upset us considerably, since he wrote that the enemy was again at the gates of Rostov, which was subjected to almost daily air raids. We are really anxious about them, in particular about Volodya, because he is the one who is particularly exposed to danger, on account of his service in the Extermination Battalion under the NKVD. If the enemy approaches Rostov, they will be deployed near the frontline. This was the case on September 25, and possibly [*this will happen*] also now. It may be that the enemy will be pushed back again, away from Rostov, but it is difficult to believe that it won't happen again [*that the Germans won't reach Rostov again*]. All the time we write home, so, if need be, Aunt Anya and [*Aunt*] Liza could make their way to us, and then all of us could leave, in whatever direction. But generally speaking, the situation is terrible. We do not have strength any more to withstand it.[171]

From now on, Tamara would become an important correspondent, providing us (and Efim Ginsburg) with additional information, supplementing the news that came from Anya and Liza Ginsburg. Tamara's point of view frequently

---

171   From Tamara Meerovich in Budennovsk, November 18, 1941, 82–87.

differed from that of her aunts. She perceived the situation as an evacuee, living in another location. She also had a very different mindset: the Ginsburg sisters were born in the nineteenth century (Anya in 1893 and Liza in 1895), and raised to no small extent in Tsarist Russia. In contrast, Tamara Meerovich was only twenty-eight years old in 1941 and had been brought up mainly during the Soviet period. It is to be expected that Anya and Liza would be more broad-minded in their appraisals, while Tamara would be more influenced by her entirely Soviet upbringing, as she had been raised at a time when the Bolshevik state was most forceful in imparting its values to the new generation of Soviet citizens.[172] We shall soon see whether these assumptions were correct.

It is also suggested that the personal relationship with their correspondent might have had a different effect on the letters written by Anya and Liza, on the one hand, and on those written by Tamara and Tsylya, on the other. The sisters were already adults when Efim was arrested. As a result, they would probably have faced discrimination at their places of work in the 1920s, when Efim was in prison. And even if he was no longer being persecuted in the 1930s, the threatening atmosphere of this period must have had a strong and lasting impact on them.

In contrast, Tamara and Tsylya were still adolescents at the time of Efim's arrest. There is no doubt that they would have had a difficult time at school, but still, this pressure was more bearable than it would have been, had he been imprisoned in the 1930s. Later on, in the 1930s, when Efim was presumably no longer in prison, Tamara and Tsylya might have faced some problems at work on account of his previous record, but overall, it would have been less severe than what Anya and Liza encountered in the 1920s. As a result, Tamara apparently had less fear of censorship. Assuming that the entire family received the same information while they were in Rostov-on-Don, we see that Tamara penned the developments in Rostov-on-Don that led to her family's evacuation, while Liza refrained from putting any of it down on paper. For example, the older generation did not mention how the German seizure of the city of Mariupol influenced the mood of Rostov's population, most specifically within their own family.

Why were the sisters so cautious? The explanation seems to involve several factors: first, fear of the Soviet censors with all that this entailed; second, the

---

172 See, for example, David Brandenberger, *Propaganda State in Crisis: Soviet Ideology, Indoctrination and Terror under Stalin, 1927–1941* (New Haven, CT: Yale University Press, 2011). Cf. David L. Hoffmann, *Cultivating the Masses: Modern State Practices and Soviet Socialism, 1914–1939* (Ithaca, NY: Cornell University Press, 2011).

sisters' desire not to upset their brother too much. Given Efim's prewar background as a "marked individual," they might have been particularly restrained, as they did not want to provoke a sharp reaction from him, which in turn, might have alerted the Soviet censors. To compensate, Liza made up for the lack of factual information with sentiments. Finally, the sisters appeared to indeed be "frozen" by their fear of the Germans.

In contrast, for Tamara Meerovich, these events became the critical point that led to her evacuation, together with some other members of her family. Her account reveals that the situation on the frontlines—or, to be more precise, its perception by the local population—affected the people's mood and their opinions about the need to escape. As noted above, there was no official announcement that the Germans had taken Mariupol; only two short reports mentioning fighting near the city, but somehow the population got wind of this news.

In Budennovsk, Tamara also had to rely on rumors. News communicated through hearsay circulated faster than official pronouncements—and was perhaps more accurate—especially considering the chaotic situation in the North Caucasus in the fall of 1941. However, there was still room for mistakes: Tamara was unintentionally misled by her husband Volodya, who wrote that the enemy had been pushed back beyond Taganrog. This was not true, but apparently this was what Volodya himself had been told.

Tamara's account is also illustrative of how people managed to escape from the beleaguered city of Rostov-on-Don (and apparently from the entire threatened region of the North Caucasus). The role of personal connections proved to be crucial to this enterprise.[173] For Tamara's family, particularly important were the connections of her husband Volodya in the local administration, without which the family could not have obtained the desired evacuation permits. Likewise, were it not for the connections that Tamara succeeded in making on the journey to Budennovsk with some wives of the Red Army commanders, another sizable subgroup of the Soviet population, who, along with Jews and various Soviet functionaries, fled en masse before the advancing German armies, she would not have obtained even a modest accommodation. Tamara's letter also clarifies why Liza and Anya Ginsburg remained in Rostov-on-Don: not only was it difficult to get permits for them, but the sisters themselves were inclined to stay.

The letter also shows the extent of the chaos that reigned in the North Caucasus at that time, with respect to evacuation. The evacuees were not moved

---

173 The point is reiterated in Shternshis, "Between Life and Death," 499–504.

far enough away from the frontlines. No financial support, food, or workplaces were provided, so the evacuees had to provide for themselves on the journey and in their temporary accommodation. In addition, the evacuees did not comply with the government regulations that had them settle in specific places. Instead, they often attempted to get closer to rescue routes. This last point is particularly meaningful: their willingness to violate Soviet rules indicates that for some of these evacuated Jews, the Nazis seemed more dangerous than non-compliance with Soviet orders, which, because of the chaotic wartime situation, could not be enforced. However, since the breakdown of the Soviet power happened suddenly, not everyone realized how weak the regime had become.

Overall, Tamara viewed her evacuation, at least at this stage, as "an unforgivably foolish thing," that is, as a very bad mistake. She had weighed up the considerations in favor of evacuation (escaping from the German air strikes, or against evacuation (the problem of attaining comfortable living conditions, heating and food). The dimensions of the German threat to her Jewish family obviously remained unclear to Tamara, as this factor was not included in her balance sheet. Possibly, Tamara's statement was predicated on the assumption that the evacuated branch of the family would be no safer in Budennovsk than in Rostov-on-Don. And yet, in my opinion, Tamara's letter is not completely pessimistic until the last two sentences. Rather, she deplores having been influenced by collective hysteria, and, as a result, having left her home city for a far worse location in terms of *living standards*.

In contrast to her aunts, who were too prone to believe the Soviet assurances, the young Tamara Meerovich demonstrated a clear-headed ability to judge the situation at the front and assess it in relation to her prospects for evacuation. We can imagine that, in family discussions centering on the dilemma of whether to leave their home city or not, she was the most serious and down-to-earth participant. Whether Tamara succeeded in convincing her overcautious opponents (especially Anya and Liza), we shall see from the following letters.

Volodya Meerovich's enlistment in the Extermination Battalion was also mentioned in Tamara's letter. Extermination Battalions were set up in accordance with the decision of the Politburo of the Central Committee of the VKP(b) from June 24, 1941: "On the actions to combat saboteurs and parachutists." The members of these paramilitary units—who continued to work at their place of employment—were recruited from the most politically reliable elements and served to protect strategic facilities, such as plants and bridges. When the German armies approached, the Soviet military command often used the Extermination Battalions to supplement the army. Altogether, 186,000 people were drafted into Extermination Battalions in Russia alone. Volodya was the second member of the Ginsburg clan to be conscripted into the Red Army, or, to be more precise, into a paramilitary auxiliary unit. Unlike David, the first member of the family who joined the army, Volodya's enlistment seems to have more aptly reflected the fighting spirit of the family. Tamara clearly took pride in the military actions of her husband, although it was obvious that in her family he would be the only one to serve in the military. Tamara did not consider joining up, despite the fact that women did fight in the Soviet army. Her role was first and foremost that of mother, wife, and daughter.

On November 21, 1941, the Nazi German army captured the city of Rostov-on-Don, putting Anya and Liza, as well as all the other Jewish residents, in mortal danger. This catastrophic event was not reported in a timely fashion in the Soviet media. In order to get an idea of the strategic situation in Southern Russia in 1941, at the time of the maximum German penetration into this sector of the front, a contemporary reader would have been obliged to consult the foreign press. An article in *The Washington Post* dated November 24, 1941 explained:

> The Russians have suffered many blows in the five months that have elapsed since the beginning of the German attack, but none of greater potential menace than the fall of Rostov, whose capture the German High Command announced Saturday. Forty miles from the mouth of the Don, Rostov is the gateway by rail and road to the Caucasus and Iran. With both Rostov and Kerch in their possession, the Nazis are now in a position to launch a drive on towards Europe's richest oil fields. … The stiff resistance offered by the Russians and the casualties they inflicted on the invaders do not alter the fact that, in losing Rostov, they have lost a point of major strategic importance.[174]

Indeed, the seizure of Rostov-on-Don was of paramount importance for the planned German invasion of the Caucasus. The Wehrmacht was probably not in a position to advance further eastwards in the southern sector during the winter of 1941–1942. Had the Germans been in possession of Rostov-on-Don at the beginning of their summer offensive in 1942, it would have taken them much less time to reach the Caucasian mountains, as compared to what actually

---

174 "Fall of Rostov," *The Washington Post*, November 24, 1941.

occurred.[175] The Wehrmacht would have been in a considerably more favorable position to achieve its strategic goal for the 1942 campaign: the capture of the entire Caucasus. As for the Ginsburg family, we can say with certainty that Anya and Liza Ginsburg would have had little chance of surviving a lengthy German occupation of Rostov-on-Don, which almost certainly would have resulted in the annihilation of the city's Jewish population.

> ### The First Occupation of Rostov-on-Don and Its Impact on the Rostov Jews
>
> Within two days, November 21 and 22, 1941, the Wehrmacht (the First Tank Army under *Generaloberst* Ewald von Kleist) attacked and captured the city of Rostov-on-Don. The first German occupation of the city only lasted one week, and therefore, it was not well documented. Nevertheless, it is evident that the city's Jews were immediately required to register, and, according to some sources, to wear badges bearing six-pointed stars, attached to their outer clothing. On November 22, the German authorities (army or *Sonderkommando* 10a deployed in the city)[176] ordered the establishment of a Jewish Council. Failure to comply with these orders was made punishable by death.[177]
>
> However, it appears that these orders were largely ignored by the Rostov Jews, because they, like the rest of the population, had spent that week in underground shelters. The city was heavily shelled by Soviet artillery poised very close to Rostov-on-Don. As a result, the German troops, including those in *Sonderkommando* 10a, refrained from patrolling the city and enforcing their orders. During that week, the Germans "only" had time to kill several dozen Jews and non-Jews in Rostov-on-Don.[178]
>
> There is one well-substantiated report about German reprisals against the local population. In this incident, witnessed by many inhabitants of the city, the Germans set fire to a house near the place where a Wehrmacht officer had been killed, and then shot all the residents of the house, regardless of their

---

175 Alexander Statiev, *At War's Summit: The Red Army and the Struggle for the Caucasus Mountains in World War II* (Cambridge: Cambridge University Press, 2018).
176 YVA: O.51/165 II.
177 Movshovich, "Rostov-na-Donu," 867. Cf. Krut, *Povest' o podarennoi zhizni*, 10. Cf. Testimony of M. Vdovin in Smirnov, *Rostov pod sen'iu svastiki*, 60.
178 Angrick, *Besatzungspolitik und Massenmord*, 357. Cf. GARO: 32/11302/30, pp. 134, 139, in Tatyana Blumenfeld, *The Holocaust in the Southern Part of Russia*, PhD diss., Haifa, Haifa University, 2014, 119–120. There is a report that on the very first day of the occupation, Soviet prisoners of war marked with numbers on their uniforms were marched through the main streets of the city, guarded by German soldiers shouting "Jude." GARO: 32/11302/30, p. 139, in ibid., 119–120.

nationality.[179] The total number of victims that week among the civilians and prisoners of war, including Jews, seems to have been slightly more than a hundred. Fearful of encirclement by the Soviet army, the Wehrmacht pulled out of Rostov-on-Don on November 28, 1941.

The German policy towards the Jews during the week of occupation conveyed an ambiguous message to the local Jews. On the one hand, the Germans only killed a small percentage of Rostov's Jews at that time and the extent of their murderous intentions were not made clear to the remaining Jews. On the other hand, the German administration in the occupied city carried out an "iron fist" policy towards all Rostov inhabitants, irrespective of their ethnic origin, and many dozens were summarily executed. To this, we should add the very meaningful fact that the Red Army had been able to recapture Rostov-on-Don within a very short period, which testified, as many local Jews assumed, to its willingness and ability to hold on to the city at any cost.

As a result, after the first German occupation many Rostov Jews (as well as other North Caucasian Jews) remained confused about what to do.[180] Everyone shared the view that the Germans discriminated against Jews and persecuted them. However, this was interpreted differently by various groups. Some of Rostov's Jewish survivors, very frightened by the German occupation, decided to flee eastwards at any cost, regardless of the difficulties and dangers involved. However, others, such as the Ginsburg sisters, concluded that the Germans would limit themselves to discriminating against the Jews, and so there was no need for them to leave Rostov-on-Don, suffer from privations along the road, and risk losing their accommodation in their home city. Among this group were those who had previously left Rostov-on-Don (like Tamara and Tsylya), but later chose to return to the city.[181] The third group opted for a short-term solution, assuming that the city was indeed threatened, but that the German drive would soon spend itself. They moved out to the east of Rostov-on-Don but stayed not too far away from the city, in the familiar North Caucasus surroundings.[182] This sums up the saga of decision and indecision in the Ginsburg family.

---

179 Testimony of Klara Shcheglova, b. 1931, September 6, 1997, YVA: O.93/35826. Cf. Krut, *Povest' o podarennoi zhizni*, 10. Cf. Testimony of V. Varivoda in Smirnov, *Rostov pod sen'iu svastiki*, 63.
180 Testimony of Kalnitskaya, ICJ: TC 2759. Cf. Testimony of Mandelblat, YVA: VT/1911.
181 Solomon Shvarts, *Evrei v Sovetskom Soiuze s nachala Vtoroi Mirovoi voiny (1939–1965)* (New York: American Jewish Working Committee, 1966), 58. Cf. Report of Evenson, YVA: P.21.2/1.
182 Shvarts, *Evrei v Sovetskom Soiuze*, 58. Cf. Report of Evenson, YVA: P.21.2/1.

Although the Soviet media often failed to report Soviet losses, when the tides of war began to turn, this news was immediately reported by the Budennovsk newspaper, to which Tamara Meerovich and her family had access in the evacuation. On November 26, 1941, a local newspaper reported on a successful Soviet counter-offensive "to the west of Rostov."[183]

The Red Army was able to recapture Rostov-on-Don from the Germans on November 28. The event made a strong impression on a number of Jews from Rostov-on-Don, who had previously fled the city. Enthusiastic over the Soviet victory, they immediately returned to the city. After the War, a Jewish witness recalled the story of her uncle, who had been evacuated from Rostov-on-Don to Stalinabad in Central Asia: "On November 29, 1941, when Soviet troops recaptured Rostov, my uncle decided to return to Rostov. He could not be persuaded [*not to rush back*] and left with his wife and children."[184] This enthusiasm was not shared by everyone, but is indicative of the sense of euphoria that swept over some Jews in the region. It would prove a dangerous emotion.

On November 30, Rostov's Municipal Committee of Defense, which had just returned to Rostov-on-Don, called upon local civilians to return to work on December 2[185] and "to keep up the revolutionary order, to help the Red Army and the authorities to catch and destroy fascist agents."[186] This announcement was the first indication to the local populace that the stability in the city was restored, and also the first official suggestion that there were collaborators in Rostov-on-Don.

Around November 30, slightly more than one day after the liberation of the city, the command of the Red Army published an account, "On the German Atrocities in Rostov."[187] The report also provided relatively complete details about the German abuse of the local population. One case of mass murder of civilians (some two hundred people were shot in the Armenian cemetery) was highlighted, but, same as previous articles, this report did not mention that the Jews were singled out for persecution.

The fact that such a report was published so soon after the return of Soviet rule in the city, suggests several things. First, the Soviets relied on a preexisting,

---

183 "Udar po chastiam vraga," *Bol'shevistskaia pravda*, no. 154 (1736), November 26, 1941.
184 The story of her uncle Boris Naumovich Shagin, his wife Maria, and their three little daughters. Testimony of Anna Shagina-Blokh, b. 1919, April 1965, YVA: O.3/3146, pp. 1–4.
185 TsDNIRO: 3/2/2, p. 204. In Zelenskaia, *Kul'turno-prosvetitel'nye uchrezhdeniia*, 75.
186 Partiinyi arkhiv Rostovskoi oblasti (henceforth PARO): 3/2/2, p. 204. In Rezvanov, *Na zashchite Rodiny*, 98–99.
187 Not earlier then November 30, 1941. PARO: 3/1/5, p. 14. In Rezvanov, *Na zashchite Rodiny*, 99–101.

well-developed network of agents and/or sympathizers, who remained in the city after it was conquered, to gather intelligence and set up a nucleus of resistance under German rule. Second, the quality of the Soviet report was very dubious, since it was impossible to conduct a thorough investigation only one day after recapturing the area. Unless the details in the report were revised later, the findings cast doubt on the credibility of the entire Soviet investigation of the German occupation of the city. Third, the Soviets were interested in documenting the results of the German occupation as early as November 1941, almost a year and a half before the establishment in March 1943 of the Extraordinary State Commission, whose purpose was to investigate Nazi atrocities.[188]

December 1941

The German retreat from Rostov-on-Don was the first German withdrawal during the Second World War, and, therefore, widely covered by the foreign media. This is what *The New York Times* wrote about the retreat, in an article published on December 2, 1941:

> Hordes of Russians are blocking the German path to the Caucasus at Rostov and in attacks of extreme recklessness are striking blow upon blow in a mighty effort to reach Taganrog [*held by the Germans until August 1943*], the German military spokesman admitted yesterday. … The withdrawal from Rostov, it was said, was carried out in good order, because of the Russians' great superiority in numbers and "the abandon with which they were used," which made it "expedient" to retire to more favorable positions to meet the onslaught. Nothing further was said of reprisals against Rostov for civilian fighting, which was given at first as the reason for the German retirement.[189]

The Germans used the reports on civilian fighting in Rostov-on-Don to justify their abuse of the city's civilian population.

The Red Army regained control of the city but failed to push the frontline more than fifty kilometers away from Rostov-on-Don. The city was still

---

188 On this Commission see, for example, Marina Sorokina, "People and Procedures. Toward a History of the Investigation of Nazi Crimes in the USSR," *Kritika: Explorations in Russian and Eurasian History* 6, no. 4 (2005): 797–831. Cf. Kiril Feferman, "Soviet Investigation of Nazi Crimes in the USSR: Documenting the Holocaust," *Journal of Genocide Research* 5, no. 4 (2003): 587–602.

189 "Berlin concedes Rostov retreat," *The New York Times*, December 2, 1941.

under siege, and the Soviets had trouble keeping the population inside it. Their approach combined limitations on leaving Rostov-on-Don[190] (issued, in all probability, in early December) and propaganda aimed at portraying the city as a safe and stable locale.

Consequently, the Soviet victory at Rostov-on-Don came to occupy a central place in the Soviet media coverage of the War during this period. The celebration of the recapture of Rostov-on-Don was particularly emphasized in newspapers published in southern Russia, until the next Soviet victory, the battle for Moscow itself, eventually overshadowed the triumph at Rostov-on-Don. For instance, on December 2, 1941, a Krasnodar newspaper reported extensively on the Soviet recapture of Rostov-on-Don.[191] On the very same day, the country's second most important newspaper, *Izvestiya*, published a report, "In Liberated Rostov," which emphasized the cruelty of the German occupation of Rostov-on-Don and the Nazi policies towards the city's Jews:

> As elsewhere, Jews received the Germans' special attention. They were subjected to particular humiliation and insults. They were permitted to walk in the streets only from 6 am to 2 pm (all other civilians from sunrise to sunset). The experience gained by the Fascist Black Hundred[192] men was fully used by them here. First, they ordered Jews to knit green stars on their sleeves and to paint such stars on the doors of their apartments. By branding and marking Jews, the Germans made it easier for them to perform their dirty work. Then, they declared a general registration of all Jews living in Rostov. Mass murders in Kiev and Odessa had also begun with mass registration. Fascist pogromists planned the destruction of tens of thousands of people in Rostov. Fortunately, they did not have time [*ne uspeli*] to carry it out].[193]

This frank description of specifically Jewish suffering during the War indicated that new winds were blowing from Moscow regarding policies of presenting the Jewish tragedy. The tone for this change was set by Joseph Stalin in his speech at the twenty-fourth anniversary of the October Revolution on

---

190 Movshovich, *Ocherki istorii evreev na Donu*, 127.
191 "Kak byl vziat Rostov," *Bol'shevik*, no. 285 (1267), December 2, 1941.
192 The name "Black Hundreds" quickly became synonymous with the extreme anti-Semitic right.
193 Ezra Vilenski, "V osvobozhdennom Rostove," *Izvestiia*, no. 284 (7660), December 2, 1941. Cf. Berkhoff, *Motherland in Danger*, 125–126.

November 6, 1941. At that time, the Soviet leader explicitly alluded to "medieval Jewish pogroms" perpetrated by the Germans in the USSR.[194]

And yet, even this article framed Nazi anti-Jewish policies rather as a propaganda motive than as objective reporting. The article's central claims were predicated on a conjecture (apparently accurate, but still, only a conjecture). As mentioned previously, it is still an open question whether Rostov's Jews were particularly targeted for physical assault within the one short week of the German occupation and domination of Rostov-on-Don. There is almost no evidence corroborating the assertion that Jews and their dwellings were marked during this period.

Another article published in the same issue of *Izvestiya* admitted that the Germans had only been pushed back fifty kilometers from Rostov-on-Don.[195] This meant that the Germans remained dangerously close to the city. Local people, including the Ginsburgs, would have heard the sounds of artillery—a fact that no propaganda could conceal—and must have lived in constant fear of the Germans returning.

Izvestiya was one of the few Soviet newspapers delivered to every part of the country, even if not always in a timely fashion, due to logistical problems. From its articles, the evacuated branch of the family (Tamara Meerovich, Tsylya Pinchos, and their families), as well as Efim Ginsburg, could have learned of the Nazi oppression of the city's Jews and the current situation in Rostov-on-Don as early as the first week of December, 1941. The news was ambiguous: it was a source of both terrible anxiety (as special measures against the Jews were mentioned) and of hope (as mass killings of Jews had not taken place). For the evacuated Ginsburgs, this information would certainly not have sufficed to work out what had happened to their Rostov relatives.

Let us return now to the information that nurtured the perceptions of Anya and Liza Ginsburg in the city of Rostov-on-Don. The local newspaper *Molot* had just resumed publication in early December. It was an important—probably the most important—source of information for this branch of the family. On December 3, 1941, *Molot* reprinted on its front page an encouraging note about the advance of the Red Army on the southern front near Rostov-on-Don, information which had appeared in *Pravda* on the previous day:

---

194 Iosif Stalin, *O Velikoi Otechestvennoi Voine Sovetskogo Soyuza*, 5th edition (Moscow: Gosudarstvennoe izdatel'stvo politicheskoi literatury, 1950), 50–52.
195 E. Borskii, "Nemtsy otbrosheny na 50 km ot Rostova," *Izvestiia*, no. 284 (7660), December 2, 1941.

> Upon ousting the German occupiers from Rostov-on-Don, this morning the warriors from General Kharitonov's and General Remezov's units continued to pursue the retreating enemy. ... By 10 a.m., Comrade Kharitonov's units threw the enemy out of localities B. and K.[196]

The importance of this Soviet victory and of the recapture of Rostov-on-Don was also emphasized in foreign media reports. On the same day, *Molot* cited extensively, again on its front page, reports from the United Kingdom newspapers such as *The Daily Mail, The Manchester Guardian, The Liverpool Daily Post, Reuters,* and *The Times,* United States media such as *The New York Times and New York Herald Tribune,* and radio broadcasts.[197] However, the articles did not refer to the names of specific localities captured by the Red Army, so the Ginsburgs would not have been able to obtain authentic information on the extent of the Soviet offensive in the region. The lack of such pertinent information was camouflaged by the newspaper's stress on the magnitude of the Soviet victory at Rostov-on-Don. The question was, how long could the Red Army use the momentum it had gained after its seizure of Rostov-on-Don, and could the Soviets translate that momentum into other gains on the ground?

In its ongoing efforts to bolster the fighting spirit of its citizens, Soviet propaganda also made a special effort to draw the attention of the local public to the suffering of civilians and captured Red Army soldiers under German rule in occupied Rostov-on-Don. On December 4, 1941, *Molot* published an important letter purportedly written by the inhabitants of Rostov-on-Don, "We Will Never Forget." The letter, which described in details the German atrocities against Rostov's civilians, was signed by the "inhabitants of liberated Rostov" and addressed to the "soldiers, commanders, and political workers of the Ninth and Fifty-Eighth Armies," active in the Southern sector.[198]

The rationale behind such messages was clear. They aroused feelings of vengefulness in civilians and soldiers and helped to boost their fighting spirit. Despite the ghastly details, the excessive emphasis that the suffering was in the past may have misled the Ginsburgs, along with other Rostov Jews, into ignoring the dangers that threatened them at that time. It is also noteworthy

---

196 "Nashi voiska presleduiut otstupaiushchego vraga," *Pravda,* December 2, 1941. Reprinted in *Molot,* no. 285 (6163), December 3, 1941.
197 "Inostrannaia pechat' o pobede Krasnoi Armii na Iuge," *Molot,* no. 285 (6163), December 3, 1941.
198 A. Shevchenko, A. Sirota, I. Burechko, G. Dulov, N. Galin, V. Prut, A. Gamenian, G. Lomonosov, et al., *Molot,* no. 286 (6164), December 4, 1941.

that, in the traditional Soviet policy framed the German persecution of Jews as part of their hatred for all Soviet people. As a result, *Molot*'s these messages did not stress that the Germans singled out the Jews for abuse. Moreover, it could not be claimed with certainty that there was a particularly brutal persecution of Jews during the first German occupation of Rostov-on-Don in November 1941, which further obscured this issue.

On the same page, *Molot* printed another encouraging announcement about the Soviet advance in the south: "The Troops of the Southern Front Continue to Pursue the Enemy." Quoting a December 3 *Pravda* article, the Rostov newspaper declared that the Germans fled in panic, abandoning their tanks and canons.[199] The triumphal spirit of the publication, which was part of a well-orchestrated propaganda campaign, was bound to affect the mood not only of the Ginsburg sisters but of all the family members in various parts of the country, and to convince them that the Soviet advance in the region was gaining momentum and would avert the danger of a new German occupation of Rostov-on-Don.

It is from this perspective that we should view another article boasting of the Soviet victory at Rostov-on-Don. On December 5, *Izvestiya* published another survey of the foreign press to sum up the Battle of Rostov-on-Don. The article quoted, albeit not verbatim, *The New York Times*, the Associated Press, the *Daily News*, *The Washington Post*, and a Turkish newspaper, *Ulus*. A report by *The New York Times* was highlighted: "Nazis hounded near Rostov. Russian assault is mounting. Anticipating the destruction of the Germans at the southern trap near Taganrog."[200]

On December 7, *Molot* published an editorial, "Let's Clean Out the Germans from Rostov":

> Our troops have seized Matveev-Kurgan [*situated on the eastern coast of the Mius River, 94 km to the west of Rostov-on-Don*]. A fierce battle is being waged on the outskirts of Taganrog. It won't take long before the hordes of German fascists will be entirely ejected outside of the bounds of our district… The streets and squares of the city are flooded with the blood of absolutely innocent women, old men, children. …[201]

---

199 Ibid.
200 "Inostrannaia pechat' o bor'be na Vostochnom fronte," *Izvestiia*, no. 288 (7664), December 6, 1941.
201 *Molot*, no. 289 (6167), December 7, 1941.

This article differed significantly from what we have previously read. First, it gave the name of a specific locality captured by the Soviet troops, so that the readers could work out how far away the Wehrmacht had been driven back from Rostov-on-Don. Moreover, the article also claimed that the Red Army was fighting on the outskirts of Taganrog, the second most important city in the Rostov district.[202] This "news" (or rather propaganda) was a cause for optimism, bound to boost the morale of Rostov's inhabitants. Also of interest is the type of local patriotism around which local people were expected to rally: Rostov's citizens were called upon to believe in the coming liberation of their district. This message showed that the government in Moscow was certain of the victory in the Soviet South, and even in the War as a whole, at this stage already.

On the same day, the Rostov newspaper published an announcement by the Army Command, the District Party Committee, and the District Executive Committee of the Workers' Soviets, that is, all the major Soviet authorities in the region at that time. Rostov's inhabitants were called upon:

1. To strictly observe order and Soviet discipline.
2. To expose fascist henchmen and hangers-on (*prikhvostni*), people who proved to be traitors of the Fatherland, robbers and marauders, and to hand them over to the Soviet authorities.
3. To take a most active part in the restoration of the economy destroyed by the fascists.
4. To be engaged in the most active way in the defensive work around Rostov performed at the direction of Army leaders, because an insidious enemy may again encroach on our city.[203]

These seemingly strong messages reflected both confidence and uncertainty. Emphasizing the Soviet resolve to resume normal economic life and to prosecute collaborators, the Rostov media aimed to persuade their citizens that the Soviets were determined to secure their control over the city at any cost. At the same time, the emphasis on defensive work being carried out around the

---

202 I was unable to validate the claim that the Red Army was indeed poised on the outskirts of Taganrog at that time. At most, I could find a sentence that the "Red Army opened its offensive in the general direction of … —Taganrog" (Boog et al., *Germany and the Second World War*, vol. 4, 885). So it follows that Taganrog was the direction in which the Russian army wanted to advance in the long term, but in early December 1941, it remained an unattainable goal.
203 *Molot*, no. 289 (6167), December 7, 1941.

city highlighted Rostov's continued vulnerability in the face of another possible German assault.

Several front-page articles published in *Molot* on the same day emphasized the firm Soviet hold on Rostov-on-Don and the magnitude of the Soviet victory. Such were the editorial, "To Swiftly Do Away with the Consequences of the Germans Lording It [*khoziainichaia*] over Rostov." Another article, entitled "American Press on the Seizure of Rostov by the Red Army," referred to publications in *The Baltimore Sun*, the Associated Press, and *The New York Sun*, as well as radio broadcasts. Finally, a short news update on the situation in the southern sector of the War, "The Advance of Our Units on the Southern Front Proceeds Successfully," mentioned the Soviet retaking of village D. The piece continued: "The Germans hastily build trenches on the western bank of the Mius River. … Our forces are engaged in fighting on the outskirts of Taganrog.[204]

The article on the second page, "First Days in the Liberated City," returned to the issue of Germans shooting civilians in Rostov-on-Don.[205] The continuous stress placed by the Soviet propaganda on this episode, apparently the only case of a German atrocity against civilians in Rostov-on-Don that could be documented, made a strong impression on the readers. The emphasis on reporting this murder created the effect of suggesting that a large-scale German abuse of civilians had taken place in the occupied city.

Of particular importance for understanding what occurred in Rostov-on-Don, not only after its liberation but also during the German occupation, is a long article entitled "Traitor," published on the second page in the section, "In the Military Tribunal":

> Usharov A. P., an inhabitant of Rostov, was hostile towards Soviet rule, but concealed his real disposition under the guise of a loyal citizen. On November 23, 1941, when Rostov was temporarily occupied by the German fascist occupiers, Usharov went to citizen Kolesnikova's apartment and in the company of his acquaintances began to lash out at Soviet organizations. Citizen Mizyaev, who was staying here, stopped the insolent fellow short. "I'll show you, I will bring Germans and they will do away with you!" Usharov cried, and ran out in order to bring some Germans. Mizyaev was able to exploit his short absence and leave the building. Several minutes after his departure, German officers broke into Kolesnikova's apartment and threatening with

---

204 Ibid.
205 I. Krivenok, ibid.

weapons started to demand that those present turn the Soviet supporter over to them. Komsomol members Kolesnikova and Tanya Stromus bravely stated to the German occupiers that they were unaware of Mizyaev's whereabouts. The fascists immediately shot Komsomol member Stromus. The Military Tribunal … that examined the traitor Usharov's file condemned him to execution and confiscation of his property. The verdict was carried out.[206]

To begin with, this was probably the first time that the Rostov newspaper presented a lively and personalized story instead of a major tragedy with a considerable number of nameless victims. This specificity gave more plausibility to the account. However, a careful reader could also see things hidden between the lines. The Germans questioned two Komsomol members; both of them gave misleading answers that apparently angered the Germans; but only one was shot. Why? The answer most probably is that, as her name indicates, she was Jewish. If so, this fact, apparently, was no secret to Usharov, who must have informed the Germans. The Germans killed Stromus on the spot, sparing Kolesnikova, even though both girls were affiliated with the Komsomol, the Bolshevik youth organization. Komsomol membership was never an asset in German-occupied territories, but not as dangerous as being Jewish. This episode—of course, if we accept that it really happened as described in the article—shows what it meant to be a Jew facing the Germans in Rostov-on-Don in this crucial week of November 1941. Rostov's Jews could interpret this report as a warning against their staying any longer in the city. If the Germans retook Rostov, it would mean mortal danger for the Jews.

On December 8, *Molot* published a lengthy report of German atrocities against Rostov's civilian population. The article "Fascist Beast" mentioned that the "German occupiers killed several thousands of Rostov's inhabitants, men, women, children."[207] This article provided a highly inflated estimate of the death toll among Rostov's inhabitants. Over time, the Soviets quietly stopped referring to these numbers. Furthermore, it is not clear from the report under what circumstances, or rather, under which pretext the Germans allegedly killed the civilians. For a cautious reader, this could sound like another Soviet propaganda spin.[208] However, it is likely that, since they had no other sources of information,

---

206 Ibid.
207 M. Shtatskii, *Molot*, no. 290 (6168), December 8, 1941.
208 The reference to "several thousands" of Rostov's inhabitants killed, without details, this was understood as another propaganda gimmick. In contrast, the mention of the death of "three hundred," if accompanied by exact details, was likely perceived as a real event, and therefore would resonate with the Jews much more powerfully.

the inhabitants of Rostov-on-Don who had stayed in the city during the German occupation would have believed such news. But what conclusions could they draw? Reports of the indiscriminate murder of civilians, regardless of nationality and apparently for no reason, further confused the issue for the Rostov's Jews.

On December 9, *Molot* informed its readers in a short note that on the last day of the German occupation, three hundred Jews were shot in one of the city's neighborhoods, Nakhichevan.[209] This information provided specific details, so, coupled with other disturbing news about the Germans' persecution of Jews, it must have had a strong impact on Rostov's Jewish inhabitants, impelling them to leave the city as soon as possible.

On December 9, *Izvestiya* published another article about Rostov-on-Don. Alongside a detailed depiction of the murder of local civilians during the German occupation, the newspaper described the fate of German collaborators: "City dwellers help police seize provocateurs and traitors. They are tried in open trials and death verdicts are applauded."[210]

The news of the murder of civilians might have confused those members of the Ginsburg family who were not living in Rostov-on-Don. It was not clear from the article on what grounds the civilians were killed and whether this operation was directed specifically against Jews. Regarding the fate of collaborators, the article conveyed a message of renewed stability and confidence under Soviet rule. However, in common with other Soviet publications of this kind, the newspaper did not make clear how widespread was the collaboration with the Germans.

Despite reassuring messages that the Red Army would prevent any further German assault on Rostov-on-Don, the Soviet authorities also took care to set up additional loyal local forces that would strengthen the city's defenses. On December 9, the Bureau of the Rostov District Committee of the VKP(b) issued an order "On the formation of workers' battalions." In all eight neighborhoods in the city a workers' battalion would be set up, which would include:

a) Communists [*party members*] living in the given neighborhood headed by the neighborhood's Party Committee. [*There were 4,624 Communist party members in Rostov-on-Don as of January 1, 1942.*]
b) Komsomol members headed by their neighborhood's Komsomol committee. [*There were 5,248 Komsomol members in Rostov-on-Don as of January 1, 1942.*]

---

209   *Molot*, no. 291 (6169), December 9, 1941.
210   P. Nikitin, "Na ulitsakh Rostova," *Izvestiia*, no. 290 (7666), December 9, 1941.

c) Elements loyal to Soviet power in the midst of non-affiliated workers and employees.

   The battalions will number 500 people each. ... From December 11, these units will begin their training, first of all in the tactics of street fighting.[211]

This important order was, however, not made public. The inhabitants of Rostov-on-Don could not know that the authorities did not believe in successfully defending the city. However, the content of another decree issued on the same day could not be concealed, because its implementation was widely visible and because it applied to many people. Presumably, had Volodya Meerovich stayed in the city, the decree would have affected him, too.

On December 9, the Bureau of the Rostov District Committee of the VKP(b) ordered the enlistment of citizens of Rostov-on-Don over the age of sixteen for the construction of defensive lines inside and outside the city.[212] Such clearly visible steps might have been interpreted by the inhabitants of Rostov-on-Don as a sign of Soviet doubt about thwarting another German offensive on Rostov-on-Don.

On December 9, 1941, *Molot* continued covering various aspects of the short-lived German occupation of Rostov-on-Don and the recent Soviet recapture of the city. A note published on the front page described the Soviet victory through the eyes of the foreign media, this time referring to articles published mainly in newspapers from the neutral Turkey: *Vakyt*, *Eli Sabah*, and *Vatan*, and to broadcasts by Radio London.[213] V. Vatin's article "Murderers" appeared on the second page, revealing another mass execution of Soviet civilians, during which more than a hundred local residents were rounded up and shot near an Armenian cemetery.[214] Taken together, the articles continued two basic Soviet propaganda messages: the magnitude of the Soviet victory and the suffering of local people under German rule.

Molot did not limit itself to simply depicting the macabre consequences of the German occupation of Rostov-on-Don. The entire front page of its December 10 issue appeared under the large headline "Blood for Blood, Death for Death!," reminiscent of the well-known biblical commandment, "An Eye for an

---

211 PARO: 9/1/318, p. 154. In Rezvanov, *Na zashchite Rodiny*, 101.
212 PARO: 9/1/318, p. 153. In Rezvanov, *Na zashchite Rodiny*, 101.
213 "Inostrannaia pechat' o bor'be na vostochnom fronte," *Molot*, no. 291 (6169), December 9, 1941.
214 Ibid.

Eye." The editorial article, entitled "Atrocities of the German Occupiers," was reprinted from *Pravda*'s editorial (December 8). Referring to the murder of Jews at Babi Yar, it read:

> Without taking heed of age or gender, Hitler's hangmen machine gunned thousands of civilians, Russians, Ukrainians, Jews. 52,000 people were annihilated in Kiev. ... Terrible atrocities were committed by the Germans in Rostov.[215]

Thus, the Rostov Jews, together with the other inhabitants of Rostov-on-Don, may have learned that Jews were targeted by the Germans. Yet, they could not infer from this terse item of information, a typical propaganda understatement, how comprehensive the Nazi program was, and that its goal was total annihilation. Soviet propaganda almost never mentioned that other groups, such as Gypsies, homosexuals, and developmentally or physically disabled people, were targeted, possibly because the Soviets were unaware of this fact. Moreover, in the occupied Soviet territories, the Nazi persecution of these three groups was never as comprehensive as the murder of Jews.

On December 10, Soviet propaganda cited the foreign media again, to emphasize the scale of the victory in the south. This time, *Molot* referred to the American media: *The Nation* and *New Republic* magazines, and a newspaper, *The Philadelphia Bulletin*.[216] Once more, an article published on the second page dealt with the German occupation of Rostov-on-Don, emphasizing the suffering of the populace, in order to rally its inhabitants around the Soviet regime in the city. The article covered the funerals of the victims of the occupation and made reference to German plunder of local people's property.[217]

Then came the first letter written by the Ginsburg sisters after the liberation of Rostov-on-Don. On December 10, 1941, they wrote to Efim:

> We are still alive and in good health, but as for the future, it is difficult to say what awaits us. We endured a lot; God grant you never know [*ne dai Bog*] [*the details*]. But if it recurs, then it will be all over with us [*togda nam budet uzhe konets*]. But we want to believe that maybe it will not be repeated, and these barbarians will not have any chance here [*again*].

---

215 *Molot*, no. 292 (6170), December 10, 1941.
216 "Amerikanskaia pechat' o bor'be na vostochnom fronte," ibid.
217 I. Iudovich, "Gitlerovskaia banda ubiits i grabitelei," ibid.

> For the time being, evacuation permits are not being issued, but as soon as they are given, we will abandon everything and go away, because one cannot sell anything now (since the consignment shop does not accept goods). But we may go with what we can take with us. When you wrote that it was better to die at home, you would have done better to write that we should have moved away immediately. It would have been better; we would have arrived, but now it looks like we won't manage to leave.[218]

The sisters carefully avoided putting on paper whatever had happened to them during the German occupation. From what they did write, it seems that they definitely suffered considerably, but it is difficult to say whether they were especially targeted as Jews, or were merely persecuted as ordinary Rostov civilians. Still, judging by some of the more ominous remarks (for example, "if it recurs, then it will be all over with us"), it seems that they—or other Jews close to them—were abused just because they were Jews. Clearly, the two sisters recognized that if the Germans were to return, they would be killed.

Also of note is the fact that the word "Jewish" was conspicuously absent in their letters, even in referring to the horrors of the German occupation. This omission may have been due to their fear of the censor, or, conversely, may suggest that they accepted the message emphasized by the Soviet propaganda machine: that the Germans persecuted all Soviet people, regardless of ethnicity. Possibly, the German persecution of Jews may have been so obvious as to render all mention of it superfluous, or the sisters may have considered it one of the "bad news," which they tried to avoid mentioning.

The fear that the Germans instilled in the Ginsburg sisters sufficed to make them decide to flee, at any cost. They were no longer paralyzed by their fear. Now, for the first time, economic arguments no longer loomed large, even though their finances were still problematic: we learn that they no longer had the option of preparing themselves financially for their journey by selling their possessions through state-owned commission shops. Other troublesome issues—no man to accompany them, poor health, age, winter, etc.—still existed but were no longer regarded as a deciding factor. We will soon see whether this was a lasting stance.

The November 1941 issues of the Rostov newspaper are not available in centralized archives or libraries. But a local researcher who did have access to

---

218 From Liza Chazkewitz and Anya Greener to Tamara Meerovich in Budennovsk, December 10, 1941, YVA: O.75/324, p. 89.

these issues mentioned that in early December 1941, the local Soviet media published a letter written by Rostov inhabitants, in which they depicted the horrors that they had endured during the week of the German occupation.[219] It seems that this letter was also published in the North Caucasus, and the Ginsburg family residing there could have had access to this source of information.

This Soviet report considerably exaggerated the German atrocities in Rostov-on-Don, so it is not easy to guess how the Ginsburg sisters would have reacted to it. It is possible that it reinforced their fear of the Germans; however, it is also likely that the report merely accentuated the sisters' mistrust of everything produced by the Soviet media.

It is likely that the report, published in newspapers available in the area where they lived, came to the attention of the evacuated branch of the Ginsburg family, who were probably closely following the news from Rostov-on-Don. As suggested by the letters, to them it seemed enlightening, reinforcing the belief that their escape from Rostov-on-Don was, despite all the hardships, the correct move. And certainly this report was bound to significantly raise their anxiety about the relatives who had stayed in Rostov-on-Don.

Despite obvious Soviet military successes in the south—and the recapture of Rostov-on-Don was the most visible sign of the Red Army's achievements— the regional Soviet media warned its readers that the danger of a German counter-offensive was still real. On December 11, 1941, Stavropol's newspaper published an article, "To All Former Red Partisans," explaining that "the time has come when we are again … getting prepared for battle."[220]

On December 11, *Molot* published an important article, highlighting one of the critical messages that the local leadership was eager to convey to the inhabitants of Rostov-on-Don. From the editorial, "To Further Enhance Revolutionary Vigilance":

> It would be erroneous to fall into a state of complacency. We are well aware of the insidiousness and cunning of the German robbers. There is no doubt that they will attempt to disrupt the resumption of normal life in the city and to impair our cause. In the first days after the liberation of the city, the Military Command, the District Committee of the VKP(b), and the District Executive Committee issued an appeal to the inhabitants of Rostov:

---

219 Zhuravlev, *Kollaboratsionizm na iuge Rossii*, 175.
220 "Ko vsem byvshym Krasnym partizanam," *Ordzhonikidzevskaia pravda*, no. 293 (2357), December 11, 1941.

"Fascists may have left their people in the city in order to carry out diversions and murders. Keep utmost vigilance! Watch out for suspects and inform the Soviet agencies [*organy*] about them. Even if only one fascist remaining in the city for his vile purposes is disclosed." This directive should be implemented with all energy and resolve. Fascist spies may also penetrate villages and *stanitsy* close to Rostov. … We should know which people come to the villages and *stanitsy*; with particular [*udesiaterennaia, literally, "tenfold"*] care, we should guard enterprises, railway roads, bridges, roads… We should close all holes and gaps, through which fascist saboteurs and spies could penetrate. Also, we should expose fascist followers and henchmen who under German rule behaved like traitors to the Fatherland, robbers and marauders. … [*Here the article refers to the Usharov case*]. … Dogs should be given a dog's death. No mercy for the traitors to the Fatherland, people who went over [*peremetnut'sia*] to the enemy, who helped fascists commit their vile deeds! … Let us further enhance revolutionary vigilance.[221]

Given the special circumstances in Rostov-on-Don after its liberation, the publication of this article was most likely considered necessary. However, it clearly brought local people back to the gloomy atmosphere of spy hunting that had reigned in the Soviet Union for many years, an atmosphere of paranoia that reached its climax in the late 1930s.[222] Apart from making a depressing impression on the local people, such messages doubtless provided the populace with the opportunity to revenge long-standing rivalries and disputes. Furthermore, these circumstances were bound to inhibit people like the Ginsburgs from even considering flight from this endangered region without the proper paperwork, because in the absence of such documents, they could be accused of being German infiltrators.

The entire second page of the issue bore the headline "Death to German Monsters!" Among the articles published on this page, particularly notable is "Fascist Atrocities in Rostov," which included several horrific accounts by eyewitnesses: "How the Germans Killed My Husband and Son,"[223] "The Beasts Entertain Themselves,"[224] and "Peaceful Inhabitants Were Exterminated by

---

221 *Molot*, no. 293 (6171), December 11, 1941.
222 See, for example, Geoffrey Hosking, "Trust and Distrust in the USSR: An Overview," *The Slavonic and East European Review* 91, no. 1 (January 2013): 5–17.
223 "Account by Marfa Petrovna Gorbova, resident of house 11/54 on 40th Line," ibid.
224 "Account by Masparon Madosovich Yantarev, resident of house 71/52 on 2 Murlycheskaya St.," ibid.

Poisons."²²⁵ Taken together, these articles sought, as in the past, to appeal to the desire for vengeance among the inhabitants of Rostov-on-Don.

How did Tsylya Pinchos (Anya's daughter, who had been evacuated from Rostov-on-Don together with Tamara Meerovich's family) see the situation in the recently liberated city? On December 12, 1941, she wrote a letter from Budennovsk to her uncle in Alma-Ata:

> Only today we got your letter, it made us happy. Our dear one, don't be angry that we sent you money. Don't think that that is all we have. Not at all. When we left our home we sold lots of unnecessary goods. Both Tamara and I amassed some money. Besides, Volodya gets his salary in Rostov, and during this period, we received 1,500 rubles from him. We have only been living here for two weeks, and Tamara has already been able to find employment for 300 rubles; the children attend kindergarten; life is not expensive here; food is easily available, we eat a lot of potatoes; we pay 3.50–4.00 rubles for 1 kg; meat is cheap; there are many fats here.
>
> On November 27, Volodya suddenly came to join us; we were very pleased about his arrival, but at the same time, dazed with grief since our relatives [*the Ginsburg sisters*] had to stay there. Certainly, they can blame themselves; in the first ten days of November it was still possible to leave Rostov; Volodya could have helped them. However, everyone dissuaded them from doing so, and they told him that they would wait a bit longer. We bombarded them with letters and telegrams in order to convince them to join us at once. But they asked us in every letter if anyone could move, but they did not go themselves.
>
> Volodya was here only one day; he was sent to work in Ordzhonikidze, to be in charge of the relocated *arteli* [*marketing cooperatives*]. Now we wait for him to receive a room, and then we will all go there, and write to you. If you don't get along in your place till that time, you must come to us without any hesitation. So hopefully we all may gather together, in this way.
>
> Generally speaking, it does not make any sense to settle in remote areas, as the situation on the front improves every day; a lot of people are returning to Rostov; as for us, we have only one hope—to return home as soon as possible. In addition, Liza sent me 500 rubles; she sold my belongings that I had left behind; she writes that she will send me as much as she already has. It is better to sell one's possessions than to let the enemy get

---

225 "Account by Evdokiya Mitrofanovna Zvantseva, resident of house 11/54 on 40th Line," ibid.

his hands on them. ... We are now very concerned, as we are waiting for a letter from our aunt to reassure us that she is alive and in good health after those terrible days that the damned Hitler was there. But we have calmed down a little bit, after some people came here from Rostov and said that our neighborhood wasn't damaged.

We are all in good health. Initially, it was somewhat hard, but it is bearable [*now*]. Most importantly, we anticipate that the confounded enemy will be smashed. It is because of him that we are experiencing all this, and we are confident that soon the enemy will be destroyed and all of us will return home and lie on our soft beds, and most importantly, we'll be together.

One more significant thing. We are all worried that we have not heard anything at all from Dod.[226] But for some reason, I feel calm about this. I know that he was in Rostov; he wrote often that there was no mail where he was serving. So, his letters were often brought to me in Rostov by car. I think that he is alive. ... Marusya Soloveichik and Beba live and work together in Essentuki; Beba continues to invite Aunt Liza and [*Aunt*] Anya to go to them, but they cannot make up their minds to do so.[227]

The letter contained several important messages. The first one is the story of sending money. The Ginsburgs were, no doubt, ready to help each other when in dire straits, but there were also undercurrents in this story about who would admit that they needed this money the most. When Tsylya and her evacuated family sent Efim money, they tacitly admitted that their own situation was not so disastrous. Tsylya confirmed this impression by providing us with a new item of information. As mentioned above, the departure of Tsylya and other family members from Rostov-on-Don was too hasty, and they were only able to take with them their most essential possessions. They managed to subsist by selling or exchanging their belongings for food, coal, and other necessities, and Tamara Meerovich's employment gave the family an additional source of income. However, we now discover that, in addition, the Ginsburg sisters who stayed in Rostov-on-Don were able to sell more of their goods. Perhaps they capitalized on a propitious moment and sold them at a good price? At that time, many people were returning to the city; so that the increased demand led to higher prices.

---

226 Diminutive for David, her husband.
227 From Tsylya Pinchos in Budennovsk, December 12, 1941, YVA: O.75/324, pp. 90–93.

Tsylya also reiterated the claim that the Ginsburg sisters could have left Rostov-on-Don when it was still possible, but refused to do so of their own volition. Tsylya's letter reveals to us how the decision regarding the sisters' evacuation was made. The family was split: the already evacuated branch wanted Anya and Liza to join them, while the latter looked for every pretext not to do so. Evidently, even though this could in no way be acknowledged in the letter, the Ginsburg sisters did not want to leave; before they actually experienced the first Nazi occupation of Rostov-on-Don, they were not so afraid to face the Germans. A clue to their behavior lies in their ages: we do not know exactly where they spent World War I, but the odds are high that they experienced the German occupation, whether in Rostov-on-Don or elsewhere, and, like many other Jews, didn't have such bad memories of it—in sharp contrast to other periods of the Russian Civil War.

Tsylya, despite being far away from Rostov-on-Don, proved well aware that Jews did not face special persecution during the German occupation of the city. This suggests, in turn, that she remained less influenced by Soviet propaganda reports about the German atrocities that had occurred in Rostov-on-Don. Furthermore, the only reason that she gave as to why her aunts could have been killed during this week was, if "our neighborhood was … damaged." This elliptical expression conceals the unpalatable fact that Rostov-on-Don was bombarded during the German occupation. Since the Germans were in control of the city, she must have referred to the Soviets' bombardments of Rostov-on-Don.

However, we should not overestimate Tsylya's ability to judge the situation entirely objectively. Like her aunts, Liza and Anya, she also viewed her situation too optimistically. After the victory of the Soviet troops at Rostov-on-Don, she invited her Uncle Efim, residing in Alma-Ata, to join them in Budennovsk if his situation were to deteriorate. Encouraged by Soviet reports that also influenced other Jewish evacuees, who had made their way back to Rostov-on-Don ("the situation at the front improves every day"),[228] Tamara assumed that the Germans would soon be vanquished.

Finally, this is one of a very few letters where people outside the family were mentioned in the correspondence. The entire family, as we remember, did not seem particularly traditional or religious: no Yiddish words were used in the letters; there were almost no references to Jewish holidays; even the German occupation was described without making any reference to the word "Jewish." Still, one implicit feature is manifest in the correspondence and in this

---

228 For example, Testimony of Anna Shagina-Blokh, b. 1919, April 1965, YVA: 0.3/3146, p. 1.

specific letter: from the names cited, it appears that all the people outside the family circle who are mentioned were Jewish. If we wish to categorize them in terms of identity, the family seems to have belonged to the secular Jewish world and firmly embedded in Soviet Russian culture.[229] Because of their residence outside of the former Pale of Settlement, the impact of Yiddish and the Jewish religion was apparently lower on the Ginsburgs than on families living in places such as the present-day Belarus.[230]

On December 12, 1941, Tamara sent a new letter from Budennovsk to her uncle in Alma-Ata:

> Dear Efim!
>
> Today we finally received your postcard, which made us incredibly happy. But it immensely saddened us [*to learn*] that you were in such a precarious situation. We wept bitterly ... what has the confounded war against the fascists done to us all?
>
> But our dear one, despite all the difficulties we bear, we firmly believe in our imminent victory over these beasts and scoundrels who commit unheard-of atrocities against people.
>
> But so far, we, evacuees are in dire straits. Volodya succeeded in leaving Rostov before the Germans. Their plant was evacuated to Ordzhonikidze, and now he is there. ... We hope that they [*the two sisters??*] are alive, although we have not heard anything from them.
>
> We are all in good health. I am working. [*My*] mother is feeling well, but is grieving for our people in Rostov, and now for you, too. Don't feel despair, our dear one. We will support each other. We will endeavor to answer you, at least partially, for all your good deeds towards us. Be healthy, write to us more often at this address: Ordzhonikidze, to be called for. For the time being, this is the only comfort. We all send you kisses.[231]

The expression employed by Tamara, "unheard-of atrocities against people," was coined by the Soviet propaganda. Its usage in the letter indicates that, by that time, Tamara, like her aunts, had either begun to internalize Soviet propaganda

---

229 On this issue, see Anna Shternshis, *Soviet and Kosher: Jewish Popular Culture in the Soviet Union, 1923–1939* (Bloomington: Indiana University Press, 2006), 143–181.
230 See Elissa Bemporad, *Becoming Soviet Jews: The Bolshevik Experiment in Minsk* (Bloomington: Indiana University Press, 2013), 81–144. Cf. Arkadii Zeltser, *Evrei sovetskoi provintsii: Vitebsk i mestechki, 1917–1941* (Moscow: ROSSPEN, 2006), 229–316.
231 From Tamara Meerovich in Budennovsk, December 12, 1941, YVA: O.75/324, pp. 94–95.

phraseology or had become more cautious, fearing that her letter might be intercepted by Soviet censors.

On the same day, Liza wrote to Efim from Rostov-on-Don:

> I have already written to you that our relatives left, but Anya and I stayed; it was impossible to join them at that moment. Later, we decided that probably we would not [*have to*] leave at all. But now, as soon as the evacuation permits are issued, we will move away immediately, since we have endured many horrors.[232]

In their description of events, only the circumstances were to blame for their failure to leave: "It was impossible to join them at that moment." The sisters still refused to disclose exactly what happened to them during the last week of November 1941, and we can only guess what transpired. It is quite likely that, because of the continuous shelling by the Soviet artillery, the sisters spent the week in one of the city's shelters. Probably, this shelter was close to their home, as they did not walk around in the city in order to avoid encountering any Germans. Consequently, they could have quickly learned about the murder of Rostov civilians by the Germans in Engels Street, which was close to their home—or actually seen the corpses. This crime apparently made such a strong impression on them that, regardless of the reassuring messages conveyed by the Rostov newspaper, the sisters were adamant about the need to escape at the first opportunity.

On December 13, 1941, Liza and Anya wrote another letter to Efim from Rostov-on-Don. It began with an explanation of how Tamara had obtained employment in Budennovsk, followed by a description of the extremely difficult physical and financial conditions that the evacuated branch of the family were facing in Budennovsk:

> … Now they are deprived of the room and the fuel; their conditions have deteriorated. They are thinking about leaving (I don't know where to), despite the fact that they are not permitted to leave. I don't know what will happen and in what way.
>
> Now we have also made up our minds to move away as soon as the evacuation permits are given. Then, it might be possible for us go to Beba in Essentuki. God grant we won't need to leave, but rather our family will return to us soon. …

---

232 From Liza Chazkewitz and Anya Greener to Tamara Meerovich in Budennovsk, December 12, 1941, YVA: O.75/324, p. 97.

It is all about suffering, especially in winter. I'd like [to see] these German barbarians pushed away as far as possible and forever; bandits, robbers, murderers, let them be destroyed as soon as possible![233]

The sisters stressed the apparently insurmountable difficulties confronting the family members who had moved to Budennovsk. Although Liza and Anya suggested that these problems might cause them to leave sometime in the future, at this stage, their return to Rostov-on-Don still remained out of the question. The sisters did not remark on the substantial improvement in the lives of the evacuated branch of the family, as described by Tsylya Pinchos. Either they were ignorant of it, or it did not fit in well with their outlook. They saw evacuation as a tragedy tantamount to staying under German rule, to be avoided if possible.

In this letter, the balance between "stay" or "go" was not as clear-cut as it had been only several days previously. Liza and Anya's resolve to leave Rostov-on-Don was weakened. Previous reasons for not moving, such as the hardships suffered by evacuees on their journey, had been critical in their decision not to leave before the trauma of the German occupation of Rostov-on-Don. But now they had a new point of view. Their vacillation is manifest in musing about the destination of their evacuation, if permits were given. If it were up to the sisters, at this point they would not run as far as possible away from the Germans, but only go as far as Essentuki, a small resort city in the Stavropol territory, 523 kilometers to the east of Rostov-on-Don, and currently home to thousands of Jewish refugees.[234] They could not know that Essentuki would be spared the German occupation in 1941, but would be occupied by the Wehrmacht in the summer of 1942, and that all its Jews would be killed in early September 1942.[235] Also, as previously, Liza and Anya voiced their unflagging optimism, too reminiscent of official Soviet propaganda, for a Soviet victory. But the sisters' tone was somewhat more realistic: they wished above all that the Germans would be pushed away from Rostov-on-Don. The possibility of an absolute victory was a more remote event, not within reach.

On December 14, 1941, *Molot* published a report "Meeting of Rostov's Working People":

---

233 From Liza Chazkewitz and Anya Greener, December 13, 1941, YVA: O.75/324, pp. 98–99.
234 Feferman, "A Soviet Humanitarian Action?," 816–821.
235 Statement of the Commission of the Town of Essentuki, July 10, 1943, GARF: 7021/17/4, p. 1.

> Several days ago, there was a meeting of Rostov's working people with the soldiers and commanders of the Red Army. It was dedicated to the liberation of Rostov from the fascist yoke. … Stalin was elected as honorary chairman. … The meeting unanimously accepted an appeal "To cities threatened by the invasion of German fascists, to all citizens of the Soviet Union."[236]

Among other lessons to be learned from Rostov's example, the report emphasized the need to strengthen defenses. This article shows an instrument that the Soviet propaganda used widely throughout the entire history of the USSR, "meetings of working people." It is absolutely clear that such events were staged and closely controlled.[237] They were an opportunity for free expression of what local people really thought. However, there was one important message that the authorities (certainly not the working people) were eager to convey: Rostov-on-Don was still threatened, and it clearly remained a dangerous place to stay. This was the message that the Ginsburgs might have received upon learning about the meeting.

The only letter written by Efim himself that was saved as part of the collection (apparently because it did not reach the addressee, and was returned to the sender) was sent on December 16, 1941. He wrote to his niece Tamara in Budennovsk:

> Today I received an unsigned telegram and a telegraph money transfer for 200 rubles. I appreciate your not having forgotten me. It is good to know that I'm not the only one in this world, that there are people who are really close to you, who think about you.
>
> Let me begin with the most important thing. Since I learned that the fascist hangmen were in Rostov, when I learned about (and imagined) the atrocities they had committed there, I have had no peace; I was close to going mad. Anya, Liza and Volodya stayed there. Our poor, unfortunate sisters. … I telegraphed to Rostov, I wrote and telegraphed to you … I made special inquiries about Liza, but there was no reply. Even from you … I am ready to learn the most terrible news. Don't be worried about me on account of money; you had to take care of something much more impor-

---

236 *Molot*, no. 296 (6174), December 14, 1941.
237 For example, Brandenberger, *Propaganda State in Crisis*, 216–248. Cf. Hoffmann, *Cultivating the Masses*.

tant. ... I had to send a telegram there and to ask for a clear reply about the fate of Anya and Liza. My God! Didn't they get out of Hitler's Hell? My life is as of old—bad. But as compared to the tragedy in Rostov and the cruel fate of my beloved sisters, my problems pale in significance. ...[238]

The letter gives us a rare glimpse of Efim Ginsburg's perspective. Although he began his letter with a reference to money transfer, which we have frequently seen addressed in the rest of the letters, he clearly put things into proportion. To Efim Ginsburg, more than anyone else in the family, it was crystal clear that the German occupation meant the death verdict for his relatives, as well as for many other Jews. We do not know how or where he gained this knowledge. My supposition is that he had greater exposure to pertinent information as he had lived before the War in Moscow, the capital city of the Soviet Union, while his family continued to live in the periphery. After the outbreak of war, it is likely that Efim was evacuated with his plant or factory, and during his ongoing migration—Alma-Ata was his second stop after Omsk—he came into contact with many other refugees and evacuees, which doubtless enhanced his awareness of the genocide of the Jews. On the whole, Efim Ginsburg was the only member of the family who, despite having suffered enormously during his evacuation, regarded it as the only viable option for his family in the North Caucasus. Furthermore, he favored their making a long-distance evacuation, which would have brought his relatives as far as possible away from all the likely directions of the Germans' attack, and not the short-distance evacuation made by Tamara Meerovich's group, which still brought them too close to the frontline.

On December 16, 1941, *Molot* published a decree of the Executive Committee of the Rostov District Committee of Deputies "On the need for the citizens to hand over all radio sets." It was issued in accordance with the decree of the Soviet government (SNK SSSR) dated July 4, 1941. Rostov's inhabitants were given three days to turn in their radios. Even spare parts had to be handed in.[239] Given the proximity of the Wehrmacht, the local inhabitants were able to listen to German broadcasts. This would have given the Germans the opportunity to broadcast orders to their agents, and to receive replies. In this sense, the Soviet step did have a certain logic. But overall, this decree severely impaired the ability of the pro-Soviet Rostov populace, including the Ginsburg sisters, to

---

238 From Efim Ginsburg in Alma-Ata to Tamara Meerovich in Budennovsk, December 16, 1941, YVA: O.75/324, pp. 101–103.
239 *Molot*, no. 297 (6175), December 16, 1941.

access Soviet broadcasts, however outdated they were, and reduced the sisters' chances of being updated in good time about critical advances of the German forces.

A short note, "In the Areas of the Rostov District Recently Liberated from the Fascist Gangs," published by *Molot* on December 17, described the German atrocities as well as the assistance given by the Soviet authorities to the Red Army and the restoration of Soviet rule. Perhaps the most important message in the article can be summarized by its statement that "working people in the liberated areas are confident about their tomorrow."[240]

However, the Red Army was not yet within reach of victory in the region, and Rostov's inhabitants were warned to prepare for a long period of uncertainty. The article "Germans Put Up Stubborn Resistance in the South," published in *Molot* on December 18, admitted that "in spite of enormous losses, Fascist troops offer stiff resistance."[241] Pictures of the victims of German atrocities in Rostov-on-Don were published on the second page.

On December 18, 1941, Anya and Liza wrote to Efim Ginsburg:

> We are relieved and happy to learn that you, our dear one, are alive and in good health. Thank God, we also are all alive and in good health. So far we are in Rostov, and God grant that there will be no need to go anywhere, as we have not gone anywhere up to now. …
>
> Now our only wish is to see our dear [*relatives*] coming back soon, so that we will all be together, so that we should not need to go to them, because they are leading a difficult life. We have endured a lot…
>
> We do not need money; don't worry, everything will be fine; the enemy will certainly be smashed.[242]

Only five days had passed since the sisters' previous letter, but the change in their mood is obvious. The letter begins with their statement that "we are relieved and happy to learn that you… are alive," as if it were Efim Ginsburg whose life was in danger. This is followed by a number of other remarks, which demonstrate the extent of Anya and Liza's unwillingness to move anywhere. The letter is filled with unusual references to God (in marked contrast to their previous silence on the subject).

---

240   *Molot*, no. 298 (6178), December 17, 1941.
241   *Molot*, no. 299 (6179), December 18, 1941.
242   From Liza Chazkewitz and Anya Greener, December 18, 1941, YVA: O.75/324, p. 105.

Anya and Liza refused to be evacuated, and they hoped that the rest of the family would soon join them in Rostov-on-Don. Evidently, within these five days, the sisters had learned something that made them change their minds. This change of heart could have been the result of Soviet propaganda, which did its utmost to convince Soviet civilians that the recapture of Rostov-on-Don by the Red Army was only the beginning of a long Soviet drive westwards. In the case of Anya and Liza, these messages found eager acceptance. In fact, however, the Wehrmacht was able to check the Soviet advance in the south in December 1941.

The curious document that follows is also significant. In August 1942, when the German armies had already occupied a significant part of the Soviet North Caucasus, Einsatzgruppe D compiled a report on the situation in the region. Among other things, it claimed that:

> After the German troops left in November, 1941, the administration of Rostov fell into the hands of the NKVD, which mobilized Jews to identify collaborators. The persons who had supported the Germans, 800 people, were executed.[243]

The report, like all German documents of this sort, is strongly biased against the Jews. Still, some factual details of the report may be cautiously accepted as true. In particular, the statement regarding harsh Soviet measures taken against German supporters in the midst of the Soviet civilian population is very believable, especially since, as we have seen, the Soviet newspapers did not try to conceal these measures. Furthermore, when the Red Army liberated a locality from the Germans, the Soviet authorities usually questioned the local Jews in order to find out how the Germans had abused them, so this element of the report also rings true. Particularly important for our concerns is the fact that Soviet resolve, however predictable, in tracking down German collaborators in Rostov-on-Don might have reinforced the feeling of the inhabitants of the city, including the Jews, that the Red Army would not let the Wehrmacht enter the city again.

The article "On Rostov's Streets," published in *Molot* on December 19, 1941, showed the city functioned in those days. The article described the

---

243 EG D der SP und des SD. Meldungen aus den besetzten Ostgebieten, nu. 16 Berlin, Chef der SP und der SD. Kommandostab, August 14, 1942, RGVA: 500/1/775, p. 423. In Blumenfeld, *The Holocaust in the Southern Part of Russia*, 132.

construction of defensive infrastructure in the city itself. At the same time, the article also showed how routine daily life was resumed: water pipes and the municipal library began working again.[244] Along the same lines, on December 20, 1941, *Molot* reported that Rostov's blood bank continued recruiting volunteers to donate blood for the Red Army. In return, blood donors were paid compensation and provided with food rations.[245] Certainly, there was a degree of propaganda exaggeration in this description of the return to routine city life, but this testimony is nevertheless indicative of a strange feeling of normality in this city caught between war and peace.

On December 20, 1941, Liza and Anya wrote another letter to Efim Ginsburg, presenting their account of why they did not escape from Rostov-on-Don:

> Our dear, dear Efim!
>
> First, … we are all alive and healthy. Anya and I are still in Rostov and are working as of old. Monya, Tamara, Tsylya and [*our*] dear children are in Budennovsk, Ordzhonikidze territory, Postal Office at the Railway Station, to be called for by T. Meerovich.
>
> Then, on October 13, we could not move away with them [*the rest of the family*], as it was impossible to get evacuation permits for us. Later, we were afraid to leave, because the roads were bombed. So, we stayed, and, of course, endured a lot. Now, we want to go either to our relatives (although things are very bad there), or to Berta Markovna in Essentuki. However, we cannot leave, because evacuation permits are not being issued. Recently, as Berta Markovna came to pick up her Aunt Polya, she wanted to take us with her. But unfortunately nothing came of it; she took her aunt and left on December 17. Again, we stayed here. It seems that it is our fate not to leave Rostov.
>
> We would be enormously happy and glad if we did not need to leave, if our relatives returned soon to Rostov to their places and their own beds, because they are really suffering from all this. Nonetheless, we are not thinking about leaving, even for a while, since I want to believe that the confounded barbarians will never be able to return here. For the time being, there is no mass evacuation. I wish there would be none! So, we are waiting. Our dear one, we received all your postcards and your telegram, it took it so long to get here. Yesterday we received the telegram, in

---

244 D. Iashenko, "Na ulitsakh Rostova," *Molot*, no. 300 (6178), December 19, 1941.
245 *Molot*, no. 301 (6179), December 20, 1941.

which you advised us to move away to the East. It is a difficult thing [*to do*], especially now, in winter, and [*besides,*] we aren't all together. ... But for the time being, we are all in the same situation. ... Our dear one, don't worry about money, we don't need it now, as we are sitting in one place. When need be, we will write to you. And if need be, we will move away. Of course, we would like to see everyone together. But how can we arrange all this? I wish only that the damned enemy be destroyed as soon as possible, and then it will surely be over. No doubt it will happen. ... We wish, God grant, to receive more and more of your letters. ... With our kisses, Anya and Liza. Write back [*soon*].[246]

In this letter, Anya and Liza confirmed what we already know from other sources: there was a ban on leaving Rostov-on-Don. And yet, we see that this ban could be circumvented, as one of their Jewish friends was able to take her aunt out of the city. Thus, the letter leaves us in doubt as to whether anyone in the family, including the sisters themselves, was really pushing to get Anya and Liza evacuated from Rostov-on-Don. This letter gives the impression that only two days after stating that they would not move away, the sisters again were hesitating about whether to leave or not. This time, they envisaged a "local evacuation," not far from Rostov-on-Don, apparently to wait until the Red Army firmly secured the area around the city.

Soviet propaganda in Rostov-on-Don endeavored to maintain a very delicate equilibrium between the "business as usual" mood and preparing the population for another German onslaught. On December 21, *Molot* appeared under the slogan: "Let Us Mark the Arrival of the New Year with New Achievements in Strengthening Rostov's Defense." On the other hand, its editorial article on the front page was entitled "To Get Prepared for the Spring Sowing in a Timely Fashion."[247]

The important article that was only published on the second page of the newspaper, "Under Hitler's Foot," sheds light on the fate of the Jewish population in Taganrog, which had been occupied by the Wehrmacht since mid-October 1941. This report was presented as a personal account, most likely by a Soviet agent writing under the name Nikolai Kostantinovich P., who spent two months in the occupied city, from October 17 to December 17:

---

246 From Liza Chazkewitz and Anya Greener, December 20, 1941, YVA: O.75/324, pp. 106–109.
247 *Molot*, no. 302 (6180), December 21, 1941.

… Soon after the takeover, the Hitlerites issued an order. All the Jews were required to wear yellow armbands with six-pointed stars, go to School no. 27, and take warm clothes and [enough] food for three days. Afterwards, these people, who did not suspect anything, were marched to trenches near the instruments plant; their executioners fell upon them, took their clothes away, and killed them all, including elderly people and infants, by shooting them with machine guns.[248]

Unusual in the Soviet press, this was an unequivocal acknowledgement[249] that the Jews were being annihilated in the German-controlled territories. As the reference was made to events in a city in the Rostov district, very close to Rostov-on-Don, it was bound to affect the newspaper readers profoundly (provided they believed what was published).

Simultaneously, *Molot* continued to convey the message that the situation in the city had returned to normal. Announcements that were also placed on the second page of the issue informed the Rostov public about the films being screened in the city's theaters, among them *Sisters-in-Arms* (*Frontovye Podrugi*), *Spartacus*, and four others. Local citizens were also notified that New Year decorations were available for sale in the Rostov Model (*pokazatel'nyi*) department store, located at 77 Moskovskaya Street.

On the same day, December 21, 1941, the sisters sent a letter to their family in Budennovsk:

> All the time we think that as soon as the evacuation permits are given, we will put everything aside and go to you or to Beba, although Beba is very unreliable in her behavior. She came here to take us and went without us. She lost the invitation for us.[250]

From this letter we learn that the only reason why Anya and Liza had not left Rostov-on-Don was due to a technical problem—their acquaintance's failure to obtain the necessary invitation. If the sisters' description of events was accurate, this was the first evidence that they were really ready to be evacuated. However,

---

248 Ibid.
249 On this topic, see, for example, Altshuler, "The Holocaust in the Soviet Mass Media." Cf. Berkhoff, "'Total Annihilation,'" 61–105.
250 From Liza Chazkewitz and Anya Greener to Tsylya Pinkhos in Budennovsk, December 21, 1941, YVA: O.75/324, p. 111.

Anya and Liza were only considering a local move, not a fully fledged flight to Central Asia.

On December 22, 1941, *Molot* reported on "terrible atrocities against civilians" committed by the Germans in the recently liberated areas of the Rostov District.[251] Such a message, not infrequently found in the Soviet propaganda,[252] probably had an ambiguous impact on the Ginsburgs, because the article was unclear about whether the Germans specifically targeted Jews.

On the same day, Tsylya Pinchos wrote a letter to Efim in Alma-Ata, another demonstration of the mood that reigned in the extended Ginsburg family prior to the German occupation of Rostov-on-Don:

> Our departure from Rostov was entirely accidental. We all cried that we would not abandon Rostov under any circumstances, that if we are doomed to perish we'd better stay together at home. Aunt Anya expressed it differently: when we considered moving, she said that she would not go away to be killed. And suddenly, within two hours, we had to collect our possessions and go. The most awful thing for us was that we [*thought at first that we*] had to go alone; we could not imagine then that the children were not included automatically in the evacuation permit. Tamara was still at work, Volodya rushed to bring her, the neighbors in the yard carried our possessions; at that time, Doda was here for some days. ... Mother was shocked to learn that I would go with them, I rushed to bring Dod. ... When we left we were accompanied by a terrible outcry: it was ... the most dreadful bombardment of the city.
>
> Now, our aunts kept asking us in every letter, if they had to go and what was the situation with [*respect to*] employment. We did not stop writing to them and we sent a priority telegram, in order to urge them to leave immediately. Apparently, it worked the other way about. The situation with employment is terrible here, fuel costs 20–30 rubles a day, and we live in a cold room. If they came, and, of course, found no employment, we could not sustain ourselves. Beba did not stop writing to them; in Essentuki there was both an apartment and work. But they took advice [*from others*]. It would have been possible for Volodya to transfer them, but they answered him, "We'll wait a little bit longer." Maybe it is for the best that we experience the hardships here on our own.

---

251 *Molot*, no. 303 (6181), December 22, 1941.
252 Berkhoff, *Motherland in Danger*, 116–133.

> Tomorrow we are leaving for Ordzhonikidze, to Volodya's place. We won't be worried if the children are sick: they've got doctors there. When we get your money, we'll send it back to you at once. Shame on you! You sell your last possessions there and send us money. I have already written to you that we do not need anything.[253]

From the letter, it appears that the decision to leave Rostov-on-Don, made by that part of the Ginsburg family, was entirely spontaneous. What determined their decision was a combination of several factors. First, it was the large-scale distribution of evacuation permits to non-organized evacuees, after many weeks of waiting. These permits could be used within a very limited period of time. It appears that many local inhabitants, among them the Ginsburg family, interpreted this change in policy as the authorities' tacit admission that the military situation around Rostov-on-Don had got out of control and the danger of takeover by the Germans loomed much larger than previously thought. To this, we should add other factors, which were already at play before these events, but coupled with the issuing of evacuation permits, they grew in significance. These included rumors emanating from refugees and increasing whenever there were German air strikes. For some of the Ginsburgs, all this tipped the balance in favor of immediate evacuation.

Also of note are the never-ending "honor games" between Efim Ginsburg and his North Caucasian relatives. All of them were in dire straits, yet everyone refused to accept presents from the other side, claiming that the conditions of the others were even worse and that the others should take care of themselves first.

Molot continued calling upon the Rostov public to display vigilance and self-sacrifice in carrying out defensive works. On December 23, the newspaper published on its front page the "Resolution of the Plenary Meeting of the [*Rostov*] District Committee of the VKP(b) Following the Report of Comrade Dvinsky[254]":

- To accelerate as much as possible the pace of defensive works because [*the city of*] Rostov and Rostov District are located in a battlefield zone. …
- To increase the pace of exposing enemy henchmen, who proved to be anti-Soviet elements [*pokazavshikh svoe antisovetskoe litso*] during the German occupation.[255]

---

253 From Tsylya Pinkhos in Budennovsk, December 22, 1941, YVA: O.75/324, pp. 112–113.
254 Boris Dvinsky was the First Secretary of the District Party Committee.
255 *Molot*, no. 304 (6181), December 23, 1941.

Such warning messages were bound to instill fear in the Ginsburgs and to lead them to escape from the city once the opportunity presented itself.

A short note on the second page, "In the District Police Administration," informed readers that:

> For speculation, collection, and concealment of a small amount of Soviet money, two persons [*one Russian and one Armenian, judging by their names*] were arrested. Three people were prosecuted for speculation. For the evasion of defensive work, six people were arrested and will stand trial by court martial.[256]

This article had several objectives. First of all, it was important for the authorities to demonstrate their efficiency to the local population, including the restoration of law and order in the beleaguered city. Therefore, this news was a soothing message for people like the Ginsburg sisters. At the same time, the emphasis on the defensive work meant that the situation in the city continued to be fraught with danger. The menace implied by continued defensive construction was only partly sweetened by the announcements placed on the second page, which advertised five films being shown in theaters all over Rostov-on-Don.

On December 23, 1941, newsreel no. 114, "In liberated Rostov," was released and screened in cinema theaters all over the country.[257] In contrast to local print publications, which were mostly limited to circulation in Rostov-on-Don and available only to a limited extent in other parts of the country, this newsreel could have been seen by Efim Ginsburg in Alma-Ata and by the Pinchos and Meerovich branches of the family in Ordzhonikidze. The newsreel section called "We Won't Forget, We Won't Forgive" featured the Germans' harsh treatment of Rostov's population to the point of physical assault, although the newsreel did not mention whether the Jews were singled out for persecution.[258]

Given the particular power of video propaganda, a newsreel informing people about the brutalities of the German occupation could have influenced the members of the Ginsburg family in several ways. For people such as the two Ginsburg sisters, who were aware that the German abuse of civilians during the short occupation of Rostov-on-Don had been quite limited, the newsreel

---

256 Ibid.
257 Hicks, *First Films of the Holocaust*, 47–56.
258 *Soiuzkinozhurnal*, no. 114, December 23, 1941, RGAKFD: record 4672, http://pobeda-vov.ru/Lib/pages/item.aspx?itemid=10523, accessed November 12, 2011. Cf. Altshuler, "The Holocaust in the Soviet Mass Media," 161.

pointed to the gap between the facts they witnessed and the assertions presented in the film—one case of German brutality was shown as representative of the German terror directed at the local population. Likely, the film further undermined Anya and Liza's opinion about the trustworthiness of the Soviet media. At the same time, those family members who were unaware of the details of the German occupation could have interpreted the newsreel as an urgent call to escape not only from Rostov-on-Don, but from the North Caucasus as well, in order to get as far away as possible from the Germans.

Yet, as Tsylya's letter from December 12 indicates, the evacuated family members were not entirely ignorant of the occurrences in occupied Rostov-on-Don. We can speculate that, since this information could not be obtained from the official media, it was leaked through other channels, most specifically by the refugees who fled Rostov-on-Don immediately after its liberation by the Red Army. However, Efim Ginsburg, having no access to such informal sources (we may safely surmise that no refugee from liberated Rostov-on-Don reached Alma-Ata at that time), could have been more susceptible to official Soviet propaganda on the German atrocities in the city.

On December 24, 1941, *Pravda* published a report on the German genocide of Jews in Taganrog, which had been occupied from October 17 onwards:

> On a certain day, the order was given: the Jews must report to the places of assembly and bring warm clothing and enough food for three days. … Some 500 people gathered. An officer appeared and announced that they would now be sent away to work a short distance from town. They loaded the women and children aboard trucks, and arranged the men in ranks. They ordered them to undress and shot them all. Then it was the women's turn. The soldiers took their children away. The women were also shot with automatic weapons. These matters were retold by people who had managed to escape from the fascist hell.[259]

This report was not complete. The Soviets did not know or were loath to admit that the *entire* Jewish population in Taganrog was wiped out in late October 1941. This detailed information was only published in March 1942. Nevertheless, a report that highlighted the mass murder of Jews—not abroad, not even in a faraway Soviet territory, but in the Rostov District itself—would

---

259 "Zverstva nemtsev v Taganroge," *Pravda*, December 24, 1941. In Altshuler, "The Holocaust in the Soviet Mass Media," 137.

have made a strong impression on the members of the Ginsburg family. *Pravda*, the country's most important newspaper, was sent to every corner of the Soviet Union, including Rostov-on-Don and Ordzhonikidze.

An editorial, "Military Tasks of the Don Bolsheviks," which appeared in *Molot* on December 24, 1941, emphasized the need to reveal those who had collaborated with the Germans:

> In Rostov and in other areas of the District, there are people who betrayed the interests of the Fatherland, who helped the enemy. These people are not numerous… The population should provide (and it does provide) active aid to the Soviet agencies [*organy*] in this cause [*denouncing these people to the authorities*].[260]

Again, the newspaper called upon the population to maintain its vigilance. Perhaps justifiable as a security measure, this incessant spy hunt may have also impeded inhabitants of Rostov-on-Don from receiving timely updates the military events in the area surrounding the city and forming their decisions to escape. Asking questions had become dangerous: people who asked too many questions about the proximity of the German forces could be denounced as German spies. So, the inhabitants of Rostov, including Jews, stifled their inquiries, and as a result, they did not receive vital information.

In a similar vein, the Rostov media continued reporting news with contradictory impact on the population. On December 25, *Molot* reported that eleven people were tried for evasion of defensive work construction and sentenced to prison terms of three to ten years.[261] This news item pointing to the continuous threat to the city was counterbalanced by the report that Rostov's state university, named after Molotov, would resume regular courses after January 1, 1943.

Normality quickly returned to the city, or at least, this was the impression created by the local newspaper. On December 27, *Molot* informed its readers that, starting from January 1, 1942, telephone communications would resume between Rostov-on-Don and all other Soviet cities. Telephone calls could be made from the communication center at 57 Engels Street. The same issue announced that, starting from December 26, Rostov Central Telegraph had begun to accept congratulatory telegrams, which could be sent to all Soviet cities.[262] The telegraph

---

260 *Molot*, no. 305 (6183), December 24, 1941.
261 *Molot*, no. 306 (6185), December 25, 1941.
262 *Molot*, no. 308 (6187), December 27, 1941.

was an important means of communication for the Ginsburg sisters, and they soon made use of it, as we will see later. On the face of it, this report seemed to imply that Rostov's inhabitants could also be kept abreast of developments by means of the telegraph. But, in practice, this was not the case, as Soviet censors effectively barred customers from transmitting such information.

On December 28, 1941, *Molot* published the announcement of the Commander of the Rostov Garrison:

> Persons who, during the period set in accordance with the order of the Commander of the garrison from November 30, 1941, failed to hand over the property taken [*by them*] during the temporary German occupation of the city, should [*now*] hand it over to the police [*militsiia*], or the institutions and enterprises from which it was taken. This should be done no later than January 1, 1942. Those failing to hand over the property will stand trial at military tribunals as looters.[263]

This measure aimed to redress, in part, the economic hardships plaguing Rostov-on-Don. Moreover, this announcement let the population know that of law and order were being restored in the city. As such, it may have assuaged the Ginsburgs' fears.

On December 29, *Molot* published more notes emphasizing Rostov-on-Don's return to normality: it reported that studies in the city's schools would resume from January 1, 1942,[264] and the first performance at the Rostov Puppet Theater would be staged on December 31. With actors recruited from other theaters, the Puppet Theater also planned to stage in January 1942 a new performance, *Rostov-on-Don Speaking*, about the struggle against the Fascist occupiers.[265]

On December 29, 1941, Tamara,[266] wrote to Efim Ginsburg on behalf of the entire evacuee part of the family:

> From December 24, we are inhabitants of Ordzhonikidze. We have a big, quite comfortable room located not far from the center; we were given two beds and some furniture; provision of fuel is our problem. It is expensive:

---

263 "Ot nachal'nika garnizona goroda Rostova-na-Donu," *Molot* No. 309 (6188), December 28, 1941.
264 V. Zolotarev, "V shkolakh goroda vozobnovliaiutsia zaniatiia," *Molot*, no. 310 (6189), December 29, 1941.
265 Ibid.
266 The letter was signed by Tsylya, but from its content it is clear that her sister Tamara wrote it.

we pay 150 rubles a month; those are the prices for rooms here. But as we hope not to stay here too long and to return home soon, we want to live in a normal apartment; after all, we suffered enough in Budennovsk. Certainly, within several days, I'll begin working. As for Tsylya, probably she'll do manicures, as it does not suit her to go out to work, since in this case, my mother will have problems with the children and with the household management.

Life is very expensive; the only cheap things are potatoes: 8–10 rubles for a pail; fats are expensive; there is almost no meat. There are long lines to get bread, but there is also bread sold in commercial stores. After famous Budennovsk, we feel here as if it is paradise; this is a big city and quite beautiful; it is not worse than Rostov. At present, there are very many inhabitants of Rostov here; even our relatives, Semeon Aisenstark with his wife and son, are here. … When the Aisenstarks left Rostov on December 13, Aunt Anya went to see them: they [*the aunts*] are in good health and seem to have decided not to go anywhere, as they hope that everything will be all right. However, we wrote to urge them to leave, and then they should go to Beba at Essentuki, where they may find a dwelling and employment.[267]

Several old and new motives are apparent in this letter. This branch of the Ginsburg family had relocated to Ordzhonikidze. What was the reason for their moving? It was not a result of a worsening security situation in this specific area. Rather, it seems that the Pinchos and Meerovich families relocated in pursuit of a better place to live. Yet, they did not return to their home city of Rostov-on-Don, because they deemed, and justly so, that the situation there was too perilous. This being the case, their move from Budennovsk to Ordzhonikidze seems to have combined security concerns and economic considerations.

The family could not know at that time that, by moving from Budennovsk to Ordzhonikidze, they escaped from the region that would be occupied by the German armies in the second half of 1942, when its entire Jewish population would be destroyed. The Wehrmacht advance stopped precisely on the outskirts of Ordzhonikidze, despite the Germans' attempts to seize this city, capital of the Autonomous Republic of North Ossetia, in the fall of 1942. If the Meerovich and Pinchos families had remained in Ordzhonikidze for the rest of the War, they would in all likelihood have survived the Holocaust.

---

267 From Tsylya Pinkhos in Ordzhonikidze, December 29, 1941, YVA: O.75/324, pp. 114–115.

Also of note are numerous references to the high, and apparently hardly bearable, cost of living in Ordzhonikidze for evacuees. The family did not have any savings, so they had to work. However, the situation was not disastrous: Tsylya could still afford not to find an official job, contented with her occasional work as a manicurist, which could be done at home, but carrying unclear remuneration. The disadvantage was that Tsylya did not receive the invaluable food coupons, for which only people who were officially working were eligible, and which constituted the most precious part of the salary package. That some of Ordzhonikidze's women could indulge in manicures at that time shows that the civil life continued in the city, even though it was close to the battlefields. Overall, Tamara's considerations at this stage do not fall, strictly speaking, into one of the two evacuation-related categories, "stay" or "go." Her mood was improved when she heard of Soviet victories; she thought that her troubles were almost over and contemplated an eventual return to Rostov-on-Don in the not-too-distant future.

Finally, this is one of the few letters that refers to other people outside the narrow circle of the Ginsburg family. Again, as indicated by the names, only Jews were mentioned in the letter. One possible explanation is that Jews were, more than others, affected by the fear of the German enemy and felt the need to escape, to get away from the advancing Wehrmacht. But perhaps, there is more here than meets the eye. The Ginsburg family appeared thoroughly assimilated in its Russian setting. They wrote their letters in very good Russian (especially the younger generation), which almost certainly was their mother tongue. Their letters do not contain a single word of Yiddish or Hebrew. However, judging by their correspondence, the Ginsburgs still tended to socialize primarily with fellow Jews. Coupled with the fact that the family continued to only marry Jews, they seemed to still continue observing their separate Jewish identity, in spite of, or along with being well integrated into the Russian culture.

On December 31, *Molot* informed its readers of the decision of the Rostov City Committee of Defense, "On the Construction of Defensive Borders," made one day previously:

> 1. To set for Rostov's population an average assignment for digging land. Each mobilized person will dig 30 cubic meters throughout the entire period of the work of building the defensive borders. Upon the completion of this norm, the mobilized persons will be released home and given an appropriate certificate. …

5. To authorize police to check houses in order to establish whether their tenants are participating in the construction of the defensive borders, and to punish those evading this labor quota.[268]

From January 1, 1942, a new "military" task was imposed.[269] The decree did not apply to the Ginsburg sisters, nor did it affect them directly. But this New Year "present" indicated the gravity of the situation in the city and was likely to prompt the sisters to leave.

This major news item was "diluted" by the newspaper's routine advertising films screened in Rostov's cinema theaters. The program included not only war films, but also "light" entertainment, such as *Anton Ivanovich Is Angry*, and an animated movie, *The Tale of the Fisher and the Fish*.[270]

On December 31, 1941, Anya and Liza sent a New Year's greeting from Rostov-on-Don to Efim in Alma-Ata:

> Dear Efim!
> We congratulate you on the New Year. We are in good health.
> Hugs and kisses, Anya and Liza.[271]

Written only one month after they had survived the first German occupation of Rostov-on-Don, this note claims that return to normal life, when people celebrate with each other on various occasions, was within reach.

---

268 *Molot*, no. 312 (6191), December 31, 1941.
269 Ibid.
270 Ibid
271 From Liza Chazkewitz and Anya Greener (radiogram), December 31, 1941, YVA: O.75/324, p. 116.

CHAPTER 3

1942–1943

1942

January 1942

The start of 1942 was a time of important military developments in the immediate vicinity of the North Caucasus. The Soviet counter-offensive, which began in late December 1941 on the Crimean peninsula, led to the recapture of Kerch and Feodosia.[1] This tangible result was viewed, first of all by Soviet propaganda, but also by many of the Soviet population, as a natural continuation of the victories near Rostov-on-Don and Moscow. Now, the entire German hold on the Crimean Peninsula was threatened. The more confident the Red Army felt in the Crimea, the smaller seemed the danger of a new German offensive in the direction of Rostov-on-Don. Of course, we cannot be sure that the Ginsburg family perceived its situation in the beleaguered Caucasus in these terms exactly, but they no doubt thought that the successful Soviet advance in the Crimea boded well for them.

On January 1, 1942, *Molot* published a call, "To the soldiers, commanders and political workers of the Southern Front." It was signed by Rostov's two strongmen, the Secretary of the Party District Committee, Boris Dvinsky, and the head of the local administration, Matvei Motinov. It read that "1941 was the year when the destruction of Hitler's gangs commenced. 1942 must become the year of their complete annihilation."[2]

This was a big promise. There was no doubt that it was sanctioned by Moscow and promoted by other means of Soviet propaganda. Arguably, it resonated heavily with the Soviet population, in particular with people like the Ginsburg sisters, who wished to believe in such messages.

Now, let us see how the Soviet counter-offensive in the Crimea was viewed in the West. On January 2, 1942, *The Washington Post* mentioned the Soviet

---

1 Sovinformburo, *Bol'shevistskaia pravda*, no. 1 (1750), January 1, 1942.
2 *Molot*, no. 1 (6192), January 1, 1942.

recapture of Kerch in the Crimea (the status of Feodosia remained unclear, and after two weeks, in mid-January, the Soviet forces had to leave the city):

> When Kerch fell six weeks ago the Nazis hailed it as a victory of great magnitude, which it was—potentially. …Where the Nazis had failed—namely, in crossing the Kerch Strait which separates the Crimea and the Caucasus—the Russians succeeded.[3]

The US newspaper openly stated what the Soviet media fell short of saying: that control of the Crimea was the key to control of the North Caucasus. This strategic consideration, which was not very sophisticated, was always (to the best of my knowledge) absent from Soviet reports. If Soviet citizens, including the Ginsburg family, had been able to sense that there was a link between these developments in real time, this would most likely influence their decision on whether to evacuate.

On January 3, 1942, a newspaper in Ordzhonikidze drew the attention of its readers to the newsreel "Liberated Rostov": "The newsreel was screened throughout December 1941 in Rostov and in Ordzhonikidze. A communal grave of victims of the German occupation of Rostov was shown."[4] Thus, as we have already suggested, the information about the German atrocities against civilians in Rostov-on-Don was available to the younger branches of the Ginsburg family, who were living at that time in Ordzhonikidze. However, judging by the contents of Tsylya Pinchos's letter dated December 12, 1941, the Ginsburg evacuees were less worried than Efim Ginsburg in Alma-Ata regarding the fate of Anya and Liza during the first German occupation.

Tamara Meerovich and Tsylya Pinchos, on the one hand, and Efim Ginsburg, on the other, had access to similar information duing the war. However, the North Caucasian Ginsburgs knew which rumors circulated among those who had recently come from Rostov-on-Don. In this case, the rumors proved to be relatively more trustworthy than the Soviet propaganda (for example, there was no mass murder of civilians, including Jews, at that time, as claimed in the Soviet newsreel). Yet, in the long run, this disregard for all information disseminated by the Soviet propaganda machine, and exclusive reliance on rumors, proved to be dangerous.

---

3 "Kerch retaken," *The Washington Post*, January 2, 1942.
4 G. Pavliashvili, "Osvobozhdennyi Rostov," *Sotsialisticheskaia Osetiia* (Ordzhonikidze), no. 2 (2557), January 3, 1942.

What news actually reached the Ginsburg sisters in Rostov-on-Don? A significant note published by *Molot* on January 3 was entitled "Fighting for Feodosia." Signed by Major-General A. Pervushin, it reported that the Soviet troops had recaptured Kerch and Feodosia in the course of a recent advance.[5] Rostov-on-Don itself continued its return to normal life, as indicated in another note, "Regular movement of trolleybuses commenced." Trolleybuses ran from 7:00 to 17:00, and trams from 6:30 to 17:30. This was encouraging news for the Ginsburg sisters, who by that time were becoming more inclined to remain in Rostov-on-Don.

Keeping in mind the information available to the two branches of the Ginsburg family, in Ordzhonikidze and Rostov-on-Don, let us now look at the next letter, sent by Tamara Meerovich from Ordzhonikidze, on January 3, 1942, to her uncle Efim Ginsburg in Alma-Ata:

> Dear Efim!
>
> We haven't heard from you for so many days and are terribly anxious. Poor you, all alone there; you are faring worse than all of us, you still can't settle down, and moreover, you are worrying so much about the family. …
>
> We think that at least you received our telegram that our people in Rostov are all right, and that you have calmed down. We were also awfully worried about them, and it was only on December 20, 1941, that we received a message from them. They can only blame themselves: if they didn't leave with us when we were evacuated, why didn't they go when it was made possible to leave freely? Besides, while he was in Rostov, Volodya offered to sort it all out and help them, so that they would be able to get here. But they could not make up their minds and said that they might wait a bit longer. Now, without any justification whatsoever, they blame Volodya and me. After all, they aren't children. …
>
> The fuel problem is fairly acute here. …
>
> It would be great if all of us could be together. Certainly, it is not easy to get registered[6] here, but we will make every effort to bring them here. But what I wish even more is that our situation at the fronts would improve, and that they wouldn't need to come here, and that we could go home. It is not easy to live in a foreign land. We have had a lot to bear, in particular concerning the children.

---

5 A. Pervushin, "V boiakh za Feodosiiu," *Molot*, no. 2 (6193), January 3, 1942; "Nachalos' reguliarnoe dvizhenie trolleibusov," ibid.

6 That is, to obtain a permit from the authorities to live in a certain place.

Dear Efim! Write to us about your intentions, with an eye to your arrival here. Do you want to come here, if it is possible? If so, what type of work would fit your profession? Let us know, so that we can find out whether such employment is available here.

Dear Efim! We would like very much to see you here. Volodya says that, provided he is at home, there would be no problem with your registration and employment.

… coal is extraordinarily expensive here, houses are heated with wood; we need 300 rubles [*for fuel*]. Food products are very expensive here. We are waiting impatiently for your decision.[7]

This letter shows that the younger branch of the Ginsburg family was very anxious about Anya and Liza's fate in German-occupied Rostov-on-Don. However, there are some signs indicating that their anxiety was less acute than that of Efim Ginsburg. Even though Tsylya had left her mother Anya in Rostov-on-Don, both she and Tamara Meerovich already had families of their own, and the children became the primary focus of their care and apparently their major concern. In contrast, Efim Ginsburg did not have a family of his own in 1941, and Anya and Liza Ginsburg were his closest relatives. Probably he remained emotionally very attached to them from his childhood, when his older sisters had taken care of their little brother. However, Tsylya and Tamara could not admit their relative calm to Efim, because it would mark a clear departure from the official Soviet position on "unheard-of atrocities committed by the Germans in Rostov," and would also portray them, in Efim's eyes, less concerned about the fate of his two sisters. This would be especially applicable to Tamara, for whom Anya and Liza were only aunts, whereas her own mother, Manya (Monya), had been evacuated with her.

It is worth noting that the "North Caucasians" were in a state of confusion. This is seen from Tamara's question to her uncle—whether and when he intended to move to the North Caucasus (but not to Rostov-on-Don itself, as it seemed too dangerous), with its better material conditions, as compared to Alma-Ata—and her contention that Efim fared worse than the rest of the family.

We also get a glimpse into a rift between the two branches of the Ginsburg family. There was evidently a dispute as to who was to blame for the fact that Anya and Liza Ginsburg had stayed in the city, under threat of German occupation? We have already seen from other letters that Anya and Liza claimed

---

7   From Tamara Meerovich in Ordzhonikidze, January 3, 1942, YVA: O.75/324, pp. 127–132.

it was impossible to leave Rostov-on-Don ecause they did not get an evacuation permit. The sisters also suggested, albeit in a most delicate way, that Volodya Meerovich, the best-connected person among the Ginsburgs, who arranged the evacuation of his immediate family, did not do enough to get Anya and Liza evacuated, too. Tamara, as we see from her letters, disagreed with this interpretation of events and put all the blame for their failure to leave Rostov-on-Don on Anya and Liza themselves. Judging by the sisters' evasive letters to Efim, Tamara's point of view seems more acceptable.

On January 4, *Molot* published on its front page an order by Rostov City Committee of Defense, "On renewed registration (*perepropiska*) of the population of Rostov-on-Don":

> Owing to inadequate registration of the population in Rostov-on-Don resulting from evacuations as well as due to the need to have a precise account: ...
>
> 2. Renewed registration will take place from January 1 to February 10, 1942. ...
>
> 6. Those evading registration will stand trial according to the laws of the War period.[8]

These measures can be understood in part as the Soviet struggle against infiltration by German agents. They might adversely affect Jewish refugees living in the city, but could hardly affect permanent residents like the Ginsburgs. Moreover, the growing number of announcements on routine business affairs, such as buying and selling household goods (page 2 of the same issue of the newspaper) hinted that life in the city was gradually returning to normal.

On January 6, a new Soviet newsreel—which highlighted, among other topics, the advance of the Soviet forces in the southern sector of the Soviet-German front—was shown in cinema theaters.[9] It featured huge columns of Red Army soldiers and transports moving through the city of Rostov-on-Don, and the newsreader emphasized that the Soviet offensive westwards was continuing unabated. Such pictures had the potential to reinforce the optimism of the Ginsburg family, especially since they could not be refuted by any other source, such as the refugees' rumors.

---

8 Predsedatel' GKO B. Dvinskii, "O perepropiske naseleniia goroda Rostova-na-Donu. Postanovlenie gorodskogo komiteta oborony Rostova-na-Donu ot 3.1.42," *Molot*, no. 3 (6194), January 3, 1942.

9 *Soiuzkinozhurnal*, no. 1, January 6, 1942, RGAKFD: record 4673, http://pobeda-vov.ru/Lib/pages/item.aspx?itemid=10527, accessed on December 5, 2011.

The Soviet authorities continued to make strenuous efforts to enforce the compulsory work order calling on every adult to participate in the construction of various defensive lines in and around the city. On January 6, *Molot* published an article reporting on a conversation with Polozkov, the Prosecutor of the Rostov district, "The duty of every worker is to participate in the construction of defensive installations." The article mentioned two cases of evasion of duty. One of the transgressors was condemned to ten years' imprisonment, the other to five years.[10] The Ginsburgs could understand from this article that the military situation around Rostov-on-Don remained precarious.

As previously mentioned, the Soviet recapture of Rostov-on-Don in late November 1941 was highlighted in the newsreel "Liberated Rostov." From January 6, 1942, it was also screened in Rostov-on-Don itself; if the Ginsburg sisters had watched the newsreel, it would have boosted their morale.

On January 7, 1942, the Soviet radio broadcast a short report on the resumption of normal life in Rostov-on-Don:

> Economic and cultural life has quickly resumed in the city of Rostov-on-Don, and in those areas of the district that have been liberated from the German occupiers. Hundreds of state and cooperative enterprises have started working again. Plumbing, the electric network, trams and trolley-buses have been set in operation. Saunas, stores, movie theaters, theaters, libraries, reading rooms, elementary and middle schools, as well as vocational schools have opened their doors.[11]

This report was broadcast all over the country and was available, among others, to the evacuee branch of the Ginsburg family. It could serve as another soothing signal, which, in due time, would prompt their return to Rostov-on-Don.

On January 8, 1942, Tamara Meerovich and her relatives residing in Ordzhonikidze, as well as the Rostov Ginsburgs,[12] could have read several remarkable articles in the local newspapers. By far the most important of them was the publication of the entire note by Soviet Commissar of Foreign Affairs,

---

10 "Dolg kazhdogo trudiashchegosia—uchastvovat' v stroitel'stve oboronitel'nykh ukreplenii. Beseda s Prokurorom Rostovskoi oblasti tov. Polozkovym," *Molot*, no. 4 (6195), January 7, 1942.

11 Sovinformburo update, January 7, 1942, http://army.lv/ru/Istoriya-Rossii/Velikaya-Otechestvennaya-voyna-%281941-1945%29/Ot-Sovetskogo-Informbyuro/1942-god/Yanvar-1942-goda/975.

12 The Note was reproduced all over the country. However, we do not know the exact number of issues of *Molot* in which the Note was published. I was unable to access these issues.

Vyacheslav Molotov, delivered on January 6 to all the countries with which the Soviet Union maintained diplomatic relations. Reprinted in the regional press across the Soviet Union on January 8, the note enlarged on the murder of Jews by the Germans, mainly in Kiev:

> Horrible slaughter and pogroms were committed by the German invaders in the Ukrainian capital, Kiev. In only a few days, the German bandits killed and tortured 52,000 men, women, old men and children, mercilessly dealing with all Ukrainians, Russians and Jews, who in any manner displayed their loyalty to the Soviet Government. Soviet citizens who have escaped from Kiev described the astounding picture of these mass executions. A large number of Jews, including women and children, were assembled together in the Jewish cemetery. Before being shot, all of them were stripped naked and beaten up … and were shot with automatic rifles. …[13]

Molotov's Note did not state explicitly that the Jews were singled out for extermination by the Germans. Still, it did indicate that Jews were among the groups of Soviet citizens that were purposefully targeted by the Germans for criminal mistreatment. Thus, the Note could serve as a warning light to the Ordzhonikidze branch of the Ginsburg family. When they had to decide whether to escape further eastwards, to stay where they were, or to return westwards to Rostov-on-Don, this Note would be a proof of the tangible German threat. Possibly, this Note had a more powerful impact than many ordinary reports, because it expressed the official position of the Soviet government.

The Note also included sentences relating to Rostov-on-Don, which probably had particular resonance for the Ginsburgs. It stated that the Germans claimed that they made a total registration of all the Jews in Rostov-on-Don. It was further mentioned that "Fascist pogromists prepared another extermination of tens of thousands of people. Fortunately, they were unsuccessful." Definitely this sounded frightening, especially as the sentence was read in the context of the tragedy of the Kiev Jews. However, it was not frightening enough to convince the Rostov Jews to flee immediately and at any cost.

Other messages coming from the Soviet media with regards to evacuation remained ambiguous. On the same day, the same newspaper showed

---

13 "O povsemestnykh grabezhakh," *Sotsialisticheskaia Osetiia* (Ordzhonikidze), no. 6 (2561), January 8, 1942. The translation is in *Soviet Government Statements on Nazi Atrocities* (London: Hutchinson, 1946), 22. On Molotov's Note, see, for example, Berkhoff, *Motherland in Danger*, 126. Cf. Lukasz Hirszowicz, "The Holocaust in the Soviet Mirror," *East European Jewish Affairs* 22, no. 1 (1992): 40.

advertisements from local theaters and cinema theaters,[14] emphasizing the normality of life in the city and conveying the message that the area was strongly under Soviet control and there was no need to leave.

In her letter sent on January 8, 1942, Tamara Meerovich had to first defend herself against apparently harsh accusations from her uncle. Evidently, Efim believed that Tamara, or the evacuated branch of the family, had not done enough to bring about the evacuation of the Ginsburg sisters

> Dear Efim,
> We have just received your letter dated December 26. Yes, your letter is far from being delicate but most important, none of the charges are justified. We have written to you frequently, but as regards our people in Rostov, we only learned on December 19 that they were alive, and immediately thereupon sent you a telegram. If you did not receive it until December 29, it is not through any fault of ours, but because of the Telegraph [*Office*].[15]

Then, Tamara repeated to Efim Ginsburg the saga that led to the evacuation of her part of the family, and to Anya and Liza staying in Rostov-on-Don:

> As for inviting our people from Rostov, it was impossible for them to go with us. But then, it became possible but they decided to wait, and asked us endlessly what it was like to live in our town. At the same time, we bombarded them with letters and telegrams pleading with them to leave. You shouldn't blame Volodya; he left Rostov on November 21, when the enemy's bullets were dropping near him. Then, he went on foot from the frontline towards the Kavkazskaya station, and not the way you suggest. These are facts, they speak in our favor, and therefore, it was painful [*literally "hurt to tears"*] for me to read your letter. You are the closest and the dearest person for us, our dear one. We are terribly anxious and concerned about you.[16]

The exchange between Efim and Tamara can be summed up as follows: Efim repeatedly blamed Tamara's husband, Volodya Meerovich, for his sisters' failure to leave Rostov-on-Don; Tamara defended her husband. To Efim in remote

---

14 *Sotsialisticheskaia Osetiia* (Ordzhonikidze), no. 6 (2561), January 8, 1942.
15 From Tamara Meerovich in Ordzhonikidze, January 8, 1942, YVA: O.75/324, p. 136.
16 Ibid.

Alma-Ata, Volodya appeared to be the only person able to arrange the sisters' evacuation. Tamara explained to her uncle that her aunts were simply reluctant to move away. In passing, we learn that Volodya apparently was engaged in the fighting. We will learn more about the nature of his involvement in the War in 1941 from Tamara's future letters.

The Soviet authorities continued to demonstrate to the local population that peace and normal life had returned to Rostov-on-Don. On January 8, *Molot* informed its readers that pre-schools had reopened in the city.[17] Furthermore, the newspaper published an order signed by the military commander of Rostov's garrison, which sanctioned free movement of privately owned trucks in the city, without special authorization, until 20:00. Public transport could operate longer than previously: trams until 18:00 and trolleybuses until 18:30.[18] Such measures gradually made the life of Rostov's inhabitants more convenient, and could have further strengthened the Ginsburgs' desire not to move away from the city.

Finally, as we remember, the Soviet authorities had already issued warnings urging civilians to return the goods that had been looted from public stores and warehouses during the period (of just a day or two) between the withdrawal of the Soviet forces and the establishment of the German occupation (November 19–21, 1941). It looks as if few people responded to this call. On January 8, *Molot* reported that the financial police (OBKhSS)[19] "arrested a group of major looters, who, during German rule, had engaged in looting Soviet institutions, stores, warehouses." Five people, all of them bearing Russian or Ukrainian family names, were arrested, and, it was promised, would stand trial.[20]

On January 9, 1942, the sisters, Liza and Anya, sent a new letter to Alma-Ata:

> We have written you so many times that we are alive and well, and that the confounded Fascist barbarians did not have enough time to hurt and exterminate us; they failed, because they were soon expelled from our Rostov by our heroes, the warriors of the Red Army, who came in good time to our aid. However, these bandits and robbers committed so many atrocities and killed so many innocent people. Of course, you would take it very hard.

---

17 "Otkrylis' detskie iasli," *Molot*, no. 6 (6197), January 8, 1942.
18 Order no. 19 by Svinitsky, the military commander of Rostov's garrison, ibid.
19 OBKhSS [*Otdel bor'by s khishcheniiami sotsialisticheskoi sobstvennosti*] was the abbreviation for the Department for Combatting the Embezzlement of Socialist Property, acting under the People's Commissariat of Internal Affairs.
20 "Arest maroderov," *Molot*, no. 6 (6197), January 8, 1942.

> Now we are staying here and are not considering evacuation. In recent days, many people have come back. In all probability, we won't need to leave. It will be better [*for us*] to see all our dear people, including you, coming back [*here*]. We will be truly happy. When will this happy day come, when we will all gather together?! I think it will be soon, by May 1, 1942.[21]

The first paragraph of the letter sheds light on the sisters' mindset at that time. Some of their remarks deserve to be emphasized. This was the first acknowledgement made by Liza and Anya that they only survived because the Germans "did not have enough time to hurt and exterminate us." This, in turn, indicates that, whatever they thought about the Germans before and during the first occupation, the sisters were now determined to do their utmost so as not to find themselves under German rule a second time. The only new item of information that the sisters acquired at this time about the German policies towards Jews could have come from the Soviet sources. This demonstrates that the sisters were receptive to both explicit and implicit Soviet propaganda messages. (That Anya and Liza accepted Soviet phraseology is manifest in many of their letters, including the current one.)

Still, their decision does not seem final at this stage. To support their decision to stay in Rostov, the sisters cited examples of the mass return of evacuees to Rostov-on-Don. This is in accordance with what we know from other sources, although the sisters' stress on a mass return appears to have been remarkably exaggerated. Furthermore, they demonstrated to what extent they were in agreement with the intentions of the Soviet propaganda, not supported by the developments on the ground, by falling for its gimmicks promising quick victory over the Germans, by May 1942.

Not having heard back from her uncle, on January 10, Tamara made another attempt to inform Efim that the Rostov Ginsburgs had fortunately survived the German occupation: "Staggered so many telegrams [*were*] not received. Our [*people*] in Rostov [*are*] in a good health. Tamara."[22]

On January 11, 1942, a newspaper in neighboring Stavropol reported on the mistreatment of Jews in Warsaw, by the Germans. The article mentioned

---

21 From Liza Chazkewitz and Anya Greener, January 9, 1942, YVA: O.75/324, pp. 137–138.
22 From Tamara Meerovich in Ordzhonikidze (telegram), January 10, 1942, YVA: O.75/324, p. 139.

the Jews, the Warsaw Ghetto, congestion and malnourishment.²³ This report was not reproduced, either in Rostov-on-Don or in Ordzhonikidze, and therefore was unavailable to any branch of the Ginsburg family.

On January 13, 1942, Anya and Liza Ginsburg wrote a letter to Alma-Ata:

> Don't worry and don't be upset with us, our dear one! We turned out to be alive and well. The damned Fascist bandit and barbarian did not manage to reach us. And he will never do so, because we want to believe that there would no way back for him here.
>
> For the time being, we are not thinking about going anywhere. Instead, we think that probably it would be better for us to wait for our dear people, including you, to come here, back to Rostov.²⁴

The sisters sound more confident now regarding their decision not to leave Rostov-on-Don, albeit not absolutely convinced ("for the time being"). Still, they had to admit, though half-heartedly, that their decision was based mainly on emotion and opinion ("we want to believe …").

The next item of information of relevance to our subject, published in the local North Caucasian media, differs from what we have analyzed to date. It has nothing to do with the course of the Soviet-German War, but rather with the economic problems caused by the movement of evacuees into the North Caucasus and out of it. The central Soviet government as well as local administrations went to some lengths to alleviate the lot of refugees. One of the steps in this direction involved the allocation of special funds, both money and goods, to meet the specific needs of the evacuee population. As I already wrote elsewhere,²⁵ this policy was also applied in the North Caucasus. To some extent, these measures did produce the desired effect. But as the War severely aggravated the chronic shortages of all goods and services that were plaguing the country's economy, these special allocations, along with conventional supplies for local inhabitants, inevitably drew the attention of those whom the Soviets castigated as "speculators."

This was the subject of the next newspaper clip. In the winter of 1941–1942, North Ossetia's OBKhSS was in charge, among other things, of policing Ordzhonikidze, where Tamara Meerovich, Tsylya Pinchos, and their families were now living. The article revealed that there were robbers in the local food industry and

---

23   *Ordzhonikidzevskaia pravda* (Stavropol), no. 9 (2384), January 11, 1942.
24   From Liza Chazkewitz and Anya Greener, January 13, 1942, YVA: O.75/324, pp. 141–142.
25   Feferman, "A Soviet Humanitarian Action?," 822–824.

in bakeries, and reported that, "The following were confiscated: 3 tons of wheat, 200 kilograms of groats, 40 kilograms of salt, 60 kilograms of butter, 200 kilograms of meat, 1 ton of potatoes, 1,000 packets of cigarettes, 100 tablets of soap."[26]

This was the economic reality with which the evacuees had to cope. Although the lot of the local inhabitants was also very difficult, they at least had some food reserves they could use. In contrast, the evacuees—I mean here average people with average means at their disposal, which sooner or later ran out—could only rely upon state supplies.

On January 14, 1942, Tamara Meerovich sent a letter from Ordzhonikize to Efim Ginsburg:

> Dear Efim!
>
> Finally, today we received a money transfer from you. And we hurry to notify you about it. Today I am sending it [on] to Rostov. On [January] 8, we sent you a postcard and a telegram. It is a pity that, though I write to you often, apparently you don't receive my letters.
>
> Yesterday, one of Volodya's colleagues came here from Rostov; he went to see our relatives and brought us their letters. They are in good health; their state of mind has improved and we are very glad about that. We urge them to come here, but do not know what decision they will make.
>
> They are living in our apartment, together with Polina Tilli's relatives, whose [own] apartment was apparently damaged. It is good because they are not alone. Sima Svirsky received your letter and came to see us with it. They are all in good health. We really want to know that you received [our] good news and have calmed down. Don't take offense with us; we did and do everything we could. Write back more often. Be healthy. We wish you all the best. Kissing you. Tamara.[27]

Evidently, at least some of the Ginsburg letters went unnoticed by the Soviet censors. We do not know how often that was the case. In all probability, only letters within the North Caucasus could be hand-delivered in this way, as it is difficult to imagine that any of the family's trusted friends travelled from

---

26 Gosudarstevnnyi Arkhiv Respubliki Severnaia Osetiia: P-639/1/80, pp. 12, 16, 21. In Aleksandr Israpov, *Gosudarstvennye organy upravleniia i narod v 1941–1945 gg.: aspekty politicheskogo, ekonomicheskogo i organizatsionno-pravovogo vzaimodeistviia na materialakh avtonomnykh respublik Severnogo Kavkaza*, PhD diss., Makhachkala, Dagestanskii nauchnyi tsentr Rossiiskoi Akademii nauk, 2004, 203.

27 From Tamara Meerovich in Ordzhonikidze, January 14, 1942, YVA: O.75/324, p. 144.

the North Caucasus to Alma-Ata, back and forth. Furthermore, we do not have these uncensored letters at our disposal and cannot compare them to letters sent by ordinary mail and screened by the censors. However, it must have been an especially intimate channel, through which the North Caucasian Ginsburgs could keep each other informed about news that they were reluctant to share by phone, by telegram, or in conventional letters.

As in previous lettes, Tamara again hints that those family members living with her were in favor of the evacuation of the Rostov relatives to Ordzhonikidze. But here, probably for the first time, Tamara did not insist on their evacuation, as she had probably begun to view the situation in Rostov-on-Don as more stable than previously. This mood was manifest in her letter, even though some local people suffered from the War's privations, having to host other Soviet people in their homes—either local inhabitants, as was the case with Tamara's relatives, or refugees.

Rebuked by the propaganda campaign emanating from the center,[28] the local authorities in those North Caucasian areas that were flooded with refugees began a massive campaign to help the uprooted people. The place where Tamara Meerovich settled was no exception to the rule. On January 14, 1942, the local administration (*Oblispolkom*) of Ordzhonikidze gave orders for monetary aid to be rendered to the evacuees, totaling 200,000 rubles.[29]

From early 1942 to October 1, 1942, the newsreel "The North Caucasus" was shown all over the region. It highlighted "the destruction of German [*forces*] near Rostov-on-Don,"[30] and was, like other similar steps, intended to instill confidence and raise the morale of the Soviet people.

On January 15, 1942, Tsylya Pinchos wrote a letter from Ordzhonikidze to Alma-Ata:

> … yesterday I received the first letter from Dod; I was very glad. He is presently in the Stalingrad District and is supposed to be transferred to Rostov.
>
> Recently, we had a greeting from our relatives in a letter dated January 9. Their mood has improved; they write that a lot of people are returning to Rostov, and that they are waiting for us impatiently. But, at the same time,

---

28 Feferman, "A Soviet Humanitarian Action?," 827–828.
29 Israpov, *Gosudarstvennye organy upravleniia*, 167.
30 Malyshev, *Sredstva massovoi informatsii Iuga Rossii*, 47–48.

they report that it would be better for us not to come immediately. We are all in good health and that's what we wish for you.

[*We are*] waiting impatiently for good news and the final defeat of the Fascists.[31]

Tsylya's testimony shed some light on her husband, David (Dod), about whom we know next to nothing. Communication between the home front and the Army was complicated in the wartime Soviet Union. It is no wonder that Tsylya was happy about receiving just one, albeit the most precious, item of information from her husband.[32] Still, it seems that overall, Tsylya was quite reserved in expressing herself about her husband, compared to Tamara's reports about Volodya.

Efim Ginsburg with Tsilya Pinchos and Tamara Meerovich. 1932. Courtesy of Yad Vashem Photo Archive.

The letter also indicates that mid-January 1942 was a precarious period, when no one in the family was certain of anything. On the one hand, Tsylya claimed that the Rostov branch of the family was "waiting for us impatiently." On

---

31 From Tsylya Pinchos in Ordzhonikidze, January 15, 1942, YVA: O.75/324, p. 146.
32 Three excellent collections of letters written by Red Army Jewish soldiers are available, in the three-volume edition, *Sokhrani moi pis'ma. Sbornik pisem evreev Velikoi Otechestvennoi voiny*, ed. Il'ia Altman and Leonid Terushkin (Moscow: Tsentr i Fond "Kholokost," Izdatel'stvo "MIK," 2007, 2010, and 2013).

the other hand, there was no certainty regarding the situation in Rostov-on-Don, either. Unlike her cousin Tamara, Tsylya Pinchos does not reveal her own grasp of the situation, but rather conveys ideas expressed by other family members.

On January 15, 1942, it was Tamara's turn to write to Efim in Alma-Ata:

> Yesterday we received the money transfer and reported it to you immediately. At first, we thought about returning it to you. But then Liza wrote that you might be offended, and therefore we sent it to Rostov.
>
> All is quiet in Rostov; life is going all right again. …We are living now better than we did previously. The room is not bad; the city reminds us of Rostov. But the thing is that there is talk that Volodya's plant might be moved back to Rostov. This is not good news, since the general situation has not improved enough for us to go back.[33]

As the material conditions of both branches of the family in Ordzhonikidze and Rostov-on-Don improved somewhat, they didn't refer to this subject as often in their letters. It appears that, other things being equal, Tamara was inclined to go on living in Ordzhonikidze as long as her husband could stay with her. But this was a unique situation, which could not last long. Volodya Meerovich was a man of draft age and he could be enlisted at any moment. As long as he was still working on the plant, it could also be relocated back at any time, as the Soviet authorities began to consider the situation in Rostov-on-Don quite stable. The letter captures this ideal situation—as far as the Meerovich family was concerned—but also reflects the uneasiness because this fragile state of affairs could easily change.

Volodya's plant could be brought back to Rostov-on-Don, but Tamara clearly did not see the situation in the city and its surroundings as stable enough. These lines reveal her more realistic—and therefore, more pessimistic—views, which differed from those of the rest of her North Caucasian relatives.

The city and district of Rostov-on-Don, where one of the branches of the Ginsburg family stayed, was still a focal point for refugees who had fled from the Western Soviet areas, away from the advancing German armies. According to official Soviet statistics, as of January 20, 1942, the number of evacuees in the Rostov District was very large—183,000 people.[34] The mindset of some of these people must have been similar to that of Anya and Liza Ginsburg. The

---

33 From Tamara Meerovich in Ordzhonikidze, January 15, 1942, YVA: O.75/324, p. 148.
34 Summary of the lists of evacuees from the areas close to the front line, as of February 15, 1942, SNK RSFSR, Department of economic accommodation of the evacuated population, For service use only, YVA: JM/24678. Source: GARF: A-259/40/3517.

refugees probably had better knowledge about the German policies towards Jews than the Ginsburg, and, having already fled once to escape the Germans, they were more dynamic. Still, some of them viewed the Soviet recapture of Rostov-on-Don in late November 1941 as a reassuring sign that the Soviets would never let the city fall again.

On January 21, 1942, Tamara Meerovich sent this letter to Efim Ginsburg:

> We've received a letter from them, dated January 17. They are in good health; Aunt Liza is working at a pharmacy, while Aunt Anya isn't working yet. She is in charge of the house and buying food. They are not considering coming to us, and hope to see us at their home. We all are in good health; it is difficult to purchase anything.[35]

Evidently, there was a further change in the family's assessment of the situation. Anya and Liza were firm about staying in Rostov-on-Don, and, for the first time, Tamara and Tsylya were not urging them to leave. They did not even express their concern about the sisters remaining in Rostov-on-Don. Now, the North Caucasian Ginsburgs were more and more preoccupied about their financial difficulties. The problem was how to procure food. It seems that the Rostov Ginsburgs were more successful at doing that than the evacuee members of the family—presumably because they had long-established connections and more possessions at their disposal, as the Rostov branch were still living in their home city.

On January 28, 1942, Liza and Anya Ginsburg sent a short note to their brother:

> Our dear one!
> Right now we are not considering going anywhere. Our relatives are bursting to come back here. It would be better, if both they, and you, our dear one, were to come here.[36]

Notable here is the sisters' emphasis on how their relatives were "bursting" to return to Rostov-on-Don. This contrasts sharply with what Tamara and Tsylya wrote in their letters. All the same, this description should not be dismissed out of hand as wishful thinking. It is possible that, in their internal correspondence or in their phone calls, some evacuee members of the family did express their willingness to return. Even if that was the case, at this stage it must have been

---

35 From Tamara Meerovich in Ordzhonikidze, January 21, 1942, YVA: O.75/324, p. 152.
36 From Liza Chazkewitz and Anya Greener, January 28, 1942, YVA: O.75/324, p. 160.

just one person, most likely Tsylya. This may have to do with the fact that, unlike Tamara, she was not employed; nor did she have her husband and mother close to her. Consequently, for both financial and psychological reasons, Tsylya might have been more inclined to return to Rostov-on-Don, a place where her mother was living. Thus, the sisters' account seems to indicate an apparent turnabout in the mindset of their evacuee relatives.

On January 28, 1942, Anna and Liza sent a long letter to Efim Ginsburg:

> ... Get better—in your health, nerves, and general appearance. We want to see you, our dear one, in our midst this summer, in July, as we were used to do, as we saw [*you*] last year. It is our only wish. Very soon, at least before May 1, I wish that that damned barbaric Fascism will be destroyed forever. [*We hope*] that, together with the whole Soviet people, we will all celebrate the great proletarian holiday, May 1, 1942 with a great victory over our enemy. [*We hope*] we will all be [*alive*] and living together, as we were until recently.
>
> Our dear one! We are not considering going anywhere, for the time being, because now it is said that there is no need to do so. Our relatives are dreaming about coming here. Certainly, it would be better for them to come here [*than*] if we were to go to them. ... I can state firmly that this day will come, very soon. That's what I want and that's what is needed. The enemy will be smashed and the triumph will be ours. ...
>
> We are in good health. Anya is not working at present, because there is no work to be found, as yet. But it does not matter, since she is busy enough, keeping house. We are living at Monya's place, because our house is not heated yet. But they say our house will soon be included [*in the list of those heated*]. ...
>
> On December 31, we sent a telegram to congratulate you for the New Year. Be happy and let us have big victories. ...
>
> Our [*people*] [*Tamara and the other evacuees*] sent your money back [*to you*] because they learnt you were not working. ...
>
> Greetings from the Svirsky [*family*]; his son is at Baku. The Epiles [*family*] remained at home. ...
>
> See you soon. Yours, survivors of the occupation of the German beasts. They will never be here again!!!
>
> Yours, Anya and Liza.[37]

---

37   Ibid., pp. 159–170.

This is one of the letters in the Ginsburg collection of correspondence that particularly abound with Soviet propaganda clichés, some of them rendered verbatim (such as "the whole Soviet people", "the great proletarian holiday"). The sisters may have used this assertive style for the Soviet censors, but it seems most likely that it mainly resulted from Soviet wartime propaganda resonating significantly with them. As a result, Anya and Liza occasionally came to identify with its messages, as they precisely reflected the sisters' inner thoughts,[38] helped them to soothe their concerns, and reinforced their desire not to leave Rostov-on-Don.

Of note is the reference to Anna's unemployment. This fact is recognized both by the sisters and Tamara, albeit in a different way. The sisters indicate that if there was work available, Anna would work, apparently because she would in this case provide the much needed money and the even more precious food coupons that only working people could receive. In contrast, Tamara implies that, while unemployed, Anna took upon herself the important task of procuring the food for herself and her sister. It looks like the sisters were reluctant to report this detail to Efim: it might have revealed their miserable situation, and thus compromise the picture they wished to present to the evacuee Ginsburgs: a quiet and self-sufficient family living at home.

Only one day later, on January 29, 1942, the sisters sent a slightly different message:

> They [*the evacuee branch of the family*] strongly desire to come back home; they have become very tired and exhausted. But I am writing to them to say that they should not hurry. When they are permitted to do so, they may come. I hope it will be as soon as possible.[39]

This time, Anna and Liza appear to have been less insistent on their relatives' urgent return to Rostov-on-Don. The letter suggests that such permits would be issued by the authorities when they deemed the general situation around the city to be stable enough. The sisters implied that, despite all their previous assurances that it was quiet and peaceful in Rostov-on-Don, for the time being they could not take the responsibility for their relatives' return to the city.

---

38 On this topic, see Feferman, "To Flee or Not to Flee."
39 From Liza Chazkewitz and Anya Greener, January 29, 1942, YVA: O.75/324, p. 158.

February 1942

The situation in the city of Rostov-on-Don indeed stabilized, to some degree. At least, the Soviet authorities and the media did their utmost to demonstrate that the city was firmly under control and that the residents had normal lives. On February 1, the Rostov newspaper reported extensively about a ski cross event, held jointly by the Komsomol and the Trade Union and dedicated to the twenty-third anniversary of the Red Army. According to this report, tens of thousands of people took part in the competition.[40]

On February 1, 1942, Liza and Anna sent another letter to Efim Ginsburg:

> Our dear one!
> Everyone wishes to return to Rostov. You urge us in the strongest terms to join our relatives in Ordzhonikidze. So, I am writing to you in this regard. First, they are longing to come home and they do not know how to do it: the thing is that, so far, they have not been permitted to return. Even Volodya himself wishes to return to Rostov. Indeed, I wrote to them not to hurry and to move at the right time, when they are entitled to do so. For us, there will be no evacuation from here; evacuation permits are not being issued. So we think that it does not make sense to apply for evacuation permits, especially as such good news is being broadcast every day on the radio. These barbarians, [these] German murderers, will never come here; death to the German occupiers, death! [Death to] these barbarians, army of robbers! The enemy will be smashed and the victory will be ours. So, we'd better wait for a speedy return of our dear ones. I also hope to see you among us.
>
> Therefore, for the time being, we have decided, our dear one, not to leave. Don't take offense! You see, now we don't need to move, while later there will be absolutely no need to move anywhere. It is our firm decision to wait for all of you, our dear ones, to come back here. …
>
> We are in good health, but our nerves are really frayed; we are also growing thin. But all this is no problem. The important thing is peace of mind; it will settle our nerves and improve our general appearance. Please write to us, our dear one, about what you think regarding our firm decision not to go anywhere, but rather to wait for you here.[41]

---

40 *Molot*, no. 27 (6218), February 2, 1942.
41 From Liza Chazkewitz and Anya Greener, February 1, 1942, YVA: O.75/324, pp. 175–182.

This time, Anya and Liza provided a solid and balanced account of their evacuation prospects. In many respects, this letter differs from their previous more emotional declarations. It seems that Anya and Liza wanted to persuade their brother that, given the circumstances, they had made the only right decision.

Their reasoning in this letter is probably more refined than ever, but their basic arguments against evacuation remain the same: psychological ("so many people have returned to Rostov; all our relatives also want to do so") and pseudo-rational ("such good news is being broadcast every day on the radio"). As we do not have precise data pointing to the scale of return of Soviet civilians to Rostov-on-Don, the impact of the first factor cannot be gauged. However, we are able to evaluate the impact of the Soviet radio broadcasts. In January 1942, there were, indeed, many of them, highlighting the Soviet advance on the southern front.[42] Although, with one exception, the broadcasts did not mention specific localities recaptured by the Red Army, their cumulative jubilant mood and intensity, especially by late January 1942, must have affected the Soviet listeners, including the Ginsburg family. Evidently, by early February 1942, the weight of all these factors on the sisters' calculations had increased considerably. Coupled with their initial reluctance to move away, the broadcasts reinforced the sisters' decision to stay.

It's worth noting that Anna and Liza continued expressing themselves through the use of Soviet propaganda clichés ("death to the German occupiers, death! …"). Perhaps they repeated these phrases to convince themselves, but it is also possible that they did embrace the clichés as their own.

A new item of information disclosed by Anna and Liza in this letter referred to their physical and mental condition. It turned out that the War, the German occupation, wartime privations in their home city, and the ongoing uncertainty surrounding the two sisters had cost them dearly, and their health had deteriorated significantly. Moreover, the sisters were compelled to admit that, despite their unflagging optimism, they were far from feeling peace of mind. Implicit is the idea that this feeling could only be regained when the German threat against Rostov-on-Don was entirely alleviated.

The report on "A new thrust against the German occupiers in the south," published in the Rostov newspaper on February 4, 1942[43], is an example of the

---

42 Of note are the broadcasts from January 6, 13, 23, 24, 26, 27, 28, 29, 30, 1942. See http://army.lv/ru/Istoriya-Rossii/Velikaya-Otechestvennaya-voyna-(1941-1945)/Ot-Sovetskogo-Informbyuro/1942-god/974, accessed November 22, 2012.

43 *Molot*, no. 29 (6220), February 4, 1942.

"good news" mentioned by the sisters in their previous letter. However, the report—quite characteristically—did not provide any specific details about Soviet military achievements. Indeed, as we now know, the Red Army did conduct an offensive in the region in February and March of that year, but it failed to advance in the German-held territory in the Donbass region.[44]

Meanwhile, the evacuee branch of the Ginsburg family had a very difficult life, as seen from Tamara's next letter, sent from Ordzhonikidze on February 5, 1942:

> We are in good health. Volodya and I are working. It is frosty here and it is very costly to heat [the apartment]. We are sick and tired of the "refugee" life; we'd like to get home soon. But it is difficult to say when this will take place.[45]

This is the first time when the Ginsburg refugees acknowledged that they were considering returning home, even though at that time it was not feasible. Importantly, the desire to eturn was even shared by Tamara Meerovich, the person who got along during the evacuation better than anyone else in the family (remember that she had a job, and her husband and mother were living with her).

Two days later, Tamara wrote another letter to her uncle:

> It is a long time since I wrote to you. Of course, it is my fault—but there is nothing to write about. Especially since Liza keeps you informed about all the events. … Our son is growing bigger. Time will pass quickly, we won't even notice how quickly, before he goes to school. … I have registered him in the children's library, [he] listens with attention and demands that I change them [the books] for new ones.
>
> Dear Uncle Efim! Come to see us; we are going to wrestle. … Soon I am going to visit Voroshilov. …[46]

This is one of the few letters in which the correspondents did not complain about the difficulties they were facing. Amidst the mess and the War's privations that surrounded them, Tamara saw what really counted for her—her son, who wrote the last two lines of the letter. He was supposed to start school in

---

44 David M. Glantz, "The Red Army's Donbas Offensive (February–March 1942) Revisited: A Documentary Essay," *The Journal of Slavic Military Studies* 18, no. 3 (2005): 369–503.
45 From Tamara Meerovich in Ordzhonikidze, February 5, 1942, YVA: O.75/324, pp. 203–204.
46 From Tamara Meerovich in Ordzhonikidze, February 7, 1942, ibid., pp. 185–186.

September 1943. Why did Tamara stress the "long time" that had passed since she wrote to Efim, when she had written to him only two days earlier? It may show that intellectually, she was lonely, and most likely wanted to contact her uncle, probably the only person in the family who shared her opinions regarding the evacuation, as often as possible.

This statement was sent by a local police inspector in Rostov-on-Don to Efim Ginsburg in Alma-Ata on February 8, 1942: "Citizen Ginsburg E. G. This is to announce that Ginsburg A. G. and Chazkewitz E. G., who you were inquiring about, are residing in the city of Rostov; they are alive and in good health."[47] Efim had made an official inquiry to the Rostov authorities regarding the fate of his relatives under the German occupation. This is a strong indicator that the powerful Soviet bureaucratic machine was back in operation in the city. Once again, the Soviets were in charge of population movement, and, if need be, able to help ordinary people locate their relatives.

On February 9, 1942, the sisters sent another letter to Efim in Alma-Ata:

> Again, our dear one, you are urging us to move to be with our relatives. I wrote to you in all our recent letters that so far there is no need to leave without evacuation permits; in this case, we might lose our room [*here*]. It is very frosty now; we can hardly endure such weather. Besides, our dear one, I must say outright that when I start to think about our departure as an immediate enterprise, I feel terrible, since I am afraid of travelling, because of my health. I get truly disturbed; my heart palpitates wildly. In addition, there are possessions that we must surely take with us. But I can carry absolutely nothing. Even light things, let alone getting on a train with [*our*] possessions. As soon as I begin to think about it, I feel ill. Certainly, if there was someone to accompany us to the destination point and to help us handle our possessions during the trip, to put us on the train and to arrange everything, then we would [*consider it*] more willingly. But in any case, there is no need; we shall stay here, however difficult it is for us and regardless of the outcome. Our health is not quite strong, let alone our nerves. ...
>
> Anya is at home; she is very nervous. ...
>
> We have received reports that these barbarians are beaten and destroyed and driven westwards. All the same, it will soon be all over with them. These bandits will be destroyed to the last man. So that we won't need to go anywhere. So that everyone will come back.[48]

---

47 From divisional inspector Tkachev in Rostov-on-Don, February 8, 1942, ibid., p. 187.
48 From Liza Chazkewitz and Anya Greener, February 9, 1942, ibid., pp. 188–195.

In this letter, the sisters added a new reason for not evacuating, namely their fear of losing their room. This argument might indeed have been valid: unauthorized evacuation, that is, leaving one's home town without obtaining prior permission from the authorities, could lead to a family being deprived of their only asset: an apartment, or, for most families, a room in an apartment.[49] This shows us the conditions in which the Ginsburg family lived, and which were typical at that time for Soviet citizens.

This letter also depicts the decision-making process among the family members, at this stage of the War, in a new light. Evidently, the sisters gradually ceased to think that the situation was fraught with deadly danger. As a result, the weight of all other considerations, including the economic ones, increased dramatically. A journey away from Rostov could lead to many privations, which Anya and Liza wanted to avoid, or, at least, minimize. In fact, these were largely the same reasons that Anya and Liza had given before the German occupation. They were disregarded for several weeks, while the sisters were suffering from post-occupation shock.[50] However, this shock had faded by early February 1942, influenced by real or imaginary Soviet military successes in the region.

Liza's very vivid description as to why neither she nor Anya could leave Rostov-on-Don sounds convincing at first reading. But we should remember that, only a few weeks before, the two sisters had said that they were ready to run away, regardless of these same considerations. In addition, we should keep in mind that people who have made a definite decision to become evacuees have time to make preparations, and could at least partly have overcome the difficulties listed by the sisters. For a start, Anya and Liza should have exchanged their possessions for money and valuables. This was certainly a risky thing to do, since they would then have become easy targets for thieves and burglars. But if they chose to move to Ordzhonikidze, the sisters could have received protection from Volodya Meerovich and the younger Ginsburgs, and could have solved the problem of their inability to carry heavy objects. However, none of this was even on their agenda, showing that the sisters simply did not want to leave.

---

49 On the importance of having their own dwellings for Soviet people, see Susan E. Reid, "The meaning of home: 'The only bit of the world you can have to yourself,'" in *Borders of Socialism: Private spheres of Soviet Russia*, ed. Lewis H. Siegelbaum (New York: Palgrave Macmillan, 2006), 145–170.

50 There are no letters describing the sisters' experiences during the first German occupation of Rostov-on-Don. I am inclined to believe that they were reluctant to write about that period, mainly in order to avoid upsetting their brother Efim.

Finally, their only seemingly reliable source of information on the course of the Soviet-German War was the reports of the Soviet media. As we have seen, these reports boasting about Soviet successes in the southern sector of the War were quite frequently propaganda spins. On a macro level, this was an entirely justified means of psychological warfare against Nazi Germany. But on a micro level, the Ginsburg sisters could not have known whether the reports were true or not, as there were no independent sources to corroborate or reject the official Soviet reports. Ultimately, this ambiguity led to a disaster for the Ginsburgs.

On February 10, 1942, Tamara Meerovich in Ordzhonikidze sent a lengthy letter to Alma-Ata:

> It is possible that you did not receive those letters, and therefore I am describing the situation to you once again, but for the last time. Volodya's wishes had nothing to do with the number of persons listed in the evacuation permit. Those permits are issued by the District Executive Committee (*oblispolkom*), by means of the organizations that provide the data concerning the number of dependents. Fortunately, the chairman of their Union knew David, and thanks to this, Volodya was able to persuade him to include two more people, that is, Tsylya and her child [*in the permit*]. He received the evacuation permit on October 13, 1941, at 2 p.m., when I was at work. Of course, if we had had experience in the evacuation process, we would have known that the children should not have been counted.
>
> Within an hour, we somehow collected our possessions,[51] and Volodya ran to bring me from my working place, because we were due to board the train at 2 p.m. So, I went straight from my job to the railway station. We went to the station in the middle of an air-raid alarm and firing. When we got to the boarding platform, it was pouring with rain, and it was an open platform without a roof. Just imagine the feeling of terror that seized us! Some people had tried to dissuade us from evacuating, saying it was tantamount to certain death for the children. But we had decided to leave Rostov—for the sake of the children. So we were ready to go in whatever direction, just not to stay and witness our children being killed. As for me, in those terrible moments, I was not concerned about my own death.

---

51 "We" cannot be correct, because Tamara was still at work, and her husband could not carry all their belongings to her work place. I assume that because of the rush they took only a few possessions with them. But this discrepancy may also indicate that some seemingly illogical parts of the account were due to the fact that Tamara was in an emotional turmoil, and she as well as other correspondents might have forgotten some details.

Fortunately for us, finally, we found ourselves travelling in a passenger train in normal conditions.

… During recent months, Volodya has been a member of the Extermination Battalion under the NKVD, and he was in combat readiness. Therefore, he left the city on November 21, when the Germans had already captured part of it. The Battalions retreated towards Kavkazskaya on foot, together with the Red Army units, while under constant attack. So, no one can complain that he didn't make our aunts leave with him. …

We did not receive any message from our aunts until December 19, 1941, when we learnt that they were still alive. When we came to Budennovsk, we described local conditions [*to the aunts*] in detail; if they have made up their minds to relocate here, they should not hesitate. But they wrote all the time that they were no longer considering evacuating, that it was cold, and that in addition, they were confident that the Germans would never again reach Rostov. All we can do is write to them and call them to come here. Neither Volodya nor I can travel to Rostov to bring them here, since we cannot get released from work. Besides, we are unable to help them now, when it is not permitted to move out of here. Provided they have a permit, they can come here on their own. We gave them detailed instructions regarding their possessions [*they can take with them*] and the travel arrangements. But they decided not to move and to wait for us in Rostov. We are not opposed to this option, either; [*in fact*] we have reconciled ourselves to the idea that they won't move and prefer to wait for us in Rostov. …

See you soon at our place in Rostov, after the final defeat of the Fascist bandits. I hope that it will happen as soon as possible.[52]

In this letter, Tamara again, in greater detail, explained why she and her side of the family were evacuated from Rostov-on-Don, while Anna and Liza stayed behind. Visible here is of the fascinating aspects of this correspondence: the Ginsburgs could never be certain that their letters would reach their destination, and so they had to provide essentially the same information over and over again. However, each time they added some important details, sometimes also changing the perspective.

We see how the desired evacuation permits could be obtained, in a time of crisis. Even though, in theory, it was possible to receive a permit for every

---

52   From Tamara Meerovich in Ordzhonikidze, February 10, 1942, YVA: O.75/324, pp. 196–200.

Soviet citizen, who was eager to evacuate, sometimes it could only be achieved by pulling strings. We also learn more details about the general setting of the Ginsburg family's evacuation. It seems that the idea of evacuation was frowned upon by many Rostov inhabitants, because they thought the way eastwards was extremely dangerous. Choosing to leave amid intensifying German bombardments was doubtless a brave and risky step.

Worth noting is the reasoning used by Tamara and people who objected to her opinions when discussing the need to leave Rostov-on-Don. All their arguments were based on their care for the children. Apparently, if there had been no children in the family, the decision would have been different. This could also implicitly explain why Anya and Liza chose to stay. Viewed from this perspective, the sisters emerge as more rational players, opposed to the emotionally driven younger generation of the Ginsburg family.

Also of note is Tamara's description of their exodus from Rostov-on-Don. Thanks to this letter, we see that for her and for many people in a similar situation the evacuation was an escape from certain death. But Tamara and those members of the family who opted to flee did not seem to take into account the fact that they were Jewish: they did not think that the German occupation would bring about their destruction primarily because they were Jews. Rather, they chose to evacuate because they viewed the general security situation in Rostov-on-Don, most specifically the intensifying bombardments, as truly unbearable.

Finally, we see how influential were the Soviet directives, aimed at limiting or entirely preventing population movement in an area so close to the frontlines. Due to these directives, Tamara and her husband Volodya could not return to Rostov-on-Don or bring their elderly aunts out of the city. For every movement, a permit was required, and the family could not obtain one. Even a relatively well-connected man such as Volodya could not get the necessary documents. Thus, the Soviet measures, which could be understood in terms of internal security, adversely affected the family's chances of survival.

The provision of food for the civil population was low on the Soviet scale of priorities even in peaceful periods before the Soviet-German War.[53] During the War, when the country lost its most fertile lands, and all its efforts were subordinated entirely to the military victory, food supplies became an

---

53 Elena Osokina, *Our Daily Bread: Socialist Distribution and the Art of Survival in Stalin's Russia, 1927–1941* (Armonk, NY: M. E. Sharpe, 2001).

enormous problem.⁵⁴ As the shotages increased, there emerged "resourceful" people, ready to sell and buy unofficially. Unable to solve the problem by economic methods, the Soviet authorities resorted to their proven weapon—repression. In addition, they did not shy away from publicizing these measures. In an article "To relentlessly wipe out speculation," published in *Molot* on February 12, 1942, Z. Mazanov, head of the police department (*militsiia*) in the Rostov District, mentioned that the inhabitants of certain villages, who sold produce (food and alcohol) in Rostov-on-Don at a high price, would stand trial.⁵⁵

The overall ban on leaving Rostov-on-Don, enforced since after the city was liberated from the Germans in early December 1941, was slightly moderated in mid-February 1942. On February 14, 1942, the Rostov newspaper published the order of the local military commander permitting to sell train tickets without his specific authorization, if business travel orders [*komandirovochnye predpisaniia*] or evacuation permits [*evakolisty*] were presented.⁵⁶ It appears that by authorizing business trips in the region, even though it remained vulnerable, the Soviet authorities demonstrated their confidence that they could control the situation in the North Caucasus. In addition, these measures were necessary for the smooth functioning of the city. For the Ginsburgs, this meant that Volodya Meerovich, the only family member to whom the order regarding business trips could apply, would now be eligible—but not necessarily able (as it depended on the needs of his plant)—to travel to Rostov-on-Don and see Anya and Liza from time to time. In addition, this order implied that the responsibility for evacuation of the city's residents was now with the local civilian administration. This could have also benefitted the two sisters, who would have been able to use their connections with these authorities in order to obtain evacuation permits.

The ban on leaving Rostov-on-Don turned out to be effective. As of February 15, 1942, the central Soviet authorities in charge of evacuation recorded that 33,724 refugees remained in the region.⁵⁷ If granted permission to leave, these refugees, who had already fled from the Germans once, would most likely escape Rostov-on-Don and its vicinity to avoid the Germans.

---

54 Feferman, "Food Factor," 74–78 and 85–87.
55 *Molot*, no. 36 (6227), February 2, 1942.
56 Order by Military Commander Borsh dated February 13, 1942, *Molot*, no. 38 (6229), February 14, 1942.
57 Summary of the lists of evacuees from the areas close to the front line as of February 15, 1942, YVA: JM/24678. Source: GARF: A-259/40/3517.

As we have seen, faced with the influx of refugees who had lost almost all their possessions, the local administration in the North Caucasus endeavored to alleviate their lot. Although this was done largely as a response to pressure from the central government,[58] the impact of these measures should not be underestimated. The local Soviet authorities in the region were severely underfunded, and every allocation of food and goods for the benefit of evacuees was very precious. This was the background to the article published on February 15, 1942 in Ordzhonikidze, which highlighted bureaucratic indifference to the fate of eighteen adolescent evacuees, placed in a trade school (only two of them had arrived with their parents). It was stressed that the situation improved after the start of the school year, and some children received clothes and boots.[59] This is a good example of the dire poverty that many evacuees faced.

On February 20, 1942, Tamara Meerovich sent a new letter from Ordzhonikidze:

> We are terribly worried following the decree concerning the evacuees' apartments. On the face of it, it has nothing to do with us, since neither I nor Volodya were evacuated at the same time as our plants. But we fear that, without any announcements, it may be applied to us. We do not know what to do: we have no idea. It is an unpleasant prospect to lose an apartment in Rostov and not find one here. We can imagine that it might be a blow for you (provided the decree applies to you). If we knew that these damned Germans were squeezed out of Taganrog, we could move there. Otherwise, it is too risky to get into an "unpleasant situation," after all our experiences.
> … We are in good health but in a dreadful [*ubiistvennyi*] mood. …[60]

The letter shows the extent to which economic factors influenced at this stage the decision-making process within the Ginsburg family. The fact that economic considerations were considered so important, even predominant, is a strong indicator that the military situation seemed more or less stable to the Ginsburgs; they described it as merely "unpleasant."

We do not know much about the Soviet decree that sanctioned the requisitioning of rooms from a certain category of evacuees, namely those who were

---

58 Feferman, "A Soviet Humanitarian Action?," 824–825.
59 T. Belova, "Bol'she vnimaniia evakuirovannym podrostkam," *Sotsialisticheskaia Osetiia* (Ordzhonikidze), no. 39 (2594), February 15, 1942.
60 From Tamara Meerovich in Ordzhonikidze, February 20, 1942, YVA: O.75/324, p. 201.

forced to evacuate when their plants were relocated. It looks like this was a local initiative aimed at accommodating the refugees, thousands of whom were still living in Rostov-on-Don.

Yet, Tamara Meerovich's fears were not unfounded. The Soviet government decree published in *Pravda* on February 17, 1942, indeed, stipulated that families of evacuees and refugees would be deprived of the housing provided by their employers.[61] The ensuing German occupation led to even more turmoil. In its September 1943 report, the Rostov District Committee of the VKP(b) mentioned that, as of September 9, 1943, 1,345 apartments were seized in an arbitrary manner, while 2,945 more apartments were seized following German housing orders.[62] Although the report did not explain who the people were whose property was seized, it is evident that they had either fled the city or perished under German rule. Jews, as we have seen, formed a noticeable percentage of both categories.

In the meantime, the decree worsened the mood of all the Ginsburgs (on this issue there were no divisions within the family), who feared to lose their housing. Instead of an apartment or rooms in a city considered, by Soviet standards, "first-class," the Ginsburgs, if evacuated, would be entitled to receive a dwelling in a second- or even third-rate town, to which they would be evacuated. To protect their property rights, Tamara even considered returning to Rostov-on-Don, but the proximity of the German forces prevented her from doing so. Despite all the Soviet authorities' triumphant declarations, Tamara appeared less optimistically disposed than her aunts in Rostov-on-Don; and when she saw that even Taganrog, 67 kilometres away from Rostov-on-Don, was still in German hands, Tamara understood that Rostov-on-Don was very vulnerable. Since the "successful" Red Army advances had not led to the recapture of any large cities to the west of Rostov-on-Don, Tamara, unlike her aunts, was less inclined to fall for the Soviet propaganda spin describing the continuous victories of the Red Army in the south. Tamara was haunted by this uncertain situation, as she made clear with a single phrase, "we are still in a desperate mood."

Of note are Tamara's remarks on the manner in which her branch of the family communicated with the Rostov Ginsburgs. Despite the distance that separated them, the family managed to stay in contact and keep each other

---

61 Decree of the SNK SSSR "Ob osvobozhdenii zhiloi ploshchadi mestnykh Sovetov i predpriiatii, zanimavshcheisia ranee rabochimi i sluzhashchimi, evakuirovannymi na Vostok," February 16, 1942. In *Pravda*, February 17, 1942. Cf. Manley, *To the Tashkent Station*, 259.
62 Tatyana P. Khlynina, "Zhilishchnyi vopros i praktiki ego razresheniia v gody Velikoi Otechestvennoi voiny," *Nauchnyi dialog* 5, no. 29 (2014): 18–19.

abreast of their wishes and decisions. At the same time, given the information vacuum in which both branches of the family found themselves, it is clear that they used the frequent letters to influence each other. We have already seen how various members of the Ginsburg family tried to influence the others' opinions on evacuation and financial matters in the previous weeks.

On February 21, 1942, Anna and Liza sent a new letter from Rostov-on-Don:

> We are living alone, as before; things are boring. Our nerves are a bit strained, but hopefully this will pass. Our health is not good, either, but the important thing is to get good news from the front, to learn that the enemy is in flight and is about to be smashed. Then, everything will go on well. This is all we desire and hope for. [*The rest*] is not that important. What matters is that the Germans have not caught us and that there is no need to leave Rostov.[63]

This short letter summarizes Anya and Liza's mood well: they had extremely high hopes pinned on a decisive Soviet victory, presumably in the very near future. These hopes were based on the Ginsburg sisters' emotional attachments, while also nurtured by Soviet propaganda. By late February 1942, it seemed to Anya and Liza that the situation had changed for the better. Now, their nerves were only "a bit" strained, an improvement compared to what they wrote in their letter dated February 1 ("Our nerves are really frayed").

On February 26, 1942, Tsylya Pinchos sent a letter from Ordzhonikidze to her uncle:

> We have received interesting letters from our relatives. Some days ago, Tamara spoke to Aunt Liza on the phone. We were concerned over the apartment problem, but we learnt that it did not apply to us, so we are very pleased. They keep on asking us in every letter and on the phone: when are we coming back? They say that everything is quiet and we all hope that everything will be quiet; very many [*former*] inhabitants of Rostov have returned and are returning home. In the days to come, Volodya should be returning to Rostov, in order to work there.
>
> My dear Uncle [*diaden'ka*]! I am going to give you some very good news: Doda has come back to us here; the commission has granted him leave from his [*Army*] unit, due to his illness. He arrived a month ago; I

---

63 From Liza Chazkewitz and Anya Greener, February 21, 1942, YVA: O.75/324, pp. 348–349.

did not write about it [*before*], since he was placed at the disposal of the *voenkomat*; yesterday, the commission declared him unfit for army service; he is ill.

Life is becoming harder; we are mostly preoccupied with the problems of fuel and the apartment; these are the chief reasons that urge us to go back to Rostov: fuel is available there, and the apartment there costs almost nothing.

Today we received unpleasant news that a malaria epidemic has allegedly broken out in Alma-Ata. We are really concerned about this; maybe if it is possible you could come to us; after all it would be great; and then, all of us could move to Rostov.[64]

This letter describes what was happening to the evacuee branch of the family from Tsylya's standpoint, which was different from that of Tamara. Even the way she addresses Efim Ginsburg differs from Tamara's letters: the word *diaden'ka*, which children used to address adults in Russian, shows her great respect and tenderness.

The contents of Tsylya's letter also illustrate her primary concern. Volodya Meerovich's return to Rostov-on-Don, which would, without a doubt, have been a most traumatic event for Tamara, is only briefly mentioned here. On the other hand, Tsylya writes much about the return of her own husband, Doda (David), demobilized from the Army. It is apparent that his state of health was too poor even to meet the Red Army requirements in 1942. Tsylya herself admitted that her husband was ill. But at least, he was now save from death or wounds on the battlefield, and was living with her, so Tsylya was overwhelmed with joy. In retrospect, we can say that this development would likely cost David Pinchos his life, as he was then doomed to stay, together with his civilian relatives, in the North Caucasus.

The letter provides another example of how Anna and Liza exerted mounting pressure on the evacuee branch of the family, urging them to return to Rostov-on-Don. Nevertheless, at this stage, it seems that the evacuees were still able to remain largely immune to this pressure.

Tsylya's letter also shows the growing importance of economic considerations for the evacuee branch of the Ginsburg family. Evidently, they did not consider that their new location was threatened by a German attack. Nor is there any reference to scarcity of food or even to its poor quality. From these

---

64 From Tsylya Pinchos in Ordzhonikidze, February 26, 1942, ibid., pp. 207–208.

omissions, we can infer that these problems had largely ceased to preoccupy the evacuee Ginsburgs in late February 1942. Likewise, the apartment problem in Rostov-on-Don was solved—in all probability, the local authorities recognized that Volodya Meerovich returned to the city within three months after its abandonment; so that the harsh decree of February 16 did not apply to any of his family who were registered as living in the same apartment.[65]

What may have now become a decisive factor in the family's considerations was the sharp increase in prices of lodging and fuel. (The winter of 1941–1942 was an especially cold one.) What was not written in the letter, but implied, was that the local people whose apartment the Ginsburgs rented in Ordzhonikidze, and who sold them wood for fuel, were charging them exorbitant prices. This was the harsh reality of the War: unless the authorities intervened and set fixed prices, or provided services free of charge, the evacuees had to pay for everything. The local administrations were frequently overstretched, and did nothing to prevent this exploitation. This being the case, the local population could take advantage of the situation and demand very high payments for lodging, food, and fuel.[66]

March 1942

On March 2, 1942, Liza and Anya sent a long letter to Alma-Ata:

> Our dear one!
>
> We are living as we did previously: I am working. Anya is in charge of the household. Don't worry so much about us! Our health is feeble, nothing good. ...
>
> Our dear one! We agree ... with you completely. Your advice is absolutely correct. It is quite possible that in the future we will be very sorry that we did not follow your wise and good advice concerning the possibility of going to our relatives, as the worst option, and the possibility of moving even further away from Rostov with them, as the best option. However, our dear one, when we stay here we want to believe that maybe there will no longer be a need to move, and that the German bastards have no chance [*of coming*] here again.
>
> Anya feels terrible, as soon as she thinks about evacuating. If we did not move with the rest of the family, let us stay here and not go anywhere. I

---

65 Manley, *To the Tashkent Station*, 258–259.
66 Feferman, "A Soviet Humanitarian Action?," 826–829.

have a presentiment that we must stay here and wait for all of you, our dear relatives, to come back here soon. Our relatives are striving with all their might to come back here; they dream about the day when they can return home. Volodya is supposed to be coming here [*very soon*]. We expected him today. ... Many people are returning from there [*Ordzhonikidze*]. So you see, we don't know what to do, since in this case everyone will have problems with employment and accommodation, with possessions and furniture. If [*a home*] is put up for sale, then the price is ridiculously low; but you can only buy it back if you pay thousands. We have already run out of money. But of course, all this is nothing but talk that will have to wait until the situation here becomes quieter; we are also aware of hardships in a foreign land (*na chuzhbine ne med*). But if these barbarians arrive soon, if something bad happens, then we will move away or [*even*] walk away on foot; then, we will not stay here. Most important, don't worry about us! Come what may! [*chemu byt', tomu ne minovat'*]. But we will flee from the German barbarians without fail, despite our poor health and weak strength, lest we be killed, especially by these murderers. Again, I say that they will not get this [*far*]; they will be crushed and destroyed. And the victory will be ours!!! ...

As for money for us, don't bother so much! First, you should provide for yourself, because now life is very expensive and food costs a lot. Don't sell any possessions of yours in order to send us money. When you have a surplus [*of means*], then we will ask you to send us [*money*]. As for now, everything is very costly in the markets, since no food is supplied [*from the countryside*], due to [*bad*] weather. When it gets warmer and the weather stabilizes there will be a lot of foodstuffs and certainly the prices will go down. Of course, all this is triviality and we can and must put up with such privations, because all this is passing. ...

On Sunday, February 22, I spoke on the phone to Tamara and Grinechka when they called directly to the pharmacy. I was very happy and enormously excited.[67]

This important letter contains another acknowledgement by Anya and Liza—that their refusal to leave Rostov-on-Don and their attempts to bring their relatives back to the city could probably put them in deadly danger. The sisters explicitly admitted this when they wrote that their behavior was based mainly on

---

67   From Liza Chazkewitz and Anya Greener, March 2, 1942, YVA: O.75/324, pp. 211–214.

their hopes. We can imagine how difficult it was for Efim Ginsburg to win them over in such discussions. We do not have any of his letters to help us, but this letter from his sisters demonstrates that, when unable to present rational replies to their brother's arguments, they resorted to apparently agreeing with him.

The sisters' financial calculations were also irrational. If many people, as they claimed, returned to Rostov-on-Don, they would indeed have been in need of furniture and home accessories, which would have led to an upsurge in market prices. So, upon their return to Rostov-on-Don, the evacuee Ginsburgs would indeed have had to pay a high price, as Anya and Liza wrote. But what they omitted to say in this letter is that, at this stage, their own departure from the city was required more urgently than their relatives' return to it, and the situation could benefit people eager to sell their possessions and furniture in order to finance their evacuation.

It is along these lines that we should view the sisters' statement, "We have already run out of money." It implies that they had evidently spent all their savings on buying food in the first months of the Soviet-German War. It also means that they could not make ends meet in Rostov-on-Don without selling their possessions and/or exchanging them for food and maybe other essentials, such as fuel. Their difficulties were similar, in fact, to the problems of the family's evacuee branch, whom Anya and Liza urged to return. We learn from this letter that there was simply not enough food available in Rostov-on-Don at that time. So the only big financial advantage of staying in Rostov-on-Don was not having to spend money on a costly evacuation and not having to pay in full to rent a room.[68] This was indeed important, but had to be weighed against the danger of remaining in the beleaguered city.

The strained economic situation in the Rostov District during this period was summarized in the official Soviet statistics, as reflected in a study produced by a Russian researcher in 2006.

- In April 1942, a military loan was imposed for the first time on the Soviet population. It was implemented under the slogan "Three, four days' wages—for the 1942 state loan." The inhabitants of the Rostov District fulfilled the loan plan in 1942 by 130.9% (155,794.000 rubles).

---

68 Very few people owned their own homes in Soviet Russia. Overwhelmingly, all property belonged to the state. However, since it was a socialist state, it did not set a full market price on the property lease. So the tenants had to make a certain payment for the dwellings they lived in (which was in fact a form of tax), but it was far below the market rent price. The evacuee Ginsburgs felt this difference all too well.

- Retail prices for vodka, tobacco, etc., were increased, but prices for staple products issued against food stamps remained stable.
- Withdrawal of money by the local inhabitants from the only state bank (*Sberkassy*) was temporarily limited.[69]

These terse details shed light on how Soviet victory was being achieved in this region. It meant, for example, that, although the entire Rostov District had been occupied by the Germans since August 1942, the local inhabitants were forced to pay for this loan from their income in April and June 1942. We see that Soviet citizens paid heavily to enable the Soviet military machine to gain ground after the disasters of 1941.[70] There is no doubt that these harsh economic measures were applied to the Ginsburg family—those who continued to live in the city of Rostov-on-Don and those who were evacuated from it—and this explains to no small extent what they delicately referred to in their letters as "economic hardships."

On March 3, 1942, Tamara Meerovich sent a long letter to Alma-Ata:

> Volodya left yesterday for Rostov. His departure resulted from the following [*factors*]: first, the plant where he was employed all the time stayed in Rostov, and is now producing armaments. So it seems that upon his arrival in Rostov, he will take up his previous position. Second, when the decree was issued regarding the evacuees' apartments, we became alarmed, and this factor has also played some role in his going back home: we need to retain [*zakrepit'*] our apartment there. Although it is still premature to think about our return, we feel some relief at the thought that we have some corner [*ugolok*] of our own, somewhere [*to go to*]. As a result of his departure, our mood has become terrible. Certainly it was easier for us in every respect while he was here. If he works there it won't be so awful, since he will try to provide for the family. In this regard, he is an extraordinarily exemplary husband and father. But if he is drafted, which is quite possible, and that's what we have got to be prepared for, it would certainly be most difficult for us. …

---

69 N. G. Dubrovskaia. "Finansovaia sistema Rostovskoi oblasti v gody voiny," in *Istoricheskie i sotsial'no-ekonomicheskie problemy Iuga Rossii. Materialy IV mezhvuzovskoi nauchno-prakticheskoi konferentsii (23 dekabria 2006 g., g. Azov)*, ed. V. Naukhatskii (Rostov-on-Don: Rostovskii universitet ekonomiki, 2007), 39.

70 On this subject, see Kristy Ironside, "Rubles for Victory: The Social Dynamics of State Fundraising on the Soviet Home Front," *Kritika: Explorations in Russian and Eurasian History* 15, no. 4 (Fall 2014): 799–828.

Most important, we are paralyzed with fear for the future. It is difficult to say what awaits us in the future; in particular, given the fact that spring will soon arrive, because it is to be feared that the enemy is in a state of mortal agony, but may still use all its forces to attack the Caucasus, on the way to [*try to*] seize the oilfields. Then we will find ourselves in a trap, since it makes no sense to think about our further retreat, because to come to your area means to die there from starvation. All these thoughts are driving [*us*] crazy.

How strongly we desire to quickly see our victory and the complete defeat of this reptile, Fascism, which has broken and twisted [*pokalechil*] all our lives! However much we are suffering now, we all want to live, in order to witness the end of this conflict and to take part in [*celebrating*] our victory. I can imagine how our relatives will rejoice over Volodya's arrival! Now they won't feel so alone. He took with him a *pood*[71] of potatoes [*for them*] … But it doesn't make any sense [*for them*] to come here now from Rostov, since it is possible that in the near future we might have to flee [*from here*]. Furthermore, it is even probable that Rostov may be in a more favorable position than the Caucasus, as the road [*towards the Caucasus*] not only goes through Rostov but also through the Krasnodar district. But generally, come what may… We are all in good health, but our nerves are frazzled.

Foodstuffs are getting more expensive every day. Potatoes cost 150–160 rubles a sack; grain—250 rubles for a pood; fats—100–120 rubles.[72]

In my opinion, this is one of the most important letters in the entire collection. It was written at a crucial point, when the family members were still able to make up their minds more or less voluntarily and without haste: first, the Germans' summer advance had not yet begun; second, the Soviet authorities still tacitly allowed evacuation from the North Caucasus. So let us see what considerations guided Tamara Meerovich, probably the most original thinker in the Ginsburg family, in her decision-making process.

The most significant factor for Tamara was the departure of her husband, Volodya, for Rostov-on-Don. We see that his movements occupied a special place in her letter, in contrast to Tsylya Pinchos, for whom they were only of secondary importance. Thanks to his connections Volodya was able to provide,

---

71 Russian measure of weight equaling 16.38 kg or approx. 36 lb.
72 From Tamara Meerovich in Ordzhonikidze, March 3, 1942, YVA: O.75/324, pp. 215–218.

more or less satisfactorily, for his family (as we have seen, he was able to obtain the evacuation permits). A low-ranking member of the local establishment, he was also employed, and therefore received an increased food ration. Once Volodya left Ordzhonikidze, his family's prospects of economic survival as evacuees would have diminished considerably. The only viable option remaining for Tamara and her family (as she gradually became convinced) was to return to Rostov-on-Don, regardless of the situation at the front, and to try to survive the period by pooling the entire family's resources and using their connections in the city where they had lived for so many years.

Worthy of note is Tamara's remark that Volodya's return to Rostov-on-Don was in accordance with the Meerovich family's wishes. Otherwise, Tamara and Volodya could probably have tried to work out a scheme to avoid moving. But they wanted to keep their apartment in Rostov-on-Don, which shows the importance of financial considerations in their decision.

It is also worthy of notice that, in Tamara's eyes, at least as of March 1942, Volodya's departure from Ordzhonikidze was far more significant than his possible drafting into the Red Army. This important letter shows that the need to withstand the German aggression, clearly shared by Tamara on a macro level, was counterbalanced by her desire for the survival of the family, as the Army could by no means guarantee her husband's safety.

Tamara's personal reflections are followed in the letter by her analysis of the situation on the Soviet-German front. She clearly feels that the momentum of the German offensive had not exhausted itself. But Tamara expresses her fears in a very cautious way, as her letter might easily have fallen into the hands of a Soviet censor. So, her analysis of what could happen in the summer of 1942 begins with the formula "the enemy is in a state of mortal agony," which could protect her from accusations of spreading defeatism if the letter were intercepted by the Soviet censors. At the same time, it is quite possible that Tamara Meerovich here said what she really meant: she truly believed in a general Soviet victory in the Soviet-German War.

Whatever Tamara thought about the possible outcome of the entire War, she was obviously very anxious about the military situation in the Caucasus in summer 1942. She noted that the city of Rostov-on-Don and the adjacent area, both places where members of her family stayed for the time being, or where they could move to without a great effort, were not by themselves desirable targets for the Germans. The Germans were attracted by the Caucasian oil. It is fascinating that this woman, without access to any independent source of information (such as *The New York Times* or *The Washington Post*), let alone contemporary German and Soviet military reports, could have quite accurately guessed what would happen in the summer of 1942, namely, the German thrust in the direction of the Caucasus. It is particularly surprising to read these lines, because the Soviet military command, with much more information at its disposal, failed to draw this conclusion and to deploy its forces accordingly.

Nevertheless, Tamara still cherished hope that the city of Rostov-on-Don might be a safe haven, even under these circumstances. She assumed that the city was heavily defended by the Soviets, and the Red Army would do its utmost to thwart a possible German assault on Rostov-on-Don. In a way, the German advance in 1941 did provide certain grounds for such assumption. In 1941, the Wehrmacht tended to advance by encircling Soviet pockets of resistance, which could be wiped out at a later stage. So Tamara assumed that it would not make much sense for the Germans to waste precious time storming Rostov-on-Don, and that they might prefer to encircle it. In this case, Rostov-on-Don could become a sort of a fortress in German-occupied territory, like Odessa and Sevastopol in 1941–1942. Both these cities, especially Sevastopol, had been able to withstand a protracted German assault. It was sober reasoning; but in retrospect, it is apparent that Tamara grossly exaggerated the Soviet ability to defend Rostov-on-Don in the summer of 1942.

However, Tamara's otherwise in-depth analysis is followed by a somewhat paradoxical conclusion. It seems that her own harrowing experience as an evacuee, together with the information that she received from her uncle Efim, and probably from other informal sources, led her to conclude that evacuation as a rule meant starvation, and had to be avoided at any cost. This had to be done, even if it meant exposing her family and herself to deadly danger, by continuing to stay in such a vulnerable place as the North Caucasus in spring 1942. Tamara did not even consider the option of fleeing further eastwards and possibly joining her uncle. Efim's letters, in which he openly described the hardships he had suffered during his evacuation, now backfired on him. Well aware of the difficulties that he had encountered, the North Caucasian Ginsburgs ignored his pleadings to flee from their region and to join him. For them it would be tantamount, as Tamara put it, to "death from starvation."

On March 3, 1942, the Department of Agitation and Propaganda of the Central Committee of the Bolshevik party issued a decree, "On the work of regional newspapers": "all regional newspapers will appear in two pages."[73] The Soviet authorities did not want to cut the impact of their propaganda machinery in half, they were simply confronted by a severe shortage of paper. In absence of any other legal ways of obtaining news about the situation at the fronts and the Nazi persecution of the Jews, the Soviet newspapers remained the only sources of information apart from the infrequently working public radio. Thus, for the Ginsburg family dispersed in the North Caucasus this meant a reduction in the amount of critical information, however censored and brief, that was available to them.

On March 8, 1942, Tamara Meerovich sent a letter to Efim in Alma-Ata:

> Apparently you have already received the letter in which I wrote that the Pinchos family had left for Rostov. In Rostov, things are looking like this: Volodya is working; for the time being, he is not exempt [*from conscription*]; besides, unfortunately, he has been ill for a long time with tuberculosis. …
>
> David appeared again before the Commission and received complete exemption from [*military*] registration. In the next few days, he is supposed to begin working; so their financial situation will be somewhat clearer.
>
> Now it is quiet in Rostov, but prices are very high. In contrast, as we have relatively cheap potatoes, it is definitely easier to subsist here. …
>
> However, if the [*military*] situation changes for the better, we will not be discouraged by the high prices there. …We are all in good health and yearn to see all the others. How we want to see a quick end to the war! With love from Mom, Grisha, and me.[74]

The family had split up several times. Now Tsylya Pinchos, together with her husband and daughter, left Ordzhonikidze and rejoined Anya and Liza in Rostov-on-Don. Tamara mentioned the reasons behind Tsylya's departure in her previous letters. Here they are: Tsylya's husband David had been exempted from military service due to his illness. He could only earn his living in Rostov-on-Don, where the family could pull some strings. Certainly, the same held true for Tsylya herself. In addition, she must have wanted to join her mother, Anya, in Rostov-on-Don. Finally, it seems that Tsylya did not share, or chose to overlook, Tamara's skepticism regarding the situation

---

73 Zhuravlev, *Kollaboratsionizm na iuge Rossii*, 166–167.
74 From Tamara Meerovich in Ordzhonikidze, March 8, 1942, YVA: O.75/324, pp. 221–222.

in Rostov-on-Don. It is quite possible that this factor did not seem important to her. At any rate, her letters do not show the same analytical approach to the situation. Rather, it is likely that Anya and Liza were able to persuade her to return to Rostov-on-Don.

In the meantime, judging by Tamara's letter, the economic situation had changed somewhat for the better in Ordzhonikidze and worsened in Rostov-on-Don. Viewed from this perspective, Tsylya's return to Rostov-on-Don had less to do with strictly economic considerations, but was based more on emotions. So, at this stage, the economic argument could no longer be employed to justify return to Rostov-on-Don; but all Tamara's rationality suddenly gave way to her all-encompassing desire to rejoin her relatives in Rostov-on-Don. Uncertainty resulting from the city's continued vulnerability prevented her from immediately travelling back. But is appears that the departure of Tsylya Pinchos for Rostov-on-Don, without paying any heed to security factors, made an impression on Tamara and laid the foundations for her own future decisions.

An interesting glimpse at the mood of some segments of Rostov Jewry can be found in the recently published memoirs of a local North Caucasian Russian junior military commander in the Red Army. During the War, his unit was stationed in the region. It appears that a wave of patriotism that swept over many Soviet people at the start of the War[75] continued to affect the attitudes of many young people, among them some Jews. He mentions some girls who studied in Rostov's institutes of higher education, were Komsomol members, and had volunteered to serve in the Red Army. They were brought to his unit for training in the spring of 1942. Among them were some Jewish girls.[76] It is, of course, an open question whether and to what extent these girls really volunteered or were forced to enlist.[77] But in any case, we can speculate

---

75 See, for example, Richard Bidlack, "The political mood in Leningrad during the first year of the Soviet-German war," *Russian Review* 59, no. 1 (2000): 101–102.
76 Skorokhodov, *Takoi dolgii, dolgii put'*, 184–185.
77 As Anna Krylova indicates, women were frequently not forcibly conscripted, but had to literally beg to get into the army. See her *Soviet Women in Combat: A History of Violence on the Eastern Front* (Cambridge: Cambridge University Press, 2010). However, in other cases we do have references to mandatory conscription of women (for example, Gel'fand, *Dnevnik 1941–1946*, 157). Furthermore, local dissertations on this topic (Natal'ia Klimova, "Trudovoi i ratnyi podvig molodezhi Stavropol'ia v gody Velikoi Otechestvennoi voiny, 1941–1945 gg," PhD diss., Pyatigorsk, Piatigorskii lingvisticheskii universitet, 2005; Galina Kameneva, "Zhenshchiny Severnogo Kavkaza v gody Velikoi Otechestvennoi voiny, 1941–1945 gg," PhD diss., Stavropol, Stavropol'skii gosudarstvennyi universitet,

that Rostov's young Jewish people, similar to other young Soviet Jews, but in contrast to many non-Jewish youngsters, might have been especially motivated to serve in the Red Army, and saw no other way but to fight for the Soviet Union until the end, largely because they couldn't consider surrendering to the Germans.[78]

The next item of information comes from another letter written by Anya and Liza, on March 8, 1942:

> It is already the fourth day since Volodya came here! We feel more joyful; now, God willing, all our relatives will return quickly. Then, it will be truly wonderful. Then, we won't need to go to them [in Ordzhonikidze], as you keep urging us to do when you ask us to move to live near them, without a moment's thought. ...
>
> We only urge you not to worry so much about us. We are in good health; though it is not as good as it used to be. I want to believe that you will come to us soon. And we all, including the children, will welcome you with flowers as we did last year. Then, you will see your beautiful sisters. What matters to us is to survive until then; the rest are petty matters. So far, we choose not to be evacuated.
>
> Volodya says that poor Monya longs to come home; and if someone tells her not to be in a hurry, then she shouts at him. And she says that in two weeks she will definitely return home. Poor Monya! She keeps saying every two weeks that she is about to move.[79]

The sisters were obviously very pleased to be joined by Volodya Meerovich. Not only was he a loved member of the family, he was also the best-connected person in the family, who could and did bring about some alleviation of their difficult economic conditions. However, they seem to have interpreted his return to Rostov-on-Don as a sign that the situation in the city had become safer. Characteristically, the sisters again expressed hope that their brother Efim might soon come to see them. However, as we shall soon see, Volodya's return to Rostov-on-Don made his conscription in the Army

---

2004) have not found the same degree of enthusiasm in the North Caucasus. This may possibly be explained by the fact that the region as a whole was less pro-Soviet than other territories.

78 Kiril Feferman, "'The Jews' War.'"
79 From Liza Chazkewitz and Anya Greener, March 8, 1942, YVA: O.75/324, pp. 223–224.

more likely. Yet, the sisters were unaware of this at that time. Only Tamara, Volodya's wife, sensed that this might happen soon.

The letter provides a rare evidence of the relationships within the Meerovich family in Ordzhonikidze. There were only two adults there, Tamara Meerovich and her mother, Manya. Although not mentioned so far (Tamara carefully avoided writing about it), there seems to have been a conflict between them. Manya, the oldest Ginsburg, seems to have suffered greatly when her closest family was split up: her daughter and grandson were with her, but her sisters remained in Rostov-on-Don. Manya longed to return to Rostov-on-Don in order to escape from the privations of an evacuee's life and to rejoin her sisters, regardless of whether or not the German threat had been fully alleviated. Pesumably, Manya's arguments resembled those of her sisters, and were largely emotional. Judging by what Tamara wrote and what we learn from this particular letter, Manya was much more sober in her assessment of the situation and was primarily concerned with security in Rostov-on-Don. In terms of clear-headed reasoning, no one in the family had a solid argument against what Efim Ginsburg, and, to a lesser extent, Tamara Meerovich said. Yet, in contrast to Tamara's husband, Manya's weight in the decision-making process was, apparently, negligible.

On March 8, 1942, Volodya Meerovich sent a letter to Efim Ginsburg:

> On March 5, I arrived in Rostov to start permanent work. On March 6, I began working and I am living at home with A. G. [*Anya*] and E. G. [*Liza*]. We are all alive and in good health.
>
> The situation in Rostov is favorable, and, for the time being, there is no imminent danger. I am considering bringing my family from Ordzhonikidze, as soon as the situation improves somewhat. … As of now, I do not regret having come back to Rostov.[80]

There is an obvious difference of style between Volodya, a rare correspondent, and the rest of his family, which consisted exclusively of women. He gives no news about his own wife and child, left behind in Ordzhonikidze, assuming that this information was already known to his correspondent. Volodya simply wrote a short businesslike note without giving way to his sentiments. Regarding the contents of the letter, the focus seems to be on such words as "for the time being" and "as of now." Although Volodya was

---

80 From Volodya Meerovich in Rostov, March 8, 1942, ibid., p. 225.

glad to return to his home city and to see members of his extended family there, he expressed caution regarding the situation in Rostov-on-Don. It is also obvious that he viewed the situation around the city in the same way that his wife did.

This letter, one of the few authored by Volodya in the collection gives us the opportunity to reflect on his position in the local Soviet society. His enlistment in the NKVD-run Extermination Battalion indicates that he was, most likely, a member of the Bolshevik party and a part of the Soviet establishment in the city, although at a low level. The fact that he was able to procure evacuation permits by pulling strings reinforces this impression. We can gain more information from Tamara's letters, which say that Volodya was evacuated together with his plant and was not drafted immediately in the Army. Also, as we see later, he was occasionally able to travel around the region on business trips. Therefore, it is probable that he occupied a mid-level position in the management of his plant. However, Volodya's exemption from active military service proved only temporary, which means that his position in the plant administration was not absolutely essential; otherwise, the plant would have tried to keep him as one of the "indispensable employees."

On March 9, a Soviet newsreel featuring the continuing advance of the Red Army troops on the southern front was screened in cinema theaters. Against the background of the successful assault on a village defended by the Wehrmacht, the announcer proclaimed that "the Fascists roll back westwards but fiercely cling to every inch of land."[81] However, there was no information about the location of the village that had been recaptured by the Soviet troops, and we can only presume that it was somewhere in the vicinity of Rostov-on-Don, because the southern front troops were fighting in that area. Nor did the newsreel include the name of any other locality, whether large or small, which had been recently liberated by the Red Army. The impact conveyed by this and similar propaganda newsreels on the Ginsburgs was extremely ambiguous. On the one hand, it strengthened their belief in an overall Soviet victory in the War. On the other hand, the family members were misled into believing that the Red Army would also overwhelm the Germans in the spring 1942 campaign in southern Russia.

On March 12, 1942, Liza sent a short message to Efim: "For the time being, I have not been ordered to work. … Anya is not affected [by this decree] since

---

81 *Soiuzkinozhurnal*, no. 20, March 9, 1942, RGAKFD: record 4691, http://pobeda-vov.ru/Lib/pages/item.aspx?itemid=10546, accessed November 20, 2011.

it applies only to those under forty-five."[82] The note begs for an explanation. I was unable to verify for what kind of work Rostov's civilians were conscripted at that time. But judging by all the known precedents, including those related to Rostov-on-Don but in different periods of time, it seems almost certain that the adult inhabitants of the city, of both sexes, were required to construct new defensive lines or to strengthen the already existing lines around the city. This mainly involved building trenches to prevent tanks from rapidly breaking through the Soviet defenses.

Although the decree did not apply to the Ginsburg sisters, it is not clear whether the younger members of the family, like Tsylya and David Pinchos, were also lucky to be exempt from it. This order had the unintended side-effect of making clear to Rostov's inhabitants, including the Ginsburg family, that despite all their aggressive rhetoric, the Soviet authorities were not sure whether they would be able to check another German assault on the city without massive civil support. Ironically, these defense lines proved of no use in thwarting the Wehrmacht advance, not only near Rostov-on-Don but in many other places, too. At most, they made the Germans change the direction of their main thrust in order to circumvent the anti-tank trenches. Once the tables were turned and the Germans succeeded in occupying the Soviet territories, they frequently used such trenches to dispose of various "enemies of the Reich," including Jews.

Liza and Anya Ginsburg continued to express their hope for a speedy reunification of the family, in a letter sent on March 13, 1942:

> Now [all we want] is the speedy arrival of all our relatives here, and your return to Moscow. But if it is possible, first come to see us and only then move to your place in Moscow. We will all see you off but before that we will welcome you here! I firmly believe that it will happen very soon. … The most important thing is to destroy the German vampires forever. …[83]

The sisters went as far as to assume that it would be quite possible for Efim Ginsburg to arrange a courtesy visit to Rostov-on-Don before his return to Moscow. We do not know how Efim himself viewed the situation at that time, but in all probability he continued to regard it as extremely perilous. It should be noted that the Soviet authorities, despite all their desire to demonstrate

---

82 From Liza Chazkewitz and Anya Greener, March 12, 1942, YVA: O.75/324, p. 351.
83 From Liza Chazkewitz and Anya Greener, March 13, 1942, ibid., p. 229.

that the situation in the country had been stabilized, were opposed to bringing evacuees back to Moscow. The partial return of refugees was authorized only to some minor towns around Moscow, which had been liberated by the Red Army during its winter offensive of 1941–1942.[84]

That the situation in Rostov-on-Don had been stabilized and that the city had returned to normal life was strongly emphasized in a new Soviet newsreel, shown in cinema theaters on March 13.[85] In section "Rostov today," the announcer stressed, supported by the newsreel pictures, that in Rostov-on-Don the movement of trams and trolleybuses had been resumed and studies at educational institutions began again. Shoppers were going in and out of stores, and one of Rostov's maternity homes was in operation. The newsreel was part of the background—since we can assume that such or similar information was conveyed through various channels from Rostov-on-Don to Ordzhonikidze—for the decision of the Pinchos family, who were very unhappy with their experience as evacuees, to return to Rostov-on-Don.

On March 13, 1942, it was Tamara Meerovich who described a dramatic split in the family:

> I think that I … wrote to you on March 3 or 4 that Volodya has left for Rostov. Today, David, Tsylya and Anechka moved away. … Why did Tsylya decide to go? The thing is that it became impossible for her to remain here. It was impossible for her to find employment, as she had no profession. So we exhausted our modest savings resulting from the sale of our possessions.[86]
>
> As Volodya has left for Rostov, my financial situation has worsened, too. Even in the best scenario, if he is not drafted and he continues to work, he will not be able to send us much [money]. Yet, my expenses here are very high: one room costs 100 rubles and every day the food is getting more and more expensive. Just to give some examples, there is almost no meat; if we manage to procure some, it costs 35–40 rubles; fats—120–150 rubles, eggs—25 rubles. The main foodstuff, potatoes, has also become

---

84 Feferman, "A Soviet Humanitarian Action?," 816.
85 *Soiuzkinozhurnal*, no. 21, March 13, 1942, RGAKFD: record 4692, http://pobeda-vov.ru/Lib/pages/item.aspx?itemid=10547, accessed on November 14, 2011.
86 It looks like Tamara's and Tsylya's branches of the family had a common budget where all money from sold items accumulated. In addition, Tamara worked as a bookkeeper, and thus brought more money into the family budget. It is likely that Tsylya's branch felt too dependent on Tamara, or, as she indicates, after selling all their possessions, Tamara's salary simply did not suffice to keep both branches of the family afloat.

more expensive. When we came here, one sack cost 60–70 rubles; now it is 200 rubles. At present I have two sacks of potatoes, and this is good news. But it is difficult to foresee the future: prices are jumping up all the time, but salaries don't change. All this caused Tsylya to move away to Rostov, because she has an opportunity to find employment in her profession there.

Certainly, the general situation is not really favorable now for departure to Rostov. But it is getting more and more difficult here; so they decided to take a risk and chance it [*avos'*]; probably, Rostov will no longer be under threat. In any case, they have experience in being evacuated and can flee again. Of course, our relatives will be pleased about their arrival.

We remain here alone; it is very difficult and depressing. … We live hoping solely to return home quickly, but only when the situation improves in a marked fashion.[87]

As we suggested previously, the return of the Pinchos branch of the family to their home city of Rostov-on-Don was largely motivated by their financial situation. The logic was simple: once they had run out of money, or, to be more precise, of possessions to be exchanged for food, they could no longer afford to live in Ordzhonikidze. This shows how important it was for evacuees to have a profession with which they could earn their living. Ideally, this should be a skill that was in demand in a given area. This was, for example, a tough time for teachers, but doctors, nurses and those able to make various repairs were in high demand almost everywhere. Viewed from this angle, the Ginsburg family, we must admit, was badly prepared for the difficulties involved in surviving as evacuees, and Tsylya Pinchos was the first to realize this. We are informed that in Rostov-on-Don she would have been able to find employment, even without having a formal profession, while in Ordzhonikidze she hoped to work as a pedicurist. Finding steady work with reliable income in this profession depended on long-term connections, which arguably existed in the family's home city of Rostov-on-Don, but could hardly be established quickly in a new location.

Unlike the Pinchos family, Tamara was still adamant about her decision not to return to Rostov-on-Don for the time being, because she saw no improvement in the military situation in southern Russia. Yet, from her letter, it is evident that her financial difficulties had increased considerably. As her husband had

---

87 From Tamara Meerovich in Ordzhonikidze, March 13, 1942, YVA: O.75/324, pp. 232–233.

returned to Rostov-on-Don with his plant, no one was left in Ordzhonikidze to help Tamara, her child, and her mother. As the rest of her large family were in Rostov-on-Don, Tamara's loneliness certainly depressed her. Evidently, this situation could not last indefinitely.

On March 15, 1942, citing *Sovinformburo*,[88] *Molot* informed its readers about a successful Soviet offensive in the southern sector of the front. The newspaper highlighted the quantity of ammunition seized by the Red Army and the German manpower losses.[89] This could have reassured people like the Ginsburgs, who were looking for any indication that the German forces were being pushed away from Rostov-on-Don.

Soviet troops on Rostov-on-Don's streets on their way westwards. Central Archive of Moscow's Electronic and Audio-Visual Materials, 0-94364. Courtesy of Russian Holocaust Center.

However, the report did not mention any particular locality seized by the Red Army during this offensive. Obviously, if there was something to report, the Soviet media would have done so. Then the Ginsburgs, who, in all probability, knew the geography of the area well, could have figured out whether the Soviet hold on the area around Rostov-on-Don had become firmer or not.

---

88 The *Sovinformburo*, the Soviet Bureau for Information under the Central Committee of the Bolshevik party and the Soviet Government, was established on June 24, 1941, and was tasked with overseeing the Soviet and foreign press, journalists, and radio, and reporting on the events of the war and life in the USSR. Altshuler, "The Holocaust in the Soviet Mass Media," 129 (note 30).

89 "Trofei, zakhvachennye nekotorymi chastiami Iugo-Vostochnogo i Iuzhnogo frontov s 7 po 12 marta," *Molot*, no. 63 (6254), March 15, 1942.

Another interesting item of information was published in Rostov-on-Don on March 19, 1942, when *Molot* reported that a certain Lubov Rogozhina had illegally entered an apartment belonging to "citizen Vinogradova, evacuated in October 1941 from the city of Rostov-on-Don, [*and*] stolen possessions from there." Rogozhina was sentenced to five years' imprisonment; her property was confiscated.⁹⁰

Such news would be of great interest to the members of the Ginsburg family, as they indicated that in case of their evacuation, all possessions left in their abandoned rooms could easily fall prey to local thieves. Thus, such announcement could have made the Ginsburg sisters feel even less willing to leave Rostov-on-Don. Even if they nevertheless opted for flight, they would have had to take with them as much as they could.

As we have seen already, the Soviet authorities in the North Caucasus attempted to provide aid to evacuees, with special attention to children. On March 19, 1942, the Ordzhonikidze newspaper reported: "For the children studying in the Nikolaevsk secondary school (Irafsky *raion*) four hundred rubles were collected, several pairs of gloves and woolen socks were brought."⁹¹ Such aid was mostly provided for orphans or children who were evacuated without their parents, but it cannot be ruled out that such aid was also given to Tamara's son. However, given the fact that these efforts were only sporadic, they must have hardly sufficed to solve the evacuees' problems.

On March 19, 1942, the sisters Anya and Liza, confirmed that the Pinchos family had returned to Rostov-on-Don:

> Our dear Efim!
>
> I hasten to report to you that, on March 14, our dear Tsylya, Anechka and David came back to us quite unexpectedly. ... As for David, we had talked about his possible arrival. But regarding the others, there was no talk. Certainly we knew that Tsylya had been longing to come back and mentioned it at every opportunity. In any case, we are very glad to see at least half of our relatives. Now, God willing, we'll see the second half as soon as possible, including you, our dear one.
>
> Here the situation is pretty much the same. We look forward to hearing good news on the radio. ...

---

90 "Marodery," *Molot*, no. 66 (6257), March 19, 1942.
91 "Pomoshch' evakuirovannym detiam," *Sotsialisticheskaia Osetia* (Ordzhonikidze), no. 66 (2621), March 19, 1942.

Thank God, our family has grown bigger. Tsylya looks quite good; Anechka does not look well, since she has been sick for a lot of the time. They send you their best wishes.[92]

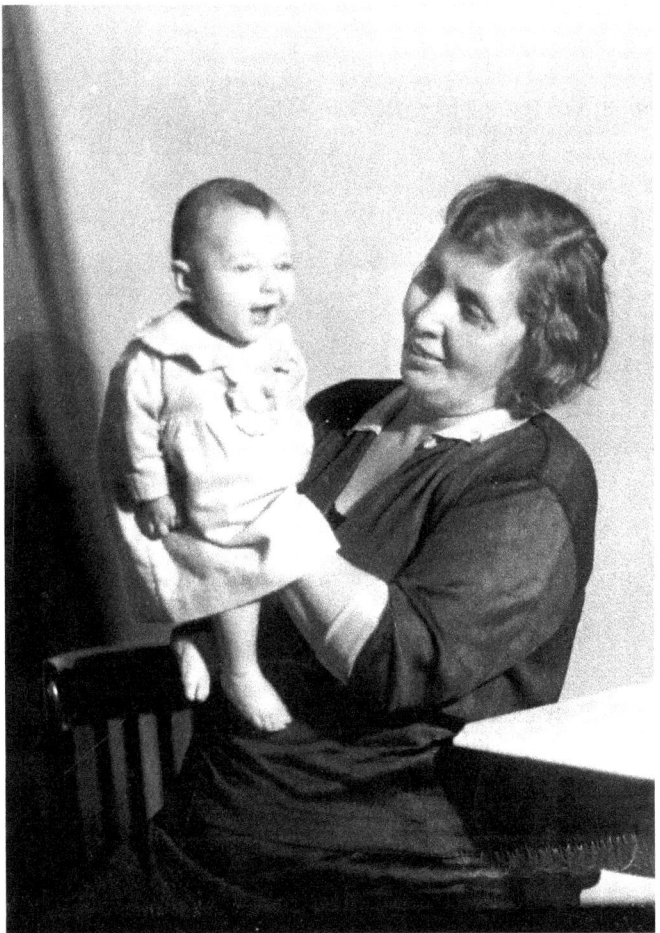

Anna Greener (Ginsburg) holding her granddaughter, Anya Pinchos.
Yad Vashem Photo Archive, 5902_35.

The letter emphasized that the return of Tsylya, David, and their daughter Anya to Rostov-on-Don was based on emotions rather than careful planning. Indeed, these feelings may have played an important role in the Pinchos family's decision. But apart from that, there may also have been pragmatic motives

---

92 From Liza Chazkewitz and Anya Greener, March 19, 1942, YVA: O.75/324, p. 245.

behind this relocation, which were not mentioned in the letter by the rather emotional Anya and Liza, but which were described by Tamara Meerovich. Given their lack of skills, connections and resources, the Pinchos family simply had more chances of surviving financially, as well as of taking care of their sick daughter, in their home city.

Notable are several mentions of God in this letter. The sisters' hopes were based not only on the might of the Red Army—this turned out to be far from certain, when it came to withstanding the Germans in the fall of 1941—but also on the power of heaven.[93]

An important article, "Terrible atrocities committed by the Germans in Taganrog," of direct relevance to the saga of the Ginsburg family, appeared in the Rostov newspaper on March 20, 1942. It reported on the "murder of several thousands of Soviet civilians, inhabitants of the city," committed by the Germans on their entry to the neighboring city of Taganrog in October 1941; but there was no reference to the fact that all these victims were Jews.[94] This was the second time that *Molot* reported on mass Jewish murders (the first time was in December 1941). But arguably, these separate items of information, however important, did not give sufficient grounds for the Ginsburgs to draw conclusions on what might happen to them if the Germans were to reach Rostov-on-Don for the second time.

On March 20, 1942, Tamara Meerovich sent a new letter to Efim Ginsburg:

> Volodya writes us that he hopes to bring us back soon [*to Rostov-on-Don*]. But I think that he is writing this in order to give us comfort. It is perilous to go back there before Taganrog and some towns close to Rostov are liberated. In particular, since this is springtime, which brings the danger of a new offensive by the Fascist beasts.
>
> True, life is becoming difficult here, whereas foodstuffs in Rostov are cheaper and more varied. Very many inhabitants of Rostov are returning home. Now we feel anguish, loneliness; sometimes we are really swept by despair. The future scares us. We anticipate the end, the victory, impatiently; but for the time being, no one can see when the war will end.[95]

---

93 On the religious renaissance in the wartime Soviet Union, see, for example, Daniel Peris, "'God is Now on Our Side': The Religious Revival in Unoccupied Soviet Territory during World War II," *Kritika: Explorations in Russian and Eurasian History* 1, no. 1 (Winter 2000): 97–118.
94 "Uzhasnye zlodeianiia nemtsev v Taganroge," *Molot*, no. 67 (6258), March 20, 1942.
95 From Tamara Meerovich in Ordzhonikidze, March 20, 1942, YVA: O.75/324, pp. 242–243.

Analyzing the military situation around Rostov-on-Don, Tamara realistically assumed that the situation had not changed to an extent that would justify her return to Rostov-on-Don, despite the psychological pressure from her own family. She saw no visible change for the better. In addition, Tamara made an astounding assumption—that the Wehrmacht might soon resume its offensive. This statement was all the more striking as it was made in the light of constant Soviet propaganda brainwashing, on the one hand, and the danger that her letter might be intercepted by Soviet censors, on the other.

The letter is very pessimistic, to the point that it could have been interpreted by the censors as defeatist. But, unlike her aunts, Anya and Liza, Tamara did not take care to disguise her thoughts. It is possible that for a moment Tamara lost her fear of the censors. Tamara still hoped for a Soviet victory in the future, but the present situation seemed to her a dead end. Financially, her family could hardly make ends meet in Ordzhonikidze. But the return to Rostov-on-Don—where Tamara expected to fare better economically—was filled with deadly danger. A prerequisite for such a return, Tamara noted wisely, would have to be at least the Soviet recapture of Taganrog. As a result, Tamara remained in exile: her heart told her to return to Rostov-on-Don, but her head persuaded her not to do so, in spite of the pressure from her own husband, as well as from the Ginsburg sisters.

If the Ginsburg family had any doubts about the religion and the nationality of those Soviet citizens whom the Germans had killed in Taganrog in the fall of 1941, these were soon dispelled. On March 24, 1942, an article in the Rostov newspaper mentioned the destruction of "almost the entire Jewish population of Taganrog" by the Germans.[96] If the Ginsburg family had juxtaposed this information with a previous notice about Taganrog, published on March 20, and the experiences of Anya and Liza Ginsburg during the German occupation of Rostov-on-Don in November 1941, they could have reached an almost certain conclusion: the survival of Anya and Liza during German rule in Rostov-on-Don in November 1941 was some sort of a miracle, which would certainly not be repeated if there was another German occupation.

Two days later, on March 26, 1942, the Rostov newspaper published Order No. 12 by the local military commander, "On the restoration and full military readiness of the anti-aircraft defenses."[97] The order was a sign for those used to

---

96 V. Vatin, "135 dnei v Taganroge," *Molot*, no. 70 (6261), March 24, 1942.
97 Order no. 12 of Kochenov, the Commandant of the Garrison of Rostov-on-Don, dated March 24, 1942, *Molot*, no. 70 (6263), March 26, 1942.

reading Soviet newspapers between the lines that German air-raids against the city might soon be resumed. This in turn indicated that the strategic situation on the southern part of the Soviet-German front might soon change in favor of the Germans. Indeed, by all accounts, the Soviet counter-offensive near Rostov-on-Don finally got bogged down at the end of March 1942.[98]

To counterbalance the negative effect of this development, the Soviet propaganda did its best to maintain the impression that the Soviet hold on Rostov-on-Don remained firm. It was a large city, whose residents were trying to go back to living their normal lives. So any article highlighting the various civil projects that were underway in Rostov would serve the propaganda goal. The following example underscores this point. On March 28, 1942, in a short article, "From the District Police Administration," the Rostov newspaper informed its readers that a new, regular technical examination of vehicles, due to take place every six months, would commence on April 1, 1942. The article added that for the inhabitants of the Rostov District, the regional branch of the State Insurance Agency would issue "voluntary individual insurance," depending on their age categories.[99]

The fact that Soviet civilians had been murdered by the Germans in occupied Taganrog was also reported in Ordzhonikidze, where Tamara Meerovich and her small family were still living. On March 29, 1942, the local newspaper published a special TASS report on the situation in Taganrog, versus activities on the Soviet southern front.[100] In contrast to what had been published in Rostov-on-Don, the report that appeared in Ordzhonikidze contained no reference to the total annihilation of Taganrog's Jews. This omission is important, since no circulation of newspapers between the various Soviet districts was permitted, and Rostov-on-Don and Ordzhonikidze belonged to two different regions. This meant that Tamara could not have learned about the murder of Taganrog's Jews from the local newspaper, although it was of course possible that she had heard rumors.

In late March 1942, Anya and Liza sent another letter confirming the arrival of Tsylya Pinchos and her family in Rostov-on-Don and saying:

> Let's hope to see big victories before May 1. The enemy will be destroyed. The enemy must be smashed to the last Fascist beast. So there would be no need to escape anywhere. But instead, you will all be able to come back here.[101]

---

98 Glantz, "The Red Army's Donbas Offensive."
99 *Molot*, no. 74 (6265), March 28, 1942.
100 "Chto tvoritsia v okkupirovannom nemtsami Taganroge?," *Sotsialisticheskaia Osetiia*, no. 75 (2630), March 29, 1942.
101 From Liza Chazkewitz and Anya Greener, late March 1942, YVA: O.75/324, pp. 343–346.

Note the stress on May 1 as the date when great Soviet victories were anticipated. Such hopes were not without foundation, as it was known that the Red Army attempted to achieve major victories on the days when the Soviet Union celebrated public holidays. In retrospect, we know that many thousands of Soviet soldiers paid with their lives for such celebrations.

Note the bizarre way in which the sisters managed to combine in a short note elevated phrases, borrowed word for word from Soviet propaganda ("… The enemy must be smashed to the last Fascist beast") with their personal dreams ("… you will all be able to come back here").

On March 31, 1942, Anna and Liza Ginsburg wrote another letter to Alma-Ata:

> We are looking forward with impatience to seeing our relatives, Monya, Tamara, and Grishechka. All I wish is to hear good news on the radio about our side!!! …
>
> It is far too muddy there [*in Ordzhonikidze*]. It is very difficult to bear, for those who are not used to it. Still, our dear one, don't worry! These are nothing but temporary difficulties. …What really counts are our successes on all our fronts.[102]

The letter shows that, delighted over the return of their relatives and "good news on the radio," the sisters remained in an uplifted mood. They hoped to bring the rest of the family back to Rostov-on-Don, and there is almost no doubt that this was the message they conveyed to Tamara Meerovich. But deep inside, the sisters remained far from feeling calm, and felt that everything hinged upon hearing "good news on the radio."

April 1942

On April 2, 1942, Tamara sent another letter to Alma-Ata:

> For the time being, Tsylya does not regret having left for Rostov. It is all quiet there. …If things continue to go on like this, they definitely won't regret having moved back. It is most important that David is there. He was reviewed by the Commission, deemed unfit for [*military*] service and received a final exemption. Now he will start to work and it will be easier for them.

---

102 From Liza Chazkewitz and Anya Greener, March 31, 1942, ibid., pp. 352–354.

> Volodya continues to work but has no exemption yet, and it greatly upsets me. Apparently he won't be spared the common fate. I do not know what we should do in this case; but I think that as soon as I learn that he has been drafted, I won't stay here and will relocate to Rostov. Then, it will be all the same, come what may. …
>
> It is rumored that life is easier here than elsewhere. …With our means, we can only buy potatoes; for the child we do our utmost and try to buy milk and eggs. Grisha looks very well. So do we.[103]

This letter is of great importance for understanding Tamara's state of mind at this unique point in time. She noted with satisfaction and probably some degree of jealousy that her relatives, who had left for Rostov-on-Don, felt quite calm there. There is no doubt that this would have had a certain effect on her state of mind. Then Tamara revealed what would guide her decisions in the future. It would all revolve around whether her husband, Volodya, would be drafted in the army or not. Tamara seemed certain that Volodya's military service would have a dramatic end, a kind of a sealed verdict ("he will not be spared the common fate"). Her considerations are understandable, but her next step was far less obvious. Rostov-on-Don continued to draw her like a magnet, and if her husband was drafted she was inclined to drop her own objections and run the risk of returning there, to be closer to her relatives, but at the price of exposing herself and her family to the danger of a German attack.

It is worth noting Tamara's remark, "It is rumored that life is easier here than elsewhere." This phrase implies that the communications between the two cities, Rostov-on-Don and Ordzhonikidze, as well as between the two branches of the family, were frequently interrupted and delayed. Coming closer to the point when she would have to make a crucial decision—whether or not to return to Rostov-on-Don—Tamara could only depend on rumors, an extremely unreliable source of information.

Apparently on the very same day, April 2, 1942 (the date of the letter is very difficult to read)—testifying to her growing nervousness—Tamara Meerovich sent another letter to her uncle, Efim Ginsburg:

> Despite all this, your situation is far better than ours, since you are so much further away from the front line. In contrast, here we can hear the air-raid alarms. On the other hand, the food situation is more favorable here.

---

103 From Tamara Meerovich in Ordzhonikidze, April 2, 1942, ibid., pp. 240–241.

What I mean is that, although food is expensive, those with funds can buy everything [*they need*]. We sustain ourselves with potatoes; without them, we would have no doubt have starved. In general, our situation is very bad.

As I have already written to you, Volodya left for Rostov, and since then he has been suffering from furunculosis.[104] He was on sick leave for a whole month. Now he has recovered [*from the boils*]. We have just received a letter from him. He wrote that the *voenkomat* has summoned him. Due to his illness, the summons was temporarily postponed, until he recovered. Now he will be screened by a Medical Commission and will no doubt be sent to the front. His fate will be sealed in the next few days. Poor man! He is in a state of despair; not for himself, but rather for our sakes, since in this case we will be left without any assistance from him.

He assumes that when he is drafted we will return to Rostov. Then, we'll be all together. In this respect, my considerations are as follows: if Rostov were not threatened so much and if at least Taganrog, Mariupol and some adjacent towns were liberated, then we would not hesitate. But this is not the case at present. In addition, it is extremely expensive in Rostov; so it would be even more difficult for us there. Besides, I'm not sure whether I can find employment there, whereas here I am able to earn at least four hundred rubles. …Given all these considerations, we have decided to stay here for two more months, and then we shall see. Write what you think about this question, since I am feeling at a loss. …

Tsylya is working in a school cafeteria [*in Rostov-on-Don*]; Anechka is going to kindergarten; David is working. Mother is grieving all the time why all our people are in Rostov but we have to be here.[105]

The letter begins with Tamara's sober appraisal that her situation was very serious. Her family faced financially problems: they could hardly make ends meet, and now there was also danger from the Germans. For the first time, we learn that the air-raids could even be heard in Ordzhonikidze, some five hundred kilometers away from Rostov-on-Don. Tamara noted that her uncle's situation in Central Asia was much safer—a notable admission for a person who in early January viewed Efim's conditions as the worst in the family. And yet, she did not consider joining him in Alma-Ata; the only viable option for her was returning to Rostov-on-Don.

---

104 An acute skin disease characterized by boils or successive crops of boils that are caused by staphylococci or streptococci.
105 From Tamara Meerovich in Ordzhonikidze, April 2, 1942, YVA: O.75/324, pp. 240–241.

The letter also provides an insight into whether the Jews were willing to participate in the Soviet military effort. Many books have been already written on this issue, proving convincingly that in relative terms, the Jewish contribution to the Soviet victory over Germany probably exceeded that of other Soviet population groups.[106]

Authentic evidence from the Ginsburg family correspondence gives us an example of another type of Jewish behavior that fell between the two extremes: on the one hand, maximum readiness to fight the Nazis, to the point of sacrificing one's life, and, on the other hand, maximum desire to preserve one's life in order to outlive the Nazis, and to this end, reluctance to join the Army to the point of evasion, as the odds on surviving the War in the ranks of the Red Army were very low. Volodya Meerovich had already made a contribution to his country's military effort, when, without proper military training, he fought in the ranks of the Extermination Battalion, defending Rostov-on-Don in November 1941. Now, in spring 1942, he was about to be conscripted into the Red Army. At this point in time, the Soviet authorities decided that his enlistment was more important for the country than his continuing to work at his plant. There is no doubt that the major factor behind this change in policy towards him was due to the shortage of recruitable manpower in the North Caucasus: by spring 1942, the great majority of men of military age (from 18 to 46 years) in the North Caucasian Military District had already been drafted.[107]

However, Volodya Meerovich did not express any particular willingness to join the Army. At the same time, judging by the letters (certainly not everything could be put down on paper, but the spirit of the letters is clearly indicative), the Meerovich family did not do anything to try to prevent Volodya's imminent

---

106 For example, Yitzhak Arad, *In the Shadow of the Red Banner: Soviet Jews in the War against Nazi Germany* (Jerusalem: Yad Vashem, The International Institute for Holocaust Research; Gefen, 2010); Dov Levin, "Unique characteristics of Soviet Jewish soldiers in the Second World War," in *The Shoah and the War*, ed. Asher Cohen, Yehoyakim Cochavi, and Yoav Gelber (New York: Peter Lang, 1992), 233–244; Aron Abramovich, *V reshayushchei voine. Uchastie i rol' evreev SSSR v voine protiv natsizma* (Tel Aviv: n.p., 1981); Yosef Guri, "Jewish Fighters in the Red Army," *Dispersion and Unity* 5–6 (1966): 172–177. These books and articles address the challenge that has never been explicitly posed, namely that Jews evaded army service, or had "fought on the Tashkent front." Tashkent was situated in Soviet Central Asia and was very remote from any of the battlefields of the Soviet-German front. So whenever a reference was made to someone fighting on the Tashkent front, it was a hint that he was evading his duty. This accusation was frequently made against the Jews.

107 TsAMO RF: 144/1389/91, pp. 16–17. In Aleksei Bezugol'nyi, "Narody Kavkaza v Vooruzhennykh silakh SSSR v gody Velikoi Otechestvennoi voiny, 1941–1945 gg.," PhD diss., Stavropol, Stavropol'skii gosudarstvennyi universitet, 2004, 38.

conscription—they merely succumbed to the inevitable. But there is no doubt that, if it had depended on them both, Volodya Meerovich and especially his wife Tamara would have preferred him to have made his contribution to the War on the home front. By doing so, he would have been able to help his family.

In addition, economic considerations began to affect the decisions of the Meerovich family. Tamara assumed that it would still be easier for her to survive in Ordzhonikidze, as she had until that point, than in Rostov-on-Don. And yet, for Tamara, Rostov's "pull of gravity" felt, for example, in the psychological pressure exerted on her by her mother, was very difficult to resist. Nevertheless, having considered all the pros and cons, Tamara postponed making a decision until the end of May.

On April 6, 1942, Liza and Anya wrote to their brother Efim:

> Please forgive us because, in this unhappy year, we forgot about your birthday and did not congratulate you. Your postcard, dated March 24, arrived yesterday. You described the conditions in which you celebrated your fiftieth birthday. It is very sad and painful to us, and makes us feel so sorry. Yesterday, our dear one, after your postcard arrived, we received your money transfer for two hundred rubles. Why have you done this? Considering your awful conditions. … After your letter dated March 14, we decided to send you money, in order to help you improve your living conditions. I sent you money and what did you do? You sent us money! We are in no need, since we are living at home and hope to continue to do so.[108]

Despite all their attempts to maintain a "business as usual" attitude, Anya and Liza seem to have been under enormous and constantly growing psychological pressure. Most of their letters do not show this. Yet, in view of their warm relationship and frequent communications, the sisters' failure to congratulate their brother on his birthday (as was their custom before the War) in a timely manner is very indicative of the state of mind of the Ginsburg sisters in Rostov-on-Don at that time.

It is also significant that, despite their very strained finances, Anya and Liza decided to give their brother financial support. It was the first time that they did so. Previously, it was Efim who tried to help them, but without much success. This could be attributed to the sisters' desire to show Efim who was really in need in their family.

---

108 From Liza Chazkewitz and Anya Greener, April 6, 1942, YVA: O.75/324, p. 254.

Given the military significance of the city, the Soviet authorities did their utmost to keep any suspicious characters out of Rostov-on-Don. One of the obvious signs of this was an announcement by the District Police Administration published by on April 11, 1942. The police required Rostov's inhabitants to have their passports registered anew, between April 15 and July 7. Failure to comply with the requirement would lead, according to the announcement, to a fine of up to a hundred rubles.[109]

On April 21, 1942, Liza sent a long letter to her brother Efim in Alma-Ata:

> Our dear Efim!
> … We expect to hear good news on the radio concerning our southern front. Today, there was great anxiety, because Volodya was drafted into the army. He left the house today. So far, he is still here, in the city, but God knows what will happen next. God grant him luck and complete well-being so that he will come back alive and unhurt. Right now there was a very moving letter from Tamara. He read it and wept bitterly; then Anya and Tsylya saw him off at the *voenkomat*. … We feel great pain, because Volodya has been taken away from us. Again, we remain alone. He is a very good man. … Tamara is taking it terribly badly; she is grieving over this; we don't know how to console her. She doesn't know yet that he has already been drafted. She has only just learnt that he was due to be reviewed by the military commission. …
> That's all for the time being, our dear one. Of course, there is no good news, but nothing to be done about it… Still, there will be some good and happy news soon enough. All we have to do is to be patient and to wait a bit longer… No doubt each of us will outlive this German barbarian and we will all be together!!! … All we wish now is to hear good news on the radio concerning our southern front. …Tsylya and Anechka send you their best wishes. She is working at a school cafeteria until May. David is working on a stall; Volodya arranged this work for him. … [110]

An event feared by the entire family, the conscription of Volodya Meerovich, finally occurred. His departure was painful for all the Rostov Ginsburgs. They were now very attached to him, since he had become part of the family, even though at first he had only been a stranger who had married one of the members

---
109 *Molot*, no. 86 (6277), April 11, 1942.
110 From Liza Chazkewitz, April 21, 1942, YVA: O.75/324, pp. 255–267.

of the clan. Also, he was the one who took care of all of them. In this letter, we learn that, before his conscription, he was able to make a farewell present to his family, by finding a job for David Pinchos. Now he had gone away and it appeared that there was no one else capable of replacing him and fulfilling his family duties. However, Volodya's mobilization was particularly devastating for his wife, Tamara. So far, she had managed to rein in her feelings in her letters to Efim, but apparently in the above-mentioned letter that she sent to the sisters, she was completely overwhelmed by grief.

This is a letter full of personal, family-centered events. Even when the Ginsburg sisters continued to express hope for future Soviet victories, their real concerns were local. They were primarily preoccupied with the stabilization of the military situation in their own region ("our southern front") and the survival of their family members ("No doubt each of us will outlive this German barbarian"). Even though in the last sentence the sisters indicated their confidence in the final victory in the War, it served as a sort of an answer to a question asked by many, among them Efim's sisters and other Rostov Jews: "What will happen next?"

That the situation in and around Rostov-on-Don had begun to look less stable can be seen in a curious announcement placed in the Rostov newspaper on April 22, 1942. In the "Lectures" section, the newspaper reported on the lecture "The significance of a defense line in the defense of the city," organized for the Bolshevik party leadership (*aktiv*) corps in Rostov-on-Don.[111] There were several important aspects to this short report: the very fact that the lecture was given at all, its intended audience (selected personnel from the Party's mid-level echelon), the fact that no more details were provided about the event, and, last but not least, the fact that the news was made known to the wider public through the newspaper. How did the ordinary local inhabitants interpret this announcement? They might have concluded that the city's situation was growing more dangerous, as they must have realized already from several previous events such as the order to dig defensive lines, but the Soviet authorities duly made preparations to face the threat.

On April 24, 1942, Tamara Meerovich for the first time commented in writing on her husband's mobilization. She wrote to her uncle from Ordzhonikidze:

> Volodya's future is at stake. I have been terribly anxious, and therefore I put off writing to you. …Yesterday, we received a letter from him, dated

---

111 *Molot*, no. 95 (6286), April 22, 1942.

April 18, saying that the Commission has declared him fit [*for service*] and that he had been drafted. It was bound to happen, sooner or later. He wrote that, for the time being, he would probably stay in Rostov. And then, he would surely be dispatched somewhere else. I am particularly preoccupied with the question—where he might be sent to. I fear only one thing: that he may be transferred immediately to the front; he is still feeling weak after his illness. …

If we were at home, it would probably be easier for us. But here we don't know what awaits us. A future that has no hope. Of course, I should pull myself together [*and say*]: let's take the chance; probably the fates will have pity on us and won't let us perish. For the time being, I am going to stay here, and then we will see. Of course, were it not for our damned Jewish [*iudeiskii*] origins, I would not stay here for a moment, and would go to Rostov. In spite of the hardships that probably await us there …; but at least, we would share the same fate as the rest [*of the family*]. I think that you will understand me. Mother is also concerned and is growing weaker. It is spring here, but inwardly there is a terrible feeling of anguish. Every day, living here is getting more and more difficult; prices are soaring astronomically.[112]

Tamara hadn't written to her uncle for some time, and in this letter we are told the reason: she was extremely worried over the fate of her husband; all her letters were concerned with his fate. She felt that she might never see him again. It was likely that Volodya would be killed in action, as the huge number of casualties in the Red Army were no secret to the Soviet people.[113] He could also disappear into the vast spaces of Russia or simply lose contact with his family. At any rate, for Tamara, his conscription meant the loss of her husband and the break-up of her family. Also, it appeared, although she did not say so explicitly, that her own evacuation into the country's interior would only increase the chances that she would lose her husband forever. The poor woman could clearly see no way out, whether in Ordzhonikidze, Rostov-on-Don, or elsewhere.

Her extremely pessimistic letter contained one of the very few references to the impact of their being Jewish on the family's decisions. Almost always, the

---

112 From Tamara Meerovich in Ordzhonikidze, April 24, 1942, YVA: O.75/324, pp. 270–271.
113 See, for example, Boris V. Sokolov, "Estimating Soviet War Losses on the Basis of Soviet Population Censuses," *The Journal of Slavic Military Studies* 27, no. 3 (2014): 467–492.

Ginsburgs preferred not to touch on this subject. This could either be ascribed to their desire not to draw the attention of the Soviet censors to the family, or to their preferring not to mention something that was clear to all of them. In this letter, however, Tamara makes an exception and writes with striking frankness about her "damned Jewish origins." This phrase is so emotionally charged and so meaningful that it must be analyzed carefully.

First, Tamara felt the heavy burden of her belonging to the "chosen people," when their own survival and the survival of their families was at stake. Therefore, Tamara's statement should not come as a surprise. Under the circumstances, she, like almost every Jew, would have been willing to relinquish any trace of her affiliation with the Jewish people, that is, anything that could be held against her by the Nazis.

Her statement could alert the Soviet censors, too. On the face of it, she claimed that, were it not for her being Jewish, she would not have hesitated to return to Rostov-on-Don, as long as the city remained in Soviet hands. But it is clear that Tamara's hesitation had nothing to do with whether or not the city was held by the Soviet authorities. After all, there was nothing that could endanger her and her family in that situation. Rather, her statement, however vague, referred to the possibility of a German takeover of the city. Not only did she mention this possibility, which could on its own have alerted the Soviet censors. Rather, she implied that, in principle, if it wasn't for her Jewish origins, she would not have been opposed so fiercely to living under German rule.[114]

On April 24, 1942, Liza supplied a few more details about Volodya's military service:

> On April 21, Volodya was drafted into the Army. So far, he is here [*in Rostov-on-Don*] for a course that will last from six weeks to five months. Then, we'll see. …
>
> We want to believe and hope that everything will be all right, otherwise it is impossible. …[115]

---

114 Such ideas were occasionally articulated by Jews elsewhere. See Shternshis, "Between Life and Death," 494. Cf. Mordechai Altshuler, "Escape and Evacuation of Soviet Jews at the Time of the Nazi Invasion: Policies and Realities," in *The Holocaust in the Soviet Union. Studies and Sources on the Destruction of the Jews in the Nazi-Occupied Territories of the USSR, 1941–1945*, ed. L. Dobroszycki and J. S. Gurock (Armonk, NY: M. E. Sharpe, 1993), 90.

115 From Liza Chazkewitz, April 24, 1942, YVA: O.75/324, pp. 272–273.

How can we understand this letter? Volodya Meerovich was still in Rostov-on-Don, but he was already in the Army, with all that this entailed. He could not visit his relatives, nor could he help them. However, he was still in a relatively safe place and this was the only good point, in the opinion of the family, about his service. However, they realized that this equilibrium could be upset at any moment. They still believed in a happy ending to their saga, but we can see the cracks in this belief: they had not given up hope yet only because there was no other way out.

In the meantime, the military situation around Rostov-on-Don did not seem to have changed. In spite of this, the Soviet military authorities endeavored to alleviate the misgivings of Rostov's inhabitants, and succeeded, to some extent. On April 25, 1942, *Molot* announced that the city's military commander permitted the free movement of civilians until 22:00. Previously, they had only been allowed to move around until 20:00.[116]

On April 26, 1942, Liza sent a new letter to her brother in Alma-Ata:

> We are very glad to learn that your superiors hold you in high esteem and that you have been given bonuses. It could not be otherwise, since they had never had such an employee as you. …
>
> We anticipate hearing good news from all the fronts from our valiant heroic Red Army!!! … Which is moving ahead towards the great victory!! Death to the German occupiers. …
>
> It's almost May; it is going to be warm, in particular after everything we have endured. That's why we have decided to go on waiting. Despite the fact that you have urged us not to sit and wait, but to go, while all our relatives are longing to come home. So, we have decided to wait until they all come back to Rostov. …
>
> Some days ago, we were visited by people from the police (*militsiya*); according to your request, they checked whether we were still alive; we were really touched by this.[117]

It is worthy of note that Liza was not entirely preoccupied with the situation in Rostov-on-Don. She was still able to respond to the news mentioned by Efim Ginsburg in his own letter, and to praise him for his success at work. This may indicate that at that point in time she did not view the situation in Rostov-on-Don as absolutely desperate.

---

116 Order No. 36 of the Commandant of the Garrison of Rostov-on-Don of April 24, 1942, *Molot*, no. 98 (6289), April 25, 1942.
117 From Liza Chazkewitz, April 26, 1942, YVA: O.75/324, pp. 276–281.

As in previous correspondence, the sisters' letter is full of expressions of grand Soviet patriotism, not modest wishes for some improvement in the situation around their home city. It is difficult, almost impossible, to establish whether this was due to their suspicions that their letters might be intercepted by the Soviet censors, or, alternatively, whether they really thought this way. On the one hand, in late April 1942, there were slightly fewer reasons for Russian citizens to believe in a resounding great Soviet victory in the foreseeable future. On the other hand, it is likely that Anya and Liza's pronouncement would be read in the context of the intensive propaganda campaign that preceded May 1, one of the major Soviet holidays. And yet, the sisters did not seem to repeat Soviet slogans automatically, as such statements still reflected their inner, however shattered, beliefs.

In the letter, Liza once again replied negatively to her brother, who had urged his sisters to leave the city immediately. Were there any changes in the sisters' viewpoint regarding their possible evacuation, as compared to the previous periods of time? At this stage, Anya and Liza continued to claim that Tamara Meerovich and her family were endeavoring to join them in Rostov-on-Don. But significantly, they no longer mentioned crowds of refugees coming back to the city. This return stream, as far as we now know, had long since been exhausted. The sisters' arguments may have been intended to cover the fact that it was still more convenient for them to stay at home than to wander around the Soviet hinterlands, suffering extreme privations. This letter was written in mid-spring, and the sisters could no longer use the excuse of the cold winter as the major obstacle on the way eastwards. In this sense, it was now easier for them to escape than previously. However, in contrast to previous periods, they could not have hoped to receive the help of Volodya Meerovich, both physical and financial, as he was already in the Army. Evidently, the only other adult male in the family, David Pinchos, could not be counted on in such a long, difficult enterprise. He had been declared unfit for military service and doubtless had a serious medical problem, which meant that he would have needed to receive care himself during their evacuation. So, viewed from this angle, it had actually become more difficult now for the Ginsburgs to escape from Rostov-on-Don, not easier.

May 1942

On May 2, 1942, the Ordzhonikidze newspaper published an order from Stalin, signed in his capacity as the People's Commissar of Defense: Let 1942 be the year of destruction and liberation of Soviet soil from the Hitlerite scoundrels."¹¹⁸ This pledge was widely disseminated by the Soviet propaganda machine.¹¹⁹ As we see, the Ginsburg sisters' optimistic forecast that the Red Army would triumph in 1942 was well grounded, but only in the world of Soviet propaganda.

Rostov inhabitants reading the order of the People's Commissar of Defense, Iosif Stalin, on May 1, 1942. Source: Central State Archive of the City of Moscow. Central Archive of Moscow's Electronic and Audio-Visual Materials, 0-94260. Courtesy of Russian Holocaust Center.

Rostov inhabitants in one of the city parks. Apparently May 1–2, 1942. Source: Central Archive of Moscow's Electronic and Audio-Visual Materials, 0-94266. Courtesy of Russian Holocaust Center.

---

118   Order No. 130 by the People's Commissar of Defense from May 1, 1942, *Sotsialisticheskaia Osetiia*, no. 104 (2657), May 2, 1942.
119   Berkhoff, *Motherland in Danger*, 45.

Echoing Stalin's pronouncement, Liza and Anna wrote to Efim Ginsburg on May 3, 1942: "Comrade Stalin has said that the War will be over in 1942. The confounded enemy will be destroyed without fail."[120] They wrote this despite the fact that that it was difficult to see any signs of a noticeable Soviet advance on the ground, either in the southern sector of the fighting, or anywhere else. The sisters' attitude towards Stalin was remarkable. In my opinion, this went beyond what was expected of them as loyal Soviet citizens. Rather, it was due to their unshakable belief in Stalin's genius.[121] There are several references to Stalin in the correspondence, and the role attributed to him here is more or less that of a god. This is indicative of the sisters' optimism, based mainly on belief and emotions, rather than on rational thought. In contrast, the younger generation (Tamara and Tsylya) never spoke about God, and Tamara only mentioned Stalin's name once. They, too, were sometimes carried away, and let their emotions affect their decision-making, but on the whole, they tended to resort to logic.

The optimistic mood of the Ginsburg family members living in Rostov-on-Don might have been boosted, among other things, by the news that Rostov's leading theaters, including the Gorky Theater and the Theater of Musical Comedy, had returned to the city after evacuation in April and May 1942.[122]

On May 6, Tamara Meerovich commented on the situation as it was seen from Ordzhonikidze:

> Dear Efim!
>
> … Your last letter saddened us truly. It is apparent that the food situation in your area has grown far worse. Where is the way out? To move to another place, for example, here, in the Caucasus, is risky now. Indeed the food situation is better here, but it is closer to the front. Actually, it is a vicious circle. …
>
> On April 21, Volodya was conscripted into the army. We have all taken it very hard, but now we have calmed down a bit, because he has been sent [to] Rostov for a two-month course for medical orderlies… He urges us to stay here for a couple of months, though we are sick and tired of it. And although we want to get home as soon as possible, it looks like we must follow [developments], as the situation dictates. No doubt the summer

---

120 From Liza Chazkewitz and Anya Greener, May 3, 1942, YVA: O.75/324, p. 299.
121 On this aspect of attitudes of the Soviet populace towards Stalin, see Jan Plamper, *The Stalin Cult: A Study in the Alchemy of Power* (New Haven, CT: Yale University Press, 2012).
122 Zelenskaia, *Kul'turno-prosvetitel'nye uchrezhdeniia*, 81. They were evacuated again from Rostov-on-Don in summer 1942.

months will be crucial in determining the outcome of the War. We believe that everything will develop as Comrade Stalin has ordered. …

I have had a small promotion: now I am a deputy chief accountant, which carries with it an additional hundred rubles. It is not big money, but now it is important for me.[123]

Tamara Meerovich. Source: Source: Yad Vashem Photo Archive. 5902_15.

It appears that Efim Ginsburg's confession about severe food shortages in Alma-Ata had made a painful impression on Tamara. She looked at the situation from Efim's point of view and felt concern for him, as if he was the one with nowhere to go. Of course, it only strengthened her own resolve against evacuation eastwards.

We see time and again how Efim's candidness in describing his privations in the Soviet hinterland played against him. In a certain sense, he provided his family in the Caucasus with arguments against evacuation. Viewed from this perspective, Efim's inability to conceal, or, at least, downplay his hardships as an evacuee affected the family's unanimous decision not to evacuate deeply into the Soviet hinterland, or not to evacuate at all.

Tamara once again demonstrates her acute strategic vision by stating that "the coming months" will be "crucial in determining the outcome of the War." Indeed, the Battle of Stalingrad, which took place to the north of the North

---

123 From Tamara Meerovich in Ordzhonikidze, May 6, 1942, YVA: O.75/324, pp. 288–289.

Caucasus from July 1942 and culminated in the encirclement and annihilation of the German Sixth Army in late January 1943, is considered to be the turning point in the entire Soviet-German War. Still, in a marked contrast to Tamara's overall strategic vision, she apparently still relied on Stalin's promises, which so far had not been kept. Or was she merely paying lip-service to the suspicious Soviet censors?

This ambivalence was best manifest in the realm of crucial personal decisions. No one in the family knew what to do. Tamara's husband did not encourage her to go back to Rostov-on-Don for the time being. These decisions depended on their feelings, presentiments, and intuition. But although Tamara's economic situation had slightly improved, there was some temporary certainty, and therefore, relief regarding Volodya's mobilization, she still had to act as a lone fighter, swimming against the stream and going against the wishes of almost the whole Ginsburg family. Evidently, Tamara was on the verge of being exhausted.

Tsylya Pinchos's letter from May 6, 1942 gives us the picture from the Pinchos family's point of view:

> Hello dear uncle!
>
> … We are finally in Rostov. I am working in a school as an assistant in the cafeteria; I am very tired, also I have to do all the housework. Doda is working; he is doing pretty well for the time being. What really matters is that he is with us. Anechka is attending kindergarten and is very happy about it. Altogether, the mood is rather somber, but let's hope that confounded Hitler will soon be done away with, and, most important, we'll be together again.
>
> I miss our relatives very much, especially little Grishechka. Volodya comes here occasionally. Last Sunday he came here with his friends and had dinner with us. I treated them well. I feel pity for him, poor one; he is really missing his son. …We are so eager to be together and to begin to live again. We are all in good health and wish you the same. Several days ago, Doda and I recalled last year and your visit, how pleasant and joyful it was. … Best wishes from Doda and Anechka.[124]

It appears that Tsylya's mood was notably better that that of Tamara. Tsylya preferred to look at the bright side of the picture: almost the entire family was together, most specifically, her own branch, comprising her daughter Anya,

---

124 From Tsylya Pinchos in Rostov-on-Don, May, 6, 1942, ibid., pp. 1–2.

husband David, mother Anya, and herself, were all living in Rostov-on-Don and managing to make ends meet. Tsylya did not concentrate simply on her own situation; she also felt compassion for Volodya Meerovich, whose family had been split up and who felt heartbroken. Overall, she seems a warm-hearted woman and a good hostess. However, her judgment seems to lack the intellectual depth and strategic vision characteristic of Tamara Meerovich.

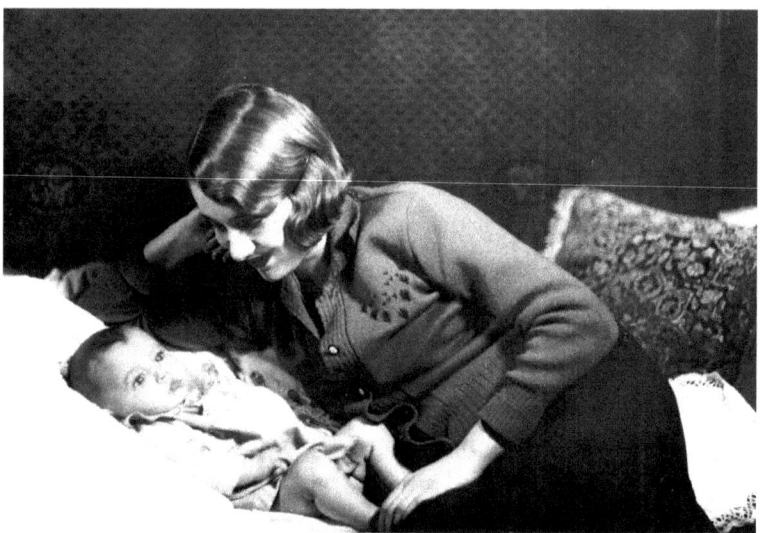

Tsylya Pinchos with her daughter Anya (Anechka). 1936. Yad Vashem Photo Archive. 5902_36.

Like the older generation of Ginsburgs, Tsylya's hopes for a better future were connected with the past, with the return to prewar peace. Although we learn Tsylya's views on life before the War, as seen from the perspective of 1942, it seems that they differ markedly from those of her cousin, Tamara Meerovich, who was only a year older than her. In her letter written in April 1941, the only good thing Tamara had to say about the prewar "fat years" was that there was no war then.

On May 8, 1942, Tamara sent a short note to Efim Ginsburg:

> We are living as of old, anticipating changes for the better, dreaming about our house and meeting all our relatives, including you. Volodya is still in Rostov; he writes to us almost every day, calms us down and cherishes the hope for himself and for us of a quick end to all the horrors.[125]

---

125 From Tamara Meerovich in Ordzhonikidze, May 8, 1942, ibid., pp. 282–283.

The letter accurately captures a delicate "in-between" period, a deceptive lull before the storm, one of many in the Ginsburg saga, spanning the moments between their major decisions. Some traces of a possible volte-face in Tamara's mindset regarding the return to Rostov-on-Don are noticeable in this short letter. She no longer wrote about her life in Ordzhonikidze. Rather, her thoughts and dreams were now devoted to Rostov-on-Don, where all her family were staying.

This letter also stresses the important role played by her husband Volodya in the family decision-making. On the one hand, he was doing what he was supposed to do, namely supporting his wife. On the other hand, by assuaging her fears, he contributed to her choosing to return to Rostov-on-Don, despite her deeply rooted doubts and reservations. In retrospect, it appears that the best-connected member of the family was, like the rest of the Ginsburgs, poorly informed about the current military situation in the region.

In the meantime, important military developments were taking place in the neighboring Crimean Peninsula. These were reported in *The Washington Post*, which on May 12, 1942, published an article, "Hitler opens drive in the Crimea for gateway to Caucasus oil":

> Heavy fighting has erupted in the Kerch peninsula, [a] narrow neck [of land] leading from the eastern Crimea to the oil [fields] of Caucasus, and the Red Army is fighting stubbornly there against a new German offensive, the Russians announced officially tonight.[126]

The article suggested that, after the capture of Kerch, the Caucasus would be the natural direction of the next German thrust. At this point in time, the Ginsburg family was still unaware of these military developments and their repercussions.

Consequently, Liza and Anna's short note, dated May 13, 1942, contained only patriotic messages, as if taken straight from the first page of a Soviet newspaper: "No doubt it will be like that. The enemy will be destroyed and we shall triumph! Death to the German barbarians!"[127]

The sisters' assessment, if it may be regarded as such, is sharply contrasted with the appraisal of the situation in the US media. The possibility that the Wehrmacht would strike at the Caucasus was at the time freely discussed by the US newspapers. Furthermore, even the German sources, despite the secrecy surrounding the direction of the 1942 summer offensive, implied that the battle

---

126 *The Washington Post*, May 12, 1942.
127 From Liza Chazkewitz and Anya Greener, May 13, 1942, YVA: O.75/324, pp. 284–285.

for Caucasian oil had just begun. On May 14, 1942, *The Washington Post*, citing German sources on the impending fall of Kerch in the Crimean Peninsula, wrote:

> Germans say Kerch is about to fall.
> (UP). Berlin, May 13. Nazi spokesman tonight predicted the early fall of Kerch, Russia's besieged bastion of the Eastern Crimea, and said the Germans already had loosed across the adjacent four-mile water gap "the first blows in the great battle for Caucasian oil".[128]

On May 16, 1942, Tamara sent a new letter to Efim Ginsburg:

> Today I received a letter from Volodya, dated May 10. He writes that until June he will stay in Rostov; generally, he hopes that everything will turn out well concerning his future. He excels himself in his studies, and on May 1 he was praised for his achievements in the unit order. He is in a good and cheerful mood; he frequently goes to Tsylya's place; but he is really worried about us. …
> During the last few days, we have been terribly worried by the events in Kerch. Every morning we listen to radio broadcasts with a sinking heart; we anticipate getting good news, but instead we are getting entirely the opposite. …
> Mother is all right; she feels good and is getting used to the hardships in life. Sometimes she is more cheerful that I am, and she cheers me up. She misses you greatly. Every day she tells fortunes; it is her only entertainment. She also tells fortunes for the neighbors and gives comfort to everyone.[129]

The letter gives another example of Volodya Meerovich's misguided judgment. He remained in Rostov-on-Don and was still able to walk around, almost in a free manner: he still could contact his friends and colleagues in the city. What is more, he was exposed now to a new, important influx of information, emanating from the Red Army personnel with whom he was in contact on a daily basis. But despite all this, he expressed optimism regarding the general situation and state of anxiety in Rostov-on-Don, and the situation of his family in Ordzhonikidze, a city located relatively far away from the frontline, some 700 kilometers to the south-east of Rostov-on-Don. However, it is also likely that Tamara failed to grasp her husband's transformation from a civilian into a soldier, subject to severe military censorship. After his enlistment, he doubtless

---

128 *The Washington Post*, May 14, 1942.
129 From Tamara Meerovich in Ordzhonikidze, May 16, 1942, YVA: O.75/324, pp. 286–287.

remained extremely close to her, but as all his letters had to pass the military censors, he became much more cautious in providing any negative assessment of the situation around Rostov-on-Don.

We learn that Volodya Meerovich was doing well in his army course, which may be instructive of his high motivation to fight—as a Soviet patriot, and/or as a Jew, and/or in order to protect his family. The letter also mentions another person, who was rarely mentioned in Tamara's letters: her mother, Monya, who was fifty-two years old at that time. We know next to nothing about her. Apparently, she did not work, and was in charge of the household; Monya indulged herself in escapism from the cruel reality surrounding her.

We can feel how anxious Tamara was; her mood again contains elements of "freezing," which characterized the conduct of the Ginsburg family in 1941. She tried to keep herself briefed continuously about events at the front. Indeed, the *Sovinformburo* update broadcasts, which started from the evening of May 13, mentioned the gradual withdrawal of the Red Army forces towards the city of Kerch.[130] Finally, on the evening of May 16, the very day that Tamara wrote this letter, it was announced that the fighting was taking place in Kerch itself.[131] (In fact, the Soviet forces lost control of the city of Kerch and the adjacent area on or about May 14, 1942. Since then, Sevastopol remained the only Soviet-held stronghold in the region.) Tamara's words indicate that, detached as she was from other sources of information, she increasingly relied on Soviet reports as a trigger for her decisions.

To her credit, Tamara succeeded in grasping the truly important news about Kerch, even though it was "diluted" in a multitude of meaningless Soviet propaganda messages. However, she does not seem to have fully comprehended the significance of these events, and how they might affect subsequent events in the North Caucasus in the very near future. The triumph in the Crimea would enable the Germans to free up forces for the advance towards the Caucasus.

May saw the unfolding of a big battle around Kharkov, a city situated more than 450 kilometers to the north-west of Rostov-on-Don. It began in mid-May with a Soviet advance. It was reported on May 17, 1942 in *The New York Times*:

> A Stockholm dispatch, relayed by the Vichy French news agency and Reuter, said today that the Red Army, flanking Kharkov to the south, had breached the German defenses at Lozovaya in a drive to cut German communications with the entire front, south of that point.[132]

---

130 Sovinformburo updates, May 13–16, 1942, available at: http://army.lv/ru.
131 Sovinformburo update, May 16 (evening), 1942, available at: http://army.lv/ru
132 "Kharkov reported flanked. Breaching of Lozovaya Defenses Imperils Nazis in South," *The New York Times*, May 17, 1942.

Indeed, as we now know, the first days of the offensive indeed looked promising for the Soviet forces.

The ensuing jubilant atmosphere was immediately reported by the Soviet media. On May 19, 1942, the Ordzhonikidze newspaper published a TASS report, "Successful offensive of our troops in the direction of Kharkov." The main findings of this report were as follows: the Soviet forces broke through the enemy's defenses, they advanced 20 to 60 kilometers westwards, and 300 localities were liberated.[133] This news sounded good to the Ginsburgs, as the successful Soviet advance pushed the frontline further away to the north-west from the beleaguered Rostov-on-Don, and therefore made their stay in the city safer.

On the very same day, May 19, 1942, the Ordzhonikidze newspaper published another reassuring report from the central military newspaper *Krasnaya Zvezda*, "The advance of our forces in the direction of Kharkov is proceeding successfully."[134]

However, in the meantime, the Battle of Kharkov was evolving not in the manner envisaged by the Soviet command. Quoting German sources, on May 21, 1942, *The New York Times* briefly reported on recent developments in the southern sector of the Soviet-German front. Based on information from German broadcasts, the newspaper stated that the Soviet attacks on Kharkov were repulsed in heavy plane and tank fighting, with thirty-four more Soviet tanks destroyed. The London correspondent also mentioned that the Nazis reportedly plan to erect a huge parachute base at Kerch for Caucasus invasion.[135]

As we now know, the Red Army planners badly miscalculated and aimed their thrust in exactly the direction where the Wehrmacht was preparing its own attack. As a result, the Soviet forces were confronted with a well-prepared enemy, which was able to destroy the attacking Soviet troops and to turn the tables on them. The Soviet advance quickly ground to a halt, and then it crumbled in the face of a mighty German counter-offensive, for which the Red Army was ill-prepared. As a result, large Soviet forces were encircled in the Kharkov pocket, reminiscent of the 1941 Blitzkrieg advance, and were annihilated.[136] The Soviet fiasco at Kharkov was instrumental in moving the war momentum back

---

133 *Sotsialisticheskaia Osetiia* (Ordzhonikidze), no. 116 (2671), May 19, 1942.
134 P. Olender, *Sotsialisticheskaia Osetiia* (Ordzhonikidze), no. 116 (2671), May 19, 1942.
135 "Soviet push fails, Germans contend," *The New York Times*, May 21, 1942.
136 David M. Glantz, *Kharkov 1942: Anatomy of a Military Disaster Through Soviet Eyes* (New York: Ian Allan Publishing, 2010), 171–234. Cf. idem, "The Khar'kov Operation, 12–27 May 1942," *The Journal of Soviet Military Studies* 5, no. 3 (1992): 494–510.

in favor of the Germans, thus further facilitating the German move towards the Caucasus.

It is certain that the Ginsburgs were totally unaware of any of these events. Even Tamara Meerovich, apparently the most discerning in the family, failed to grasp what was happening. It was during those very days that she made the most decisive step of her life.

On May 21, 1942, Liza Ginsburg wrote to her brother from Rostov-on-Don:

> It is still the same here. I am reporting to you that our relatives in Ordzhonikidze have decided to return. Thank God. They are supposed to leave on May 31. It is difficult to say now, our dear one, what is the best thing to do and where is the better (safer) place. ... Then, our dear one, we will look forward to seeing the complete collapse of Hitler's bandits. ...
>
> We are in good health, on average. There is a canteen near me, where I get breakfast and dinner. ... Speaking frankly, it is good so far.[137]

The complete reunification of the family was of course the most important news in this note, an event that was of major importance to them, compared to all the other "trivial" happenings. The Ginsburg sisters were obviously overwhelmed with joy. Furthermore, Tamara's return served as proof that they had been right in not moving anywhere, while Tamara and Efim had been wrong. Still, the two sisters did not over-emphasize their triumph. The situation around Rostov-on-Don seems to have remained very volatile; they did not feel easy about this and remained in the dark about the future ("it is difficult to say ... what is the best thing to do").

Tamara's decision to return to Rostov-on-Don may have been reinforced by a report published on May 23, 1942 in the Ordzhonikidze newspaper. It stated that the Red Army was proceeding to push the Germans westwards. However, no further details were provided.[138]

On May 24, Liza wrote from Rostov-on-Don:

> ... [*the only thing we need is*] to repel the German barbarians and murderers as soon as possible... I am reporting to you that our relatives should

---

137 From Liza Chazkewitz, May 21, 1942, YVA: O.75/324, pages unclear.
138 L. Trifon, "Pod udarami Krasnoi Armii vrag otstupaet na zapad," *Sotsialisticheskaia Osetiia* (Ordzhonikidze), no. 119 (2674), May 23, 1942.

be coming here soon. They have made their decision. Recently Volodya sent them an invitation [*vyzov*]; Tamara called me today at the pharmacy and said that they had received it. They are thinking about moving here on May 31. Tomorrow she will begin to make her request, in order to receive the travel permit.[139]

We learn that the decision to return was not Tamara's own, but was rather coordinated with her husband. The latter sent a formal invitation, without which Tamara and her family would not be able to move back to Rostov-on-Don. This invitation had to be approved by the local authorities. Judging by the fact that Tamara was able to obtain the desired permit within a very short time, the local Soviet authorities were not opposed to letting civilians return to Rostov-on-Don. This may indicate that they, at least at the middle level of Soviet bureaucracy, had not yet been briefed on the changing situation in the region, where Rostov-on-Don was again exposed to German attack. Alternatively, it is possible that the authorities were kept informed, but were guided by the desire not to let the civilian population know that the situation around Rostov-on-Don and in the entire North Caucasian region might soon get out of control. Under such circumstances, they could and actually did approve requests, authorizing the return of some citizens to Rostov-on-Don.

In the meantime, more news of the painful Soviet defeat at Kerch, and its implications, had reached the foreign media. On May 25, 1942, *The Washington Post* reported the withdrawal of Russian troops from the Kerch peninsula, following two weeks of bitter fighting. The newspaper stated that this gave the Nazis undisputed possession of a springboard for an invasion of the oil-rich Caucasus.[140] If the Ginsburgs could have figured out what the Soviet abandonment of Kerch would mean to them, they would have realized that staying even in remote areas of the North Caucasus might jeopardize them. This drastic change in the strategic situation in the region in late spring 1942 meant that Rostov-on-Don and the adjacent area would become particularly exposed to the German thrust, in the very near future.

On May 25–26, the central Soviet press (*Pravda* and *Izvestiya*) reported on the second meeting of the "Representatives of the Soviet Jewish people," held in Moscow on May 24, 1942. The first meeting, as mentioned above, had highlighted the fact that the Jews were being especially targeted for persecution by

---

139 From Liza Chazkewitz and Anya Greener, May 24, 1942, YVA: O.75/324, p. 292.
140 "Fall of Kerch," *The Washington Post*, May 25, 1942.

the Germans. In contrast, the second meeting dealt mainly with the willingness of members of the Jewish community to fight against the German invaders. Only in a small addition to the report of the meeting, in a telegram sent by its participants to Stalin, it was noted,

> In the lengthy generations of its [*history*], the Jewish people have known much misery and suffering, persecution and torment, but all past atrocities pale in comparison with the benighted actions of the crazed Fascist beasts, the crimes of Hitler's executioners and murderers.[141]

Typically, this article was not reproduced in the Rostov newspaper. This may be indicative of the anti-Jewish sentiments of members of the *Molot* editorial board or of local censors, but also of the fact that the worsening military situation around the city led the local decision-makers to conclude that the newspaper should address more urgent tasks. If the members of the Ginsburg family somehow learned about the meeting, it might possibly have strengthened their Jewish identity and their resolve to do their utmost in order not to find themselves under German rule.

In the letter sent on May 26, the sisters inquired in a detailed way how Efim made ends meet in Alma-Ata. They further suggested lending him the money he had previously sent to them (because he adamantly refused to take it back), so that he could spend it on improving his living conditions, mainly by buying foodstuffs. This discussion overshadowed the description of the events in the Caucasus.

The sisters' again mention of Tamara's forthcoming return and demonstrated their unflagging optimism: "… They are sick and tired of living like this and tormenting themselves alone, in such poor conditions. And then, our dear one, we'll be waiting for you after the complete destruction of Hitler's gang."[142] But in the meantime, the military situation on the ground was worsening, and Moscow prepared plans for the worst eventuality. On May 29, 1942, the State Defense Committee, the highest Soviet authority during the Soviet-German War, issued decree no. 1828, "On the preparation for the disablement [*vyvod iz stroia*)]of the strategically important Maikop oil enterprises and the eviction from the Krasnodar territory and the Rostov district of socially dangerous persons, Germans, Romanians, Crimean Tatars, foreign citizens."[143] The decree was intended for the local

---

141 "Vtoroi miting predstavitelei evreiskogo naroda," *Pravda*, May 25, 1942; *Izvestiia* May 26, 1942. In Altshuler, "The Holocaust in the Soviet Mass Media," 139.
142 From Liza Chazkewitz, May 26, 1942, YVA: O.75/324, pp. 296–297.
143 Fedoseev, "K voprosu o provedenii evakuatsionnykh meropriiatii," 168.

Soviet authorities in the North Caucasus, as well as for the People's Commissariat of the Interior. Needless to say, the decree was marked "Top Secret."

Concurrently, the ordinary Soviet civilians were still being fed with the stories of a continuous Soviet advance westwards. On May 30, a Soviet newsreel was shown in cinema theaters throughout the Soviet Union.[144] It showed the completion of construction of a new bridge over the River Don and a huge number of Red Army troops crossing the bridge to advance westwards. Although no territorial gains were mentioned (and indeed, none were made during that period), the newsreel made it clear that the momentum of the Soviet offensive in the south was far from being lost.

June 1942

On June 2, 1942, Liza Ginsburg sent a letter to her brother Efim:

> Our dear Efim!
>
> ... Now I have received your second [*transfer of*] five hundred rubles. Certainly I am angry with you, but I had to accept it. When we meet, we'll talk and swear at you [*a bit*]. But not now, because our dear relatives from Ordzhonikidze, Manya, Tamara and Grishenka, have returned to us in Rostov. We are glad and happy. Now it is highly desirable that their arrival will be secure and permanent and [*that*] we are not threatened any more. ...
>
> They [*the evacuees*] look well, but it is very hard and a real pity that in two days Volodya will be dispatched to the front. ... [145]

The letter can be seen against the background of the changing military situation in the south, consisting of different elements. The first one was not easy to interpret. Recently, the Soviets had publicly acknowledged their loss of Kerch on the Crimean peninsula, but had downplayed any possible implications of this defeat on the North Caucasus area. The second element was even harder to grasp. The Soviet authorities had maintained an effective information blackout on the defeat of the Soviet forces at Kharkov, the dimensions of this fiasco, and its possible repercussions on the Soviet hold over the North Caucasus. Still, there was a noticeable absence of Soviet boasting about their victories and advances in this sector. For those able to read between the lines, this omission

---

144 *Soiuzkinozhurnal*, no. 45, May 30, 1942, RGAKFD: record 4713, http://pobeda-vov.ru/Lib/pages/item.aspx?itemid=10394, accessed November 21, 2011.
145 From Liza Chazkewitz, June 2, 1942, YVA: O.75/324, p. 303.

was a sign that all was not well. However, little change could be seen in the general situation around Rostov-on-Don, as perceived by its inhabitants, so that the difference was barely perceptible.

The Ginsburg sisters, like all the ordinary Soviet citizens in the region, were not aware of the real military situation around Rostov-on-Don. Yet, doubtlessly, there was something in the air, and the resulting anxiety was revealed in this letter. There is no talk about "our valiant army" and "forthcoming victories." Instead, the letter deals with how the family might react in case of an emergency. This ranges from expressing hope that the enlarged family will not need to flee, to reluctantly accepting money from Efim (sent almost certainly in order to help the Rostov Ginsburgs cover the costs of evacuation). Such ideas, voiced on an otherwise a very festive day for the family, which was finally reunited, were particularly meaningful. And, as if only to prove how shaky this reunification really was, it was marred by Volodya's imminent departure for the front.

This anxiety came to the fore in another letter that Liza Ginsburg sent to Alma-Ata on the same day. It repeated the previous letter almost verbatim; the only notable new theme was related to Liza's response to Efim's forceful urging to flee Rostov-on-Don, and even to leave the Caucasian region completely, as soon as possible:

> … Regarding your anxiety, dear one, of course there is what to think about and what to worry about. However, it is difficult to say anything specific regarding our prospects for the future. Anyway, if something dreadful is drawing near, then we will take our bags and walk away in whatever direction, ready for any suffering, only to avoid Hitler's hangmen. Still, I think that he won't have the opportunity to threaten our lives. Soon, there will be death for him and his hangmen.[146]

In the meantime, the local Soviet authorities in the North Caucasus took steps to put into practice the decree of the State Defense Committee dated May 29, 1942. On June 2, 1942, the Krasnodar Territorial Committee of the VKP(b) created the plan for emergency inactivation of the strategically important Maikop oil instalallations, located some three hundred kilometers to the east of Rostov-on-Don. In case of Wehrmacht breakthrough, the inactivation was scheduled to begin within forty-eight hours and be completed within eight to ten days.[147] The authorities in Krasnodar seemed confident—apparently

---

146 From Liza Chazkewitz, June 2, 1942, YVA: O.75/324, p. 307.
147 Fedoseev, "K voprosu o provedenii evakuatsionnykh meropriiatii," 168.

they had access to inside information—that nothing could prevent the Wehrmacht from rapidly pushing towards the Caucasus, once it had crushed the Soviet defenses, which were at that time only fifty kilometers from Rostov-on-Don. Furthermore, as the worst-case scenario, the regional Bolshevik leaders assumed that the Germans could break through the Soviet lines and reach Maikop as early as mid-June 1942 (June 2 plus forty-eight hours plus "eight to ten days" assigned for the disablement of the Maikop refineries). In fact, the Wehrmacht was only able to seize Maikop on August 9.

Certainly, such appraisals were not available to ordinary North Caucasians, including the members of the Ginsburg family. If they had been, they might have adversely affected the resilience of the local inhabitants, and likely would have led to panic in their midst and mass exodus of those civilians who were afraid of the Germans. These people, including the North Caucasian Jews, among them the Ginsburgs, might have had a better chance of saving their own lives. These appraisals were not publicized, however, because in most (probably all) cases where there might have been a clash between war needs and humanitarian concerns, the Soviets were only guided by military or military-economic considerations. We will see this later in greater detail when it came to the evacuation of civilians from the North Caucasus, in July and August 1942.

In this respect, it must be pointed out that the USSR was not the only Allied country to behave in this way. Suffice is it to mention the notorious refusal of the US and British Command to direct air strikes at the Auschwitz concentration camp.[148] To be sure, often implicit in such behavior was not only the priority of war needs over everything else, but also the fear of confirming and reinforcing the Nazi accusations that the Allies were fighting for Jewish interests.[149]

On June 6, the Rostov Municipal Defense Committee issued a decree, "On the tightening of the defense of Rostov-on-Don and the city's defensive installations,"[150] which envisaged the formation of units raised from the Komsomol members and non-affiliated [*nesoiuznaia*] youth in order to aid the police. This step was designed to prevent "the penetration of the city by spies, saboteurs and

---

148 Henry L. Feingold, "Bombing Auschwitz and the politics of the Jewish question during World War II," in *The Bombing of Auschwitz: Should the Allies Have Attempted It*, ed. Michael J. Neufield and Michael Berenbaum (Lawrence, KS: University Press of Kansas, 2000), 193–203. See also Danny Orbach and Mark Solonin, "Calculated Indifference: The Soviet Union and Requests to Bomb Auschwitz," *Holocaust and Genocide Studies* 27, no. 1 (Spring 2013): 90–113.
149 Jeffrey Herf, *The Jewish Enemy: Nazi Propaganda during World War II and the Holocaust* (Cambridge, MA: The Belknap Press of Harvard University Press, 2006), 50–91, 183–230. Shlomo Aronson, *Hitler, the Allies, and the Jews* (Cambridge: Cambridge University Press, 2004), 54–71.
150 PARO: 9/8/8, p. 72. In Rezvanov, *Na zashchite Rodiny*, 139.

other hostile elements," Of note is the wording of the order *"due to a certain tension in the situation"* [*the emphasis is mine*] … to exempt these youths from work.

Young women enlisted in auxiliary units designed to strengthen Rostov-on-Don's defenses. Central Archive of Moscow's Electronic and Audio-Visual Materials, 0-94267. Courtesy of Russian Holocaust Center.

On the same day, the Rostov Municipal Defense Committee ordered the reinstatement of the Extermination Battalions in the city. Two battalions, numbering 120 people each, were to be raised and armed.[151] The orders, like all similar decrees, were kept secret, and the local inhabitants were not informed about their implementation. Yet, this time, the circle of people "in the know" was widened beyond the regional leadership, and thus could have alerted more people to the German danger.

On June 7, 1942, Tamara wrote her first letter to her uncle upon her return to Rostov-on-Don:

> Because of the troubles [*nepriiatnosti*] at Kerch, it was not safe to stay there [Ordzhonikidze] any longer, either. …Besides, due to Volodya's enlistment, it was nearly impossible for us to survive there solely on my wages. The room cost us 100 rubles, and heating—10 rubles daily. … In addition,

---

151   PARO: 9/8/8, p. 76. In Rezvanov, *Na zashchite Rodiny*, 136.

> the inhabitants of Ordzhonikidze had started panicking—everyone was going to Rostov. ... Each of us was influenced strongly.
>
> All this brought about our decision: to leave with hope that if Rostov had been lucky twice [*there were two German attacks on Rostov-on-Don in the fall of 1941*], everything would be all right later. How nice it was to come back home. If the situation were better, we would be really happy. The result is that we are mentally ready to leave again at any moment [*chemodannoe nastroenie, literally 'suitcase mood'*], as if we were on a volcano. ...
>
> Yesterday Volodya was sent away ... in the direction of Voroshylovgradsk[152] [*north-west of Rostov-on-Don*].

Obviously, Tamara felt the need to explain the decision to return to Rostov-on-Don, which ran counter to her previous line of reasoning that she had so often and so convincingly expressed in her letters to Efim. Her strategic train of thought is very interesting. In a carefully worded message, Tamara assumed, and correctly so, that the German capture of Kerch in May 1942 was critical to the ongoing situation in the North Caucasus. However, her conclusion was somewhat paradoxical. She worked out that it would be equally unsafe now to stay anywhere in the region. Now that the entire North Caucasus was exposed to German attacks, Tamara argued that people had more chances of surviving in heavily fortified Rostov-on-Don than in Ordzhonikidze. She believed that Rostov-on-Don was of great strategic and military value to the Soviets, and she knew that this city had already withstood German attacks, while Ordzhonikidze was of much less value to the Soviets and had never suffered a direct German attack.

This reasoning was, indeed, justified, at least to some extent. It was, for example, referred to by an analyst from *The Washington Post,* who wrote that the capture of Kerch led to "The Nazis' undisputed possession of a springboard for their invasion of the oil-rich Caucasus."[153] It seems that Tamara, like the analyst, pointed to the possibility of German forces landing in the North Caucasus from the Crimean peninsula. But with the benefit of hindsight, this was a remote possibility, whereas in all other scenarios, there still remained a considerable difference in the level of danger between Rostov-on-Don, situated at the very edge of the Soviet-held North Caucasus, and Ordzhonikidze, situated deep inside the region. This difference turned out to be crucial: at the start of *Operation Blau,*

---

152 From Tamara Meerovich in Rostov-on-Don, June 7, 1942, YVA: O.75/324, pp. 308–309.
153 "Fall of Kerch," *The Washington Post,* May 25, 1942.

the Germans seized Rostov-on-Don, and then moved further eastwards and southwards in the North Caucasus, but failed, despite numerous attempts, to capture Ordzhonikidze.

Tamara's second argument was purely financial. This was not the first time that she mentioned her growing financial difficulties, which she faced while trying to provide for her family, first in Budennovsk and then in Ordzhonikidze. Indeed, this was an important factor, and it seems that it was becoming more and more difficult for Tamara's family to survive the hard life of evacuees in the North Caucasus. In April and May 1942, the family's conditions deteriorated further, following Volodya's conscription and consequent inability to help his family. Still, it appears that this factor was only secondary to Tamara's strategic considerations. It was very difficult for a family consisting of three persons, one of them a child, to subsist only on her wages. Yet, as Tamara acknowledged, "it was nearly impossible," that is, it was still just about possible, although the family's resources were almost exhausted. Moreover, confronted time and again with growing financial pressure, Tamara's family did not consider moving to a less expensive area, such as the countryside in the North Caucasus. They remained, even in those harsh times, urban dwellers, for whom their quality of life, even though it decreased sharply during the War, still mattered a lot. This was a costly enterprise to maintain in a Soviet city during the Soviet-German War, and the family gradually ran out of means with which to do so in a strange locality.

Finally, Tamara refers to panic among the refugees, who were eager to return to Rostov-on-Don. This evidence is not corroborated by what we know from other sources. Yet, it is plausible that like Tamara Meerovich, the Jewish refugees also sensed a change for the worse following the German successes in the south. Some of them rushed to Rostov-on-Don, guided by the same calculations as Tamara.[154] Still, a flight eastwards from the North Caucasus would presumably have been a more reasonable step in such a situation. At any rate, it seems strange that Tamara mentioned this factor, because she had previously demonstrated a formidable presence of mind and immunity to what other people, especially her own relatives, advised her to do. It appears that Tamara, the woman whom the War had made into the family decision-maker, not only for herself but also for her child and her mother, must have now succumbed to the enormous psychological pressure exerted on her by other members of her clan, Soviet propaganda, and probably her refugee milieu, and decided to take her

---

154 For example, letter written by Zinaida Serpik, March 1943, Archive of Russian Holocaust Center, Personal collections (S-28).

chances ("to leave with hope that, if Rostov-on-Don had been lucky twice ..."). But she was still terribly anxious, as the last lines of her letter demonstrate ("we are mentally ready to leave again at any moment").

On June 7, Liza and Anna sent a new letter to Efim. Most of this letter deals with the sisters' concern about their brother. The lines related to Rostov-on-Don mostly repeat what we have already seen in the previous letters from the sisters (for example, describing once again how the Ordzhonikidze relatives had returned). Some relatively new motifs include calls to display calmness (apparently directed at Efim but probably also to themselves) and then: "Everything would be absolutely fine. The enemy must and will be completely destroyed."[155] Also noteworthy is the sisters' disclosure that they were able to provide support to their relatives in Ordzhonikidze through acquaintances who frequently travelled there from Rostov-on-Don and took with them parcels of essentials such as soap.[156] It is quite likely that, through this informal communication channel, the family was able to share sensitive news, which they feared to put down on paper. Also, it is possible that parcels sent from Rostov-on-Don eventually contributed to the image of the city as being a safe haven, and, hence, to the return of the evacuees.

On June 8, the Rostov Municipal Defense Committee ordered the creation of an armed defense unit attached to the Committee and numbering four or five hundred people.[157] This order further expanded the circle of those "in the know" about the real situation in the area surrounding the city. Despite the secrecy characteristic of Soviet orders, the cumulative effect of all these decrees was such that, over time, the number of Rostov inhabitants who were aware of the deterioration in the situation in the area surrounding the city increased considerably.

On June 12, a new newsreel screened in Soviet cinema theaters showed fighting in the Kharkov region.[158] The Soviet advance, the recapture of unnamed localities, the trophies of war, and the German prisoners-of-war were highlighted, although, as we know, the Red Army offensive in that region had ended some ten days before this date, in a humiliating defeat and the destruction of the Soviet forces. The Soviet failure in Kharkov facilitated the entire German offensive towards the Caucasus, due to begin in early July 1942, but the Ginsburgs, like most ordinary Soviet civilians, were left unaware of this disaster, which would bring deadly danger for the family.

---

155 From Anna Greener and Liza Chazkewitz, June 7, 1942, YVA: O.75/324, p. 313.
156 From Anna Greener and Liza Chazkewitz, June 7, 1942, ibid., p. 315.
157 PARO: 9/8/8, p. 75. In Rezvanov, *Na zashchite Rodiny*, 139.
158 *Soiuzkinozhurnal*, no. 25, June 12, 1942, RGAKFD, http://pobeda-vov.ru/Lib/pages/item.aspx?itemid=10440, accessed November 24, 2011.

To prepare the ground for the destruction of the oil refinery facilities, as prescribed by Moscow, Seleznev, the Secretary of the Krasnodar Territorial Committee of the VKP(b), and Timoshenko, the Head of the NKVD Territorial Administration, issued on June 16, 1942 a joint directive to the local Party and NKVD leaders: "On the preparation and conduct of special actions [*spetsmeropriiatiia*], in case the Krasnodar territory is occupied by the enemy":

> We give warning that the conduct of preparatory works should be organized in a clandestine manner [*konspirativno*], without affecting the course of the work. This is only preparatory work, nothing more [*than that*].[159]

These special actions included, first of all, the destruction of the oil refinery facilities, so that the Germans would not be able to make use of them. Of particular note is the continuous stress on two major aspects of these activities, interwoven one with the other. The first aspect is secrecy, intended for the local population that was supposed to continue to stay and work in the region, as if nothing had changed, even if the danger of German occupation was growing daily. The second aspect involved a soothing message to the local leaders to whom the directive was issued. It was no longer possible to conceal from them that their region might soon be seized by the Germans. To prevent panic, since the German occupation would jeopardize their lives, they were told that all this was nothing but preparation.

On June 16, 1942, Liza sent word to Efim from Rostov-on-Don:

> Of course, it looks like something terrible is about to happen, but it may be that nothing bad will occur. Then, the dark clouds will be scattered and nice bright days will come again. No doubt this is what will happen!!! Let's not worry in advance. And let's not think about what threatens us. These barbarians have already been thrown out of here once, and next time they will not come here, since our valiant regiments will not let them. But if, God forbid, [*it does happen*], we shall leave everything here and walk away in whatever direction, regardless of whatever may happen, in order to get as far as possible away from these beasts. But my heart tells me that nothing

---

159 Directive by Seleznev, the Secretary of the Krasnodar Territorial Committee of the VKP(b), and Timoshenko, the Head of the District NKVD Administration, to the local party and NKVD leaders: First Secretary of Adygea Regional Party committee, secretaries of municipal committees, and respective local heads of the NKVD in the Krasnodar territory, June 16, 1942. In Fedoseev, "K voprosu o provedenii evakuatsionnykh meropriiatii," 169.

bad will happen to us and that we won't need to run anywhere. We will live with this hope. ...We would like, our dear one, to be together with you and to wait calmly for the victory [*to come*]. But alas! It cannot be done now, no matter what your and our wishes may be. ...[160]

Almost no real information on the situation regarding the fighting in the southern sector of the Soviet-German front reached the Ginsburg family. Soviet propaganda continued to persuade them that the counter-offensive still continued. No refugees came from the war-affected areas to tell the Jews that the artificial status quo in the south, where the Wehrmacht and the Red Army had been engaged for months in trench warfare, had been broken. Such information might have tipped the balance in favor of immediate flight. Nevertheless, the Ginsburgs, even the most optimistic among them, appear to have sensed a change for the worse. Furthermore, Liza wrote about it in no uncertain terms, as something that was self-evident.

Then, as usual, Liza tried to reassure her brother that the situation was still under control. She based her hopes, first, on logic (the German occupation had already taken place once and could not re-occur); second, on Soviet military might ("our valiant regiments"), and then, on her intuition ("my heart tells me that nothing bad will happen to us"). God (with a capital letter) is also mentioned in this list. If all this was of no use—Liza realized that all these arguments could prove futile—then they would flee. As another sign of awakening, however belated, Liza acknowledged that Soviet victory, despite all official pronouncements, could not be achieved at that time.

On June 21, 1942, Liza sent a short note to Efim Ginsburg. Its most important new message was condensed in several lines:

> It is such a good season but it is so bad, so difficult at heart for everyone. Tomorrow it will be a whole year since the attack by our barbaric enemy on our country. Our enemies act in a bestial fashion, but it does not matter; they are as good as dead, their downfall is close.[161]

The note is remarkable because Liza cited almost verbatim one of the main Soviet propaganda slogans, which always resurfaced whenever the position of the Soviet forces sharply deteriorated. At that time, all other means of persuasion turned out to be useless, as Soviet propaganda proved inadequate for

---

160 From Liza Chazkewitz, June 16, 1942, YVA: O.75/324, pp. 336–343.
161 From Liza Chazkewitz, June 21, ibid., p. 324.

enlisting the support of the local population, using its conventional "ammunition." In retrospect, we know that the publication of the above-mentioned joint directive to the local Party and NKVD leaders meant that the Soviets sensed they were on the verge of military collapse in a given (but unnamed) area.

Six days later, on June 27, 1942, Liza wrote another letter:

> … we'll hope that everything will be all right and that under no circumstances will the damned enemy get here; everyone is talking in this way and no doubt this is what should happen. We are alarmed since the confounded enemy is paying many air visits here. …
>
> We are all in good health; our food provision is not bad. Tamara wants to find a job in a *sovkhoz* in the Salsky *raion*. This question will be solved in the coming days. If it is possible, we'll also go with them. It is in the Rostov District.[162]

The family still appeared opposed to the idea of escaping, as they thought that the situation was not critical. However, something new had occurred in the meantime. German air-raids, to which the family had got accustomed by now (they commenced as early as August 1941), intensified to such a point that it was next to impossible to stay in Rostov-on-Don. As a result, the family decided to move away in order to save themselves from the bombardments.

For the second time, we encounter the problem of how the Ginsburgs interpreted air strikes, most specifically if they constituted the prelude to a land offensive. As in 1941, the family viewed the bombardments as a stand-alone phenomenon, unrelated to land warfare. The family's behavior can possibly be explained by the fact that the German bombardments, albeit on a smaller scale, had begun months before the Wehrmacht reached the city overland and threatened it. The Rostov inhabitants, including the Ginsburgs, had become accustomed to these strikes, but had difficulty working out when the intensification of bombing would be followed by a ground assault on their city. One way or another, as in 1941, the family miscalculated.

However, there was one difference now—unlike 1941, the family was united in its decision. Since it was intended to be a flight away from the bombing, not one caused by their fears as Jews, they envisaged evacuation only on a very local scale, within the boundaries of the Rostov district (the main city of Salsky *raion* was situated approximately 170 kilometers from Rostov-on-Don), as compared

---

162 From Liza Chazkewitz, June 27, 1942, ibid., p. 326.

to long-distance journeys during their previous flights to Budennovsk (530 kilometers from Rostov-on-Don) and Ordzhonikidze (500 kilometers).

On June 30, 1942, all three sisters wrote a letter to their brother in Alma-Ata:

> The most important thing is your quick return home, to your Moscow apartment. Then, in winter, you must come to see us.
>
> We are all alive and well and living as of old. The mood is somber, for some reason. It has changed somehow and we don't know why. Let's see what is going to occur. Maybe it will pass [us by] and ... there will be no need to do anything.[163]

It is remarkable what Anya, Liza, and Monya regarded as the "most important thing," only a few weeks before their destruction at the hands of the Germans. This was not about saving their own lives. They depicted an idyllic picture of a peaceful future, which would come after the Germans somehow disappeared from the scene.

However, we should not take what they wrote entirely at face value. The sisters were, as previously, moved by the desire not to upset their "little brother" too much. It is difficult to imagine that they stopped worrying about their own fate. Rather, it was more likely that they preferred to conceal their feelings from Efim Ginsburg. They hinted at their anxiety in phrases such as "The mood is somber, for some reason. It changed somehow, and we don't know why." The sisters understood the reason for this change but preferred not to write about it.

July 1942

By early July 1942, the German armies were poised to attack the North Caucasus. The German advance[164] envisioned the seizure of the Caucasian oil fields and was earmarked as one of the major goals of *Operation Blau*, along with the capture of Stalingrad. This attack involved units of Army Group A (*Heeresgruppe A*),

---

163 From Liza Chazkewitz, Anya Greener, and Monya Ginsburg, June 30, 1942, ibid., p. 319.

164 For the analysis of the Battle of the Caucasus in 1942–1943, see Bernd Wegner, "The War Against the Soviet Union, 1942–1943," in *Germany and the Second World War*, vol. 6: *The Global War: Widening the Conflict into a World War and the Shift of the Initiative 1941–1943*, ed. Werner Rahn, Reinhard Stumpf, Bernd Wegner, John Brownjohn, Patricia Crampton, Louise Willmot, and Horst Boog (Oxford: Clarendon Press, 2001), 1022–1048, 1173–1177. Cf. Joachim Hoffmann, *Kaukasien, 1942–1943: Das deutsche Heer und die Orientvölken der Sowjetunion* (Freiburg: Rombach Verlag, 1991), 63–66, 80–81. Cf. V. Gurkin and A. Kruglov, "Oborona Kavkaza: 1942 god," *Voenno-istoricheskii zhurnal* 10 (1992): 11–18. Cf. Andrei Grechko, *Bitva za Kavkaz* (Moscow: Izdatel'stvo Ministerstva Oborony SSSR, 1971), 17–27.

which included some fifteen German divisions (among them the Waffen SS "Viking" division), six Romanian divisions, and one Slovak Division. Army Group A was initially led by Field Marshall Wilhelm von List.[165]

As we saw, the Soviet authorities took note of this, and, starting from late May, they began the preparations for the destruction of the strategic oil facilities. But this policy was not matched by a similar effort to evacuate the civilian population from the endangered region. In summer 1942, this neglect not only involved the failure to alert the civilian population to the growing danger of staying in the North Caucasus, but also failure to urge people to leave. In retrospect, the Soviet authorities grossly overestimated their own strength, leading them to bring many refugees into the Rostov District and the other parts of the North Caucasus region in the first six months of 1942. According to official Soviet statistics, following the arrival of more evacuees and refugees from Leningrad and from other North Caucasian localities, by July 1, 1942, the total number of evacuees in the Rostov District had increased to 48,100 people.[166]

> Shortly before the Germans broke through the Soviet defense lines near Rostov-on-Don, in July 1942, many Jews endeavored to escape from the city and adjacent areas. It proved to be extremely difficult for those living in the Rostov district to get out of reach of the German armies, as the area was the closest to the frontline. There is no valid evaluation of the numbers of those evacuated from the city and District of Rostov at that time;[167] in my estimate, their number was very low. The estimate of 22,000 out of 40,000 local Jews, provided by a Soviet Jewish newspaper in 1945[168] appears to be out of touch with reality. More Jews managed to flee from other North Caucasian areas, further away from the Soviet-German frontline, such as the Territories of Stavropol and Krasnodar.[169]

---

165 Field Marshall Wilhelm von List was later superseded by Hitler himself, and then by *Generaloberst* Paul Ludwig Ewald von Kleist.
166 Information on the number of evacuated people accommodated in the rear areas of the RSFSR, SNK RSFSR, Secret, YVA: JM/24678. Source: GARF: A-259/40/3096.
167 Ben Tsion Pinchuk, *Soviet Jews Face the Holocaust: A Research of Exile or Evacuation Issues* (Tel-Aviv: The Association for the Study of Jewish History, the Institute of Diaspora Study, 1979) [Hebrew].
168 *Einikait*, May 29, 1945, cited in Pinchuk, *Soviet Jews*, 118, 124.
169 Statement of Efrem Peikhvasser, July 2, 1943, GARF: 7021/17/1, p. 26. Cf. Testimony of Aron Gurevich, no date, GARF: 7021/17/206, p. 329. Cf. Testimony of Khanya Knor, b. 1918?, no date, HUJ, ICJ, DOR, cassette no. TC 2772 (not transcribed).

> The sudden and rapid advance of the Wehrmacht forces, coupled with intensifying bombardments in the summer of 1942, led to the panic and partial paralysis of the Soviet bureaucratic machine. Under such circumstances, it was not easy to be evacuated, even for those Jews who belonged to privileged groups that were earmarked for evacuation from the North Caucasus. In Stavropol, a Jewish police captain, a high-ranking, influential, and well-connected official of the local administration, could only get an evacuation permit for himself; he was unable to take any of his family with him.[170] But even when the evacuation of the target groups was successfully organized, it could fail later, because the Soviet authorities had lost control of the general situation.
>
> An ill-defined, lawless interim period, stretching from the abandonment of the area and its civil population by the Red Army, to the entry of the Wehrmacht troops in the North Caucasus, could have lasted several days.
>
> Faced with imminent danger from the German army and the collapse of the transportation system,[171] masses of Jews in the North Caucasus resorted to fleeing eastwards independently. This happened in the last two or three weeks of Soviet rule in the region and during the interim period, regardless of any official Soviet pronouncement on evacuation. Most Jewish refugees were forestalled by the advancing Wehrmacht troops or by local anti-Soviet insurgents,[172] and only a small minority succeeded in escaping from the area that was overrun and occupied by the German army.[173]

In early July, 1942 the Battle of the Crimea reached its climax. In broadcasts on July 1 and 2, Soviet radio reported, albeit in a very abrupt fashion, the German assault on the Soviet positions at Sevastopol.[174] On July 3, it was acknowledged that the Red Army had "left the Crimean peninsula in accordance with the order from the Supreme Command."[175] This development was soon reported in the printed media. For example, an article published by the Krasnodar newspaper

---

170 Statement of Peikhvasser, GARF: 7021/17/1, p. 26.
171 Izobilnoe village, Krasnodar. Report of the Commission of the Izobilnensky *Raion*, June 29, 1943, GARF: 7021/17/10, p. 121. Testimony of Gadleva, YVA: 0.3/4391, p. 9.
172 Testimony of Fanya Sklyar, September 1975, YVA: 0.3/3934, p. 3. Cf. Poppe, *Reminiscences*, 160.
173 Testimony of Knor, ICJ: TC 2772. Testimony of Mikhail Milgrom, no date, GARF: 7021/17/206, p. 43.
174 Sovinformburo updates, July 1 and 2, 1942, http://army.lv/ru/01-Iyulya-1942-g./1016/1601 and http://army.lv/ru/02-Iyulya-1942-g./1016/1602.
175 Sovinformburo update, July 3, 1942, http://army.lv/ru/03-Iyulya-1942-g./1016/1603.

on July 5, 1942, mentioned the Soviet defeat at Sevastopol and the complete abandonment of the Crimean peninsula by the Soviet forces.[176]

Thus, it is suggested that information about this most important military development reached the members of the Ginsburg family more or less soon after it actually occurred (Sevastopol was captured by the Wehrmacht on July 2). But Soviet propaganda refrained from explaining what implications the capture of Sevastopol would have on the German advance in the Caucasus. It freed up considerable German forces, which had been previously constrained by the fighting in the Crimean peninsula (this process had already begun with the German capture of Kerch in May), for the attack on the Caucasus. It also deprived the Soviets of the chance to threaten the German advance towards the Caucasus by hitting them in the Crimean "underbelly." However, it seems that people such as Tamara Meerovich, who possessed strategic skills, could work out the probable repercussions of the final German victory in the Crimea.

That the big German advance in the North Caucasus was imminent was sensed by *The New York Times*. On July 5, 1942, it wrote:

> Now Herr Hitler has launched his drive for the Caucasus and its wealth of oil. His "Spring" drive has been considerably delayed, but there is no room for doubt that his armies are now starting their 1942 effort to crush the Russian forces and open the way to Batum and Baku.[177]

Of note is the assessment of the Soviet military efforts in the region in the previous few months: they were not entirely in vain and led to delay in the German plans. In retrospect, it is likely that this delay would be crucial in thwarting the goals of the German summer offensive: the seizure of the entire Caucasus, and, most specifically, the Soviet oil reservoirs near Baku. At the same time, the Germans succeeded in achieving the short-term aims of their advance by seizing vast territories in the North Caucasus.

On July 9, 1942, Liza and Anya wrote one of their last letters to their brother in Alma-Ata:

> Dear Efim,
>   Enough time has passed and there is no letter from you. The last letter we got from you was dated June 13. It greatly preoccupies us [*worrying*] whether you are in good health.

---

176 "250 dnei geroicheskoi oborony Sevastopolia," *Bol'shevik*, no. 158 (1451), July 5, 1942.
177 Edwin L. James, "Herr Hitler launches drive for Caucasus," *The New York Times*, July 5, 1942.

On July 7, our [*people*] left for *zernosovkhoz* in the Rostov District. Anya and I would also have gone with them, but, to my great sorrow, I, <u>a high-ranking employee</u> [KF—*emphasis in the original text*], was not permitted to leave under any circumstances, as a matter of principle; this is my opinion. Anya stayed, because of me. She did not want to go and to leave me alone. For the time being, Anya and I are alive and well. Let's hope that it will continue like this. But in any case, anything may happen to us. We ask you not to worry. It is war, and nothing can be done about it.

I am writing to you while at work and right now there is an air-raid warning; so far it is quiet; it is the second time today. It has passed now. Well, it was so good and so quiet. Probably it'll be again like this. Our relatives are not happy: they returned and soon afterwards, it began.

Be healthy and happy. We kiss you and embrace you strongly. Anya and Liza. Waiting for your letter.[178]

The Luftwaffe continued to pound the city, and this affected the daily life of the Ginsburgs more than anything else. We learn from this letter that Tamara Meerovich and her family were extremely alarmed by the developments. For her, it signaled that her family might have made a grave mistake by returning to the beleaguered Rostov-on-Don from the relatively quiet Ordzhonikidze. To save themselves from the bombardments, Tamara, her son, and her mother moved away from Rostov-on-Don to the countryside, not far away from the city. Tamara's evacuation to a distant area of the Rostov district may indicate that she did not consider the possibility that the Germans would break through the Soviet positions and capture the entire North Caucasus. At the same time, it is also possible that a fully fledged evacuation out of Rostov-on-Don eastwards was no longer feasible, so Tamara attempted to escape at least from the German air-strikes.

Anya and Liza were not opposed, as we saw, to leaving the city for the countryside. But now, it was not up to the sisters to decide whether and when to leave Rostov-on-Don. Their case is indicative of the complexities surrounding the evacuation of Soviet civilians. In 1942, Liza was only forty-six or forty-seven, and she was still working. She became a victim of the Soviet policy of preventing the evacuation of "visible" figures, which might have created an impression that the city was endangered. Probably justifiable, on a macro level, this policy frequently led to the deaths of these unfortunately "visible" people.

---

178 From Liza Chazkewitz and Anya Greener, July 9, 1942, YVA: O.75/324, pp. 330–331.

The Soviet authorities always secured the evacuation of truly influential persons belonging to regional elites, as well as their families. It is also clear that Liza was *not* a high-ranking official. We saw that she had been left in Rostov-on-Don during the first occupation, as the authorities did not make the effort to evacuate her and her family.

Liza's failure to obtain an evacuation permit before the first German occupation of Rostov-on-Don helps us to understand that people who applied for a permit were not necessarily better off in terms of evacuation prospects if they were employed and occupied a valued position in the wartime Soviet Union. The answer seems to be clear: such a person received a higher salary and a higher food ration, and also, could be evacuated with their plant. But as Liza's and Volodya Meerovich's examples demonstrate, there was also the other side of the coin. These people were not masters of their own destiny—their freedom was more constrained. Volodya, as we remember, was enlisted in the Extermination Battalion, and then was evacuated to rejoin his plant, which had been relocated to Ordzhonikidze; later, he was sent back to Rostov-on-Don, and wound up going to the Army. By the same token, Liza was prevented from leaving Rostov-on-Don at the most critical moment because in the wartime Soviet Union, abandonment of one's working place was considered a serious crime.[179]

In contrast, for those family members who had modest employment (such as Tamara Meerovich and David Pinchos), it was easier to receive evacuation permits or try to run away independently, since in theirs employer were not likely to veto their departure. In this regard, the family members who had no permanent work (such as Anya Greener and Tsylya Pinchos) were in the best position, since they could, at least theoretically, make their escape much faster, without violating any employment law.

The letter ends with a macabre presentiment ("anything may happen to us"), which contrasts with the sisters' previous overwhelmingly positive assessments of the future. They said that their possible victimhood should be viewed in the context of the War ("It is war and nothing can be done about it"). Although these last lines may sound like a sort of farewell to their brother, it is more likely that the sisters were not here to the German occupation and the anticipated mistreatment of Jews. Rather, they implied that they might perish from an accidental German bomb. Despite the worrying atmosphere at the front, the Soviet authorities all over the North Caucasus did their utmost

---

179 Martin Kragh, "Soviet Labour Law During the Second World War," *War in History* 18, no. 4 (2011): 531–546.

to demonstrate that their hold on the region remained firm. One of the most recurrent themes in the Soviet media, even at that time, was the duty of all Soviet people to continue working, according to previously elaborated plans. An editorial article published by the Stavropol newspaper on July 10, 1942 "On the expanding [*razvertyvanie*] of harvest collection"[180] underscores the point.

On July 10, 1942, Liza sent her last letter to Efim Ginsburg:

> Our relatives left three days ago; so far we have not heard from them. Of course, it is not good there, either, since it is too close. But as of now, it may be quiet there; there are no air strikes there, as are taking place [*here*].[181]

No news had arrived so far from Tamara and her family. It could be that, due to the German air attacks, it was not possible to receive information from the area to which they had relocated, situated in the south-west of the Rostov district, that is, relatively far away from Rostov-on-Don. Liza was concerned over the lack of communication with Tamara and her family. But as it turned out, the two branches of the family soon managed to resume communication. At the same time, the situation in Rostov-on-Don calmed down: immediately prior to the assault on the city, the Germans reduced the intensity of air strikes, either to divert the Luftwaffe to other areas or to mislead the Soviet command about the possible direction of their next attack.

The situation of the Red Army in the North Caucasus continued to deteriorate. This was acknowledged even by official Soviet sources. Quoting the Soviet midnight communiqué from July 12, *The Washington Post* wrote that the German spearhead east of the River Don had pushed forwards a few miles to the outskirts of Voronezh, on the Moscow-Rostov railway line.[182]

The worsening of the situation in Rostov-on-Don led many Jews to try to escape—but it became extremely difficult to do so. Referring to another Jewish family residing in Rostov-on-Don, a Jewish refugee from this city later described their attempt to escape during this period:

> … her daughter, Doctor Grinberg, tried to evacuate with M. A. Grinberg, but to no avail. They were robbed of their possessions at the beginning of the road; they got back to Rostov and awaited their fate.[183]

---

180 *Ordzhonikidzevskaia pravda*, no. 159 (2534), July 10, 1942.
181 From Liza Chazkewitz and Anya Greener, July 10, 1942, YVA: O.75/324, p. 332.
182 "Germans gain at Voronezh, imperil the Caucasus," *The Washington Post*, July 12, 1942.
183 Testimony on Maria Abramovna Grinberg, no date, YVA: P.21.2/13.

The testimony describes an attempt to escape independently. It indicates that, during the days and probably weeks preceding the German occupation, the Soviet hold on the region already became looser, to the point where the regular transportation system ceased to function and there was no security on the roads, where refugees, mainly women, elderly people, and children, could easily fall prey to robbers.

Another Jewish escapee from Rostov-on-Don described the events in this period in the following manner:

> When the Germans seized Rostov for the second time, in July 1942, it was already impossible to escape. ... My uncle left the city and escaped into the forests. His wife and children stayed behind, because no one thought that anything bad would happen to women and children, even if they were Jewish. ... Mariya and the girls stayed; he fled to the North-Caucasian territory where he wandered about for a whole month. On August 9, he returned on foot to Rostov, and found none of his family.[184]

This testimony records several patterns of Jewish behavior during this period. Depending on how they assessed the danger, some Jews stayed in Rostov-on-Don. I assume that this was a minority: after all, one year after the beginning of the German atrocities against Soviet Jews, information about this threat had spread far and wide.

Others fled the city because they felt the coming danger, but failed to escape beyond the area occupied by the Germans. These Jews did not to seem to have fully realized what the German "mistreatment" of Jews actually signified, and the person referred to in the above testimony was apparently not afraid to return to German-controlled Rostov-on-Don. Judging by their behavior (but contrary to their pronouncements), Anya and Liza, as well as other family members, except Tamara Meerovich, might have viewed the forthcoming German occupation somewhat along those lines. Tamara was more realistic and harbored no illusions about what would await her and her family under German rule.

In the article published on July 13, 1942, *The Washington Post* summarized the fighting in the North Caucasus in the following way:

> Powerful German advance threatens to split Southern, Central Red armies.
> Eddy Gilmore (AP). German troops, sweeping through Kantemirovka

---

184 The story of my uncle, Boris Naumovich Shagin, his wife Mariya, and their three little daughters, Testimony of Anna Shagina-Blokh, b. 1919, April 1965, YVA: O.3/3146, pp. 1–2.

and Lisichansk in their push toward the Caucasus, have rolled [*back*] the Red Army 70 more miles to Boguchar, in their greatest penetration yet on Russian soil, the Soviets acknowledged officially today. Boguchar is 50 kilometers east of a line drawn due north of Rostov, the southern anchor of the Red line, which thus far held the Germans from pushing along to the Sea of Azov. Rostov, which the Germans reached last year, and then had to leave, was the previous high-water mark of eastward invasion.[185]

Drawing apparently on German sources, the writer implied that the German advance at this stage was not directed at Rostov-on-Don. Rather, it threatened to encircle the Soviet forces defending the city, in line with the strategic forecast once voiced by Tamara Meerovich.[186]

German road sign. 1942. Source: www.temernik.rugallerydisplayimage.phpalbum=482&pos=33. Public domain.

On July 14, all the family members remaining in Rostov-on-Don—Anya and Liza Ginsburg, as well as Tsylya, David, and Anya Pinchos—moved from the city to the village of Novorogovskoe (Egorlyksky *raion*) in the Rostov district. By that time, Tamara Meerovich had already moved to this village (in all probability, this was her initial destination) and was apparently already employed as an accountant in a *sovkhoz* (government-owned granary) there. A Soviet report

---

185 "New Nazi gains set the stage for Don drive towards Caucasus oil," *The Washington Post*, July 13, 1942.
186 From Tamara Meerovich in Ordzhonikidze. March 3, 1942, YVA: O.75/324, pp. 215–218.

in March 1943 stated explicitly that all the other family members, with the exception of the Pinchos family (who apparently went there independently), were evacuated "to Tamara Meerovich."[187] Evidently Tamara and the Ginsburg sisters had somehow managed to reestablish contact at that time, and Anya and Liza Ginsburg were able to inform Tamara about their destination.

Evidently, the fact that Tamara was able to find employment in the village was a weighty factor in leading her to stay there and to convince the other family members to join her. As the family had few means by which to support themselves, Tamara's salary, whether in the form of money or foodstuffs, was a very important support for the entire family. In this sense, Tamara's story repeated itself: as in the winter of 1941, once she had found a job, she decided not to move away any further. Later, Tsylya Pinchos was also able to find employment as a nurse in the village kindergarten. Now, the family had two people with jobs, which could enable them to survive financially through the difficult period of evacuation. It was a big stroke of luck for the evacuees, and it is understandable that, given their overall reluctance to move further away, they decided to stay in this village.[188]

The place to which the family moved was in the easternmost part of the Rostov district, bordering on the Krasnodar territory. The distance between Rostov-on-Don and the area's main village, Egorlyksk, was 110 kilometers. The village of Novorogovskoe was another 32 kilometers away from Rostov-on-Don. It seems that the family figured out that even if the Germans were able to capture Rostov-on-Don for the second time, their offensive would be checked very close to Rostov-on-Don, as in November 1941. Novorogovskoe was not occupied by the Wehrmacht in the fall of 1941, so it might have seemed a safe haven against German air strikes. But there was also a disadvantage—it was impossible to quickly escape from the village in case of a rapid German ground advance. It seems that all members of the family, even if they realized in the second half of July 1942 that their destruction was already inevitable, preferred to remain together at that critical hour, instead of trying to escape in separate groups.

Recognizing the looming danger to Rostov-on-Don, the Soviet authorities[189] finally authorized a limited evacuation from the city. In her work on the wartime evacuation in the Soviet Union, Rebecca Manley writes that "women

---

187 Statement of the Commission of *Stanitsa* of Novo-Rogovskaya, March 28, 1943, GARF: 7021/40/774, p. 24.
188 Ibid., p. 20.
189 In all probability, the author, who did not disclose her sources, was referring to the Evacuation Council, which would best correspond with the logic of her narrative. Manley, *To the Tashkent Station*, 71.

and children were evacuated from Rostov-on-Don on July 18."[190] Yet, insofar as we can judge, this decree was indeed issued, but not implemented. There is no indication in the German documentation or Soviet post-liberation reports that Rostov-on-Don was left without women and children. Viewed from this perspective, the Ginsburgs did the right thing by not waiting for the last-minute organized evacuation from the city.

True to their policy of convincing the local population that the situation was under control, the Soviet newspapers until the very end continued publishing many "business as usual" reports. For example, on July 16–18, 1942, when the German offensive had already made considerable progress, the Krasnodar newspaper placed advertisements for performances in municipal theaters and films in Krasnodar.[191]

However, as the situation of the Soviet troops on the southern front was becoming critical, the contents of the Soviet propaganda also changed. From July 16, *Sovinformburo* radio reports, broadcast twice a day, with the first report in the morning and an updated one in the evening, began to mention heavy fighting in the Rostov District and gradual retreat of the Red Army. It was probably easier for the Ginsburgs, who were moving from one place to another in those hot summer days, to keep abreast of the latest developments in the region through radio broadcasts than newspapers. Government radio speakers were installed at many points, while newspapers could mainly be found in Rostov-on-Don. On July 16, the *Sovinformburo* reported that,

> To the south-east of Millerovo [*The distance between Millerovo and Rostov-on-Don is 221 kilometers*], our troops withdrew to new positions amidst the fighting. Having been engaged in non-stop heavy fighting against the superior forces of the German Fascists, our units cause big losses to the Germans. …Our air forces are bravely striking the columns of the advancing German troops.[192]

Similar *Sovinformburo* messages mentioned a slow withdrawal, but the disorganized flight of the Soviet forces was not announced on the radio in the twice-daily reports, on July 17, 18, 19 and 20.

On July 19, the information was published in the country's newspapers, for the first time. The tone was set by the country's main newspaper *Pravda*. Its

---

190 Ibid.
191 *Bol'shevik*, July 16, 17, 18, 1942.
192 Sovinformburo update, July 16, 1942, http://army.lv/ru/02-Iyunya-1942-g./1015/1572.

editorial article, "To beat the enemy for sure" was reprinted on July 19, 1942, by the Stavropol newspaper, which acknowledged "a fierce battle going on now in the Don [*area*]."[193]

But many Soviet propaganda messages designed for both domestic and foreign consumption remained ambiguous. On July 19, 1942, quoting a correspondent of the Soviet TASS news agency, *The New York Times* mentioned that harvesting was already in process in the North Caucasus and Central Asia.[194] Directives to proceed with the harvest were issued almost simultaneously (as we know today) with the orders to remove food stocks from the North Caucasus. What could not be removed was destroyed. A small part of the food reserves was distributed to the local population.[195]

> In the Soviet regions adjacent to the Rostov District, the situation was finally understood to be extremely serious. On July 21, 1942, the Krasnodar newspaper highlighted in its editorial article, "In the South," the grave situation in the North Caucasus. It was admitted that the German armies were breaking through towards the Don and Volga Rivers.[196] On the same day, a similar article entitled "The duty and obligation of every patriot" appeared in the Stavropol newspaper. It stated that "The German Fascist bandits are breaking through towards the Volga, towards the Caucasian oil, towards the expanses of the Don."[197]

On July 22, the Soviet radio acknowledged for the first time that the Germans had attacked the city of Novocherkassk, situated some forty-five kilometers north of Rostov-on-Don:

> Our troops were engaged in heavy fighting in the area of Novocherkassk. ... In another sector, our troops carried out heavy fighting against the enemy's superior forces. ... Our forces also suffered considerable casualties, and, by the end of the second day, withdrew to new positions, in accordance with the orders from command.[198]

This piece of information was likely known to the Ginsburgs.

---

193 *Ordzhonikidzevskaia pravda*, no. 167 (2542), July 19, 1942.
194 "Harvesting begins in the Caucasus," *The New York Times*, July 19, 1942.
195 Feferman, "Food factor."
196 *Bol'shevik*, no. 171 (1464), July 21, 1942.
197 *Ordzhonikidzevskaia pravda* (Stavropol), no. 168 (2543), July 21, 1942.
198 Sovinformburo update, July 22, 1942, http://army.lv/ru/22-Iyulya-1942-g./1016/1622.

The gravity of the situation on the Soviet southern front was growing almost hourly. This was aptly summarized by *The Washington Post*. In an article published on July 25, 1942, the newspaper cast doubt on the trustworthiness of Soviet reports pertaining to the region, and indicated that the German coverage of the military events in the region appeared to be more reliable at that stage:

> The German High Command claims that Rostov was stormed last Friday with Novocherkassk—40 miles to the northeast—captured the following day. These claims have never been confirmed by the Red Army, whose latest communiqué speaks only of fighting "in the vicinity" of Rostov. ...There seems to be little doubt, however, that Marshal Timoshenko's valiant rear-guard action has so far failed to stem the Nazi drive, and the situation for the Red Army in the Don-Volga sector is getting worse instead of better.[199]

On July 24, 1942, forces of the Seventeenth Army under *Generaloberst* Richard Ruoff, supported by the First Tank Army under von Kleist, seized the city of Rostov-on-Don for the second time.

German troops entering Rostov-on-Don, July 1942. Public domain.

---

199 "Rostov and beyond," *The Washington Post*, July 25, 1942.

The German advance in the summer of 1942 brought under their sway large sections of the North Caucasus, including the whole Rostov District, the territories of Stavropol and Krasnodar, the autonomous republic of Kabardino-Balkaria, and a large part of the autonomous republic of North Ossetia, as well as the small portion of the autonomous republic of Chechnya. The local population found itself under German occupation for varying periods of up to five months.

Only on July 28, 1942, four days *after* Rostov-on-Don was captured by the Wehrmacht, the Stavropol newspaper published an announcement from the *Sovinformburo*, highlighting the fierce battles near Rostov-on-Don.[200] The abandonment of the city by the Soviet authorities was acknowledged only a full day later, on July 29, 1942. The Stavropol newspaper reprinted an editorial article from *Pravda* from July 28, 1942, "To repel the enemy's attack!" The article stated: "After fierce battles our troops abandoned Rostov and Novocherkassk. The Soviet south is in serious danger."[201]

August 1942

On August 4, *Sonderkommando* 10a issued the order for all Jews over the age of fourteen to personally register with the German authorities between August 4 and 7, 1942.[202] The Einsatzgruppe D reported that 2,000 Jews complied with this order,[203] but this was only a fraction of the Rostov Jews who were discovered by the Germans.

In the same order, the German authorities announced that on August 2, 1942 they had set up a *Judenrat* under Dr. Lurie and his deputy Lapiner. Every Jew had to comply with the *Judenrat* directives under pain of severe punishment. All Jews were ordered to wear white ribbons or a yellow star on the sleeves of their outer clothing. Refusal to comply with the order was punishable by death.[204]

On August 9, an "Appeal to the Jewish Population of the city of Rostov," signed by Dr. Lurie on behalf of the "Jewish Council of Elders" was pasted on notice boards all over the city. In the appeal, local Jews were ordered to present

---

200 *Ordzhonikidzevskaia pravda*, no. 174 (2549), July 28, 1942.
201 *Ordzhonikidzevskaia pravda*, no. 175 (2550), July 29, 1942.
202 Ibid.
203 Meldungen aus den besetzten Ostgebieten, Nr. 16. Berlin, Der Chef der Sicherheitspolizei und des SD. Kommandostab, August 14, 1942, RGVA: 500/1/775, p. 435.
204 GARO: P-3613/1/451, p. 32, and P-3613/1/454, p. 32.

themselves on August 11 at six assembly points, "for organized relocation to a special region where they would be protected against hostile actions." On August 11, the Jews were brought from the assembly points to the Zmievskaya *balka* (ravine), situated in the city's suburbs. The Soviet investigation, which was conducted after the liberation of the region in 1943, maintained that the *Sonderkommando* 10a and its local collaborators shot and killed up to 13,000 Jews on one day, August 11, 1942.[205] The total number of Jewish victims in the city during the short period of the German occupation of Rostov-on-Don— the city was liberated by the Red Army on February 14, 1943—apparently exceeded 20,000 people.[206]

On about 16 August, 1942, two Russian women in the grain *sovkhoz* at the *stanitsa* of Novorogovskoe witnessed the following:

> The Germans took from the sovkhoz yard the family of Tamara Meerovich and Pinchus [*Pinchos*] Tsylya, altogether nine persons,[207] on a cart and moved them away in the direction of the steppes outside the *stanitsa*. Before this they had been held for a day by armed German guards.[208]

All eight members of the Ginsburg family residing in that locality were killed there. Presumably, their murderers were Germans from a police unit or the SS. Here are their names and details, as specified in the same Soviet report, compiled on March 28, 1943 (see the copy of the report preserved in Yad Vashem on the next page): 1) Meerovich Tamara, chief accountant, 2) Grigory, son, 3) mother [*Manya*], 4) aunt [*Anya*], 5) aunt [*Liza*], 6) Pinchus [*Pinchos*] Tsylya, tutor, 7) husband [*David*], 8) son [*apparently this was daughter—Anya*]. According to the report, the members of the Ginsburg family were killed together with thirteen other Jews who had been living in the village.

---

205 Statement of the Commission of the City of Rostov, November 23, 1943, YVA: M.33/585, p. 175. Cf. Gontmakher, *Evrei na donskoi zemle*, 209. Cf. Elena Voitenko, *Kholokost na iuge Rossii v period Velikoi Otechestvennoi Voiny (1941–1943 gg.)*, PhD diss., Stavropol', Stavropol'skii gosudarstvennyi universitet, 2005, 11. Cf. Winkler, "Rostov-on-Don 1942."
206 A local Jewish scholar cites the highest estimate of the Jewish death toll in the city, 30,000. Movshovich, "Rostov-na-Donu," 869.
207 There is a discrepancy in the numbers. In the following lines there is a list of only eight victims.
208 Statement of the Commission of *Stanitsa* of Novo-Rogovskaya, GARF: 7021/40/774, p. 24.

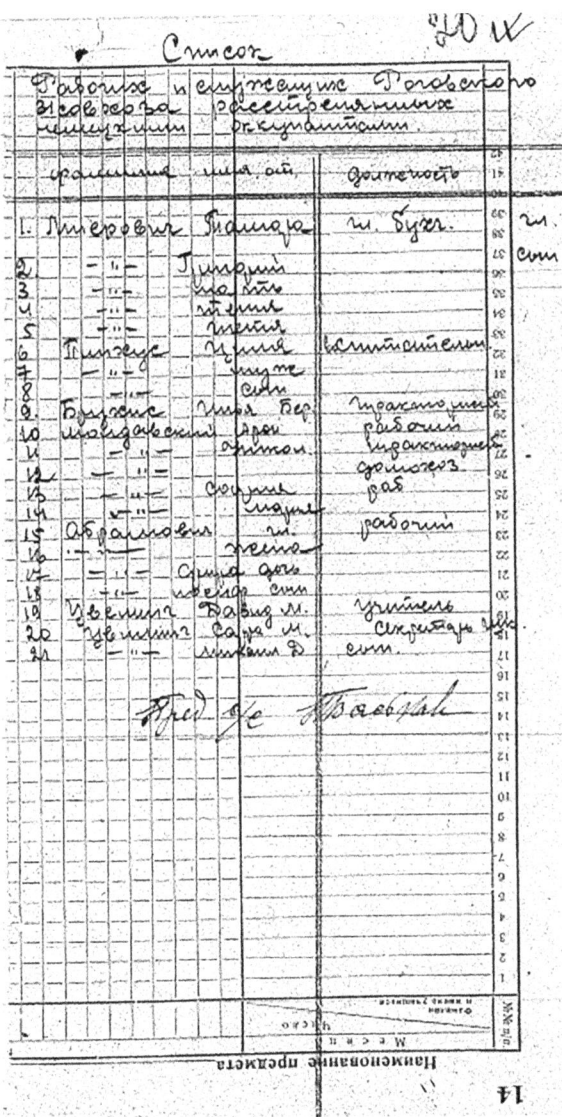

List of the workers and employers of Rogovskii *sovkhoz* executed by the German occupiers. The list includes members of the Ginsburg family. GARF: 7021/40/774, p. 103. Courtesy of Yad Vashem Archives.

1943

February 1943

The city of Rostov-on-Don was liberated by the Red Army on February 14, 1943.

In liberated Rostov. February 14, 1943. Central Archive of Moscow's Electronic and Audio-Visual Materials, 1-56978.

Rostov. Winter 1943. After the liberation. People walking to a local jail in order to look for the corpses of their relatives. Public domain.

March 1943

The next letter comes from a woman called Marusya, a non-Jewish inhabitant of Rostov-on-Don. Apparently, she was one of the Ginsburgs' neighbors and knew the entire family, including Efim, quite well. We do not know exactly why she was the one who wrote the letter to Efim. Most likely, the people living in the Ginsburgs' building saw one of Efim's letters, and Marusya took it upon herself to send him the tragic news:

> Before Rostov was seized, they moved to one of the villages in the Egorlyksky *raion*, and they were executed there by the Fascist barbarians. ...We did not believe it, hoping that probably it was not so, but unfortunately we have become convinced.
>
> I thought that Volodya was not alive and he would not have to go through this dramatic experience. But he came here to learn about the fate of his family from Anna Vasilievna Shneider and she told him everything. ...
>
> On the whole, their return was so reckless. Tamara did not tell [*me*] about it. If she did I would never have recommended that they do it. And they would have taken heed of my advice. But now it cannot be helped. But their deaths are especially painful because they could have been avoided. Especially because Anna and Liza never wanted to leave Rostov.[209]

This letter is undated, but in all probability it was written during the period from March 1943 to April 1943 (when Volodya Meerovich, who was mentioned in this letter, joined the correspondence once more).[210] The writer did not give any names at the start of the letter, but it seems that she first wrote about Anna (Anya) and Liza, whose fate was always of particular concern to Efim. The sisters finally succeeded in leaving Rostov-on-Don, but they did so on the very eve of the German occupation, only to be shot far away from their home.

The second part of the letter deals with the fate of Tamara, Tsylya, and the other family members who came back to Rostov-on-Don on the eve of the German takeover of the city. The writer of the letter considered that the entire family could have survived the German assault and that their death was avoidable. This aptly sums up the main motif of the entire Ginsburg saga. We also learn how Volodya Meerovich heard about the murder of his family, which gives us

---

209 From Marusya (?) in Rostov-on-Don to Efim Ginsburg in Alma-Ata, no date, YVA: O.75/324, pp. 337–342.
210 See the next letter.

a clue to his future behavior. We cannot be certain that he actually visited the village of Novorogovskoe, where his wife and son were killed. It is likely that he did not know where the killing took place, but he doubtless figured out that they had failed to move far enough away from the front and realized that their chances of surviving under German rule were close to zero.

April 1943

On April 25, 1943, after a very long silence, a short message came from Volodya Meerovich: "I am alive and well, currently stationed on the front line."[211] Only one member of the Rostov family was now left alive!

The very next day, April 26, 1943, he sent another letter, giving some information about his activities (if the reader knew how to read his code):

> I have just returned safely from a business trip where I visited our enemy. …We are beginning to settle accounts with our enemy. The first account was for my son; it was small; still, it made itself felt. And I hope it is not the last one. There will be accounts to settle for my beloved wife, and so on. Our dear one, you also read the newspapers. There is nothing essential [*going on*] now at the front and it is true. It will commence soon and I will definitely participate in it.[212]

Presumably, Volodya wrote this letter after he visited the newly liberated Rostov-on-Don. When he heard that he had lost his entire family, he was determined to take revenge on the Germans. Apparently, the letter described the first opportunity he had to carry out his plan and kill some of the enemy. This meant that, prior to this point in time, Volodya was either not posted on the front line and/or was unaware of what exactly had happened to his family. The letter indicated that Volodya had killed one or a number of Germans during an attack on the enemy's positions or in the course of a reconnaissance raid. (We do not know exactly in which army unit he served.)

This is the last letter written by Volodya Meerovich from the Ginsburg collection. We have no further information about him, which is significant. The survival rate in the ranks of the Soviet infantry, where Volodya was probably placed, was extremely low, compared to other branches of the Red Army.

---

211 From Volodya Meerovich in the army, April 25, 1943, YVA: O.75/324, p. 334.
212 From Volodya Meerovich in the army, April 26, 1943, ibid., p. 336.

Furthermore, since Volodya was determined to take revenge on the Germans, it seems highly possible that he did not survive the Soviet-German War and was killed in action as early as 1943. After the murder of his family, Volodya Meerovich's chief motivation was not survival but revenge, regardless of the price that had to be paid.

July 1943

On July 19, 1943, Efim Ginsburg received official confirmation of the news that he had already heard from Marusya:

> Comrade Ginsburg!
> We received your letter with the inquiry concerning the fate of your sister. Unfortunately, we are unable to answer you with anything specific. All that we know is that she (Elizaveta Grigor'evna) and her sister were evacuated from Rostov some ten days before the German occupation of the city, in July 1942. We do not know where, apparently somewhere in the direction of the Caucasus. Since then, we do not know anything about them.[213]

The only new—for us—detail revealed in the letter is the date of the sisters' evacuation from Rostov-on-Don, July 14 (ten days before it was captured by the Wehrmacht). It turned out that in mid-July Liza was finally able to have her evacuation authorized by her superiors,[214] but evidently, at that time it was already impossible to complete the evacuation process successfully, all the more so as the sisters did not intend to leave the North Caucasus.

The letter is illustrative of the administrative havoc that reigned in the region after the German occupation: six months after the Germans were expelled from the Caucasus, the Soviet authorities were still unable to find out where people had been evacuated to, according to their own official program. But the Soviets lost many archives during their hasty retreat from the North Caucasus in the summer of 1942. By the summer of 1943, when the current letter was issued, attempts were made to fully document the crimes that the Germans had perpetrated in the region. These reports, part of the general

---

213 From A. A. Karasev and V. A. Anisimov, inhabitants of the building 101–103, Engels Street, Rostov-on-Don, to Efim Ginsburg in Alma-Ata, July 19, 1943, ibid., p. 351.
214 Shternshis, "Between Life and Death," 500.

Soviet investigation of the Nazi occupation of the Soviet Union, including their criminal mistreatment of civilians, were drawn up in 1943–1944.[215] In this respect, it would appear that the report mentioning the details of the Ginsburg family members, quoted above, is a remarkable achievement in reconstructing the true facts, since it was made already one year after their deaths, and the victims were not local people known to everyone in the village.

---

215 On this investigation, see, for example, Sorokina, "People and Procedures," 797–831; Feferman, "Soviet Investigation of Nazi Crimes," 587–602.

Conclusion

The book you have just finished reading is a complex one. It serves as a memorial to the people who wrote these letters, the members of the Ginsburg family. They lived at a difficult time and they wanted to go on living, but they made a fatal mistake that cost their lives. Their cries from the embattled Soviet Union, written months, weeks, or just a few days before they met their death at the hands of the Germans, is all that is left to remind us of them.

For me, the letters written by the Ginsburgs turned out to be more difficult to analyze than I had initially expected. First of all, I had to take into account that there were several people involved in the correspondence, and it would have been wrong to see them as if they were all cut from the same cloth. Their letters differed in their degree of caution, conservatism, and emotionality. Yet, in the final account, all members of the family were inclined to make the same decision, whether or not to become evacuees (and where to go). In this vital decision-making process, the voices of the more conservative, and, as it turned out, more short-sighted, members of the family prevailed.

These letters were written by Soviet citizens living in the Soviet Union at the time of the Soviet-German War. They put their thoughts down on paper, although they doubtlessly realized that their letters might be intercepted, and they had to screen their contents accordingly. This could have reduced the quality of the letters as a historical source. But if we look at these letters, understanding that they reflect the sentiments of a Soviet Jewish family in the North Caucasus in 1941–1942, and, at the same time, taking into account their fear of Soviet censorship, we gain an additional unique insight for analysis. There appears to be a correlation between the situation at the various fronts and the contents of these letters. Paradoxically, the moments of liberation from the grip of Soviet censorship came as the German army drew closer and closer and the deadly fear that the Germans instilled in the Ginsburg family surpassed their fear of the Soviet regime.

The main motive of all the letters written throughout this period was whether to flee or not to flee. However, there is more behind this motive than the eye can see. Why did the Ginsburgs need to run away from Rostov-on-Don? The answer appears to be clear: they did not want to be killed by the Germans. Yet, what exactly did they know about the danger that the German occupation would bring them? Here we do not have a clear response based on what happened during the first German occupation in November 1941, and it cannot be ruled out that the older generation of Ginsburgs was at that time more ready to stay under German rule rather than escape into the Soviet hinterland. In short, after considering all the pros and cons, they reached the conclusion that leaving Rostov-on-Don would not be worthwhile. Certainly, the situation was reversed in the summer of 1942, when the Ginsburgs already accumulated sufficient information from various sources about the criminal abuse of the Jews by the Germans and cherished no illusions about what the arrival of the Germans would mean for them.

The Soviet media made the reliability of the information it supplied highly controversial. It failed to provide the Ginsburgs with accurate real-time information about the imminent danger threatening them specifically as Jews and about the proximity of the German forces. In fact, it was a very problematic source of information. The shortcomings of the Soviet reporting were highlighted in an internal report written by the heads of the Rostov District Committee of the VKP(b) as early as October 1, 1943:

> Due to the censorship, our [newspaper] *Molot* has turned into an ignorant, superstitious old lady [*bogomol'naia staraia dura*]. You won't see there anything to reflect the work on strengthening the defenses of the city. Future generations will be surprised [to learn this]: [for] sixteen months, the enemy stood outside Rostov's walls; [our] people fought against them, at first successfully and then unsuccessfully. But there is nothing, absolutely nothing reflected in *Molot*, because the censors had drawn such far-fetched conclusions that any scholar would envy them. It bans even references to mobilizing the workers to strengthen the defense of the city. It is no joke but a [matter of] fact that a statement like "the state bread factory is working" cannot be published. ("Excuse me, the censor reasons, but this factory is supplying the Army—so cut it out!").[1]

---

1 Letter of B. A. Dvinsky, the First Secretary of the Rostov District Committee of the VKP(b), to G. F. Aleksandrov, the Head of the Department of Propaganda and Agitation of the Central Committee of the VKP(b), October 4, 1943, RGASPI: 17/125/185, pp. 54–55. In Gennadii Kostyrchenko, "Sovetskaia tsenzura v 1941–1952 gg." *Voprosy istorii* 11–12 (1996): 87–94. See also Berkhoff, *Motherland in Danger*, 93–94.

Finally, there is one more factor in the letters that is worth emphasizing. In my opinion, it was crucial in dissuading the Ginsburgs from leaving Rostov-on-Don. The family did consider the idea of evacuation, and not only theoretically. Some family members were evacuated in an orderly fashion, and although this was not a long-distance move and did not continue for years, it was still a full-fledged evacuation. The evacuee branch of the family suffered enormously as a result of their evacuation, and their experience made an impression on all the other Ginsburgs. The conclusion they reached was, as they said more than once, "it would be better off to die at home." Their reluctance to move away was reinforced even more by a candid and detailed description of the hardships Efim Ginsburg underwent during and after his evacuation to Central Asia. This ensuing decision not to flee to the Soviet hinterland cost them their lives.

The book is an attempt to combine history from above and history from below, general descriptions of the Soviet-German War, the evacuation experience, and the Holocaust, on the one hand, and a perspective of the "little man and woman," ordinary Jewish people struggling to survive in an era when their chances for survival were very low, on the other hand. I believe that such a synthesis, whenever possible, may help us better understand the tragic events of those days.

List of Letters in the Ginsburg Collection

No	Author, origin, addressee, and destination	Reviewed by military censorship	Date	Source. YVA: O.75/324
1	From Anya Greener (Ginsburg) and Liza Chazkewitz (Ginsburg) in Rostov-on-Don to Efim Ginsburg in Moscow (telegram)		March 26, 1939	p. 378
2	From Anya Greener (Ginsburg) in Rostov-on-Don to Efim Ginsburg in Moscow		April 1939, 1940 or 1941	p. 379
3	From Anya Greener (Ginsburg), Liza Chazkewitz (Ginsburg), and Boris Chazkewitz in Rostov-on-Don to Efim Ginsburg in Moscow (telegram)		March 28, 1940	pp. 7–8
4	From Liza Chazkewitz (Ginsburg) and Anya Greener (Ginsburg) in Rostov-on-Don to Efim Ginsburg in Moscow		September 8, 1940	pp. 11–12
5	From Tamara Meerovich in Budennovsk to Efim Ginsburg in Alma-Ata		Unclear	p. 13
6	From Liza Chazkewitz (Ginsburg) in Rostov-on-Don to Efim Ginsburg in Moscow (telegram)		December 30, 1939 or 1940	p. 375
7	From Anya Greener (Ginsburg) in Rostov-on-Don to Efim Ginsburg in Moscow		Apparently prewar	p. 347
8	From Liza Chazkewitz (Ginsburg) in Rostov-on-Don to Efim Ginsburg in Moscow		March 18, 1941	pp. 15–16
9	From Liza Chazkewitz (Ginsburg) in Rostov-on-Don to Efim Ginsburg in Moscow		April 10, 1941	pp. 17–18
10	From Tamara Meerovich in Rostov-on-Don to Efim Ginsburg in Moscow		April 18, 1941	pp. 19–20
11	From Liza Chazkewitz (Ginsburg) in Rostov-on-Don to Efim Ginsburg in Moscow		April 22, 1941	pp. 21–22

List of Letters in the Ginsburg Collection | 267

No	Author, origin, addressee, and destination	Reviewed by military censorship	Date	Source. YVA: O.75/324
12	From Liza Chazkewitz (Ginsburg) in Rostov-on-Don to Efim Ginsburg in Moscow		May 31, 1941	pp. 25–26
13	From Liza Chazkewitz (Ginsburg) in Rostov-on-Don to Efim Ginsburg in Moscow		June 22, 1941	pp. 27–30
14	From Liza Chazkewitz (Ginsburg) and Borya Chazkewitz in Rostov-on-Don to Efim Ginsburg in Moscow		July 3, 1941	pp. 35–36
15	From Liza Chazkewitz (Ginsburg) in Rostov-on-Don to Efim Ginsburg in Omsk		July 23, 1941	pp. 38–39
16	From Liza Chazkewitz (Ginsburg) in Rostov-on-Don to Efim Ginsburg in Omsk	Yes	July 27, 1941	pp. 40–41
17	From Liza Chazkewitz (Ginsburg) in Rostov-on-Don to Efim Ginsburg in Omsk	Yes	August 7, 1941	pp. 42–43
18	From Liza Chazkewitz (Ginsburg) in Rostov-on-Don to Efim Ginsburg in Omsk	Yes	August 15, 1941	pp. 44–45
19	From Liza Chazkewitz (Ginsburg) and Anya Greener (Ginsburg) in Rostov-on-Don to Efim Ginsburg in Omsk		August 30, 1941	pp. 9–10
20	From Liza Chazkewitz (Ginsburg) in Rostov-on-Don to Efim Ginsburg in Omsk	Yes	August 31, 1941	p. 46
21	From Liza Chazkewitz (Ginsburg) in Rostov-on-Don to Efim Ginsburg in Omsk	Yes	September 7, 1941	pp. 47–48
22	From Liza Chazkewitz (Ginsburg) in Rostov-on-Don to Efim Ginsburg in Omsk	Yes	September 17, 1941	p. 50
23	From Liza Chazkewitz (Ginsburg) in Rostov-on-Don to Efim Ginsburg in Omsk		September 21, 1941	p. 49
24	From Liza Chazkewitz (Ginsburg) in Rostov-on-Don to Efim Ginsburg in Omsk	Yes	September 21, 1941	pp. 51–57
25	From Anya Greener (Ginsburg) in Rostov-on-Don to Efim Ginsburg in Omsk	Yes	October 3, 1941	pp. 58–59
26	From Anya Greener (Ginsburg) in Rostov-on-Don to Efim Ginsburg in Omsk		October 1, 1941	pp. 63–64
27	From Anya Greener (Ginsburg) in Rostov-on-Don to Efim Ginsburg in Omsk		October 3, 1941	pp. 66–67
28	From Liza Chazkewitz (Ginsburg) in Rostov-on-Don to Efim Ginsburg in Omsk	Yes	October 6, 1941	pp. 60–62
29	From Liza Chazkewitz (Ginsburg) in Rostov-on-Don to Efim Ginsburg in Omsk		October 6, 1941	pp. 64–66
30	From Anya Greener (Ginsburg) in Rostov-on-Don to Efim Ginsburg in Omsk		October 26, 1941	pp. 65–71
31	From Anya Greener (Ginsburg) in Rostov-on-Don to Efim Ginsburg in Alma-Ata		October 30, 1941	pp. 72–76

No	Author, origin, addressee, and destination	Reviewed by military censorship	Date	Source. YVA: O.75/324
32	From Anya Greener (Ginsburg) in Rostov-on-Don to Efim Ginsburg in Alma-Ata		November 3, 1941	pp. 80–81
33	From Liza Chazkewitz (Ginsburg) and Anya Greener (Ginsburg) in Rostov-on-Don to Efim Ginsburg in Alma-Ata		November 18, 1941	pp. 77–78
34	From Tamara Meerovich in Budennovsk to Efim Ginsburg in Alma-Ata		November 18, 1941	pp. 82–87
35	From Efim Ginsburg in Alma-Ata to Tamara Meerovich in Budennovsk	Yes	December 10, 1941	pp. 88–89
36	From Tsilya Pinchos in Budennovsk to Efim Ginsburg in Alma-Ata		December 12, 1941	pp. 90–93
37	From Tamara Meerovich in Budennovsk to Efim Ginsburg in Alma-Ata		December 12, 1941	pp. 94–95
38	From Liza Chazkewitz (Ginsburg) and Anya Greener (Ginsburg) in Rostov-on-Don to Efim Ginsburg in Alma-Ata		December 12, 1941	pp. 96–97
39	From Liza Chazkewitz (Ginsburg) and Anya Greener (Ginsburg) in Rostov-on-Don to Efim Ginsburg in Alma-Ata	Yes	December 13, 1941	pp. 98–99
40	From Tamara Meerovich in Budennovsk to Efim Ginsburg in Alma-Ata (telegram)	Yes	December 13, 1941	p. 371
41	From Efim Ginsburg in Alma-Ata to Tamara Meerovich in Budennovsk		December 16, 1941	pp. 100–103
42	From Liza Chazkewitz (Ginsburg) and Anya Greener (Ginsburg) in Rostov-on-Don to Efim Ginsburg in Alma-Ata		December 18, 1941	pp. 104–105
43	From Liza Chazkewitz (Ginsburg) and Anya Greener (Ginsburg) in Rostov-on-Don to Efim Ginsburg in Alma-Ata		December 20, 1941	pp. 106–109
44	From Liza Chazkewitz (Ginsburg) and Anya Greener (Ginsburg) in Rostov-on-Don to Tsylya Pinchos in Budennovsk	Yes	December 21, 1941	pp. 110–111
45	From Tsylya Pinkhos in Budennovsk to Efim Ginsburg in Alma-Ata		December 22, 1941	pp. 112–113
46	From Tsylya Pinkhos in Ordzhonikidze to Efim Ginsburg in Alma-Ata		December 29, 1941	pp. 114–115
47	From Liza Chazkewitz (Ginsburg) and Anya Greener (Ginsburg) in Rostov-on-Don to Efim Ginsburg in Alma-Ata (radiogram)	Yes	December 31, 1941	p. 116
48	From Liza Chazkewitz (Ginsburg) and Anya Greener (Ginsburg) in Rostov-on-Don to Efim Ginsburg in Alma-Ata (radiogram)	Yes	December 31, 1941	p. 120

List of Letters in the Ginsburg Collection | 269

No	Author, origin, addressee, and destination	Reviewed by military censorship	Date	Source. YVA: O.75/324
49	From Liza Chazkewitz (Ginsburg) and Anya Greener (Ginsburg) in Rostov-on-Don to Efim Ginsburg in Alma-Ata (telegram)	Yes	December 31, 1941	p. 122
50	From Liza Chazkewitz (Ginsburg) and Anya Greener (Ginsburg) in Rostov-on-Don to Efim Ginsburg in Alma-Ata (telegram)	Yes	December 31, 1941	p. 122
51	From Tamara Meerovich in Ordzhonikidze to Efim Ginsburg in Alma-Ata		January 3, 1942	pp. 127–132
52	From Tamara Meerovich in Ordzhonikidze to Efim Ginsburg in Alma-Ata		January 8, 1942	p. 136
53	From Liza Chazkewitz (Ginsburg) and Anya Greener (Ginsburg) in Rostov-on-Don to Efim Ginsburg in Alma-Ata		January 9, 1942	pp. 137–138
54	From Tamara Meerovich in Ordzhonikidze to Efim Ginsburg in Alma-Ata (telegram)	Yes	January 10, 1942	p. 139
55	From Anya Pinchos to Efim Ginsburg in Alma-Ata (with a drawing)		December 1941–February 1942	pp. 377–378
56	From Liza Chazkewitz (Ginsburg) and Anya Greener (Ginsburg) in Rostov-on-Don to Efim Ginsburg in Alma-Ata	Yes	January 13, 1942	pp. 141–142
57	From Tamara Meerovich in Ordzhonikidze to Efim Ginsburg in Alma-Ata		January 14, 1942	pp. 143–144
58	From Tsylya Pinkhos in Ordzhonikidze to Efim Ginsburg in Alma-Ata		January 15, 1942	pp. 145–146
59	From Tamara Meerovich in Ordzhonikidze to Efim Ginsburg in Alma-Ata		January 15, 1942	pp. 147–148
60	From Tamara Meerovich in Ordzhonikidze to Efim Ginsburg in Alma-Ata (telegram)	Yes	January 18, 1942	p. 149
61	From Tamara Meerovich in Ordzhonikidze to Efim Ginsburg in Alma-Ata		January 21, 1942	pp. 151–152
62	From Tamara Meerovich in Ordzhonikidze to Efim Ginsburg in Alma-Ata		January 25, 1942	pp. 153–154
63	From Liza Chazkewitz (Ginsburg) and Anya Greener (Ginsburg) in Rostov-on-Don to Efim Ginsburg in Alma-Ata	Yes	January 28, 1942	pp. 155–156
64	From Liza Chazkewitz (Ginsburg) and Anya Greener (Ginsburg) in Rostov-on-Don to Efim Ginsburg in Alma-Ata	Yes	January 28, 1942	pp. 159–170

No	Author, origin, addressee, and destination	Reviewed by military censorship	Date	Source. YVA: O.75/324
65	From Liza Chazkewitz (Ginsburg) and Anya Greener (Ginsburg) in Rostov-on-Don to Efim Ginsburg in Alma-Ata	Yes	January 29, 1942	pp. 157–158
66	From Liza Chazkewitz (Ginsburg) and Anya Greener (Ginsburg) in Rostov-on-Don to Efim Ginsburg in Alma-Ata		February 1, 1942	pp. 175–182
67	From Tamara Meerovich in Ordzhonikidze to Efim Ginsburg in Alma-Ata		February 5, 1942	pp. 203–204
68	From Tamara Meerovich in Ordzhonikidze to Efim Ginsburg in Alma-Ata	Yes	February 7, 1942	pp. 185–186
69	From Divisional inspector Tkachev in Rostov-on-Don to Efim Ginsburg in Alma-Ata		February 8, 1942	p. 187
70	From Liza Chazkewitz (Ginsburg) and Anya Greener (Ginsburg) in Rostov-on-Don to Efim Ginsburg in Alma-Ata		February 9, 1942	pp. 188–195
71	From Tamara Meerovich in Ordzhonikidze to Efim Ginsburg in Alma-Ata		February 10, 1942	pp. 196–200
72	From Tamara Meerovich in Ordzhonikidze to Efim Ginsburg in Alma-Ata		February 20, 1942	p. 201
73	From Tamara Meerovich in Ordzhonikidze to Efim Ginsburg in Alma-Ata (telegram)		February 20, 1942	p. 202
74	From Liza Chazkewitz (Ginsburg) and Anya Greener (Ginsburg) in Rostov-on-Don to Efim Ginsburg in Alma-Ata		February 21, 1942	pp. 348–349
75	From Tsylya Pinkhos in Ordzhonikidze to Efim Ginsburg in Alma-Ata		February 26, 1942	pp. 206–209
76	From Liza Chazkewitz (Ginsburg) and Anya Greener (Ginsburg) in Rostov-on-Don to Efim Ginsburg in Alma-Ata		March 2, 1942	pp. 211–214
77	From Tamara Meerovich in Ordzhonikidze to Efim Ginsburg in Alma-Ata		March 3, 1942	pp. 215–220
78	From Tamara Meerovich in Ordzhonikidze to Efim Ginsburg in Alma-Ata		March 8, 1942	pp. 221–222
79	From Liza Chazkewitz (Ginsburg) and Anya Greener (Ginsburg) in Rostov-on-Don to Efim Ginsburg in Alma-Ata		March 8, 1942	pp. 223–224
80	From Volodya Meerovich in Rostov-on-Don to Efim Ginsburg in Alma-Ata	Yes	March 8, 1942	pp. 225–226
81	From Liza Chazkewitz (Ginsburg) and Anya Greener (Ginsburg) in Rostov-on-Don to Efim Ginsburg in Alma-Ata	Yes	March 12, 1942	pp. 350–351

List of Letters in the Ginsburg Collection | 271

No	Author, origin, addressee, and destination	Reviewed by military censorship	Date	Source. YVA: O.75/324
82	From Liza Chazkewitz (Ginsburg) and Anya Greener (Ginsburg) in Rostov-on-Don to Efim Ginsburg in Alma-Ata	Yes	March 13, 1942	pp. 229–230
83	From Tsylya Pinkhos in Rostov-on-Don to Efim Ginsburg in Alma-Ata	Yes	March 17, 1942	pp. 227–228
84	From Tamara Meerovich in Ordzhonikidze to Efim Ginsburg in Alma-Ata		March 13, 1942	pp. 232–234
85	From Grinhaus in Ufa to Efim Ginsburg in Alma-Ata (telegram)		March 14, 1942	p. 238
86	From Liza Chazkewitz (Ginsburg) and Anya Greener (Ginsburg) in Rostov-on-Don to Efim Ginsburg in Alma-Ata	Yes	March 19, 1942	pp. 244–246
87	From Tamara Meerovich in Ordzhonikidze to Efim Ginsburg in Alma-Ata		March 20, 1942	pp. 242–243
88	From Liza Chazkewitz (Ginsburg) and Anya Greener (Ginsburg) in Rostov-on-Don to Efim Ginsburg in Alma-Ata		Late March, 1942	pp. 343–246
89	From Liza Chazkewitz (Ginsburg) and Anya Greener (Ginsburg) in Rostov-on-Don to Efim Ginsburg in Alma-Ata		Apparently March, 1942	pp. 355–359
90	From Liza Chazkewitz (Ginsburg) and Anya Greener (Ginsburg) in Rostov-on-Don to Efim Ginsburg in Alma-Ata		March 31, 1942	pp. 352–354
91	From Tamara Meerovich in Ordzhonikidze to Efim Ginsburg in Alma-Ata		April 2, 1942	pp. 240–241
92	From Liza Chazkewitz (Ginsburg) and Anya Greener (Ginsburg) in Rostov-on-Don to Efim Ginsburg in Alma-Ata		April 6, 1942	p. 254
93	From Tamara Meerovich in Ordzhonikidze to Efim Ginsburg in Alma-Ata		April 16 (?), 1942	pp. 252–253
94	From Liza Chazkewitz (Ginsburg) and Anya Greener (Ginsburg) in Rostov-on-Don to Efim Ginsburg in Alma-Ata	Yes	April 21, 1942	pp. 255–267
95	From Tamara Meerovich in Ordzhonikidze to Efim Ginsburg in Alma-Ata		April 24, 1942	pp. 270–271
96	From Liza Chazkewitz (Ginsburg) and Anya Greener (Ginsburg) in Rostov-on-Don to Efim Ginsburg in Alma-Ata	Yes	April 24, 1942	pp. 272–273
97	From Liza Chazkewitz (Ginsburg) and Anya Greener (Ginsburg) in Rostov-on-Don to Efim Ginsburg in Alma-Ata	Yes	April 26, 1942	pp. 275–281

List of Letters in the Ginsburg Collection

No	Author, origin, addressee, and destination	Reviewed by military censorship	Date	Source. YVA: O.75/324
98	From Liza Chazkewitz (Ginsburg) and Anya Greener (Ginsburg) in Rostov-on-Don to Efim Ginsburg in Alma-Ata	Yes	May 3, 1942	p. 299
99	From Tamara Meerovich in Ordzhonikidze to Efim Ginsburg in Alma-Ata		May 6, 1942	pp. 288–289
100	From Tamara Meerovich in Ordzhonikidze to Efim Ginsburg in Alma-Ata		May 8, 1942	pp. 282–283
101	From Liza Chazkewitz (Ginsburg) and Anya Greener (Ginsburg) in Rostov-on-Don to Efim Ginsburg in Alma-Ata	Yes	May 13, 1942	pp. 284–285
102	From Liza Chazkewitz (Ginsburg) and Anya Greener (Ginsburg) in Rostov-on-Don to Efim Ginsburg in Alma-Ata	Yes	May 13, 1942	pp. 360–365
103	From Tamara Meerovich in Ordzhonikidze to Efim Ginsburg in Alma-Ata		May 16, 1942	pp. 286–287
103	From Liza Chazkewitz (Ginsburg) in Rostov-on-Don to Efim Ginsburg in Alma-Ata	Yes	May 21, 1942	Unclear
104	From Liza Chazkewitz (Ginsburg) and Anya Greener (Ginsburg) in Rostov-on-Don to Efim Ginsburg in Alma-Ata	Yes	May 24, 1942	p. 292
105	From Liza Chazkewitz (Ginsburg) and Anya Greener (Ginsburg) in Rostov-on-Don to Efim Ginsburg in Alma-Ata	Yes	May 26, 1942	pp. 294–297
106	From Liza Chazkewitz (Ginsburg) and Anya Greener (Ginsburg) in Rostov-on-Don to Efim Ginsburg in Alma-Ata	Yes	June 2, 1942	p. 303
107	From Liza Chazkewitz (Ginsburg) and Anya Greener (Ginsburg) in Rostov-on-Don to Efim Ginsburg in Alma-Ata		June 2, 1942	p. 307
108	From Tamara Meerovich in Rostov-on-Don to Efim Ginsburg in Alma-Ata		June 7, 1942	pp. 308–309
109	From Liza Chazkewitz (Ginsburg) and Anya Greener (Ginsburg) in Rostov-on-Don to Efim Ginsburg in Alma-Ata	Yes	June 7, 1942	pp. 310–318
110	From Liza Chazkewitz (Ginsburg) and Anya Greener (Ginsburg) in Rostov-on-Don to Efim Ginsburg in Alma-Ata	Yes	June 13, 1942	pp. 322–323
111	From Liza Chazkewitz (Ginsburg) and Anya Greener (Ginsburg) in Rostov-on-Don to Efim Ginsburg in Alma-Ata (postcard)	Yes	June 15, 1942	p. 306

No	Author, origin, addressee, and destination	Reviewed by military censorship	Date	Source. YVA: O.75/324
112	From Liza Chazkewitz (Ginsburg) and Anya Greener (Ginsburg) in Rostov-on-Don to Efim Ginsburg in Alma-Ata		June 16, 1942	pp. 366–371
113	From Liza Chazkewitz (Ginsburg) and Anya Greener (Ginsburg) in Rostov-on-Don to Efim Ginsburg in Alma-Ata	Yes	June 17, 1942	pp. 320–321
109	From Liza Chazkewitz (Ginsburg) and Anya Greener (Ginsburg) in Rostov-on-Don to Efim Ginsburg in Alma-Ata	Yes	June 21, 1942	pp. 324–325
110	From Liza Chazkewitz (Ginsburg) and Anya Greener (Ginsburg) in Rostov-on-Don to Efim Ginsburg in Alma-Ata	Yes	June 27, 1942	p. 326
111	From Liza Chazkewitz (Ginsburg) and Anya Greener (Ginsburg) in Rostov-on-Don to Efim Ginsburg in Alma-Ata (postcard)	Yes	June 30, 1942	p. 389
112	From Liza Chazkewitz (Ginsburg) and Anya Greener (Ginsburg) in Rostov-on-Don to Efim Ginsburg in Alma-Ata	Yes	July 9, 1942	pp. 330–331
113	From Liza Chazkewitz (Ginsburg) and Anya Greener (Ginsburg) in Rostov-on-Don to Efim Ginsburg in Alma-Ata	Yes	July 10, 1942	p. 332
114	From Marusya (?) in Rostov-on-Don to Efim Ginsburg in Alma-Ata		March 1943	pp. 337–342
115	From Volodya Meerovich in the army to Efim Ginsburg in Alma-Ata	Yes	April 25, 1943	pp. 333–334
116	From Volodya Meerovich in the army to Efim Ginsburg in Alma-Ata		April 26, 1943	pp. 335–336
117	From A. A. Karaseva and V. A. Anisimov, inhabitants of the building 101–103, Engels Steet, Rostov-on-Don	Yes	July 19, 1943	p. 392
118	From Liza Chazkewitz (Ginsburg) or Anya Greener (Ginsburg) in Rostov-on-Don to Efim Ginsburg in Moscow (unsorted pages from various letters)		Spring 1939, 1940 or 1941	pp. 380–387; 390–391; 395

List of Abbreviations

EG	Einsatzgruppe (a special assignment force)
ESC	Extraordinary State Commission
Glavlit	Administration of the Plenipotentiary for the Protection of Military and State Secrets in the Press under the USSR Council of Ministers
NKVD	*Narodnyi komissariat vnutrennikh del* (People's Commissariat of the Interior)
ObKhSS	*Otdel bor'by s khishcheniiami sotsialisticheskoi sobstvennosti* (Department for Combatting the Embezzlement of Socialist Property)
RSFSR	*Rossiyskaya Sovetskaya Federativnaya Sotsialisticheskaya Respublika* (The Russian Soviet Federative Socialist Republic)
SNK SSSR	*Sovnarkom*, or *Sovet Narodnykh Komissarov SSSR* (Council of People's Commissars of the USSR)
TASS	*Telegrafnoe agenstvo Sovetskogo Soyuza* (Telegraph Agency of the Soviet Union)
TsK VKP(b)	*Tsentral'nyi komitet Vsesoiuznoi kommunisticheskoi partii (bolshevikov)* (Central Committee of the All-Union Communist Party (Bolsheviks))
VKP(b)	*Vsesoiuznaia kommunisticheskaia partiia (bolshevikov)* (All-Union Communist Party (Bolsheviks))
Voenkomat	*Voennyi kommissariat* (Military Commissariat)

Bibliography

ARCHIVAL SOURCES

Jerusalem, Israel

1. Hebrew University of Jerusalem, Institute of Contemporary Jewry, Department of Oral History (ICJ, DOH)
   Collection of oral testimonies
2. Yad Vashem Archive (YVA)
   Collection TR.10, Trials of Nazi criminals in Western Germany. Provenance: Z/s Ludwigsburg
   Collection O.3, Testimonies of the Holocaust survivors
   Collection O.75, Letters
   Collection M.31, Righteous among the Gentiles
   Collection M.33, Extraordinary State Commission. Provenance: Moscow, Russia.
   Collection M.35, Jewish Anti-Fascist Committee
   Collection M.37, Selected records from the Ukrainian Archives
   Collection M.40, Selected records from the Russian Archives
   Collection P.21, Ilya Erenburg's archive
   Hall of Names (YVHN)

Moscow, Russia

1. Gosudarstvennyi arkhiv Rossiiskoi Federatsii (State Archive of the Russian Federation, GARF)
   Fond 7021, Chrezvychainaia Gosudarstvennaia Kommissiia po ustanovleniiu i rassledovaniiu zlodeianii nemetsko-fashistskikh zakhvatchikov i ikh soobshchnikov i prichinennogo imi ushcherba grazhdanam, kolkhozam, obshchestvennym organizatsiiam i uchrezhdeniiam (Extraordinary State Commission on Reporting and Investigating the Atrocities of the German

Fascist Occupants and their Henchmen and the Damages inflicted by them to Citizens, *Kolkhozes*, Public Organizations, and Institutions), 1943–1945
2. Rossiiskii gosudarstvennyi arkhiv sotsial'no-politicheskoi istorii (Russian State Archive of Social and Political History, RGASPI)

   Fond 69, Tsentralnyi Shtab Partizanskogo Dvizheniia pri Stavke Verkhovnogo Glavnokomanduyushchego (Central Headquarter of the Partisan Movement under the Headquarter of the Supreme Commander), 1942–1944
3. Rossiiskii gosudarstvennyi voennyi arkhiv (Russian State Military Archive, RGVA)

   Fond 1323, Politseiskie i administrativnye organy Germanii i territorii vremenno okkupirovannykh ei (Police and Administrative Agencies in Germany and on the Temporarily Occupied Territories), 1936–1944
4. Rossiiskii obrazovatel'nyi i prosvetitel'nyi tsentr "Kholokost" (Russian Research and Educational Holocaust Centre, Moscow).

   Personal collections
5. Gosudarstvennyi arkhiv noveishei istorii Stavropol'skogo kraia (State Archive for Contemporary History of the Stavropol Territory, GANISK)
6. Akademiia Federal'noi Sluzhby Bezopasnosti Rossiskoi Federatsii (Academy of the Federal Security Service of the Russian Federation)
7. United States Holocaust Memorial Museum (USHMM)
8. Tsentr dokumentatsii noveishei istorii Rostovskoi oblasti (Center for Documenting Contemporary History of Rostov Territory, TsDNIRO)
9. Rossiiskii gosudarstvennyi arkhiv kino- i fotodokumentov (Russian State Archive of Cinema and Photo Documents, RGAKFD)
10. Derzhavnyi arkhiv avtonomnoi respubliki Krym (State Archive of the Autonomous Republic of the Crimea, DAARK)
11. Tsentral'nyi arkhiv Ministerstva Oborony Rossiiskoi Federatsii (Central Archive of the Ministry of Defense of Russian Federation, TsAMO RF)
12. Partiinyi arkhiv Rostovskoi oblasti (Party Archive of Rostov Territory, PARO)

NEWSPAPERS AND OTHER PERIODICAL SOURCES

Bol'shevik
Bol'shevistskaia pravda
Einikait
Ha-tsofe

Izvestiia
Molot
Ordzhonikidzevskaia pravda
Pravda
Sotsialisticheskaia Osetiia
Sovinformburo updates available at http://army.lv/ru
The New York Times,
The Washington Post
Vedomosti Verkhovnogo Soveta SSSR

BOOKS

Abramovich, Aron. *V reshaiushchei voine. Uchastie i rol' evreev SSSR v voine protiv natsizma* (Tel Aviv: n.p., 1981).

Alexopoulos, Golfo. *Stalin's outcasts: Aliens, citizens, and the Soviet state, 1926–1936*. Ithaca, NY: Cornell University Press, 2003.

Al'tman, Il'ia. *Zhertvy nenavisti: Kholokost v SSSR, 1941–1945 gg*. Moscow: Fond "Kovcheg": Kollektsiia "Sovershenno sekretno," 2002.

Angrick, Andrej. *Besatzungspolitik und Massenmord. Die Einsatzgruppen D in der südlichen Sowjetunion, 1941–1943*. Hamburg: Hamburger Edition, 2003.

Arad, Yitzhak. *The History of the Holocaust. The Soviet Union and the Annexed Territories* [Hebrew]. Jerusalem: Yad Vashem, 2004.

———. *In the Shadow of the Red Banner: Soviet Jews in the War against Nazi Germany*. Jerusalem: Yad Vashem, The International Institute for Holocaust Research; Gefen, 2010.

Aronson, Shlomo. *Hitler, the Allies, and the Jews*. Cambridge: Cambridge University Press, 2004.

Bemporad, Elissa. *Becoming Soviet Jews: The Bolshevik Experiment in Minsk*. Bloomington: Indiana University Press, 2013.

Berezhkov, Valentin. *Kak ia stal perevodchikom Stalina*. Moscow: DEM, 1993.

Berkhoff, Karel C. *Motherland in Danger: Soviet Propaganda during World War II*. Cambridge, MA: Harvard University Press, 2012.

Borovoi, Saul. *Vospominaniia*. Moscow, Jerusalem: Gesharim, 1993.

Brandenberger, David. *Propaganda State in Crisis: Soviet Ideology, Indoctrination and Terror under Stalin, 1927–1941*. New Haven, CT: Yale University Press, 2011.

Brooks, Jeffrey. *Thank you, Comrade Stalin! Soviet Public Culture from Revolution to Cold War*. Princeton, NJ: Princeton University Press, 2000.

"Byla voina": sbornik dokumentov i vospominanii o Rostove v period Velikoi Otechestvennoi voiny 1941–1945 godov. Edited by A. E. Videneeva et al. Rostov-on-Don: Gosudarstvennyi muzei-zapovednik "Rostovskii Kreml'," 2001.

Chernaia kniga o zlodeiskom povsemestnom ubiistve evreev nemetsko-fashistskimi zakhvatchikami vo vremenno-okkupirovannykh raionakh Sovetskogo Soiuza i v lageriakh unichtozheniia Pol'shi vo vremia voiny 1941–1945 gg. Edited by Vasilii Grossman and Il'ia Erenburg. Jerusalem: Tarbut, 1980.

Daigi Dashot, Avshalom. *Tiyul bi-shvil ḥayai* [*A Walk in the Ways of My Life*]. N.p., 2008.

Derzhavin, Nikolai. *Fashizm—zleishii vrag slavianstva*. Moscow: Akademiia nauk SSSR, 1942.
Distribution of the Jewish Population of the USSR 1939. Edited by Mordechai Altshuler. Jerusalem: Hebrew University, Center for the Research of East European Jewry, 1993.
Dokumenty obviniaiut. Sbornik materialov o chudovishchnykh zverstvakh Germanskikh vlastei na vremenno-okkupirovannykh Sovetskikh territoriyakh. Moscow: Gospolitizdat, 1st ed. 1943, 2nd ed. 1945.
Enstad Due, Johannes. *Soviet Russians under Nazi Occupation. Fragile Loyalties in World War II*. Cambridge: Cambridge University Press, 2018.
Evakuatsiia. Vospominaniia o detstve, opalennom ognem Katastrofy. SSSR, 1941–1945. Edited by Aleksandr Berman and Alla Nikitina. Jerusalem: Soiuz uchenykh-repatriantov, 2009.
Feferman, Kiril. *Soviet Jewish Stepchild: The Holocaust in the Soviet Mindset, 1941–1964*. Saarbrücken: VDM Verlag, 2009.
———. *The Holocaust in the Crimea and the North Caucasus*. Jerusalem: Yad Vashem, 2016.
Fischer, Ernst. *Die faschistische Rassentheorie*. Moskau: Vlg. für fremdsprachige Literatur, 1941.
Gel'fand, Vladimir. *Dnevnik 1941–1946*. Moscow: ROSSPEN, 2015.
Gershenson, Olga. *The Phantom Holocaust: Soviet Cinema and Jewish Catastrophe*. New Brunswick, NJ: Rutgers University Press, 2013.
Glantz, David M. *Kharkov 1942: Anatomy of a Military Disaster Through Soviet Eyes*. New York: Ian Allan Publishing, 2010.
Gontmakher, Mikhail. *Evrei na donskoi zemle. Istoriia, fakty, biografiia*. Rostov-on-Don: RostIzdat, 1999.
Goriaeva, Tat'iana. *Politicheskaia tsenzura v SSSR, 1917–1991 gg*. Moscow: ROSSPEN, 2009.
Grechko, Andrei. *Bitva za Kavkaz*. Moscow: Izdatel'stvo Ministerstva Oborony SSSR, 1971.
Griesse, Malte. *Communiquer, juger et agir sous Staline. La personne prise entre ses liens avec les proches et son rapport au système politico-idéologique*. Frankfurt a.M. [et al.]: Lang, 2011.
Harris, Steven E. *Communism on Tomorrow Street: Mass Housing and Everyday Life after Stalin*. Baltimore, MD: The Woodrow Wilson Center Press and the Johns Hopkins University Press, 2013.
Hellbeck, Jochen. *Revolution on My Mind: Writing a Diary under Stalin*. Cambridge, MA: Harvard University Press, 2006.
Herf, Jeffrey. *The Jewish Enemy: Nazi Propaganda during World War II and the Holocaust*. Cambridge, MA: The Belknap Press of Harvard University Press, 2006.
Hicks, Jeremy. *First Films of the Holocaust: Soviet Cinema and the Genocide of the Jews, 1938–1946*. Pittsburgh, PA: University of Pittsburgh Press, 2012.
Hoffmann, David L. *Cultivating the Masses: Modern State Practices and Soviet Socialism, 1914–1939*. Ithaca, NY: Cornell University Press, 2011.
Hoffmann, Joachim. *Kaukasien, 1942–1943: Das deutsche Heer und die Orientvölken der Sowjetunion*. Freiburg: Rombach Verlag, 1991.
Hürter, Johannes. *Hitlers Heerführer. Die deutschen Oberbefehlshaber im Krieg gegen die Sowjetunion 1941/42*, 2nd edition. Munich: R. Oldenbourg Verlag, 2007.
Iudin, I. *Sledy fashistskogo zver'ia na Kubani*. Moscow: Gospolitizdat 1943.
Iskhod gorskih evreev: razrushenie garmonii mirov. Edited by Svetlana Danilova. Nalchik: Poligrafservis IT, 2000.
Jansen, Marc. *A Show Trial under Lenin: The Trial of the Socialist Revolutionaries, Moscow, 1922*. The Hague: M. Nijhoff, 1982.
Kabuzan, Vladimir. *Naselenie Severnogo Kavkaza v 19–20 vekakh: etnostatisticheskoe issledovanie*. St. Petersburg: Izd-vo "Russko-Baltiiskii informatsionnyi tsentr BLITS," 1996.

Karol, K. S. *Solik: Life in the Soviet Union, 1939–1946*. Translated from the French by Eamonn McArdle. Wolfeboro, NH: Pluto Press, 1986.
Kenez, Peter. *Civil War in South Russia, 1919–1920. The Defeat of the Whites*. Berkeley: University of California, 1977.
Kratkaia Evreiskaia Entsiklopediia. Jerusalem: Hebrew University of Jerusalem, 1994.
Krut, Yaakov. *Povest' o podarennoi zhizni*. Petakh-Tikva: n.p., 2008.
Krylova, Anna. *Soviet Women in Combat: A History of Violence on the Eastern Front* Cambridge: Cambridge University Press, 2010.
Kuban' v gody Velikoi Otechestvennoi voiny, 1941–1945: Khronika sobytii. Edited by A. Beliaev and I. Bondar'. Krasnodar: Sovkuban', 2000.
Kuromiya, Hiroaki. *The Voices of the Dead: Stalin's Great Terror in the 1930s*. New Haven, CT: Yale University Press, 2007.
Laqueur, Walter. *Black Hundred: The Rise of The Extreme Right in Russia*. New York: Harper Collins Publishers, 1993.
Lenoe, Matthew. *Closer to the Masses: Stalinist Culture, Social Revolution, and Soviet Newspapers*. Cambridge, MA: Harvard University Press, 2004.
Manley, Rebecca. *To the Tashkent Station: Evacuation and Survival in the Soviet Union at War*. Ithaca, NY: Cornell University Press, 2009.
Movshovich, Evgenii. *Ocherki istorii evreev na Donu*. Rostov-on-Don: Donskoi izdatel'skii dom, 2006.
Mostashari, Firouzeh. *On the Religious Frontier: Tsarist Russia and Islam in the Caucasus*. London: Tauris, 2006.
Mozokhin, Oleg. *Statistika repressivnoi deiatel'nosti organov bezopasnosti SSSR na period s 1941 po 1943 gg*. http://www.fsb.ru/history/authors/mozohin.html. Accessed January 3, 2012.
Na zashchite Rodiny: Partiinaia organizatsiia Dona v Velikoi Otechestvennoi voine: 1941–1945 gg.: Sbornik dokumentov. Edited by V. M. Rezvanov et al. Rostov-on-Don: Rostovskoe knizhnoe izd-vo, 1980.
Osokina, Elena. *Our Daily Bread: Socialist Distribution and the Art of Survival in Stalin's Russia, 1927–1941*. Armonk, NY: M. E. Sharpe, 2001.
Parrish, Michael. *The Lesser Terror: Soviet State Security, 1939–1953*. Westport, CT: Praeger, 1996.
Pinchuk, Ben Tsion. *Yehudei brit ha-moetsot mul pnei ha-shoa, meḥkar bi-veayot haglayah u-finui* [Soviet Jews Face the Holocaust: A Research of Exile or Evacuation Issues]. Tel-Aviv: Ha-Agudah le-ḥeker toldot ha-yehudim, ha-Makhon le-ḥeker ha-tefutsot, 1979.
Plamper, Jan. *The Stalin Cult: A Study in the Alchemy of Power*. New Haven, CT: Yale University Press, 2012.
Poppe, Nicholas. *Reminiscences*. Bellingham: Western Washington, 1983.
Rees, E. A. *Iron Lazar: A Political Biography of Lazar Kaganovich*. London: Anthem Press: 2012.
Russian-Muslim Confrontation in the Caucasus: Alternative Visions of the Conflict between Imam Shamil and the Russians, 1830–1859. Edited by Thomas Sanders, Ernest Tucker, and Gary Hamburg. London: Routledge Curzon, 2004.
Seliunin, Vladimir. *Iug Rossii v voine 1941–1945 gg*. Rostov-on-Don: Izd-vo Rostovskogo universiteta, 1995.
Shearer, David R. *Policing Stalin's Socialism: Repression and Social Order in the Soviet Union, 1924–1953*. New Haven, CT: Yale University Press, 2009.

Shekhtman, Iosif. *Pogromy Dobrovol'cheskoi Armii na Ukraine: K istorii antisemitizma na Ukraine v 1919–1920 gg.* Berlin: Ostjüdisches Historisches Archiv, 1932.

Shneer, David. *Through Soviet Jewish Eyes: Photography, War, and the Holocaust.* New Brunswick, NJ: Rutgers University Press, 2011.

Shternshis, Anna. *Soviet and Kosher: Jewish Popular Culture in the Soviet Union, 1923–1939.* Bloomington: Indiana University Press, 2006.

Shvarts, Solomon. *Evrei v Sovetskom Soiuze s nachala Vtoroi Mirovoi voiny (1939–1965).* New York: American Jewish Working Committee, 1966.

Siegelbaum, Lewis, and Andrei Sokolov. *Stalinism as a Way of Life. A Narrative in Documents.* New Haven, CT: Yale University Press, 2000.

Skorokhodov, Anatolii. *Takoi dolgii, dolgii put'. Vospominaniia, razdum'ia, razmyshleniia.* Moscow: Izdatel'stvo Glavnogo arkhivnogo upravleniia goroda Moskvy, 2010.

Smirnov, Vladislav. *Rostov pod sen'iu svastiki.* Rostov-on-Don: ZAO "Kniga," 2006.

Sokhrani moi pis'ma. Sbornik pisem evreev Velikoi Otechestvennoi voiny. Edited by Il'ia Al'tman and Leonid Terushkin. Moscow: Tsentr i Fond "Kholokost," Izdatel'stvo "MIK," 2007, 2010, and 2013.

Soviet Government Statements on Nazi Atrocities. London: Hutchinson, 1946.

Stalin, Iosif. *O Velikoi Otechestvennoi Voine Sovetskogo Soyuza*, 5th edition. Moscow: Gosudarstvennoe izdatel'stvo politicheskoi literatury, 1950.

Statiev, Alexander. *At War's Summit: The Red Army and the Struggle for the Caucasus Mountains in World War II.* Cambridge: Cambridge University Press, 2018.

Stavropol'e: Pravda voennykh let. Velikaia Otechestenaia v dokumentakh i issledovaniiakh. Edited by V. Belokon', T. Kolpikova, Ia. Kol'tsova, V. Maznitsa. Stavropol: Stavropol State University, 2005.

Stavropol'e v period nemetsko-fashistskoi okkupatsii (avgust 1942–ianvar' 1943): Dokumenty i materialy Komiteta po delam arkhivov Stavropol'skogo kraia, Gosudarstvennogo arkhiva Stavropol'skogo kraia, Tsentra dokumentatsii noveishei istorii Stavropol'skogo kraia. Edited by Valeriia Vodolazskaia, Mariia Krivneva, and Nelli Mel'nik. Stavropol: Knizhnoe izdatel'stvo, 2000.

Stavropol'e v Velikoi Otechestvennoi voine 1941–1945 gg. Sbornik dokumentov i materialov. Stavropol: Knizhnoe izdatel'stvo, 1962.

Struve, Vasilii. *Fashistskii antisemitizm—perezhitok kannibalizma.* Moscow: Akademiia nauk SSSR, 1941.

Tanny, Jarrod. *City of Rogues and Schnorrers: Russia's Jews and the Myth of Old Odessa* Bloomington: Indiana University Press, 2011.

The Einsatzgruppen Reports: Selection from the Dispatches of the Nazis' Death Squads Campaign against the Jews (July 1941–January 1943). Edited by Yitzhak Arad, Shmuel Krakowski, and Shmuel Spektor. New York: Holocaust Library, 1989.

Tieke, Wilhelm. *Der Kaukasus und das Öl: Der deutsch-sowjetische Krieg in Kaukasien 1942/43.* Osnabrück: Munin, c.1970.

Urlanis, Boris. *Rozhdaemost'i prodolzhitel'nost' zhizni v SSSR.* Moscow: Gosstatizdat, 1963.

Vo imia pobedy: Evakuatsiia grazhdanskogo naseleniia v Zapadnuiu Sibir' v gody Velikoi Otechestvennoi voiny v dokumentakh i materialakh. Edited by L. Snegireva. Tomsk: Izdatel'stvo Tomskogo gosudarstvennogo pedagogicheskogo universiteta, 2005.

Vsesoiuznaia perepis' naseleniia 1939 goda. Osnovnye itogi. Moscow: Nauka, 1992.

Zhuravlev, Evgenii. *Kollaboratsionizm na iuge Rossii v gody Velikoi Otechestvennoi voiny (1941–1945 gg.).* Rostov-on-Don: Izd-vo Rostovskogo universiteta, 2006.

Zeltser, Arkadii. *Evrei sovetskoi provintsii: Vitebsk i mestechki, 1917–1941.* Moscow: ROSSPEN, 2006.

Zipperstein, Steven J. *The Jews of Odessa: A Cultural History*. Stanford, CA: Stanford University Press, 1985.

DISSERTATIONS AND THESES

Andrienko, Maksim. *Naselenie Stavropol'skogo kraya v gody Velikoi Otechestvennoi voiny: otsenka povedencheskikh motivov*. PhD dissertation. Pyatigorsk, Piatigorskii gosudarstvennyi lingivisticheskii universitet, 2005.

Bezugol'nyi, Aleksei. "Narody Kavkaza v Vooruzhennykh silakh SSSR v gody Velikoi Otechestvennoi voiny, 1941–1945 gg." PhD dissertation. Stavropol, Stavropol'skii gosudarstvennyi universitet, 2004.

Blumenfeld, Tatyana. *The Holocaust in the Southern Part of Russia*. PhD dissertation. Haifa, Haifa University, 2011.

Butsavage, Christopher J. *German Radio Propaganda in The Soviet Union: A War of Words*. MA thesis. College Park, University of Maryland, 2012.

Bulgakova, Natal'ia. *Sel'skoe naselenie Stavropol'ia vo vtoroi polovine 20-kh—nachale 30-kh godov 20 veka: Izmeneniia v demograficheskom, khoziaistvennom i kul'turnom oblike*. PhD dissertation. Stavropol, Stavropol'skii gosudarstvennyi universitet, 2003.

Fedotov, Viktor. *Evakuirovannoe naselenie v Srednem Povolzh'e v gody Velikoi Otechestvennoi voiny (1941–1945 gg.): Problemy razmeshcheniia, sotsial'noi adaptatsii i trudovoi deiatel'nosti*. PhD dissertation. Samara, Samarskii gosudarstvennyi pedagogicheskii universitet, 2004.

Garazha, Natal'ia. *Deiatel'nost' organov vlasti po mobilizatsii rabochego klassa na pobedu v gody Velikoi Otechestvennoi voiny 1941–1945 gg.: Na materialakh Krasnodarskogo kraia*. PhD dissertation. Maikop, Adygeiskii gosudarstvennyi universitet, 2005.

Israpov, Aleksandr. *Gosudarstvennye organy upravleniia i narod v 1941–1945 gg.: Aspekty politicheskogo, ekonomicheskogo i organizatsionno-pravovogo vzaimodeistviia na materialakh avtonomnykh respublik Severnogo Kavkaza*. PhD dissertation. Makhachkala, Dagestanskii nauchnyi tsentr Rossiiskoi Akademii nauk, 2004.

Iurchuk, Ilona. *Politika mestnykh vlastei Kubani po zashchite detstva i ee prakticheskaia realizatsiia v gody Velikoi Otechestvennoi voiny (1941–1945 gg.)*. PhD dissertation. Armavir, Armavirskii institut sotsial'nogo obrazovaniia, 2008.

Iur'ev, Vasilii. *Evakuatsiia, osushchestvlennaia sovetskim narodom v period Velikoi Otechestvennoi voiny (internatsional'nyi aspekt problemy)*. PhD dissertation. Moscow, Rossiiskaia ekonomicheskaia akademiia imeni Plekhanova, 1995.

Kameneva, Galina. "Zhenshchiny Severnogo Kavkaza v gody Velikoi Otechestvennoi voiny, 1941–1945 gg." PhD dissertation, Stavopol, Stavropol'skii gosudarstvennyi universitet, 2004.

Khachemizova, Elena. *Obshstvo i vlast' v 30-e–40-e gody XX veka—politika repressii (na materialakh Krasnodarskogo kraia)*. PhD dissertation. Maikop, Adygeiiskii gosudarstvennyi universitet, 2004.

Kiselev, Fedor. *Gosudarstvennaia politika po otnosheniiu k evakuirovannomu naseleniiu v gody Velikoi Otechestvennoi voiny. Na materialakh Kirovskoi oblasti i Udmurtskoi ASSR*. PhD dissertation. Kirov, Viatkskii gosudarstvennyi tekhnicheskii universitet, 2004.

Klimova, Natal'ia. "Trudovoi i ratnyi podvig molodezhi Stavropol'ia v gody Velikoi Otechestvennoi voiny, 1941–1945 gg." PhD dissertation. Piatigorsk, Piatigorskii lingivisticheskii universitet, 2005.

Nikulina, Elena. *Istrebitel'nye batal'ony Stavropol'ia i Kubani v gody Velikoi Otechestvennoi voiny: 1941–1945 gg.* PhD dissertation. Piatigorsk, Piatigorskskii gosudarstvennyi lingvisticheskii universitet, 2005.

Malyshev, Aleksandr. *Sredstva massovoi informatsii Iuga Rossii v gody Velikoi Otechestvennoi voiny: Na materialakh Dona, Kubani, Stavropol'ia.* PhD dissertation. Rostov-on-Don, Rossiiskii gosudarstvennyi universitet stroitel'stva, 2001.

Petrenko, Tat'iana. *Evakuatsionnyi protsess na Stavropol'e letom 1942 goda: uspekhi i trudnosti.* PhD dissertation. Pyatigorsk, Piatigorskii gosudarstvennyi tekhnologicheskii universitet, 2004.

Savochkin, Aleksandr. *Massovye repressii 30–40-kh gg. 20 v. na Severnom Kavkaze kak sposob utverzhdeniia i podderzhaniia iskliuchitel'noi samostoiatel'nosti gosudarstva.* PhD dissertation. Vladimir, Vladimirskii iuridicheskii institut Federal'noi sluzhby ispolneniia nakazanii, 2008.

Somova, Inna. *Kul'turnye i religioznye uchrezhdeniia Stavropol'skogo kraia v period Velikoi Otechestvennoi voiny.* PhD dissertation. Pyatigorsk, Pyatigorskii gosudarstvennyi lingivisticheskii universitet, 2004.

Shykhamirova, Patimat. *Kavkaz v politike fashistskoi Germanii v gody Velikoi Otechestvennoi voiny v otechestvennoi i zarubezhnoi istoriografii.* PhD dissertation. Makhachkala, Dagestanskii gosudarstvennyi universitet, 2006.

Tabunshchikova, Liudmila. *Donskie antisovetskie kazach'i struktury i Germaniia v 1918 i 1941–1945 gg.* PhD dissertation. Rostov-on-Don, Rostovskii gosudarstvennyi universitet, 2003.

Voitenko, Elena. *Kholokost na iuge Rossii v period Velikoi Otechestvennoi Voiny (1941–1943 gg.).* PhD dissertation. Stavropol, Stavropol'skii gosudarstvennyi universitet, 2005.

Zelenskaia, Tat'iana. *Kul'turno-prosvetitel'nye uchrezhdeniia Dona i Kubani v period Velikoi Otechestvennoi voiny 1941–1945 gg.* PhD dissertation. Rostov-on-Don, Rostovskii gosudarstvennyi universitet, 2005.

ARTICLES

Altshuler, Mordechai. "Escape and Evacuation of Soviet Jews at the Time of the Nazi Invasion: Policies and Realities." In *The Holocaust in the Soviet Union. Studies and Sources on the Destruction of the Jews in the Nazi-Occupied Territories of the USSR, 1941–1945*, edited by L. Dobroszycki and J. Gurock, 77–104. Armonk, NY: M. E. Sharpe, 1993.

———. "The Distress of Jews in the Soviet Union in the Wake of the Molotov-Ribbentrop Pact." *Yad Vashem Studies* 36, no. 2 (2008): 73–114.

———. "The Holocaust in the Soviet Mass Media during the War and in the First Postwar Years Reexamined." *Yad Vashem Studies* 39, no. 2 (2011): 121–168.

Ascher, Abraham. "The Mensheviks in the Russian Revolution." *Zmanim: A Historical Quarterly* 27/28 (1988): 38–53 [Hebrew].

Belonosov, I. I. "Evakuatsiia naseleniia iz prifrontovoi polosy v 1941–1942 gg." In *Eshelony idut na Vostok. Iz istorii perebazirovaniia proizvoditel'nykh sil SSSR v 1941–1942 gg. Sbornik statei i vospominanii*, edited by Iu. A. Poliakov, 15–30. Moscow: Nauka, 1966.

Berkhoff, Karel C. "'Total Annihilation of the Jewish Population': The Holocaust in the Soviet Media, 1941–1945." *Kritika: Explorations in Russian and Eurasian History* 10, no. 1 (Winter 2009): 61–105.

Bidlack, Richard. "The political mood in Leningrad during the first year of the Soviet-German war." *Russian Review* 59, no. 1 (2000): 101–102.

Blauvelt, Timothy K. "Military-Civil Administration and Islam in the North Caucasus, 1858–1883." *Kritika: Explorations in Russian and Eurasian History* 11, no. 2 (Spring 2010): 221–255.

Boeck, Brian J. "Complicating the National Interpretation of the Famine: Reexamining the Case of Kuban." *Harvard Ukrainian Studies* 30, no. 1/4 (2008): 31–48.

Budnitskii, Oleg. "Evrei Rostova-na-Donu na perelome epokh (1917–1920)." In *Rossiiskii sionizm: istoriia i kul'tura*. Moscow: Evreiskoe agentstvo v Rossii, SEFER, Dom evreiskoi knigi, 2002.

———. (as Budnitski, Oleg.) "The Jews in Rostov-on-Don in 1918–1919." *Jews and Jewish Topics in the Soviet Union and Eastern Europe* 3, no. 19 (1992): 16–29.

Budnitski, Oleg, and Jason Morton. "The Great Patriotic War and Soviet Society: Defeatism, 1941–1942." *Kritika: Explorations in Russian and Eurasian History* 15, no. 4 (Fall 2014): 767–797.

Clark, Katerina. "Ehrenburg and Grossman: Two Cosmopolitan Jewish Writers Reflect on Nazi Germany at War." *Kritika: Explorations in Russian and Eurasian History* 10, no. 3 (Summer 2009): 607–628.

Dornik, Wolfram, and Peter Lieb. "Misconceived Realpolitik in a Failing State: The Political and Economical Fiasco of the Central Powers in the Ukraine, 1918." *First World War Studies* 4, no. 1 (2013): 111–124.

Dubrovskaia, N. G. "Finansovaia sistema Rostovskoi oblasti v gody voiny." In *Istoricheskie i sotsial'no-ekonomicheskie problemy Iuga Rossii. Materialy IV mezhvuzovskoi nauchno-prakticheskoi konferentsii (23 dekabria 2006 g., g. Azov)*, edited by V. Naukhatskii, 38–43. Rostov-on-Don: Rostovskii Ekonomicheskii universitet, 2007.

Dubson, Vadim. "On the Problem of the Evacuation of Soviet Jews in 1941 (New Archival Sources)." *Jews in Eastern Europe* 3, no. 40 (1999): 37–56.

Fedoseev, A. "K voprosu o provedenii evakuatsionnykh meropriiatii na territorii Krasnodarskogo kraya v 1942 g." In *Vtoraia mirovaia i Velikaia otechestvennaia voina: aktual'nye problemy sotsial'noi istorii*, 167–175. Maikop: Adygeiskii gosudarstvennyi universitet, 2008.

Feferman, Kiril. "Soviet Investigation of Nazi Crimes in the USSR: Documenting the Holocaust." *Journal of Genocide Research* 5, no. 4 (2003): 587–602.

———. "Jewish Refugees under the Soviet Rule and the German Occupation in the North Caucasus." In *Revolution, Repression and Revival: The Jews of the Former Soviet Union*, edited by Z. Gitelman and Y. Ro'i, 211–244. Lanham, MD.: Rowman and Littlefield, 2007.

———. "Food Factor as a Possible Catalyst for the Holocaust-Related Decisions: The Crimea and North Caucasus." *War in History* 15, no. 1 (2008): 85–87.

———. "A Soviet Humanitarian Action?: Centre, Periphery and the Evacuation of Refugees to the North Caucasus, 1941–1942." *Europe-Asia Studies* 61, no. 5 (2009): 813–831.

———. "'The Jews' War': Attitudes of Soviet Jewish soldiers and officers towards the USSR in 1940–1941." *The Journal of Slavic Military Studies* 27, no. 4 (2014): 574–590.

———. "To Flee or Not to Flee: The Conflicting Messages of Soviet Wartime Propaganda and the Holocaust, 1941." *Cahiers du monde russe* 56, nos. 2–3 (April–September 2015): 526–527.

Feingold, Henry L. "Bombing Auschwitz and the politics of the Jewish question during World War II." In *The Bombing of Auschwitz: Should the Allies Have Attempted It*, editrd by Michael J. Neufield and Michael Berenbaum, 193–203. Lawrence, KS: University Press of Kansas, 2000.

Gatagova, Liudmila. "Caucasian Phobias and the Rise of Antisemitism in the North Caucasus in the 1920s." *The Soviet and Post-Soviet Review* 36 (2009): 42–57.

Glantz, David M. "The Khar'kov Operation, 12–27 May 1942." *The Journal of Soviet Military Studies* 5, no. 3 (1992): 494–510.

———. "The Struggle for the Caucasus." *The Journal of Slavic Military Studies* 22, no. 4 (2009): 588–711.

———. "The Red Army's Donbas Offensive (February–March 1942) Revisited: A Documentary Essay." The Journal of Slavic Military Studies 18, no. 3 (2005): 369–503.

Goluboff, Sasha S. "'Are They Jews or Asians?' A Cautionary Tale about Mountain Jewish Ethnography." *Slavic Review* 63, no. 1 (2004): 113–140.

Govrin, Yosef. "Ilya Ehrenburg and the Ribbentrop-Molotov agreement." *The Israel Journal of Foreign Affairs* 7, no. 2 (2013): 103–108.

Graziosi, Andrea, and Dominique Négrel. "'Lettres de Kharkov': La famine en Ukraine et dans le Caucase du Nord à travers les rapports des diplomates italiens, 1932–1934." *Cahiers du monde russe et soviétique* 30, nos. 1–2 (Janvier–Juin 1989): 5–106.

Gregor, Neil. "A Schicksalsgemeinschaft? Allied Bombing, Civilian Morale, and Social Dissolution in Nuremberg, 1942–1945." *The Historical Journal* 43, no. 4 (December 2000): 1051–1070.

Guri, Yosef. "Jewish Fighters in the Red Army." *Dispersion and Unity* 5–6 (1966): 172–177.

Gurkin, V., and Kruglov, A. "Oborona Kavkaza: 1942 god." *Voenno-istoricheskii zhurnal* 10 (1992): 11–18.

Hayward, Joel. "Hitler's Quest for Oil: The Impact of Economic Considerations on Military Strategy, 1941–1942." *Journal of Strategic Studies* 18, no. 4 (1995): 94–135.

———. "Too Little, Too Late: An Analysis of Hitler's Failure in August 1942 to Damage Soviet Oil Production." *Journal of Military History* 64, no. 3 (2000): 769–794.

Hirszowicz, Lukasz. "The Holocaust in the Soviet Mirror." *East European Jewish Affairs* 22, no. 1 (1992): 39–50.

Holquist, Peter. "'Information Is the Alpha and Omega of Our Work': Bolshevik Surveillance in Its Pan-European Context." *Journal of Modern History* 69, no. 3 (1997): 415–450.

Hosking, Geoffrey. "Trust and Distrust in the USSR: An Overview." *The Slavonic and East European Review* 91, no. 1 (January 2013): 5–17.

Humphrey, Caroline. "Odessa: Pogrom in a Cosmopolitan City." *Ab Imperio* 4 (2010): 27–79.

Ironside, Kristy. "Rubles for Victory: The Social Dynamics of State Fundraising on the Soviet Home Front." *Kritika: Explorations in Russian and Eurasian History* 15, no. 4 (Fall 2014): 799–828.

Izmozik, Vladlen S. "Voices from the Twenties: Private Correspondence Intercepted by the OGPU." *Russian Review* 55, no. 2 (1996): 287–308.

Kaganovich, Albert. "Evreiskie bezhentsy v Kazakhstane vo vremia Vtoroi Mirovoi voiny," in *Istoriia, pamiat', liudi. Materialy V mezhdunarodnoi konferentsii*, edited by Alexander Baron, 13–31. Almaty: Assotsiatsiia "Mitsva," 2011.

———. "Jewish Refugees and Soviet Authorities during World War II." *Yad Vashem Studies* 38, no. 2 (2010): 1–37.

Khlynina, Tatyana P. "Zhilishchnyi vopros i praktiki ego razresheniia v gody Velikoi Otechestvennoi voiny." *Nauchnyi dialog* 5, no. 29 (2014): 17–38.

Kindler, Robert. "Famines and Political Communication in Stalinism. Possibilities and Limits of the Sayable." *Jahrbücher für Geschichte Osteuropas* 62, no. 2 (2014): 255–272.

Klier, John (as Dzhon Klir). "'Kazaki i pogromy': Chem otlichalis' voennye pogrom." In *Mirovoi krizis 1914–1920 gg. i sud'ba vostochnoevropeiskogo evreistva*, edited by Oleg Budnitskii, 47–70. Moscow: ROSPEN, 2005.

Klink, Ernst. "The Conduct of Operations." In *Germany and the Second World War*, vol. 4: *The Attack on the Soviet Union*, edited by Horst Boog, Jürgen Förster, Joachim Hoffman, Ernst Klink, Rolf-Dieter Müller, and Gerd R. Überschär, 525–762. Oxford: Oxford University Press, 1998.

Koss, Andrew N. "War Within, War Without: Russian Refugee Rabbis during World War I." *AJS Review* 34, no. 2 (2010): 231–263.

Kragh, Martin. "Soviet Labour Law During the Second World War." *War in History* 18, no. 4 (2011): 531–546.

Kurtsev, Aleksandr. "Bezhenstvo." In *Rossiia i pervaia mirovaia voina*, edited by N. N. Smirnov, 129–147. St. Petersburg: Dmitrii Bulanin, 1999.

Kumanev, Georgii A. "Evakuatsiia naseleniia SSSR: dostignutye rezul'taty i poteri." In *Liudskie poteri SSSR v period Vtoroi Mirovoi Voiny*, 137–146. St. Petersburg: Izdatel'stvo "Russko-baltiiskii Informatsionnyi Tsentr 'Blits,'" 1995.

Levin, Dov. "Unique characteristics of Soviet Jewish soldiers in the Second World War." In *The Shoah and the War*, edited by Asher Cohen, Yehoyakim Cochavi, and Yoav Gelber, 233–244. New York: Peter Lang, 1992.

Levin, Zeev. "Antisemitism and the Jewish Refugees in Soviet Kirgizia, 1942." *Jews in Russia and Eastern Europe* 1 (2003): 191–203.

Maclean, Pam. "Control and Cleanliness: German-Jewish Relations in Occupied Eastern Europe during the First World War." *War & Society* 6, no. 2 (1988): 47–69.

Markedonov, Sergei. "Evrei v oblasti voiska Donskogo v kontse 19–nachale 20 veka." In *Trudy Vtoroi molodezhnoi konferentsii SNG po iudaike—"Tirosh."* Moscow: Sefer, 1998. http://www.jewish-heritage.org/jr2a18r.htm. Accessed November 30, 2011.

Movshovich, Evgenii. "11 avgusta—60 let tragedii v Zmievskoi balke," *Shma* (Rostov-na-Donu) 7, no. 36 (May 15—July 24, 2002): 3–4.

———. "Rostov-na-Donu." In *Entsiklopediia Kholokosta na territorii SSSR*, edited by Il'ia Al'tman, 2nd edition, 866–870. Moscow: ROSSPEN, 2011.

Nachtigal, Reinhard. "Krasnyj Desant: Das Gefecht an der Mius-Bucht. Ein unbeachtetes Kapitel der deutschen Besetzung Südrußlands 1918." *Jahrbücher für Geschichte Osteuropas* 53, no. 2 (2005): 221–246.

Nevzorov, B. I. "Sokrushenie blitskriga." In *Velikaia Otechestvennaia voina 1941–1945 gg.*, vol. 1, edited by N. M. Ramanichev, 248–284. Moscow: Nauka, 1998.

———. "Zimnee nastuplenie Krasnoi Armii," In *Velikaia Otechestvennaia voina 1941–1945 gg.*, vol. 1, edited by N. M. Ramanichev, 285–318. Moscow: Nauka, 1998.

Norkina, Ekaterina. "The Origins of Anti-Jewish Policy in the Cossack Regions of the Russian Empire, Late Nineteenth and Early Twentieth Century." *East European Jewish Affairs* 43, no. 1 (2013): 62–76.

Orbach, Danny, and Mark Solonin. "Calculated Indifference: The Soviet Union and Requests to Bomb Auschwitz." *Holocaust and Genocide Studies* 27, no. 1 (Spring 2013): 90–113.

Peris, Daniel. "'God is Now on Our Side': The Religious Revival in Unoccupied Soviet Territory during World War II." *Kritika: Explorations in Russian and Eurasian History* 1, no. 1 (Winter 2000): 97–118.

Piankevich, Vladimir L. "The Family under Siege: Leningrad, 1941–1944." *The Russian Review* 75 (2016): 107–137.

Potemkina, Mariia. "Evakuatsiia i natsyional'nye otnosheniia v sovetskom tylu v gody Velikoi Otechestvennoi Voiny." *Otechestvennaya istoriya* 3 (2002): 148–156.

———. "Evakonaselenie v ural'skom tylu. Opyt vyzhivaniia." *Otechestvennaia istoriia* 2 (2005): 93–94.

Rees, E. "The Changing Nature of Centre–Local Relations in the USSR, 1928–1936." In *Centre–Local Relations in the Stalinist State 1928–1941*, edited by E. Rees, 9–36. New York: Palgrave, 2002.

Reid, Susan E. "The meaning of home: 'The only bit of the world you can have to yourself.'" In *Borders of Socialism: Private spheres of Soviet Russia*, edited by Lewis H. Siegelbaum, 145–170. New York: Palgrave Macmillan, 2006.

Shalit, Shulamit. "Mne rekomendovali vziat' psevdonim. (Mark Kopshytser, 1923–1982)." http://berkovich-zametki.com/2005/Starina/Nomer9/Shalit1.htm. Accessed March 12, 2016.

Shpakovskaia, S. V. "Sovetskie gazety v gody Velikoi Otechestvennoi voiny." *Voprosy istorii* 5 (2014): 64–74.

Shternshis, Anna. "Between Life and Death: Why Some Soviet Jews Decided to Leave and Others to Stay in 1941." *Kritika: Explorations in Russian and Eurasian History* 15, no. 3 (Summer 2014): 477–504.

Shveibish, Semion. "Evakuatsiia i sovetskie evrei v gody Katastrofy." *Vestnik Evreiskogo Universiteta v Moskve* 9 (1995): 36–55.

Siegelbaum, Lewis H. "'Dear Comrade, you ask what we need,' Socialist paternalism and Soviet rural 'notables' in the mid-1930s." In *Stalinism: New directions*, edited by Sheila Fitzpatrick, 231–256. London: Routledge, 2000.

Skolnik, Jonathan. "Class War, Anti-Fascism, and Anti-Semitism: Grigori Roshal's 1939 Film *Sem'ia Oppengeim* in Context." In *Feuchtwanger and Film*, edited by Ian Wallace, 237–243 New York: Peter Lang, 2009.

Sokolov, Boris V. "Estimating Soviet War Losses on the Basis of Soviet Population Censuses." *The Journal of Slavic Military Studies* 27, no. 3 (2014): 467–492.

Sorokina, Marina. "People and Procedures. Toward a History of the Investigation of Nazi Crimes in the USSR." *Kritika: Explorations in Russian and Eurasian History* 6, no. 4 (2005): 797–831.

Statiev, Alexander. "Motivations and Goals of Soviet Deportations in the Western Borderlands." *Journal of Strategic Studies* 28, no. 6 (2005): 977–983.

Stone, David R. "The First Five-Year Plan and the Geography of the Soviet Defense Industry." *Europe-Asia Studies* 57, no. 7 (2005): 1047–1063

Voronina, Tat'iana. "Kak chitat' pis'ma s fronta? Lichnaia korrespondentsiia i pamiat' o Vtoroi mirovoi voine." *Neprikosnovennyi zapas* 3 (2011): 159–175.

Wegner, Bernd "The War Against the Soviet Union, 1942–1943." In *Germany and the Second World War*, vol. 6: *The Global War: Widening the Conflict into a World War and the Shift of the Initiative 1941–1943*, edited by Werner Rahn, Reinhard Stumpf, Bernd Wegner, John Brownjohn, Patricia Crampton, Louise Willmot, and Horst Boog, 1022–1177. Oxford: Clarendon Press, 2001.

Winkler, Christina. "Rostov-on-Don 1942: A Little-Known Chapter of the Holocaust." *Holocaust and Genocide Studies* 30, 1 (2016): 105–130.

Zeltser, Arkadi. "How the Jewish Intelligentsia Created the Jewishness of the Jewish Hero." In *Soviet Jews in World War II: Fighting, Witnessing, Remembering*, edited by Harriet Murav and Gennady Estraikh, 104–129. Boston, MA: Academic Studies Press, 2014.

Index

Alexander II, 5
Alma-Ata, 12–13, 89n114, 104–107, 111, 135, 137–138, 142, 148, 150–151, 156, 158–160, 165, 167, 169, 171, 178, 180, 187–188, 191, 195, 209, 211, 214, 218, 222, 231, 233, 242, 245, 259n209, 261n213, 266–273
Alperin, A., 7
Anti-Semitism, xx, 6–8, 29–31, 63, 122n192
Anton Ivanovich is Angry, 156
apartment, 45, 46n29, 48–49, 104, 122, 127, 148, 154, 168, 177, 179, 184–188, 191, 193, 204, 242
Army Group Center (*also Heeresegruppe Süd*), 65, 75, 242–243
Army Group South, 65
Ashkenazi Jews, 4, 38
atrocities, 120–121, 124, 128, 131, 133, 134, 137–138, 141, 143, 148, 151, 158, 160, 165, 206, 231, 249
Auschwitz, 234

Babi Yar, 131
Baku, 60, 112, 173, 245
Baltimore Sun, The, 127
Ban, 5, 11n48, 34, 62, 73n60, 76, 78, 83, 146, 183, 264
Batum, 245
Belorussia, 31n34, 33, 75, 138
Big Terror, 11–12

Black Hundreds, 6, 122
Black Sea, 3
Bolshevik Party (*also* VKP(b)), 18, 25, 30, 32–34, 36, 54n91, 93n127, 99, 101, 109–110, 133, 194, 199, 215, 233–234, 239
    Central Committee, 25, 62n20, 67, 116, 194, 203n88, 264n1
    Rostov District Committee, 61, 65, 67, 97, 129–130, 149, 185, 264
Bolshevik (newspaper), 36
Bolshevik, xxiin16, 6–11, 62, 70, 114, 128, 152
bombardment, xiii, xx, xxii, 41, 66, 74, 76, 79, 81–82, 89, 98–99, 106, 112, 137, 148, 182, 241, 244, 246
bourgeois, 4
Budennovsk, xiii, 18, 20–21, 104–109, 111–113, 115–116, 120, 132n218, 135–142, 145, 147, 149n253, 154, 181, 237, 242, 266, 268

Caspian Sea, 60, 112
Caucasus, *passim*
Central Asia, xv, 85, 105–106, 112–113, 120, 148, 211–212, 253, 265
Chechnya, 39, 255
Cherkessk, 42–49
children, xiii, xxiii, 3, 12–13, 16, 20, 25, 28, 35, 39, 45–46, 66, 73–74, 76, 80–81, 86, 88, 95–97, 104, 106, 110–113, 120, 125, 128, 135, 145,

148–149, 151, 154, 159–160, 163, 177, 180, 182, 184, 187, 197, 204, 249, 252
Civil War (Russian), 4, 6–7, 9, 11, 92, 137
collaborators, 9, 47, 52–53, 120, 126–129, 134, 144, 149, 256
Collectivization, 8
commission (military or medical), 209, 211, 216
Commission for Evacuation (*Komissiya po evakuatsii*), 26
community, 6, 42, 47, 231
conscription (*also* draft; enrollment), xvi, 30, 60–61, 67, 70, 80, 86, 89, 117, 171, 191, 193, 195–197, 199, 201, 210–217, 237
correspondence, xiii, xv–xvi, xxi, xxiii–xxiv, 9, 11–14, 16, 18, 20, 57, 68–69, 72–73, 80–81, 85, 96, 102, 108, 137, 155, 172, 174, 181, 212, 219, 221, 259, 263, 266–273
Cossack, 4–5, 7–9, 28n22, 33, 35
Cossackdom, 5
council (*sovet*), xiii, 5, 19n60, 24–28, 31, 36n60, 42–43, 45, 47, 49, 54n94, 60n14, 68, 97, 99, 105–106, 112, 118, 251n189, 255
Council for Evacuation, xiii, 25–28, 31, 105–106
Council of the People's Commissars (*also Sovet Narodnykh Komissarov*, SNK), 25–26, 28n22, 32n39, 34n49, 142, 171n34, 185n61, 243n166
counter-offensive, xiii, 120, 133, 157, 208, 228, 240
Crimea, xiii–xiv, 34, 75, 103, 108, 110, 157–158, 225–227, 231–232, 236, 244–245
Croatia, 59
curfew, 61, 100

Dagoe Island, 103
Daily Mail, 124
district, xiii–xiv, 5, 8, 14–18, 20–22, 28, 32, 36, 38, 61–62, 65–69, 80, 88, 97, 102, 105–106, 126, 129–130, 142–143, 147–149, 151, 152, 171, 183, 185, 190–191, 208, 231, 241, 243, 246, 248, 250–253, 255, 264
Donets Basin, 75, 93, 103, 108, 177
draft, *see* conscription
Dvinsky, Boris, 69n48, 99, 149, 157, 264

Einsatzgruppe(-n), 50, 52, 88, 106, 144, 255
Empire, 3–6, 8, 114
employment, employed, xvii–xix, xxii, 11n48, 14–15, 18–19, 25n7, 27, 31n34, 35, 40, 48, 51, 100, 116, 130, 135–136, 139, 148, 154, 160, 173–174, 185, 189, 191, 193, 199, 201–202, 211, 218, 246–247, 250–251, 257
encirclement, 91, 119, 223
enrollment, *see* conscription
Erenburg, Ilya, 101
escape, xviin4, xix, xxi–xxiii, 25, 28, 31, 40–41, 66, 71, 84, 89, 91, 105–106, 108–109, 111, 113, 115, 133, 139, 145, 150–152, 154–155, 163, 172, 182–183, 198, 208, 219, 243, 246–249, 251, 264
Essentuki, 29, 34–35, 42–50, 136, 139–140, 145, 148, 154
Estonia, 31n34
evacuation permit (*also* evacuation authorization), 40, 104–105, 109, 112, 115, 132, 139, 145, 147–149, 161, 175, 178, 180–181, 183, 193, 199, 244, 247, 261
evacuation, xiii–xxiii, xxv, 12–13, 17–21, 23–41, 71–72, 80, 85–88, 90,

92–97, 99–100, 103–110, 113–116, 120, 123, 132–133, 135–140, 142, 144–149, 151, 155, 158–161, 163–166, 169, 171n34, 175–186, 188, 190–194, 197, 199, 202, 204, 216, 219, 221–222, 233–234, 241, 243–244, 246–248, 251–252, 261, 265
evacuee, xvii–xxiii, 21, 25–35, 37, 39–40, 47, 53, 72, 80, 86–88, 92, 99–100, 106, 108, 112, 111–116, 137–138, 140, 142, 149, 153, 155, 158, 162, 166–169, 171–174, 177, 179, 183–185, 187–188, 190–191, 193–194, 198, 201–202, 204, 222, 232, 237–238, 243, 251, 263, 265
Extermination Battalions, xiii–xiv, 18–19, 61–62, 72, 113, 116–117, 181, 191, 212, 235, 247
Extraordinary State Commission (*also* ESC), 35n57, 43, 45, 51, 121

Fascism, 32, 70–71, 74, 86, 92, 98–99, 120, 122, 125–128, 134, 138, 141, 143, 151, 153, 163, 165, 167, 170, 173, 181, 192, 199, 206, 208–209, 231, 252–253, 259
fuel, 28, 32, 113, 139, 148, 153–160, 187–190
Feuchtwanger, Lion
  The Oppermanns, 63
"Final Solution," 67, 76–77
Finland, 59
flight, xvii, xx, xxii, 39, 41, 94, 105, 134, 148, 186, 204, 237, 240–242, 252
food, xix, xxiii, 7, 11n48, 15, 27–29, 32, 40, 47, 49, 52, 80, 100, 116, 135–136, 145, 147, 151, 155, 160, 167–168, 172, 174, 182–184, 187–193, 201–202, 206, 210–211, 221–222, 231, 241, 247, 251, 253

fortress, 5, 98, 101, 194
Frog Soldiers, 71

Gel'fand, Vladimir, 29
generation, xvi, 3, 6, 13, 17, 20, 63, 95, 104–105, 107, 114, 155, 182, 221, 224, 231, 264
ghetto, 42–44, 47, 63–64, 167
Ginsburg family
  Chazkewitzs
    Elizaveta (Liza), xxvi, 3, 12–13, 15–18, 57–58, 66–67, 71–74, 77, 80–81, 83, 85–86, 89–91, 93–97, 103–119, 123, 125, 131–133, 135–148, 150, 153, 156–162, 164–167, 171–183, 186–190, 195–200, 204–209, 213–215, 217–221, 225, 229–233, 238–242, 245–251, 256, 259, 261, 266–273
    Boris, 15–16, 57n3, 74, 81, 86, 89–90, 93, 99, 266
    Efim, xv–xvi, xxvi, 3, 9–15, 18, 57–59, 66–68, 70–74, 77, 80–81, 83, 85–87, 89–91, 93–96, 106–108, 111, 113–115, 120, 123, 131, 135–139, 141–143, 145, 148–151, 153, 156, 158–161, 164–166, 168, 170–175, 177–179, 186–187, 190, 194–195, 197–200, 204, 206, 210–211, 213–216, 218, 221–224, 226, 229, 231–233, 235–236, 238–240, 242, 245, 248, 259, 261, 265, 266–273
Gedaliya, 3, 9, 14–15
Greeners
  Avraham, 14, 20

Anna (Anya), xxvi, 3, 12–18, 20, 57–58, 73, 80, 90, 97, 105–109, 111, 114–115, 119, 125, 131–133, 135–144, 146–147, 150, 153, 156–157, 159–162, 164–167, 172–183, 186–187, 189–190, 197–198, 200, 204–207, 209, 213, 215, 219–221, 225, 229, 231, 233, 238, 242, 246–247, 251, 259, 261

Hanna-Rachel, 3, 14

Ida (née Dektor), 13

Manya (Monya), 3, 13–14, 17, 21, 66, 74, 104, 106, 111, 145, 160, 173, 197–198, 209, 227, 232, 242, 256

Meerovichs

Grigory (Grisha), 14, 17–18, 21–22, 58, 66, 80, 86, 195, 209–210, 223, 232, 256

Tamara, xiii–xiv, 14, 17–18, 21, 57–59, 66, 83, 104, 106, 111, 113–117, 119–120, 123, 132n218, 135–139, 141–142, 145, 148, 153, 158–162, 164–174, 177–178, 180–182, 184–187, 189, 191–196, 198, 201–203, 206–211, 213–217, 219, 221–224, 226–227, 229–230, 232, 235–236–237, 241, 245–251, 256, 259, 266, 268–272

Vladimir (Volodya), xiii–xiv, xvi, 12, 17–19, 72, 95–96, 104, 109, 112–113, 115–117, 130, 135, 138, 141, 148, 159–161, 164–165, 170–171, 175, 177, 179–184, 186–189, 191–193, 195, 197–199, 201, 206, 210–214, 216–219, 221, 223–227, 230, 232, 236, 247, 259–261, 270, 273

Pinchas (Pinya), 14, 17

Pinchos

Anna (Anya or Anechka), 19–21, 66, 80, 86, 107, 180, 201, 204–205, 211, 214, 223–224

David (Dod or Doda), xiii–xiv, 14, 19–20, 81, 85–86, 89, 93, 104, 117, 136, 148, 169–170, 180, 186–187, 195, 200–201, 204–205, 209, 211, 214–215, 219, 223–224, 247, 250, 256

Tsylya, xiii–xiv, 14, 19–21, 66, 104, 106, 111–114, 119, 123, 135–137, 140, 145, 147–149, 153–155, 158, 160, 167, 169–173, 180, 186–187, 192, 195–196, 200–202, 204–205, 208–209, 211, 214, 221, 223–224, 247, 250–251, 256, 259, 268–271

Glavlit, 76, 78

God, 214, 221, 229, 240

Goethe, Johann Wolfgang von, 38

government, xvii, 5, 11, 23–28, 31–32, 60, 62–63, 68–70, 73, 78–79, 90, 92, 106, 110, 116, 126, 142, 163, 167, 184–185, 203n88, 250

Grozny, 39, 60

Great Purges, 12

Gypsies, 131

harvest, 248

Hebrew, 155

higher education, 34, 65, 74, 88, 152, 196

Hitler, Adolf, 29, 63, 74–77, 86, 91, 95, 131, 136, 142, 146–147, 157, 219, 223, 225, 229, 231, 233, 243n165, 245

Holocaust, xv, xxi–xxii, 13–14, 36, 41–54, 142, 154, 265

Hungary, 59

"In liberated Rostov," 150–151
indemnity, 47–48
information, xviii–xxii, xxiv–xxv, 10–14, 19, 28, 36–38, 41, 64–65, 68–69, 73, 76–79, 85, 91, 94, 99, 103, 105, 110–111, 113–115, 123–124, 128–129, 131, 133, 136, 142, 151–153, 158–159, 166–167, 170, 176, 180–181, 186, 193–195, 197–199, 201, 203–204, 206–207, 210, 226–228, 232, 234, 240, 243n166, 245, 248–249, 252–253, 260, 264
Iran, 117
Iraq, 60
Israel, 13
Italy, 59
Ivanchenko, G., 109
Izvestiya, xxv, 73, 75, 77, 79, 92, 94–95, 122–123, 125, 129, 230

Jewish Council (*also* Judenrat), 42–45, 47–49, 118, 255
Judaism, 6, 90, 137–138, 207
Judenrat, *see* Jewish Council

Kabardino-Balkaria, 8, 255
Kaganovich, Lazar, 8, 26n12
Kalinin (city), 26
Kalinin, Mikhail, 92n125
kantonisty, 5
Kazakhstan, 13, 105
Kerch, xiv, 117, 157–159, 225–228, 230, 232, 235–236, 245
Kharitonov, 124
Kharkov, xiv, 41, 103, 227–228, 232, 238
Kiev, xiii, 82, 91, 122, 131, 163
Kislovodsk, 33–34, 42–43, 45–51
Kleist, Ewald, von, 118, 243n165, 254
kolkhozes, 54n91, 91, 112

Komsomol, 25, 67, 77–78, 128–129, 175, 196, 234
Krasnodar, 8, 18, 27–28, 31–37, 40, 42–45, 49–51, 70, 85, 108, 110, 122, 192, 231, 233, 239, 243–244, 251–253, 255

Ladoga, 34
Latvia, 31n34
Lenin, Vladimir, 11
Leningrad, xxi, 25n8, 31n34, 34–35, 38n71, 40, 65, 196n75, 243
letter, *passim*
Liberation, 73, 120, 126–127, 131, 133–134, 141, 151, 219, 252, 256, 258, 263
Liverpool Daily Post, The, 124
Lvov, 86

Maikop, 60, 231, 233–234
Makhachkala, 103, 112
Manchester Guardian, The, 124
Mariupol, 98–99, 111, 114–115, 211
Marxism-Leninism, 71, 92
media, xviii–xx, xxiv–xxv, 36, 39, 61, 67–68, 71, 74–79, 83–84, 91–92, 94, 98, 100–101, 103, 117, 120–122, 124, 126, 130–131, 133, 151–152, 158, 163, 167, 175, 180, 203, 225, 228, 230, 244, 248, 264
Menshevik, 10–11
Mikoyanshakhar, 43–48,
Mineralnye vody, 44–45, 50, 112
Minsk, 75
Molot, xxv, 36, 60–61, 64, 68, 70, 74, 76, 79, 83–84, 92–93, 97–99, 101, 106, 123–125, 127–131, 131, 140, 142–149, 152–153, 155, 157, 159, 161–163, 165, 183, 203–204, 206, 218, 231, 264
Molotov, Vyacheslav, 152, 163

Molotov-Ribbentrop Pact (Soviet-German Pact of Non-Aggression), xiii, 62
Moscow, xiii, xxn10, 10–13, 26, 57–58, 65, 69, 71–72, 74–76, 79, 86, 92, 98, 103, 106, 122, 126, 142, 157, 200–201, 230–231, 239, 242, 248, 266–267, 273
Mountain Jews, 4–9
movement (of population), 48, 53, 61, 66, 68, 87, 100, 159, 165, 167, 178, 182, 192, 218
Murmansk, 31n34

Nalchik, 33n43, 39, 46–48
New York Herald Tribune, 124
New York Times, The, xxv, 63, 77, 91, 102–103, 121, 124–125, 193, 227–228, 245, 253
New York Sun, The, 127
news, xviii–xix, xxii, xxv, 60, 67, 73, 77, 79, 83, 85–86, 88–89, 91, 99, 108, 113, 115, 120, 123, 126–127, 129, 132–133, 141, 150, 152, 156, 159, 168–171, 175–177, 186–187, 195, 198, 202, 204, 209, 214, 218, 221, 226–227, 229–230, 238, 248, 253, 259, 261
newspaper, xxv, 7, 36, 60–62, 64–65, 67–70, 74, 76–79, 82–85, 92–94, 98–103, 105–106, 108–111, 120, 122–123–126, 128–133, 139, 144, 146–147, 149, 152, 156, 158, 161–163, 165–167, 175–176, 183, 195, 203–204, 206–208, 215, 219, 225, 228–231, 243–244, 248, 252–255, 260, 264
NKVD (*also* People's Commissariat of the Interior), 30–31, 33, 85, 110, 113, 144, 181, 191, 232, 239, 241
North Ossetia, 8, 18, 154, 167, 255
note (diplomatic), 162–163

Novocherkassk, 253–255
Novorossiisk, 42, 44n17, 49

ObKhSS, 165, 167
occupation, xv–xviii, xx–xxi, xiii, 7, 9, 17, 22–23, 30, 32–33, 35, 37–38, 42, 44–46, 48–52, 54, 64n30, 76–77, 79, 88, 91, 93, 95, 97, 102–103, 105–106, 109–111, 118–119, 121–125, 127–133, 137, 140, 142, 144, 146, 148–151, 153–154, 156, 158, 160, 162, 165–166, 173, 175–176, 178–179, 182, 185, 191 192, 194, 199–200, 207–208, 218, 239–240, 244, 247, 249, 251, 255–257, 259, 261–262, 264
Odessa, 3–4, 6, 9, 14–15, 85, 92, 122, 194
offensive, xxii, 82, 87, 117, 124, 126n202, 130, 157, 161, 177, 193, 201, 203, 206–207, 225, 228, 232, 238, 241, 245, 251–252
oil, xiv, 60, 77, 103, 117, 192–193, 225–226, 230–231, 233, 236, 239, 242–243, 245, 250n185, 253
Omsk, 12, 71, 74, 87, 111, 142, 267
Operation Blau, xiv, 236, 242
Oppenheim Family, The, 63
Ordzhonikidze (Vladikavkaz), 18–22, 36, 54n91, 104, 135, 138, 145, 149–150, 152–155, 158–160, 162–164, 166–172, 175, 177, 179–181, 184, 186–189, 192–193, 195–198, 201–211, 213, 215–216, 219, 221–222, 224–226, 228–229, 232, 235–238, 242, 246–247, 268–272
Ordzhonikidzevskaya pravda, 36, 85–86

Pale of Settlement, 4–5, 138
Pamfilov, Konstantin, 25–26
partisans, 19n60, 23, 92–93, 133

People's Commissariat of the Interior, *see* NKVD
pogrom, 3, 6–8, 122–123, 163
Poland, xix, 64, 82
police, 218
Politburo, 25, 62n20, 116
possessions, 39, 43, 49, 92, 132, 135–136, 148–149, 172, 178–181, 184, 189–190, 201–202, 204, 248
postcard, xxiv, 69, 111, 138, 145, 168, 213, 272–273
Pravda, xxv, 63, 75, 78, 85, 123, 125, 131, 151–152, 185, 230, 252, 255
Professor Mamlock, 62, 77, 83–84
propaganda, xviii, xxv, 30, 36–37, 61–62, 64–65, 67, 70–71, 74–75, 77–78, 83–84, 90, 92, 95, 99, 122–128, 130–132, 137–138, 140–141, 144–146, 148, 150–151, 157–158, 166, 169, 174, 176, 180, 185–186, 194–195, 199, 207–209, 219–220, 227, 237, 240, 245, 252–253
property, xix, xxii, 5, 24n4, 43, 52–53, 64, 128, 131, 153, 185, 190n68, 204
province, 4–7
Pyatigorsk, 34–35, 43, 47–50

racism, 63, 70–71
radio, 36, 62, 69, 76, 78, 124, 127, 130, 142, 162, 175–176, 195, 203–204, 209, 214, 226, 244, 252–253
Ramat Gan, 13
Red Army (*also* Soviet army; Soviet forces), xiii–xvi, xx, 19–20, 24–26, 29–30, 32, 34, 37, 40–41, 65, 67, 75, 88–89, 91–92, 94, 98, 115, 117, 119–121, 123–124, 126–127, 129, 133, 141, 143–146, 151, 157–158, 161, 165, 170n32, 175–177, 181, 185, 187, 193–194, 196–197, 199, 201, 203, 206, 209, 212, 216, 218, 220, 225–229, 232, 238, 240, 244–245, 248, 250, 252, 254, 256–257, 260
refugee, xvii, xix–xxiii, 25, 27–33, 35–37, 39–41, 53, 66, 87–89, 91, 96, 99, 105–106, 140, 142, 149, 151, 161, 167, 169, 171–172, 177, 183–185, 201, 219, 237, 240, 243–244, 248–249
region, xiv–xvii, xix–xxv, 4–5, 7–9, 23–24, 26–36, 38, 40–41, 48–51, 53–54, 60–61, 66, 77, 79–80, 87–88, 91, 93, 101, 106, 109–110, 115, 120, 124–126, 133–134, 143–144, 154, 163, 169, 177, 179, 183–184, 191, 194–197, 199, 208, 215, 225, 227, 230, 233–236, 238–239, 243–245, 247–249, 252–254, 256, 261
registration, 25n10, 43–45, 51, 122, 160–161, 163, 195
relative, xxi, 72, 94–95, 100, 104–105, 109, 123, 133, 135, 139, 142–143, 145, 149, 154, 160, 162, 168–169, 171–176, 178, 186–190, 192, 196–197, 200, 202, 204, 209–210, 218, 223–224, 229, 232, 237–238, 246, 248, 258
Remezov, Fedor, 99, 124
resettlement, xvii, 24, 28, 31, 44
Reuters, 124
Revolution, 6, 10, 120, 122, 133–134
Rogovskoe, 17–18, 20, 22, 250–251, 256, 260, 262
Romania, 59, 65, 231, 243
Rosh Hashana, 90
Rostov Gorky Theater, 62, 77, 83–84, 103, 221
Rostov University, 152
Rostov-on-Don (*also* Rostov), *passim*
RSFSR, 26, 36n49, 171n34, 243n166
Ruoff, Richard, 254

Russian Holocaust Center, 89, 102, 203, 220, 235, 237n154

Schiller, Friedrich, 38
Schneerson, Sholom Dov-Ber, 6
scorched land, 23–24
Seleznev, Petr, 110, 239
Serbia, 64
Sevastopol, xiii–xiv, 41, 110, 194, 227, 244–245
Shvernik, Nikolai, 25–26, 31n31
Siberia, 12n53, 71, 87, 110
siege, 100, 115, 121–122, 150, 157, 190, 226, 228, 246
Simferopol, 108
Sisters-in-Arms, 147
Slovakia, 59
Smolensk, 31n34
Socialist Revolutionary, 6, 10
Sonderkommando, 106, 118, 255–256
Soviet army, *see* Red Army
Sovinformburo, 203, 227, 252, 255
Sovkhoz(*-es*), 54n91, 241, 246, 250, 256–257
Spartacus, 147
spy, 19n60, 32, 66, 99, 120, 134, 142, 152, 161, 234
SS, 73, 243, 256
Stalin, Joseph, xvi, 8, 11–12, 66–67, 69n46, 122, 141, 219–223, 231
State Defense Committee, 231
Stalinabad, 120
Stalingrad, xiv, 105, 169, 222, 242
Stalino (Donetsk), 103
stanitsa, 33, 35n57, 51–52, 54, 87, 92, 134, 251n187, 256
starosta, 42, 53
starvation, xxiii, 40, 64, 192, 194, 211
State Defense Committee, xiv, 26, 231, 233
Stavropol, 8–9, 28, 30–33, 35–36, 42, 44, 48–50, 52–53, 60n14, 82–83, 85–86, 93, 105, 133, 140, 166–167, 196n77, 212n107, 243–244, 248, 253, 255
Sukkot, 96
synagogue, 6, 64, 96

Taganrog, xiii, 4–5, 97, 102–103, 106, 108, 113, 115, 121, 125–127, 146, 151, 184–185, 206–208, 211
Tale of the Fisher and the Fish, the, 156
Talmudei Tora, 6
TASS, 208, 228, 253
telegram, xxiv, 50n65, 57, 83, 135, 141–142, 145, 148, 152, 159, 164, 166, 168–169, 173, 231, 266, 268–269–271
terror, 12, 29, 54n91, 151, 180
theater, 62–63, 65, 71, 74, 79, 93, 147, 150, 153, 156, 161–162, 164, 199, 201, 221, 232, 238, 252
Timoshenkov, Konstantin, 110
Times, The, 124
transport (*also* transportation), xxiii, 40–41, 89, 161, 165, 244, 249
Tula, 26
Turkey, 125

Ukraine, 8, 28, 31, 33, 37–38, 51, 65, 75, 82, 91, 98, 103, 131, 163, 165
United Kingdom, 82, 124
United States, 78, 82, 124, 127, 131, 234
Uzbekistan, 105
Vladikavkaz, *see* Ordzhonikidze
Voenkomat (*see* Military Commissariat), 211, 214
Volga, 34, 253–254
Voronezh, 248,
Vyshynsky, Andrei, 11

Waffen SS, 243
Warsaw, 63, 166–167

Washington Post, xxv, 108, 117, 125, 157–158, 193, 225–226, 230, 236, 248–249, 254

Wehrmacht, xiii–xiv, xvi, xix, xxii–xxiii, 7, 26, 30–31, 33, 35–36, 38, 40–41, 48, 51–54, 65, 73–75, 78–79, 82–84, 88, 90, 92, 95, 97–100, 102–103, 105, 109–111, 115–119, 126, 140, 142–144, 146, 152, 154–155, 171, 185, 194, 199–200, 203, 207, 225, 228, 233–234, 236, 240–245, 251, 253, 255, 261, 263–264

White Russian, 7

World War I, 4, 7–8, 24, 38, 95, 137

World War II, xiii, xv–xvi, xx, 7, 9, 38, 60, 75n67, 82, 109, 121

Yad Vashem, ix, xv, xxvi, 10, 13–22, 59, 81, 170, 205, 222, 224, 256–257

Yiddish, 6, 96, 137–138, 155

Yom Kippur War, 13

Yom Kippur, 90, 93

Zionism, 7

www.ingramcontent.com/pod-product-compliance
Lightning Source LLC
Chambersburg PA
CBHW050515170426
43201CB00013B/1962